HIPPOLYTUS AND CALLISTUS.

HIPPOLYTUS AND CALLISTUS;

OR,

THE CHURCH OF ROME

IN THE FIRST HALF OF THE THIRD CENTURY.

WITH SPECIAL REFERENCE TO THE WRITINGS OF BUNSEN,
WORDSWORTH, BAUR, AND GIESELER.

BY

JOHN J. IGN. VON DÖLLINGER.

TRANSLATED, WITH INTRODUCTION, NOTES, AND APPENDICES, BY

ALFRED PLUMMER,

MASTER OF UNIVERSITY COLLEGE, DURHAM ; LATE FELLOW AND TUTOR
OF TRINITY COLLEGE, OXFORD.

WIPF & STOCK · Eugene, Oregon

Wipf and Stock Publishers
199 W 8th Ave, Suite 3
Eugene, OR 97401

Hippolytus and Callistus
The Church of Rome in the First Half of the Third Century
By Döllinger, John J. IGN. Von and Plummer, Alfred
ISBN 13: 978-1-5326-3755-1
Publication date 7/19/2017
Previously published by T. and T. Clark, 1876

THIS Translation has been undertaken with the express sanction of the Author.

The Translator is responsible for all that appears between square brackets, thus [   ], for the italics, and for many of the headings to subdivisions of the work.

TRANSLATOR'S PREFACE.

DEAN MILMAN'S great work, the *History of Latin Christianity*, was published some years before Dr. Döllinger's *Hippolytus und Kallistus*. In it he adopts the then common view that Hippolytus was Bishop of Portus, and is disposed to believe all, or nearly all, that Hippolytus says or insinuates against his opponent Callistus. Whatever may be thought about the see of Hippolytus, few students of ecclesiastical history perhaps would agree that the narrative of Hippolytus, "though *possibly somewhat* darkened by polemic hostility, has an air of minute truthfulness." To the third edition (1867) the Dean adds a long note (pp. 44, 45), in which, after praising "the Chevalier Bunsen's very learned work," he adds: "I have also read *Hippolytus und Kallistus*, by J. Döllinger, the Church historian; I must say with no conviction but of the author's learning and ingenuity. . . . I cannot but regret that M. Döllinger's book, so able, and in some respects so instructive, should be written with such a resolute (no doubt conscientious) determination to make out a case. It might well be entitled, *Apologia pro Callisto;* and I must presume to say, in my judgment, a most unfortunate case for his own cause," etc. etc. Those who know Dr. Döllinger, whether personally or from his writings, will smile at the idea of his writing with a "resolute determination to make out a case," unless by "a case" is to be understood the truth. And surely the circumstance that Dr. Döllinger's interpretation of his facts tells against his own cause is some guarantee that what he has at heart is not the adjustment of facts to a theory, but the discovery of historical truth. Dean Milman is usually very generous in his sympathy with reputed heretics; but for once he seems to be inclined to accept the worst statements of the "orthodox" Hippolytus in blackening the character and teaching of Callistus. Canon Robertson, in his valuable *History of the Christian Church* (p. 120, 2d edition, 1874), admits that Dr. Döllinger maintains his view respecting Hippolytus "with great learning and ability," but apparently prefers the view taken in Dean Milman's note, to which he refers his readers. Many English students read the works of our two historians who have no opportunity of examining the other side of this question as set forth by Dr. Döllinger. To remedy such deficiency, this translation is now offered. Even those who do not agree with the main conclusions will gain from it a more perfect knowledge of the condition of the Church at the close of the second and opening of the third century, and will also have an example of patient and thorough investigation, such as is too often wanting in a country where literary men seldom aim higher than a telling article or review.

The *Dublin Review*, in a characteristic attack which it paid the present writer the compliment of making on the Introduction to his translation of Dr. Döllinger's *Papstfabeln*, charged him with disingenuousness in endorsing Mr. Maccabe's remarks respecting the occasion and value of the *Hippolytus und Kallistus*. The passage runs as follows: "The appearance of the *Philosophumena*, by Miller (1851), gave rise to a prolonged discussion, in which many Catholics sought to weaken the testimony of the author, whilst Protestant writers endeavoured to use his authority for the purpose of throwing discredit on the Church of Rome. In answer to both parties, especially to Gieseler, Baur, Bunsen, Wordsworth, and Le Normant, Dr. Döllinger published, in 1853, *Hippolytus and Callistus, the Roman Church in the Third Century*, perhaps of all his writings the one in which his ingenuity of combination, his skill as a logician, and his lofty tone in handling the interests of his Church [the *Dublin Review* misquotes '*the* Church'], are most conspicuous."

On this innocent passage the *Review* comments in these words: "Who would not suppose from this passage that Dr. Döllinger answered 'the Catholics who sought to weaken the testimony of the author,' by showing that his testimony was worthy of credit? [Why so? any more than that he answered the Protestants 'who endeavoured to use his authority for the purpose of throwing discredit on the Church of Rome?' It is said that he answered *both* parties, and of the names given the majority are those of anti-Romanists!] Who could for a moment guess that Dr. Döllinger himself not only weakens, but annihilates the witness of Hippolytus; and that his only difference from Le Normant is, that that writer declares for Origen, while he himself considers Hippolytus to be the author? . . . But perhaps Mr. Plummer, though suppressing the truth about the Munich divine, is himself worthy of being considered an independent authority. . . . We hardly think so," etc. etc.

The subject of all this invective knows no better way of answering the above accusation than by doing his utmost to let English readers know exactly what Dr. Döllinger does and does not say "in answer to both parties." He concludes by quoting with pleasure one more passage from the *Dublin Review* in reference to this work of Dr. Döllinger's: "We have always considered this book his *chef-d'œuvre*. He puts Hippolytus into the witness-box, and analyses his evidence as the Attorney-General tore the Claimant to pieces. In doing so he has displayed an acuteness and a knowledge of Roman law, as well as of ecclesiastical history, which are admirable." It is refreshing to hear from such a quarter that a knowledge of ecclesiastical history is an admirable thing, and still more that Dr. Döllinger posseses it.

It only remains to apologize for having allowed such a volume to remain untranslated so long. This is a fault which others must share with the present writer. As far as his wishes are concerned, this volume would have appeared some years ago; but press of other work and occupations has prevented him from fulfilling them. A. P.

DURHAM, *September* 1876.

PREFACE.

IMMEDIATELY after the appearance of the *Philosophumena*, I determined on the publication of this treatise; but I delayed going to press until the work of Herr BUNSEN (which had been announced so long and so frequently beforehand) had appeared. My hopes of gaining any information and assistance from a work which treated of the same subject in such detail were then entirely dispelled; for the investigation of what was to me the main question, viz. the personality of Hippolytus and the historical contents of his narrative, was conducted in the work of Herr Bunsen (as I soon saw) in such a way as to make it impossible for me to derive the slightest advantage from it. These historical questions are generally of secondary importance with him, the main interest of the work for the author as well as for the public lying in those much more extensive portions in which he gives expression to his long-cherished dislike of the Christian Church, its doctrine and constitution, as well as of the remnants of the primitive Church still preserved in Protestantism; and in which he has found place and opportunity for the commendation of his *Church of the Future*, now ready on paper, and to be established in fact very shortly. I have, therefore, subjected only two sections of the first volume of Bunsen's work to a more thorough criticism, convinced that the readers who follow me so far will not desire a critical investigation of the rest of the store supplied by him. In fact, the significance of the book may at once be seen by the experienced in the reception which it has found in England and Germany, and which has been totally different in the two countries. In England, where people are still wont to deal seriously, at least, with some of the first principles of Christianity, the public voice has made itself heard almost exclusively in indignant condemnation. Only the *Westminster Review* (April 1853) and a couple of kindred periodicals have bestowed a compliment upon the author, which in the eyes of religiously-minded Englishmen is equivalent to the severest condemnation. In Germany, on the other hand, in accordance with the well-known character of our daily press, all the leaves of the great market, as if moved by one and the same wind, have rustled in joyful applause, and only the specially theological ones have mingled with this exultation a few drops of objection to details.

When this treatise was already more than half printed, I received the work of Dr. WORDSWORTH, and then also the discussions of H. H. BAUR and GIESELER. Whereupon I found myself compelled to mention again and go into at greater length some portions of what had already been discussed in the two first sections of this treatise. The reader will, I trust, kindly excuse the disarrangement which has thereby resulted as regards the division of the subject-matter, and also one or two unavoidable repetitions.

MUNICH, *September* 14, 1853.

INTRODUCTION.

THE *Elenchus Hæresium* or *Philosophumena*, the subject-matter of which is critically examined in the *Hippolytus and Callistus*, was discovered entire, with the exception of Book I., in a MS. brought from Mount Athos by Minoides Mynas in 1842. This Greek gentleman was acting for M. Villemain, Louis Philippe's Minister of Public Instruction, and under his direction was searching for ancient documents. It is generally allowed that the first editor, Miller, was mistaken in ascribing the work to Origen, although right in supposing that it was a continuation of the *Philosophumena* contained in the Benedictine edition of Origen's Works. Two arguments (by no means the only ones) are sufficient to show this: (1) The author of the *Philosophumena* was a Bishop; in the *Proœmium* he says: "But we, as the successors of the Apostles and the participators in this grace of Highpriesthood and office of teaching, as well as being reputed guardians of the Church," etc. etc. (2) In the *Philosophumena* there is no reference to any of Origen's numerous works, nor in any of his works is there any reference to the *Philosophumena*. The first of these arguments is also fatal to the theory that Caius is the author. It is surprising that any one should have ascribed a work written in Rome at that time to Tertullian; the language alone is sufficient disproof of such an hypothesis.

Most scholars are now agreed that Hippolytus is the

author. The list of those who support this view contains the names of Döllinger, Duncker, Schneidewin, Jacobi, Gieseler, Bunsen, Bernays, Milman, Robertson, and Wordsworth. We may, therefore, without rashness, assume the point to be virtually settled. One voice worthy of attention is still, however, raised against this conclusion. Dr. Newman, in his *Tracts Theological and Ecclesiastical* (p. 222), regards it as "simply incredible" that the author of that "malignant libel on his contemporary Popes" can be Hippolytus. He considers the attack on Zephyrinus and Callistus wholly incompatible with "the gravity of tone in what remains to us of his writings, and mainly indeed in the *Elenchus* itself," and also with the respect paid to his memory by "Popes of the fourth, fifth, and seventh centuries."[1] This objection, even if allowed to be conclusive, would affect, and *perhaps* is intended to affect, only Book IX., and not the whole of that. But it would be difficult to separate Book IX. or any portion of it from the rest; all the more so, inasmuch as the charge of heresy against Callistus reappears in the summary contained in Book X., and in much the same position, viz. between the account of the Montanists and that of the Elchasaites. We assume, therefore, as all but certain, that the whole proceeds from one pen, and that the pen of the Anti-Pope Hippolytus.

Anti-Pope may seem a strong term to use of this celebrated Ante-Nicene theologian. Dr. Newman is disposed to place him second to none in the West during that period, except his master, S. Irenæus. "At present," he says, "we have little more than fragments of his writings; and it is a mystery how Origen's works have come down to us, who has been ever in the shade, and not Hippolytus', who has ever been in the brightest light of ecclesiastical approbation."

[1] The whole passage will be found in Appendix B.

Possibly the intrinsic merit of the writings themselves may have had something to do with this, and also the comparative fame of the two men in the East. Be this as it may, and granting that the abilities and merits of Hippolytus were as great as many of his contemporaries and successors believed them to be, yet if the ninth book of the *Elenchus* be his, it is clear that he, and not Novatian, must be considered the first forerunner of that long line of Anti-Popes which begins with Felix II. and ends with Felix V. (see pp. 92, 93.)

Callistus, the victim of his bitter invective, may, on the other hand, be regarded as the forerunner of those liberal-minded and reforming Popes who have ever met with opposition, and have generally been thwarted. There is no long line of *them*. It would be hard to point to one in a century, or perhaps even one in alternate centuries; and, so far as the present prospect reveals the chances of the future to us, there is no probability of any such Pope in this century. He would be a bold prophet who ventured to point to a future reformer in the present College of Cardinals.

It has lately been remarked, with regard to reform in the Latin Church, that when the members wished for it the head would not have it, and when the head wished for it the members would not have it. The history of the Papacy during the last eight hundred years is one long commentary on the mournful remark. The work which is the subject of this volume shows that a reforming Bishop of Rome, even in the earlier part of the third century, could not carry out generous changes which the development of Christian society had rendered desirable, or even imperative, without encountering the bitterest opposition.

Hippolytus appears to have been one of those persons, very common at the present time, and perhaps at all times, in whose eyes all change is almost necessarily for the worse,—who are victims to the fallacy latent in the term "innovation," and with whom liberalism and heresy are convertible terms. In ecclesiastical matters, it requires a calmer and clearer judgment than he seems to have possessed to recognise the important truth that "a past discipline may be a present heresy."

But, in following Dr. Döllinger as he tears to shreds the evidence of Hippolytus against Callistus, we may easily be led to adopt either or both of two conclusions, neither of which necessarily follows from the evidence, and to neither of which Dr. Döllinger himself leads us.

1. Unless the words are used in a very qualified sense, it seems hard on Hippolytus to call him the author of a "malignant libel." The charges against Zephyrinus and Callistus are made with a great deal of *animus*, no doubt, and, though true in the letter, are often quite false in the meaning conveyed. But still there is no need to tax the author with consciously writing what he knew to be utterly untrue statements about others. It is a question of pyschology. What are the limits of the influence of bias? To what extent can a man's mind be warped by a strong prejudice? At what point are we justified in saying, "This cannot be blind partiality; it is conscious dishonesty"? Charity and experience alike tell us that it is wise to regard prejudice as practically unlimited, and that there is scarcely any unfairness, whether of reasoning or conduct, which is impossible to an otherwise honest and upright bigot.[1]

2. It does not follow, because Hippolytus is grossly unfair in his charges, and some of them refer to matters worthy of praise rather than blame, that the

[1] "Without doubt Hippolytus had not the conscious intention of slandering Callistus; he did not invent the transactions and fate of this remarkable man" (p. 108).

conduct of Callistus was quite irreproachable, that there was not the faintest reason for taxing him with anything that will not bear close inspection. It would have been almost a miracle had his method of carrying on the contest with his implacable opponents been always blameless. Callistus had been a slave; and we know a great deal about the moral corruption which was the all but inevitable accompaniment of slavery in Rome. If there is one vice which slavery fosters more than another, it is deceit: falsehood and cunning are the slave's natural weapons. Few habits are more difficult to conquer than habits of untruthfulness; few habits are more difficult to regain than those of perfect straightforwardness. We shall probably not be very wrong in supposing that the passionate abuse which Hippolytus pours upon the cunning and double-dealing of his opponent is not without some faint shadow of reason. It may well have been the case that Callistus, although chastened by suffering and sanctified by his high calling, still retained in his character some slight reminiscences of the "evil communications" of his earlier life, in a tendency to sharp practice, in a love of strategy, in a preference for concealment where openness would have been quite as effectual. Still, it is only fair to him to remember that we have merely his adversary's account of him, and that much of what Hippolytus tells us must have been obtained by him at second hand. But, whatever view we may take of his character,—whether with the Roman Church we account him a saint, or with Dean Milman a crafty adventurer, there can be no doubt that he was a very remarkable man. His rise from utter obscurity to the chair of S. Peter, his influence over his predecessor Zephyrinus, the success with which he carried through his reforms in spite of the unflinching opposition of the leading theologian in the West, all prove this.

b

xviii   INTRODUCTION.

And the light which the history of this brief but serious schism in the Church of Rome throws upon the development of the Christian Church in the West in the earlier part of the third century is such as the student of ecclesiastical history can ill spare.¹

---

¹ Some weeks after the above had been written, I came upon the following passage in the late Bishop HANEBERG'S edition of the Canons of Hippolytus (*Canones S. Hippolyti Arabice e codicibus Romanis cum versione Latina annotationibus et prolegominis*, edidit D. B. de Haneberg, Monachii. 1870, p. 25): *Accidit, quod quamquam morum severitate æque ac doctrina excelleret, tamen post mortem Zephyrini papæ ab ambitione non alienus mansisse videtur. Ex eo libro* philosophumenorum, *qui ante paucos annos detectus, ipsi Hippolyto a plurimis, iisque gravissimis scriptoribus tribuitur, effici posse videtur*, Hippolytum fuisse æmulum S. Callisti et primum Antipapam egisse. *Cujus dissidii reus, quamquam martyrio maculam diluerit, quomodo apud Romanos minus æstimatus sit, quam apud Orientales, quilibet videre potest.* The extreme rigorist spirit of these canons, surpassing that of the most severe among the Fathers, agrees very well with what we know of Hippolytus; but certain evidence as to the authorship is wanting. Dr. Haneberg seems to think that the 7th canon, discouraging a celibate clergy, is inconsistent with Hippolytus' attack on Callistus for ordaining digamists. But surely one may, without absurdity, hold that it is best for a cleric to be "the husband of *one* wife," and yet object to the ordination of a man who has been the husband of *two*. (See *North British Review*, No. ciii. p. 225.)

TABLE OF CONTENTS.

CHAPTER I.

HIPPOLYTUS AND THE PHILOSOPHUMENA.

	PAGE
The author of the *Philosophumena* not Caius, but Hippolytus,	2
The *Labyrinth* and the treatise on the Universe also by him,	3
The *Syntagma* in Photius not identical with the *Philosophumena*,	7
Herr Bunsen's reasons for believing the two to be identical,	8
Order and number of heresies in each,	9
Contents and sources of each,	11
The quotations from the *Syntagma*,	15
The *Libellus* appended to Tertullian's *De Præscriptione Hæret.*,	18
Relation of the *Syntagma* to the *Philosophumena*,	20
On some lost writings of Hippolytus,	22
The statue of him found in Rome,	23

CHAPTER II.

THE HISTORY OF HIPPOLYTUS. THE SAINTS OF THE SAME NAME.

Hippolytus and Pontianus,	28
Another Hippolytus in the legend of S. Lawrence,	29
Development of this new legend,	31
The S. Hippolytus of the East and of the West not the same,	33
Churches dedicated to S. Hippolytus,	33
The development of the legend of S. Lawrence,	36
Hippolytus frequently represented in pictures at Rome,	38
Another Hippolytus from the *Acts of S. Aurea*,	39
Confusion with a Bishop Nonnus,	40
Point of connection with the Chronographer of 354,	43
The various texts of the legend of S. Aurea,	43

CONTENTS.

	PAGE
A third Hippolytus,	48
The supposed Presbyter Hippolytus at Antioch,	48
The Hippolytus of Prudentius,	51
The small value of the statements of Prudentius generally,	52
The mode of death which he assigns to his Hippolytus,	54
Probable source of his statement that Hippolytus had been a Novatianist,	57
The mode of death probably taken from a picture in the vicinity of the Church of S. Lawrence,	58
Other features in Prudentius' description,	60
What is historical in his account,	62
Is the first part of the list of Popes in the Chronographer taken from the Chronicle of Hippolytus?	63
The notice in the second part respecting the banishment of Pontianus and Hippolytus,	64
Probable cause of this exile,	65
The resignation of Pontianus,	67
Was Hippolytus Bishop of Portus?	68
Modern opinions on this point,	69
Portus neither a town nor an episcopal See before 313,	72
No Hippolytus, Bishop of Portus, known in the West till the Middle Ages,	75
Eusebius, Theodoret, and Jerome are against it,	77
Herr Bunsen's reasons for making Hippolytus Bishop of Portus,	78
The testimony of Pope Gelasius,	82
The Oriental tradition that Hippolytus was Bishop of Rome,	84
Explanation of this,	87
The statement that he was Bishop of Portus comes from the spurious *Acts of S. Aurea*,	88
And is only to be found in Constantinople,	89
The episcopate of Hippolytus in Rome made plain by the narrative in the *Philosophumena*,	92
Herr Bunsen's hypothesis that Hippolytus was at once Presbyter in Rome and Bishop in Portus,	97
The position of the suburban Bishops in Rome,	100

CHAPTER III.

THE HISTORY OF CALLISTUS. THE CHARGES OF HIPPOLYTUS AGAINST HIM.

Morretti's book, *De S. Callisto Papa, etc.*,	107
The narrative of Hippolytus,	108
Callistus banished; examination of his supposed guilt,	111
His return; his relation to Zephyrinus and the Roman clergy,	112
He is made Bishop,	115
The specific charges: 1. General forgiveness of sins,	116

CONTENTS.   xxi

	PAGE
Discipline under Zephyrinus,	117
Further relaxation allowed by Callistus,	120
2. Reception of excommunicated persons,	122
3. Protection of immoral Bishops,	124
4. Ordination of digamists,	129
Agreement with a statement of Tertullian,	132
History of this irregularity,	133
Theodore of Mopsuestia attacks the custom prevalent in the East,	136
5. Allowing clergy to marry,	139
The marriage of the lower clergy,	140
Difference between allowing a cleric to continue in the service of the Church and to continue one of the clergy,	144
The sectarian rigorism of Hippolytus,	146
6. Allowing ladies to marry with the lower orders or with slaves,	147
The charge which Hippolytus appends to this last,	148
Theory and practice with regard to marriage in Rome,	152
No state official needed in contracting a marriage,	153
Marriages forbidden on account of inequality of rank,	154
Position of the Church with regard to the Roman marriage-laws,	156
Morality in Rome at this time,	158
Groundlessness of the complaint of Hippolytus,	160
Marriage with slaves,	163
Attitude of the Church towards slavery,	164
The condition of slaves improved by the Church,	166
Roman Law on the marriage of free women with slaves,	168
The action of Callistus in this matter,	169
Impossibility of finding Christian husbands of rank or position,	171
Hippolytus' remarks on the consequences of the marriages allowed by Callistus,	172
The case of the Empress Marcia,	173
7. Countenancing second baptism,	175
The synod under Agrippinus,	176
The synod at Synnada,	177
Drey's arguments in favour of Cyprian's theory of baptism,	178
Parallel between the charges against Callistus and those against Paul of Antioch,	180

CHAPTER IV.

CONTROVERSY BETWEEN HIPPOLYTUS AND CALLISTUS RESPECTING THE DOCTRINE OF THE TRINITY.

The heresy of Noëtus,	183
Sabellius,	184
His doctrine identical with that of Noëtus,	187

xxii   CONTENTS.

	PAGE
The school of the Patripassians in Rome,	188
The doctrine of Hippolytus,	191
The development of the Logos according to him,	191
His doctrine respecting the Holy Spirit,	193
The stumbling-block in his doctrine,	194
His connection with Philo,	196
The production of the Logos by an act of the Divine Will,	197
The relation of Marcellus of Ancyra to the doctrine of Hippolytus,	201
Hippolytus accused of Valentinianism,	202
The progress of the controversy in Rome,	204
Relation between Callistus and Zephyrinus,	205
The position of Callistus between Hippolytus and the Noëtians,	206
He accuses the party of Hippolytus of Ditheism,	210
The formal separation,	212
The majority of Churches for Callistus,	213
Sabellius turns against Callistus,	214
The doctrine of Callistus as misrepresented by Hippolytus,	215
The true doctrine of Callistus,	219
A sixth-century account of the feud of Hippolytus with Callistus,	227
Who was Victorinus?	229
Probable conclusion of the schism under Pope Pontianus,	231
Festival of Pontianus and of Hippolytus on the same day,	232
The memory of Callistus in the Roman Church,	234
The Callistians,	234
The relation of Origen to Hippolytus and the Roman Church,	235
Origen's doctrine respecting the Trinity,	238
Synod at Rome against him,	240
Not only Demetrius, but even Heraclas, opposed him,	241
Fragment in Photius on the question,	244

CHAPTER V.

THE LATEST INVESTIGATIONS RESPECTING THE BOOK AND ITS CONTENTS.

M. le Normant for the authorship of Origen,	249
Herr Baur for Caius,	250
The *Labyrinth*: Was Caius its author?	251
Herr Baur's hypothesis that Theodoret quoted the *Philosophumena* as a work of Origen,	253
Herr Gieseler on Hippolytus : Was he ever a Novatianist? and is he identical with the Hippolytus of Prudentius?	256
Was Hippolytus a disciple of S. Irenæus ?	259
The fable of his journey to the East,	260
Herr Gieseler's view of the Trinitarian controversies in Rome,	263
That Sabellianism was formerly universally prevalent,	265
That the Catholics opposed the notion of a Divine Generation,	266

CONTENTS. xxiii

	PAGE
That then there came a complete change of "disposition" in the Church,	267
That both parties, in spite of their difference of creed, preserved unity,	268
Date of the statue of Hippolytus,	271
The Alogi: Were they Antimontanists?	273
The Church in Thyatira,	274
Epiphanius represents the Alogi as a party related to Montanism,	276
Irenæus the same,	278
Their rejection of the Gospel of S. John,	280
They were orthodox as regards the Divinity of Christ,	281
Reasons for their suspecting the Fourth Gospel,	283
Why they rejected the doctrine of the Logos,	286
Dr. Wordsworth's book on Hippolytus,	288
Ruggieri his authority for the episcopate in Portus,	290
Worthlessness of Ruggieri's arguments,	291
The testimony of Jerome,	292
The testimony of Gelasius,	293
Anastasius and the pretended treatise of Hippolytus against Beron,	295
Its spuriousness,	296
The title "Bishop of Portus" not taken from Hippolytus' own writings,	300
Why Hippolytus does not call Callistus Bishop of Rome,	301
The "school" of Callistus,	302
The omissions in Hippolytus' narrative,	303
Dr. Wordsworth's supposed Johannean school,	304
The Decian persecution a judgment,	306
Dr. Wordsworth on Herr Bunsen,	307
Herr Bunsen on Revelation,	307
Gross mistakes in his translations,	309
The apology which he puts into the mouth of Hippolytus in London,	311

CHAPTER VI.

EXAMINATION OF CERTAIN POINTS IN HIPPOLYTUS' FORM OF DOCTRINE.

I. The meaning of "Presbyter" in his works,	313
The meaning of "Bishop of the heathen,"	316
II. His witness to the Priesthood and Sacrifice of the Church,	317
The doctrine of the Sacrifice of Christ's Body in the Eucharist primitive, and older than Cyprian,	319
Tertullian's universal Priesthood,	320
III. The "Altar" and the "Holy Table" in primitive times,	325
IV. Ascetics already numerous in the time of Hippolytus,	327
V. The doctrine of Hippolytus respecting the descent of Christ into Hades,	328
VI. The Chiliasm of Hippolytus,	330
His doctrine respecting Hades,	331

Appendix A.—Dr. Salmon on the chronology of Hippolytus, . . 333
Appendix B.—Dr. Newman on the author of the *Philosophumena*, . 340
Appendix C.—The poem of Prudentius on the martyrdom of Hippolytus, ... 344
Appendix D.—One more theory about the Bishopric of Hippolytus, . 352
Appendix E.—One more theory about the authorship of the *Philosophumena*, ... 354
Appendix F.—Dr. Caspari's contributions to the subject, . . 355

HIPPOLYTUS AND CALLISTUS.

CHAPTER I.

HIPPOLYTUS AND THE PHILOSOPHUMENA.

THAT the celebrated Father of the Church, Hippolytus, is the author of the newly-discovered work on heresies, has been the simultaneous and independent opinion expressed by the majority of those who have investigated the question.

Origen did not write it. This is so clear, and has been so convincingly proved, that we need not detain ourselves long with the question. The single circumstance, that the author attributes to himself the ecclesiastical dignity of the ἀρχιεράτεια, is at once decisive against the Alexandrines. Four facts are evident from the book itself:—1. That it is the work of a man of rare culture, and of very varied and comprehensive information; 2. That he composed other treatises; 3. That he lived in the first part of the third century; 4. That he lived in Rome. That he was eminent among the small number of Christian writers of that time, is manifest; that he should have remained unmentioned, and above all, should have escaped the observation of Eusebius, of Jerome, and of the other writers on heresy, is inconceivable. The work is too full of material, and was too important and serviceable to the Church of that age, to have remained entirely concealed, and yet to have been able to survive to our time. Accordingly, the circle of names in which we have to look for the author becomes very small at the first glance. Clement of Alexandria is, in style and mode of thought, altogether different; Julius Africanus was a mere chronographer; of Alexander of Jerusalem we possess only a few letters; Apollonius wrote only against the Montanists; and the Presbyter of Antioch, Geminus or Geminianus, whom no one mentions but Jerome, has left nothing of importance.

It results, then, that there are only three names between which we have to decide,—RHODON, CAIUS, and HIPPOLYTUS. On behalf of RHODON it may be said, that he lived in Rome; but of his writings only those directed against Marcion and Apelles are mentioned; and as he was a pupil of Tatian and a contemporary of Apelles, he belongs to an earlier period. He must have lived at the end of the second century, under Commodus and Severus, whereas the author of the *Philosophumena* reached the reign of the Emperor Alexander, and (most probably) outlived it.

The reasons which forbid us to attribute the work to CAIUS,[1] otherwise known to us as the author of a disputation with the Montanist Proclus, have been already well put forth by Herr Jacobi. What we know of the views of Caius respecting Montanism, Chiliasm, the Apocalypse, and Cerinthus, is utterly inconsistent with the expressions and mode of thought which appear in the *Philosophumena;* only in the opinion that the *Epistle to the Hebrews* is not by S. Paul do the two appear to agree. On the whole, however, the notices of Caius current up to this date require correction, and this will at the same time throw some light on the author of the *Philosophumena*.

At the outset, it is astonishing that the more ancient

[1] [Canon Robertson seems disposed to doubt the very existence of Caius. *History of the Christian Church*, vol. i. p. 120, 2d ed.]

Fathers who mention Caius, and had his writings before them, say nothing about his having been a Presbyter in Rome. Eusebius, Jerome, Theodoret, especially the two first, appear not to have known to what Church he belonged, nor whether he was a cleric or a layman; Eusebius designates him merely as ἐκκλησιαστικὸς ἀνήρ. The dialogue with the Montanist Proclus, which Eusebius had before him, was held in Rome; but it by no means follows from that, that the author was one of the Roman clergy, or even that he always belonged to that Church only. In Rome itself no trace of him has come down to us; not one of the Latin Fathers mentions him; Jerome himself took his notice of him merely from Eusebius, and at any rate knows no other writing of Caius, except the dialogue with Proclus. Photius, however, knew that Caius composed yet another treatise,—a refutation of Artemon. He distinguishes this expressly from the so-called *Labyrinth*, which was likewise directed against Artemon (and Theodotus), from which Eusebius and Theodoret have given some quotations. Eusebius, who cites this treatise merely as directed against the heresy of Artemon, remarks that it was anonymous, as also does Theodoret, who first gives its title, *The Little Labyrinth*, and mentions the circumstance that it was attributed by some to Origen, although his style is altogether different. It is from Photius that we first learn that Caius also was believed to be the author,—an opinion in which Photius himself concurs. He found, that is to say, in the treatise *On the Nature of the Universe*, a gloss or marginal note by some one unknown, according to which a Presbyter living in Rome of the name of Caius composed it. At the end of the *Labyrinth*, however, was a note stating that the author of this treatise was also the writer of the one on the Universe. He concluded, therefore, that both belonged to Caius, yet in such a way that, though he deliberately attributes the authorship of the *Labyrinth* to him, yet with regard to the treatise on the Universe he expresses himself again very doubtfully. Photius then mentions the further theory, probably contained in the very note (ἐνπαραγραφαῖς) cited by himself, that the author of this treatise was a Presbyter in Rome, and Bishop-of-the-heathen or the-nations. Such a bishop, without either a definite see or diocese, would, however, at that time have been something otherwise unheard of, a ἅπαξ λεγόμενον. In the first three centuries we meet with no instance of a man being ordained with an indefinite mission, without a bishopric: the case of Pantænus has been appealed to, but it is nowhere asserted of him that he was ordained bishop. Accordingly, Fabricius[1] proposed long ago to read 'Ἀθηνῶν instead of ἐθνῶν in Photius; but, besides the arbitrariness of the emendation, it would then be difficult to explain how this bishop of one of the most famous Churches could have remained unknown to Eusebius and the rest of the Greek Fathers after him. But all these difficulties fall away so soon as we suppose that the author of the *Labyrinth* was either designated Presbyter and Bishop-of-the-heathen in Rome by a pupil or follower, or else assumed this title himself. As the subject under discussion was a heresy which arose and spread in Rome, and the author also (as we see from the fragments preserved in Eusebius) cited remarkable facts bearing upon the new sect there, an opportunity was brought very close for mentioning his own position in Rome; and in the case of his really having one, his being silent about the circumstance would be much more to be wondered at. But that the designation, Presbyter and Bishop (of Rome), contains no contradiction, will be admitted without hesitation by any one

[1] *Biblioth. Græc.* v. p. 267.

who notices that the author of the *Philosophumena* cites Irenæus as ὁ μακάριος πρεσβύτερος, whereby he certainly did not bring the episcopal dignity of that Father into doubt.

The treatise *On the Nature of the Universe* is a work of Hippolytus; of this fact the inscription on the statue at Rome leaves no doubt. As, then, the author of the *Labyrinth*, as well as the author of the *Philosophumena*, confesses to the treatise on the Universe, the easiest and simplest conclusion is, that these three books are by the hand of one and the same writer, viz. Hippolytus. ROUTH[1] has already recognised this as regards the *Labyrinth*. But when Herr Jacobi[2] thinks that the identity of the work cited by Photius, under the title of the *Labyrinth*, with the *Philosophumena*, is clear beyond a doubt, because in the latter also the author cites his book on the Universe, and that Photius was led to the delusion that the *Labyrinth* in Theodoret was the same work on heresies which he had before him, merely by the expression "labyrinth of heresies" used there once quite casually, —we have nothing but an entirely groundless supposition, and Herr Jacobi credits Photius with a want of critical power and a degree of carelessness which would almost border on utter blindness.

For, first: What is more natural than that a man should cite a treatise written by himself in two different works published later?

Secondly: Photius must have seen as well as we do that the *Labyrinth* was directed against a single erroneous doctrine only; whereas in the *Philosophumena* (if he knew the work) thirty heresies are handled. Further: must not Photius have been aware that the history of Natalis, which Theodoret

---

[1] *Reliquiæ Sacræ*, ii. p. 19.
[2] *Deutsche Zeitschrift für Christliche Wissenschaft*, 1851, p. 205.

quotes from the *Labyrinth*, is not to be found in the *Philosophumena*?

Professor Hergenröther [1] thinks, on the other hand, that the *Labyrinth* can scarcely be attributed to the author of the *Philosophumena*, if the σπούδασμα against Artemon (cited by Eusebius) is identical with it. He mentions as reasons, first, the difference of style. But the scanty fragments of the *Labyrinth* or of the σπούδασμα preserved in Eusebius manifestly exhibit no dissimilarity,—none at least great enough to compel us to suppose a separate author for each of the two treatises. When he further says, "The views about penance deducible from the history of the Confessor Natalis cannot easily be brought into harmony with what, according to the ninth book of the *Philosophumena*, was the conviction of the author," we may remark, on the other hand, that the narrator expresses *no* view of his own respecting penance, but merely relates a fact which does not concern him further. Just as little can one allow special weight to his third reason: "The author of our work could scarcely have allowed himself to contradict the theory, that since the times of Zephyrinus the truth had been falsified in the Church, seeing that he himself makes Zephyrinus speak heretically, although, according to him, an unresisting tool in the hands of the crafty Callistus." But, in the first place, the question under discussion was one on which Zephyrinus and the author of the *Philosophumena* were agreed, viz. the Divinity of Christ; and, secondly, it is not Zephyrinus, but his predecessor Victor, whom the writer of the *Labyrinth* defends against the suspicions of the Theodotians.

We may then, I believe, assume as a certain result that the three treatises, the *Philosophumena*, the *Labyrinth*, and the discussion *On the Nature of the Universe*, have

[1] *Tübing. Theol. Quartalschrift*, 1852, p. 423.

one and the same author, and that that author is Hippolytus.

But Photius has already briefly described to us a treatise of Hippolytus on heresies; and hence the thought at once arises, that this σύνταγμα κατὰ αἱρέσεων in Photius is none other than our work. This is also the opinion of Professor Hergenröther. Herr Jacobi, on the other hand, has endeavoured with weighty reasons to show that this is not the case. Herr Bunsen, however, has not allowed Jacobi's reasons, which were already before him, to withhold him from undertaking to prove that our newly-discovered work is nevertheless no other than the one in Photius, and we will follow his reasons step by step. We have, one may say, a double interest in this: first, to arrive at the truth; secondly, to see in this very first question what in fact is the nature of Herr Bunsen's historical criticism, respecting the sure and irrefragably certain progress of which, and its exceedingly correct results, he himself has repeatedly aroused the highest expectations.

The question then is, Can the features of the treatise of Hippolytus noticed by Photius be recognised in the *Philosophumena*?

In the first place, Photius designates the treatise read by him as a pamphlet of small dimensions (βιβλιδάριον), whereas the work which we now possess is of very considerable dimensions, and certainly does not merit that diminutive designation. Herr Bunsen maintains (p. 20) that "Photius uses the same word for a manuscript that at least contained the two letters of Clement of Rome to the Corinthians and the letter of Polycarp to the Philippians, which together would make up a book fully equal to this second part of the work of Hippolytus." An incomprehensible statement. One has only to count the number of words on each side to arrive at the result that the contents of the second part of the *Philosophumena* (from the fourth book onwards) are nearly four times as great as those of the letters of Clement and Polycarp.

Herr Bunsen then maintains further (p. 22) : "The remaining portion of the notice given by Photius is sufficiently definite and exact to prove that we have the work before us ;" and as the three leading points of his proof, he urges that—

(1.) The author of the *Philosophumena* follows the order indicated by Photius; he begins with the Dositheans and ends with the Noëtians.

(2.) The work, like that read by Photius, contains the enumeration and refutation of exactly two-and-thirty heresies.

(3.) According to Photius' account, the author describes his work as being based upon that of Irenæus, and in fact whole articles are copied from Irenæus.

Every one of these three statements is incorrect.

(1a) The book does not begin with the Dositheans, but with the Naassens, Peratics, and Sethians; the Dositheans are not mentioned at all. This manifest discrepancy with Photius' account would have seemed to any one else insoluble, but Herr Bunsen knows how to help himself. "Photius," he says (p. 22), "expresses himself but inexactly; instead of calling them (the original sect of the Judaising Christians) Ophites, as he might have done, or Naassens, which is the same thing, or Justinians, he designates them as Dositheans, a sect which in our book is not mentioned at all; nevertheless, that name designates just this earliest Jewish school." I really wish that the German language was as rich in softer periphrases and synonyms for the blunt expressions, untruth, distortions, inventions, as the Arabic is in synonyms for " camel ;" for almost at every step I am compelled to contradict

Herr Bunsen, and that in things which lie open on the surface, or can be very easily ascertained. The Dositheans were a Samaritan sect, and therefore, in the first place, not a Judaic-cabalistic sect, but rather the contrary, for they rejected the Jewish prophets and denied the existence of good and bad angels; secondly, the Dositheans had nothing in common with the Gnostic Naassens and Ophites, respecting the latter of whom Herr Bunsen himself maintains later on (p. 30) that the place of their origin was unmistakably Phrygia. It is therefore not at all easy to see how Photius was to arrive at putting the Dositheans in place of the Naassens.

No doubt there is a small treatise in which the Dositheans head the list of sects enumerated; it is the one which is printed as an appendix to Tertullian's *De Præscriptione Hæret.* Herr Bunsen knew of this. He says (p. 22): "The author of the appendix begins the list of heretics with Dositheus, which is incorrect, for Dositheus was not a Christian at all, but lived before Christ, and founded a mystic sect among the Samaritans." And (p. 89): "There is also an allusion to them (the Dositheans) as representatives of the oldest class of heretics, in the discussion appended to the treatise of Tertullian." Now, the author of the appendix distinguishes expressly between the *hæretici judaismi*, the præchristian sects, among whom he reckons Dositheus, the Sadducees, Pharisees, and Herodians, and the *hæretici ex evangelio*, of whom Simon Magus was the first; moreover, there is not a syllable to be found in it from which one can draw the conclusion that the Dositheans must have been accounted by the author as representatives of the oldest class of heretics, viz. the Jewish Gnostics. All that has been put into him by Herr Bunsen, and the most favourable supposition with regard to the latter, is that he had never looked at the appendix to Tertullian, but had only a quotation before him when he wrote this.

(1β) It is not true that, as Herr Bunsen states, in the *Philosophumena* the Noëtians are cited as the last heresy. The book ends with the Essenes, Pharisees, and Sadducees, or, if only Christian sects are to be reckoned, with the Elchasaites. Herr Bunsen (p. 88) himself counts the Elchasaites as the thirty-second and last heresy. Yet, in order somehow or other to save his statement that Photius' account is here confirmed, he says (p. 90): "Our author unmistakably treats the Elchasaite heresy, which, according to our method of counting the articles in the work, is the thirty-second, as a short appendage to the Noëtian school. In fact, Alcibiades of Apamea, who taught that heresy in the episcopate, and (so to speak) under the protection of Callistus, was closely connected with the Noëtian school." Here, again, there is not one word of truth. The doctrine of Noëtus and that of Alcibiades, the founder of the Elchasaite sect, have nothing in common with one another. The latter proclaimed a new revelation and a second baptism; and the connection into which Hippolytus[1] brings Alcibiades, not with Noëtus but with Callistus, consists merely in this, that the lax discipline introduced by Callistus, and the praise with which it was received, seem to have inspired Alcibiades with the notion of coming forward in Rome also with his new baptism as an easy forgiver of sins. Of any protection by Callistus, under which Alcibiades taught at Rome, there is not a word anywhere.

(2.) It is equally incorrect to say that the author of the *Philosophumena* enumerates thirty-two heresies, as according to Photius' account was the case in the *Syntagma*; there are only thirty, and Herr Bunsen, in order to make up the number, is obliged quite arbi-

[1] *Philosophumena*, p. 293.

trarily to insert Colarbasus, who does not occur in the book.¹ He who finds it quite natural that Photius should call the *Philosophumena* a small pamphlet, goes on, nevertheless, to assume that there are omissions and abbreviations in the text as we have it; so that Photius must have had a still more complete text than the one which we possess, and ours can be only an abstract from it. That a description of the strange doctrine of Colarbasus existed in the work, but is now missing, is deliberately maintained by Herr Bunsen. "Not only," he says (p. 54), "does the table of contents prefixed to our sixth chapter, as to all others, mention Colarbasus next to Marcus as a subject of the fifth chapter, but our author also himself concludes the book with these words: 'I believe that I have now adequately stated their miserable doctrines, and clearly pointed them out whose disciples they actually were, Marcus as well as Colarbasus, the adherents to the Valentinian doctrine.'² Now, according to our text, Hippolytus does not say a word about Colarbasus. And we cannot suppose that he meant to say that these two had

---

¹ Even with Colarbasus there are only thirty-one. Herr B. gets the still missing one by translating the words (*Philos.* p. 198): "Ἄλλος δέ τις ἐπιφανὴς διδάσκαλος αὐτῶν," "Epiphanes, another teacher of theirs." Hippolytus has here borrowed from Irenæus (i. 5, sec. 2), whose ancient translator, as well as Tertullian, took the word ἐπιφανής, not as a proper name, but as an adjective: *Alius vero quidam qui et clarus est magister ipsorum.* The editors of Irenæus and other scholars have now for some time declared this to be a mistake, and maintained that the author here spoke of the heretic Epiphanes. This is not free from difficulties, because the Epiphanes mentioned by Clement cannot well have been a Valentinian; and, moreover, the position of the words in Hippolytus in itself is not favourable to the hypothesis of a proper name. But we will not dispute further with Herr Bunsen on the point, for in this he has been anticipated by several others.

² Οἱ τῆς Οὐαλεντίνου σχολῆς διάδοχοι γενόμενοι does not mean, "the adherents to the Valentinian doctrine (die Anhänger der Valentinianischen Lehre)," but "successors in the school of Valentinus," just as later on the philosopher Proclus was called successor, διάδοχος, in the school of Syrianus, and the later teachers of the Epicurean school were named διάδοχοι λόγων.

taught exactly the same, and that as he had treated of Marcus at length, he had also spoken adequately of Colarbasus. We know just the opposite; Colarbasus gave the Valentinian doctrine a new direction. Hence there remains no other alternative but that Hippolytus certainly did insert an article on Colarbasus, and that in this case also we possess only an abstract from his original text, and that a very slovenly one."

Now, in opposition to this, we must first of all remember that no conclusion as to a missing chapter can be drawn from the table of contents, for the mere mention of a name in the text was sufficient to make the author of this synopsis of the chapters insert it in his index, while yet in other cases he entirely passes over a heretic of whom Hippolytus gives a more circumstantial account. The Assyrian Prepon[1] is an instance; of the former Lucian is a proof. This Lucian is dismissed by Hippolytus with the simple remark that he was a disciple of Marcion; but in the table of contents more is said about him than in the text, so that, according to Herr Bunsen's theory, we must suppose that the article about him also has slipped out, and he must be counted with the rest; but then there would be thirty-three heresies instead of thirty-two, and so Herr Bunsen has omitted to do this.

The article on Colarbasus, said to have slipped out, Herr Bunsen thinks he may venture to transfer without further trouble from Irenæus (p. 57), but Irenæus never once says that the doctrine stated by him is that of Colarbasus, which name was first added by Epiphanius; the Bishop of Lyons speaks only of a Valentinian school, which considered itself or was considered as the more intelligent. Whether Epiphanius was right in his statement is very doubtful, for he has also committed the error of making Colarbasus a dis-

[1] *L.c.* p. 253.

ciple of Marcus. That this is really an error is shown by the older and better authorities, Irenæus and Tertullian. According to Irenæus, Marcus designated himself as the only son of Colarbasus, who received his doctrine from Sige, and was the first to bring it into the right form.[1] And Tertullian makes Colarbasus the first disciple and successor of Valentinus; next to or after him Ptolemy trod the same path, and not till then did Marcus come next to Heracleon and Secundus.[2]

The author of the appendix to the *De Præscriptione* represents the doctrine of Colarbasus and that of Marcus as quite identical, which confirms the account of Irenæus, that Marcus was only the disciple of the other, and himself speaks of his doctrine as an inheritance that had come to him from Colarbasus. Hippolytus himself in the fourth book mentions Colarbasus as the man who would construct religion with measure and numbers, as others also did, viz. Marcus, whose doctrine he later on describes more closely, while he merely remarks in conclusion that he has now shown whose disciples Marcus and Colarbasus, the διάδοχοι of the Valentinian school, really were, viz. those of Pythagoras. It is therefore clear that Hippolytus had nothing special to say about Colarbasus, because he and Marcus were related to one another much as Cerdon and Marcion, and because his system was merely developed and attained to greater importance in the hands of Marcus.

(3.) Hippolytus, according to the testimony of Photius, had expressly declared in his *Syntagma* that he therein gave a synopsis of the refutations with which Irenæus answered heretics in lectures or sermons. There is not a word about this in the *Philosophumena*; the design would not well agree with the contents of the work. No doubt the author of the latter work

[1] I., 14, pp. 65, 66, ed. Massuet.   [2] *Adv. Valent.* c. 4.

has borrowed much from Irenæus,—as, for example, a great deal of his account of the Valentinians; his description of the doctrine of Marcus and of Saturnilus; again, the main portion of that which he communicates respecting the Carpocratians, Cerinthus, the Ebionites, and Tatian. But all this is borrowed, not from lectures or sermons of the Bishop of Lyons actually delivered, but from his known works, to which Hippolytus refers one for further description. Herr Bunsen exclaims (p. 56) in triumph: "Could we have expected to find such express testimony that the book now discovered is one and the same with that which Photius read, and which bore the title of the work of Hippolytus mentioned by Eusebius and Jerome?" And what is this clear testimony? We are to find it in a passage which, as it stands,[1] is corrupt, for which the editor, Miller, has proposed an emendation, giving a sense which can be of no service for Herr Bunsen's purpose,—in a passage which, even if one does not adopt this emendation, does not contain, and from the construction cannot contain, what Herr Bunsen puts into it. For, according to him, Hippolytus is made to say: "It is from him (the blessed Presbyter Irenæus) that I have taken the description of their inventions." But, not to mention that Herr Bunsen never once gives the word which must be inserted in order to bring out this meaning, he seems altogether to have overlooked the fact that we have here the plural παραλαβόντες, which cannot possibly refer to the author, viz. to Hippolytus, for immediately before this and immediately after it he speaks of himself in the singular. And even if Hippolytus really had said that he borrowed his account of the Valentinians from Irenæus, this would still not be the statement which Photius had read in his treatise, for in this the whole of the

---

[1] *Philos.* p. 222.

little work was designated as a synopsis of the lectures of Irenæus.

(4.) Photius had noticed a passage in his treatise in which the author says that the *Epistle to the Hebrews* was not written by S. Paul the Apostle. This passage does not exist in our work.

Herr Bunsen endeavours to help himself here (p. 21) by the supposition of a general introduction, which is now wanting in the work. This introduction is to assist him in setting aside two difficulties. In the first place, it is to have contained the statement about the *Epistle to the Hebrews;* and, secondly, in it the author is to have stated the relation of his work to that of Irenæus, *i.e.* have said that he compiled his refutation from the lectures of Irenæus. But then the work already has an introduction in front of the first book, and when Herr Bunsen says that this may have special reference to the first part, while a preceding *general* introduction has been lost, this is utterly without foundation. The existing introduction is manifestly the only one, and intended for the whole work; its contents have even more reference to the second part of the work (the drift and contents of which are therein set forth) than to the first.

(5.) In the *Chronicon Paschale*[1] a passage from the *Syntagma* of Hippolytus is quoted, in which the author makes a Quartodeciman state his main argument, and then refutes this in a few words. Now, as Herr Bunsen holds the *Syntagma* to be identical with the *Philosophumena*, and yet this passage is not to be found in the latter work, resort must again be had to the means already employed in enumerating the heresies. The very work which Photius (in Herr Bunsen's opinion), although he had the whole before him, could designate as a βιβλιδάριον, is yet, we are told in the portions

P. 12, ed. Bonn.

remaining to us, only an abstract : "We have it in this article (on the Quartodecimans), and conjecture it also in many other passages, where the text is not clear and appears to want something, in an abbreviated, and, moreover, in a very clumsily and carelessly abbreviated form."[1]

Herr Bunsen's proofs are these:—

(1.) Hippolytus cannot have handled the Easter question, a subject which he had investigated with special care, and on which he was the first authority of his time, so negligently and meagrely in a book on which he had expended so much time and zeal.

Answer: Precisely because Hippolytus had handled this subject already in particular treatises, and for the most part was not inclined to copy himself, he has not gone more deeply into the subject here.

(2.) Hippolytus opposes the theory of the Quartodecimans, that the law with regard to the Feast of the Passover on the 14th Nisan was still binding, with the well-known sentence of S. Paul, that he who holds fast to one Jewish enactment is liable to the whole law. Now, Herr Bunsen says that this is certainly a perfectly sound and apostolical proof (p. 81), but unless one supplies a second answer, which certainly is now wanting in the text, the first has no force (p. 83 above). Now, to begin with, it is sufficiently astonishing to hear of a proof which is perfectly sound and yet proves nothing; but one's astonishment cannot but increase when one observes the strange logic which Herr Bunsen with all violence insists on attributing to both parties, the Quartodecimans and Hippolytus. "The poor Quartodecimans," we read on p. 81, "when they were pressed with this argument, could answer: In that we are quite agreed, if you only prove to us that what we do is wrong. But the simple fact that we are

[1] Bunsen, p. 82.

not bound to keep the whole law, does not prove that we are doing wrong in keeping it in this point." This natural reply is then made to provoke the second proof: "Certainly you are wrong in this particular point. Christ's own conduct proves that this law ceased to be binding when He met His death. On that occasion He did not eat the typical Paschal lamb, for He Himself was the true one; and therefore He died on the day on which the Jews ate the Paschal lamb in the evening."

Herr Bunsen has evidently misunderstood the Apostle's whole line of argument, as well as that of the Bishop. Both say, Whoever in matters of religion does anything because the Mosaic law orders it, he thereby admits the obligatory power of the whole law, and must therefore fulfil it in all points. But, seeing that a Christian neither will nor can do this, he must not do anything whatever on the authority of the law. So that Hippolytus, with this single production of S. Paul's argument, proved at once to the Quartodecimans that they were doing wrong in separating themselves from the rest of the Church respecting the feast of the Passover on the authority of the Mosaic decree.

In the passage from the *Syntagma* preserved in the *Chronicon Paschale*, Hippolytus has to deal with a single person and his argument. This unknown individual, in reference to his method of celebrating the Passover, appeals not to the Mosaic law, but, on the contrary, to the example of Christ, which ought to be the pattern for Christians. The question for him was rather as to the matter, the eating of the Paschal lamb, than as to the day of the feast. Accordingly, Hippolytus answered him that on that occasion Christ did not eat the Paschal lamb at all, but rather was Himself slain as that Lamb at the time appointed for it.¹ So palpably perverse and groundless is the whole of Herr Bunsen's long argument with which he endeavours to make this passage into a fragment out of the existing text of the *Philosophumena*, that really it only needs a simple comparison of the two passages to compel one to suppose that they belong to two different works.

For the exposure of another misapprehension of Herr Bunsen in designating the passage in the *Chronicon Paschale* as a citation to be found in the text of S. Peter of Alexandria, we shall have an opportunity later on; but we cannot here leave unnoticed the deliberate unfaithfulness with which Herr Bunsen is wont to translate Hippolytus. He makes Hippolytus say, Christ is the true Paschal Lamb, *received by faith alone*. Had this Father said that, he must have accepted the doctrine of Zwingli, and have excluded the real reception of the Paschal Lamb, Christ, from the Eucharist. But Herr Bunsen has in the first place arbitrarily inserted the word "alone," and secondly, instead of "recognised" (νούμενον) has put "received." That it is faith which recognises in Christ the true Easter Lamb is universal Christian doctrine; but that this Paschal Lamb is received only through faith, neither Hippolytus nor any one else of the ancient Fathers has said.

The conjecture has long ago been put forth, that the *Syntagma* which Photius describes may be preserved to us in a Latin, although certainly only in an abbreviated form—viz. that the appendix to Tertullian's *Præscriptiones*, or the *Libellus adversus omnes hæreticos*,² is a Latin version of the *Syntagma* of Hippolytus. It

¹ ["In the *Treatise on the Passover* Hippolytus says, οὐκ ἔφαγεν, ἀλλ' ἔπαθεν, i.e. He did not eat the Passover, but suffered as the Passover."—Quotation in the *Chronicon Paschale*.]

² Routh has given this title to the treatise in his edition (the best as yet), *Scriptorum eccles. opuscula præcipua*, Oxon. 1832.

was the French (reformed) theologian Allix, a resident in England, who was the first, I believe, to maintain this hypothesis.[1] Now that Hippolytus' larger work of similar contents lies before us, the question, which before could only be treated tentatively, admits of being decided with tolerable certainty. In the first place, it is clear that the Latin translator must have left out the chief part, the refutation taken from the lectures of Irenæus. That may well have been the case, and the number of the heresies agrees exactly with that given by Photius. There are exactly thirty-two. Moreover, it is probable, almost certain, that the author of this little treatise lived in Rome. But this said, we have already pretty well exhausted the features of agreement. Instead of Noëtus, the *Libellus* gives Praxeas, whom the author of the *Philosophumena*, strange to say, never mentions at all; and when the author of an article in the *Christian Remembrancer*[2] thinks it credible that the Latin translator may have substituted Praxeas for the Noëtus of the Greek text, I am unable to agree with him. Why should the mention of so important a man as Noëtus be suppressed? He might, of course, have mentioned Praxeas next to him as one addicted to the same doctrine. Hermogenes, against whom Tertullian wrote no less than against Praxeas, and whom Hippolytus mentions more in detail in his chief work, is wanting in the *Libellus*. The Cainites, about whom the latter treatise contains fuller information, are, on the other hand, dismissed in the work of Hippolytus as quite unimportant sectaries, and as if he scarcely knew them. Specially striking is the difference between the accounts which the two treatises give respecting the doctrine of Apelles. For while the *Libellus* represents Apelles as

---

[1] See Waterland's *Works*, v. 227, London 1823.
[2] January 1853, p. 229.

a dualist, who taught that there were two divinities, the Supreme God and the Creator of the world, Hippolytus maintains in the *Philosophumena* that he supposed there were three, or, with the evil one, four divinities. These are not differences which admit of being explained by mere increase of insight, which we might otherwise easily have supposed to have taken place in a man like Hippolytus, when we take the time into account which may have elapsed between the composition of his first and smaller treatise and that of the greater, the *Philosophumena*. Rather it appears to me probable that the author of the *Libellus* made use of one of Hippolytus' treatises, and possibly of both.

The first treatise of Hippolytus on heresies is then, no doubt, lost to us, but his second is preserved to us in the *Philosophumena*. That the *Syntagma* in Photius is really the earlier, while our work is the later treatise of Hippolytus, may be seen from the commencement of the latter; for this Father refers to another one composed by him at an earlier period, in which he has given the doctrines of the heretics in a brief form, only darkly indicating their secret teaching, and refuting them in general or on the main points.[1] This was therefore a smaller treatise, a βιβλιδάριον, the contents of which were not a description of heretical systems, but only a short mention of them, and chiefly a refutation of their main tenets. This refutation he had taken from sermons of Irenæus, as we learn from Photius. But because he saw, he continues, that that charitable reserve remained without results among them, he now felt himself compelled to disclose their

[1] Ὣν καὶ πάλαι μετρίως τὰ δόγματα ἐξεθέμεθα, οὐ κατὰ λεπτὸν ἐπιδείξαντες, ἀλλὰ ἀδρομερῶς ἐλέγξαντες. These last two words are rendered by Wolf, *pinguius crassiusque redarguentes*. ἀδρομερῶς is the French "en gros." Hippolytus says that he has not entered upon a detailed refutation, but has merely combated what was most striking.

hidden mysteries and carefully-concealed teaching. In the present work, therefore, he is primarily concerned not with refutation, but with an exact and complete description of heretical systems, in order that men may perceive that the heretics have borrowed their doctrines (which they communicate only to those who have been carefully prepared beforehand, and at first kept in long suspense), partly from the philosophy of the Greeks and the doctrines of other nations, partly from the mysteries or from wandering charlatans and astrologers. Both treatises, therefore, must be completed.

Both Epiphanius and Theodoret, in their works on heresies, mention Hippolytus among their authorities.[1] The former refers to what has been accomplished by Clement, Irenæus, and Hippolytus, who, by their refutations of the Valentinians, had amply done what was necessary, and had saved him the trouble of dealing with them any further. This reference in itself makes it probable that he here was thinking of the *Syntagma*, and not of the *Philosophumena*; the latter seems not to have been known to him, otherwise he would not have passed over Justinus, Monoimus, Prepon, the Peratics, and Hermogenes. On the other hand, Theodoret certainly had our *Philosophumena* before his eyes, and used the book; yet not entire probably, but only the recapitulation, which forms the tenth book; whence he also mentions Callistus among the heretics in such a way that it would seem as if he did not know who this Callistus actually was. It is probable that some people possessed copies of this tenth book alone, for it might take the place of the larger work as a convenient summary for general use, just as even Augustine did not know the larger work of Epiphanius on heresies, but only a short abstract

[1] Opp. ed. Petav. i. p. 205.

from it.¹ The opinion of Herr Bunsen, that the tenth Book *perhaps* is that earlier treatise to which Hippolytus refers at the beginning of his book, cannot for a moment be allowed to pass as even a " perhaps," for the author himself gives the regular connection in which his tenth book stands to the earlier ones most expressly; and one has to supply only the entirely arbitrary and improbable supposition that he has re-written the first page of the tenth book, in order thus to incorporate an earlier and independent work with this one as a conclusion to the whole. In that case, what he says by way of marking the difference between his first treatise and the present work does not fit the tenth book at all—viz. that in that first treatise he had stated the doctrine of the heretics only darkly and enigmatically (δι' αἰνιγμάτων); now, however, he would describe them without reserve.

Respecting the other lost writings of Hippolytus, with which Herr Bunsen busies himself at great length, I have only a couple of remarks to make.

(1.) From the catalogue of the Syrian Ebed-Jesu we see that a treatise by Hippolytus, *Capita adversus Caium*, was translated into Syriac. In Herr Bunsen (p. 198) this is called " eine Abhandlung gegen *Cain*," apparently a misprint for *Caius*, which is the reading in the English edition. But when Herr Bunsen adds, " I agree with the conjecture of Fabricius, that this must have been a treatise against the Cainites," he more assuredly deceives himself, although Magistris also (p. 127) supposes this. If this were the case, then there must have been a Caius who founded a sect, and from him the sect of the Cainites must have borne the name, which occurs in Epiphanius and in the index in Irenæus,² of Caians. But this heretical Caius is nowhere mentioned, is an utterly unknown

---

¹ *De Hæresibus*, præf. ² P. 113, ed. Grabe.

person, and it is therefore probable that the person attacked by Hippolytus is his contemporary Caius, who wrote the account of his conference with Proclus, and a treatise against Cerinthus. The inscription on the marble statue mentions a treatise of Hippolytus' which he composed in defence of the *Gospel* and the *Apocalypse* of S. John. It seems to me probable that the portion of the treatise which dealt with the *Apocalypse* was that directed against Caius, for at this time he would not admit that it was a genuine work of S. John the apostle; and that in the Syriac translation the title mentioned above was chosen.

(2.) I also believe that the προτρεπτικὸς εἰς Σεβήρειναν in the inscription on the statue is the same treatise as that which Theodoret designates as addressed πρὸς βασιλίδα τινά. Severina must therefore have been mother, wife, or daughter of an emperor. Now the name itself is enough to show that it is not Julia Mammæa, mother of Alexander Severus, as Baronius thought, nor yet Severa, the wife of the Emperor Philip, as Lemoyne would have it; Hippolytus did not live on into this emperor's reign. The conjecture of Herr Bunsen that it is a daughter of Alexander Severus is equally inadmissible, for this emperor married in the year 229, nothing is known of a daughter, and his wife was very soon separated from him, and driven away by his mother; even if he had had a daughter, she would at the most have been only four or five years old in the year of Hippolytus' death. The treatise was much more probably addressed to Julia Aquilia Severa, the second wife of the Emperor Elagabalus.[1]

The statue of Hippolytus, which was found in Rome in the year 1551, always seemed to me to be a most

[1] See respecting this Princess, CLINTON's *Fasti Romani*, p. 233; and ECKHEL, *doctr. num.* vii. p. 260, iii. p. 342.

remarkable and extraordinary monument, even before I could suspect the revelations which the newly-discovered work discloses respecting his personality. It appeared to me that some very special motive, now no longer to be divined, must have induced the man's friends and disciples to erect this monument. No such mark of respect, so far as we know, was ever paid to any Bishop of Rome in ancient times,—perhaps one may say to any Catholic Bishop at all in the first few centuries. Only one similar monument of Christian antiquity has been preserved at all—viz. a statue of S. Peter, also in Rome, and likewise in a sitting posture. Winkelmann says the figure is beyond doubt the oldest marble statue of Christian times, of the time of Alexander Severus, and all historical analogies also testify to the same effect. We can then very easily explain how the enthusiastic adherents of a man who was not only a revered teacher and ecclesiastical author, but also a party leader sharply criticised and withal bitterly reviled by the opposite side, erected this monument to him, possibly after his banishment to Sardinia. And the objection which is commonly raised against this early origin of it—viz. that the Christians of Rome were not yet in a position to undertake such things—is of no weight. In the long rest and even favour which the Christians enjoyed after the death of Severus, and which, with slight intermission, lasted for forty years, until the reign of Decius, the Christians had acquired landed property and buildings. They possessed great cemeteries, in which were rooms or chapels two stories high, and, along with these, places of meeting above or below ground, in which such a figure might find a place. But to bring the statue of Hippolytus to a later period, and transfer it to the fifth or sixth century, as has lately been attempted, is to make the whole matter an inexplicable riddle.

For, to begin with, we are compelled to believe that the community, at the head of which Hippolytus was, cut off from the congregation of the Bishop of Rome, at any rate did not maintain itself long after his death. Twenty years later it seems already to have vanished, without leaving a trace; for in the history of the Church of Rome from 250 to 257, which we know tolerably exactly from Cyprian's collection of letters, no mention of it is found. And especially when Novatian's sect arose, which had an element kindred to that of Hippolytus, it must have given some sign of life; but not a syllable is said about it in that connection. All tells in favour of the conjecture, which is supported by the ancient common festival in commemoration of Pontianus and Hippolytus, and placed on the same day, that the separation was brought to an end by Hippolytus himself shortly before his death. But who in later times would be likely to think of paying so extraordinary and unexampled a mark of respect to a man whose history appears enveloped in obscurity from so early a point, whose writings found no diffusion in the West, and here remained as good as unknown? We cannot attribute the monument to one of the Christian Emperors, nor yet to one of the Popes, as having been erected by his order. And we are therefore, with all our conjectures, always brought back to the supposition that it was a congregation which gave to their absent or else lately-deceased teacher and leader this proof of their grateful adherence, and who wished to hand on to posterity the memory of one who in their eyes was the rightful Bishop, and successor of S. Peter.

Further, the Easter-cycle, which is engraved on the statue, begins with the year 222, and goes on to the year 333. Now, if the statue was not set up until after 333, would any one have undertaken so troublesome and at the same time thankless work? would they with great expenditure of time and toil have engraved on the hard marble a cycle which had already lost all meaning and all use whatsoever, and that, too, at a time when its faultiness must have been well known? But suppose the figure to have been made in Hippolytus' time, or soon after his death, we then can understand very well how his adherents came to have a cycle engraved upon it, according to which they hoped to keep themselves correct in the regulation of their Easter festival.

Lastly, the seat of the statue contains not only the cycle of Hippolytus, but also the titles of many of his writings, all of which, as is well known, were composed in Greek. In the second and third centuries Rome was still a chief seat and focus of Greek literature and language; moreover, the Christians of the Greek tongue formed there a considerable portion of the community, and had, beyond doubt, their places of meeting where a Greek liturgy and Greek sermons prevailed. Besides, in the second century the Greek language was still the ecclesiastical language even in the West; for, according to the testimony of Jerome, it was not until the end of this century that Pope Victor and the Senator Apollonius wrote upon ecclesiastical matters for the first time in Latin; while in Rome, Clement, Hermas, the brother of Bishop Pius, Caius (if he belonged to the Church of Rome), Hippolytus, and still at the beginning of the fourth century Pope Sylvester, wrote in Greek, and the Popes kept up a lively correspondence with the Eastern Church in Greek. This changed, however, when Byzantium became the capital of the Roman Orient, and all Orientals and Greek-speaking people turned no longer to Rome, but thither. From the time of Constantine, therefore, the Greek language disappeared from Rome by rapid degrees, so much so that in the time of Pope Zosimus (in the year 417) the Greek text of the Nicene Canons appears not to have been extant any more in Rome, and in the year 430 Pope Cœlestine apprised Nestorius that he was unable to answer his letter, because he must first get it translated into Latin, and at the moment he had not a translator at hand;[1] it appears, therefore, that among the Roman clergy at that time there was no longer any one who still had command of Greek. Accordingly it becomes utterly inconceivable that at such a time a statue should have been made with a Greek Easter-cycle and a long list of Greek works. For whose use?[2]

[1] Thus no doubt we are to understand the words (*Epp. Pontiff Rom.*, p. 1116, ed. Coust.), Ὅπερ ὡς Βραδέως διὰ τὴν ἀνάγκην ἐποιοῦμεν. The ἀνάγκη cannot well refer to anything else but the want of a translator.

[2] [Dr. Salmon, in his valuable article on the *Chronology of Hippolytus* in the first number of the *Hermathena*, 1873, fixes the date of the erection of the statue at 235, very shortly after the banishment of Hippolytus. It could not have been erected much later, for the mistakes in the cycle become considerable after that time, and by 243 its erroneous character had become notorious. It could not have been erected earlier, for one of the works mentioned on the statue was written in 235. The cycle begins with the year 222, probably because that was the first year of the Emperor Alexander's reign, pp. 88–90.]

CHAPTER II.

ON THE HISTORY OF HIPPOLYTUS.

THE SAINTS OF THE SAME NAME.

AROUND the name of Hippolytus an amount of confusion has hitherto prevailed which is almost without a parallel in ecclesiastical history. The endless interchanges have driven most scholars who have busied themselves with the subject to despair, and in consequence the history of this Father has appeared enveloped in impenetrable obscurity. Thus in the various martyrologies we find *five* persons of this name, all of them said to have been martyrs, all of them said to have lived nearly at the same time, the first half of the third century. Since the appearance of the *Philosophumena* it has, however, become possible to dispel this obscurity. A firm foothold is secured to begin with in the union of the two names Hippolytus and Pontianus, and the date of the 13th of August, which, according to the best and oldest accounts, was from the first dedicated to the memory of the two men. Here, however, we may go on to observe how into the place of the Hippolytus (who, so to speak, was the rightful owner of this day) another of the same name gradually thrust himself, simultaneously with which Pontianus vanished.

The oldest account is that of the chronographer of the year 354. In the *depositio martyrum* we read: *Idus Aug.; Hippolyti in Tiburtina, et Pontiani in*

Calisti. On the 13th of August, therefore, the commemoration of the deposition of both was celebrated, although their bodies rested in different places, viz. Hippolytus in the Tiburtina, and Pontianus in the cemetery of Callistus. That the 13th of August is not the day of their death is shown by the account in the Roman *Pontifical Book*,[1] which places the death of Pontianus on the 11th of November.[2] It is worth noticing that, in the series of Roman Bishops and martyrs whose *depositio* the old chronographer records, only one other occurs who, like Hippolytus, rested in the Tiburtina, and that is S. Lawrence. Both Pontianus and Hippolytus together appear still on the 13th of August in one of the oldest martyrologies and sacramentaries, viz. the one edited by Fiorentini, under the title *Vetustius ecclesiæ occidentalis Martyrologium*,[3] and in the calendar, which by a well-known fiction bears the name of S. Jerome, as printed by d'Achery.[4] In addition we have the weighty testimony of the oldest known liturgical codex, viz. of the co-called *Sacramentarium Leonianum*, which, according to Muratori's investigations, contains a collection of Roman liturgies belonging to the period between Leo and Gelasius (457–492). Here also we find once more on the 13th of August *Natale Sanctorum Hippolyti et Pontiani*, who are designated as martyrs in the prayers. Yet the preface in this mass is unmistakably a later insertion, for it leaves Pontianus unmentioned, names Hippolytus only, and speaks of his blood shed as a testimony to divine truth. Here the interchange or substitution of another Hippolytus, to be noticed more closely presently, has already prevailed.

For from the sixth century onwards, and to some extent still earlier, an Hippolytus appears on the 13th of

---

[1] Ed. Vignoli, I. p. 42. [2] III. idus Novb. [3] P. 750.
[4] *S. Hieronymi Opera*, ed. Paris 1846, XI. p. 470.

August, who has nothing in common with that Roman Presbyter but the name, and is brought into close connection with S. Lawrence. The history of this martyr is known to us only from the *Acts of S. Lawrence*. In these we are told that he was a military officer of high rank, into whose charge the Deacon Lawrence was given before his execution; converted and baptized by him, he had then brought his whole family of nineteen persons to the Christian faith. Along with them he was made a prisoner three days after the death of S. Lawrence. His nurse Concordia gave up the ghost under the lash of the executioner. The rest were beheaded, but Hippolytus, after numerous torments, was tied to the feet of wild horses, and by them torn to pieces.

Among all Roman martyrs, S. Lawrence is the one who from the earliest times was celebrated most, and most widely. Already in the fifth century four or five churches were dedicated to his honour in Rome. In all parts of the West, and even in the East, his festival was kept.[1] But the older and better authorities, Ambrose, Augustine, Petrus Chrysologus, Maximus of Turin, Leo the Great, all know of Lawrence only. Of the conversion of Hippolytus through him, and of his family, there is no trace. And yet it is scarcely conceivable that so remarkable an event as the conversion of a Roman officer, the extraordinary manner of his death, and the execution of a whole family of nineteen persons, should have remained unnoticed, if anything had been known of it in the fourth century. The *Acts of S. Lawrence*, in which this martyrdom of Hippolytus and of his house with him is inserted, are, as is universally acknowledged, a later invention, and historically an altogether useless document. The first mention of this Hippolytus is found in a speech appended to the works

---

[1] *Quam non potest abscondi Roma, tam non potest abscondi Lawrentii corona*, says S. Augustine.

of S. Fulgentius, and in another bearing the name of Augustine, which the editors have likewise banished to the appendix as not a genuine work;[1] that is to say, not until the 6th century. Then, in Gregory of Tours (about the year 588), who, following the anachronism spread by the false *Acts of S. Lawrence*, mentions Hippolytus, with Lawrence and Sixtus, as victims of the Decian persecution.[2] But from this time onwards in calendars, martyrologies, and a number of chronicles, the martyrdom of Hippolytus and Concordia is almost always given along with that of S. Lawrence. Even in the East, *e.g.* in the *menæum* translated from the Greek,[3] we find him mentioned, yet without a special day to commemorate him, no doubt because the spurious *Acts of S. Lawrence* had been translated into Greek.

The development of the story which surrounds the person of Hippolytus is most clearly seen in the Roman calendars and missals. The connecting link which is constituted by the narrative of Prudentius shall be spoken of separately. In the list of depositions in the year 354, Hippolytus, as already noticed, is still united with Pontianus; with Lawrence he has nothing in common but the grave on the Via Tiburtina, and it is worth remarking that in this list Lawrence and Hippolytus are the only persons whose bones are said to repose on the Via Tiburtina. The oldest Roman missal has likewise Hippolytus and Pontianus together; but from thence onwards there is no further mention of Pontianus. Hippolytus alone, or Hippolytus and Concordia, Hippolytus and his family, are mentioned as the objects of the cultus; the blood which he shed

---

[1] *Opp. S. Fulgentii*, Sermo 60, in Appendice, p. 83. *Opp. S. Augustini*, t. v. App. p. 376, Serm. 316, ed. Antwerp.

[2] *Opp.* ed. RUINART.

[3] In CANISIUS-BASUAGE, III. i. p. 455, on the 2d of August; *Sixtus, interfectus et ipse postea cum ss. Martyribus Lawrentio et Hippolyto.*

for confessing the Christian faith is mentioned, and at last we read in the Gothic missal (which was used in South Gaul at the beginning of the eighth century): *Qui beatum Yppolitum tyrannicis adhuc obsequiis occupatum subito fecisti Laurenti socium. Qui spiritali ardore succensus, dum Unigenitum Filium tuum Dominum nostrum coram potestatibus veraciter confitetur, pœnis subjicitur, vinculis inligatur, cardis configitur, equorum ferocitate disjungitur.*[1] The composition of the new story appears to me to fall within the period of about seventy years, between the time of Pope Liberius and that of Leo the Great. The oldest document in which (it seems to me) the personality of the real Hippolytus is already obscured, and the mythical Roman officer, the guard of S. Lawrence, has stepped into his place, may well have been the half-heathen, half-Christian calendar of Polemius Sylvius, which falls within the year 448; and, along with notices of the weather and the games, contains the "Natales" of the Emperor and other festivals having reference to that. Among Christian feasts one finds given in this document only Epiphany and Christmas; and of saints'-days, the martyrdom of the Maccabees on the 1st of August, Depositio S. Petri et Pauli on the 22d of February, the day of S. Lawrence and of Hippolytus on the 13th of August, S. Stephen's day, and lastly, that of S. Vincent, Deacon of Saragossa. The somewhat later Carthaginian Calendar,[2] the Calendar of Fronto, the one found in Allatius,[3]—all these have Hippolytus only on the 13th of August; the small Roman martyrology states more particularly: *Romæ Hippolyti martyris cum familia sua et S. Concordiæ nutricis ejus.* Ado makes him suffer death under the Emperor Decius and

---

[1] Ap. MURATORI, *Liturg.* II. p. 628.
[2] In RUINART, *Acta Martyrum*, ed. Amstelod. p. 618.
[3] *De Consensione Eccles. occident. atque orientalis*, Col. 1648, p. 1491.

the Præfect Valerian, quite in accordance with the confessedly false account in the spurious *Acts of S. Lawrence;* whereas it is certain that S. Lawrence was not executed until long after Decius' time, viz. under the Emperor Valerian, in the year 258. The martyrology of Bede and that of Usuard give the manner of his death—that he was torn to pieces by wild horses, and call his nurse Concordia. So also the present Roman martyrology. The Mozarabic breviary has woven the narrative into a hymn.

Thus it came to pass that Hippolytus became one of the most celebrated names in the whole Church, in the Greek-speaking as well as in the Latin-speaking parts; but that in the West an altogether different person was intended under this name from the one intended in the East. That is to say,—while in the latter it is the figure of the famous Father and Bishop to which people held fast, in the West it was only the Roman officer known from the *Acts of S. Lawrence,* and by him converted, whom this name recalled for ecclesiastical remembrance. In the Greek Church, of course, his writings were preserved till quite a late period, especially the exegetical ones, as the *Catenæ* show, and from these his ecclesiastical rank was known; while in the West the Father was so unknown and so utterly forgotten, that, with the exception of Jerome, none of the Latin Fathers—not even Augustine—so much as mentions him.

Perhaps it is feasible to get some light also from the notices which have reference to tombs and churches of Hippolytus, or to some antiquarian remains bearing his name. From the earliest times it was an established fact that he, as S. Lawrence also, was buried on the Via Tiburtina, in the Ager Veranus. But the question is, whether a special church was dedicated to him as early as to S. Lawrence; that is, at least as early as the fourth century. Prudentius describes, as an eye-witness (about the year 406), the subterranean tomb of S. Hippolytus, the representation on the wall there of his being put to death by horses, the altar erected over his bones; but then goes on to speak of a splendid church which stood close by, with a double row of columns, which, on the 13th of August, the festival of the saint, received the crowd of believers who streamed thither from far and wide. Now, it has been commonly supposed that this was a church dedicated to Hippolytus exclusively, and bearing his name. I hold this to be incorrect, and believe that it was the church of S. Lawrence, which likewise stood there, that Prudentius meant. We are tolerably well informed about the churches which stood in Rome before the sixth century, partly through the notices in the *Liber Pontificalis*, partly through the two calendars, that of Martene of the fifth century, and that of Fronto of the eighth century, which, in the list of the stations, give also the names of the Roman churches. Besides which, we have the signatures of the Roman presbyters, with their "tituli" or churches, in the Acts of the Roman Synod in the year 499. While, then, as early as the fifth century, three or four churches of S. Lawrence existed in Rome, there is no trace of a church dedicated to Hippolytus, not even in Fronto's list of the Roman churches, although that is of the eighth century. A cemetery of Hippolytus is mentioned, and first in the Roman *Pontifical Book* in the life of Pope Hadrian I., who restored it after it had long lain waste.[1] It was a bit of the cemetery of Cyriaca, near the church of S. Stephen in the Ager Veranus, lying round the crypt

---

[1] *Ecclesiam Nicomedis et cœmeterium beati Hippolyti M. juxta S. Laurentium, quæ a priscis marcuerunt temporibus, a novo renovavit. Pari modo et ecclesiam b. Christi Martyris Stephani, sitam juxta prædictum cœmeterium S. Hippolyti, similiter restauravit.* Ed. VIGNOL, II. p. 228.

described by Prudentius; and there also, in the time of Cardinal Alexander Farnese,[1]—that is, about the year 1530,—the bones of the martyrs, viz. of Hippolytus, Concordia, and the eighteen or nineteen others, are said to have been found,—that is, bones about which it was thought that they might very well belong to the martyrs who, according to the story, were to be sought for here. A basilica of Hippolytus is first mentioned in the list of places of martyrdoms given by Eckhart[2] and Frobenius,[3] and dating from the ninth or tenth century; according to which, it stood on an eminence in the Via Tiburtina; and moreover, as the description of places in Rome in Mabillon[4] of about the same date remarks, opposite the chief church of S. Lawrence. The erection of it may therefore fall about the end of the eighth or beginning of the ninth century; and as the *Liber Pontificalis* does not mention it, it appears to have been built by private persons. But how closely the cultus of Hippolytus was from the first connected with that of S. Lawrence and subordinated to it, is shown in Milan, where a church of S. Lawrence existed from the fifth century, and was accounted the most beautiful and most magnificent in the city.[5] In the interior of this church there existed, near a "sacellum" of S. Xystus, a chapel of S. Hippolytus also, in which two Bishops of Milan—Theodore, who died in the year 490, and his successor Lawrence—were interred.[6] This, then, explains also why in the canon of the Ambrosian liturgy, in the prayer *Communicantes*,

---

[1] ARINGHI *Roma Subterranea*, II. p. 54.
[2] *De rebus Franciæ Orient.*, I. p. 832.
[3] ALCUINI *Opp.* II. p. 599.
[4] *Analecta*, p. 365.
[5] So in the old rhythm, *De laudibus Mediolani*, in OLTROCCHI, *Ecclesiæ Mediol. Hist.* p. 697.
[6] SAXII *Series Archiepp. Mediol.* in the *tabula chronol. Tumulum recepi in Basilica Laurentiana ad S. Hippolyti Sacellum.*

Hippolytus stands immediately after Sixtus and Lawrence.

At an earlier date than this church near Rome dedicated to the guard and disciple of S. Lawrence, there stood a church of S. Hippolytus in the seaport town of Portus. This one, however, was dedicated neither to the soldier just mentioned, nor to the supposed Bishop of Portus; for the historical Hippolytus was never, as will be seen hereafter, Bishop of Portus; but to a mythical martyr mentioned only in the *Acts of S. Aurea* or Chryse, and said to have been drowned in a pit or tank near Portus. Here a body was preserved, which, as early as the eighth century, was held to be that of the martyr of Porto; for in the first mention of this church, which occurs in the life of Pope Leo III. in the *Liber Pontificalis*,[1] we read: This Pope had two pieces of stuff worked with crosses (*vestes de stauraci*), made for the basilica of the holy martyr Hippolytus, in the "civitas Portuensis,"[2] one as a shroud for the body, the other as a covering for the high altar.

It is unmistakable that around S. Lawrence, revered as he was at such an early date, a whole circle o myths and mythical persons gradually sprang up, and that as early as the end of the fourth century. Al ready, in the fourth century, there seems to have beer a lack of a sure and authentic basis for his history and hence ornamental myth had all the freer play Names, inscriptions, to which no definite historica knowledge was any longer attached, but which, becaus they were found near the resting-place of S. Lawrence suggested the invention of any martyrdom that migh

---

[1] Ed. VIGNOLI, II. p. 266.
[2] *The Life of Leo III.*, III. p. 117, contains the more exact descrip tion : " *Ecclesia quæ ponitur in insula Portuensi, quæ nuncupatur Arsis.*" was the cathedral.

stand in connection with that of S. Lawrence; perhaps also representations in sculpture, then localities, to which the myth would give a sacred character,—all these things were moulded together into a narrative, of which the Roman Deacon was the centre and hero. Just as in later times a tombstone representing the Count of Gleichen with two wives, has given occasion to the invention of the well-known story,[1] so from the fourth and fifth century onwards a similar process took place with reference to the history of martyrs, especially in Rome, where the people from childhood had heard of a number of nameless martyrs scattered over the great city. Let us look more closely at the short description in the *Notitia* of the ninth century; here we read: *Inde in Boream sursum in monte Basilica Sancti Hipoliti est, ubi ipse cum familia sua tota* xix. *mart. jacet. Carcer ibi est, in qua fuit Laurentius. Ibi est Trifonia uxor Decii Cæsaris, et Cyrilla filia ejus ; inter utrasque Concordia et sanctus Genesius et multi martyres ibi sunt.*[2] All this close to the church of S. Lawrence, *in qua corpus ejus primum fuerat humatum.* Originally, and down to about the year 354, it was the Roman Presbyter Hippolytus, who was banished with Pope Pontian to Sardinia, but whose body was brought back from there and interred on the Via Tiburtina, quite close to the tomb of S. Lawrence. Later on this person was forgotten; at any rate, became unknown to the vulgar. In the neighbourhood some heathen monument, on which the tragical end of the son of Theseus of that name was sculptured, may very possibly have been found, and been conjectured by the Christian folk to represent his martyrdom. Possibly it was even the name alone with which the current story, still under the influence of heathen recollections, connected

[1] [See Döllinger's *Fables respecting the Popes*, p. 54, English translation.]
[2] Alcuini *Opp.*, ed. Frobenius, II. p. 599.

itself, and gave us the saint torn to pieces and mangled by horses. A tombstone, with the name of Concordia, gave occasion to the bearer of the name being turned into the nurse of Hippolytus, and also being made to die as a martyr. A room found there is now made to be the prison in which Hippolytus had kept Lawrence, entrusted to his custody by the emperor, although such an imprisonment of the Deacon does not easily admit of being brought into harmony with the older and more trustworthy reports of his martyrdom; especially if one follows the narrative of Prudentius and others, according to whom Lawrence, during the three days' interval allowed to him, gathered together the poor of the Church, and was then forthwith martyred.

Again, the strange story about Tryphonia and Cyrilla, the wife and daughter of the Emperor Decius, is probably only a fiction invented to fit two names, for which no history was extant. For both of them, one reads in the *Acts of Lawrence*, when they saw the emperor horribly tormented by a demon as a punishment for his cruelty to Hippolytus and the rest, are said to have prayed for baptism, whereupon Tryphonia forthwith gave up the ghost; while Cyrilla, at the command of Claudius, was strangled.

The frequent occurrence of Hippolytus in the sculpture of primitive Christianity on fragments of glass goblets, etc., shows that Hippolytus was a name very much revered, but gives also the further testimony that it was always only the Roman officer of the S. Lawrence myth that was intended. We may remark to begin with, that the circle of martyrs and saints, who occur in the old Christian pictures and vessels found in Rome, in general was a very small one. SS. Peter and Paul most frequently, then S. Agnes and S. Timotheus,—not the disciple of S. Paul, as has been supposed, but most certainly the Roman martyr, whose history is not known exactly, but whose cultus was very ancient in Rome, for he occurs as early as in the list of 354, and a cemetery bore his name. Of foreign martyrs, SS. Vincent and Cyprian occur, but among the Roman ones it is chiefly S. Lawrence and the martyrs historically and mythically connected with him, especially S. Xystus and Hippolytus, which one finds represented, and very frequently all together. That the name of the last was written correctly only by those who spoke Greek, but by the common Romans was much disfigured both in spelling and pronunciation, was natural, and hence he appears in these pictures sometimes as Epolitus, sometimes as Poltus. On an old glass,[1] we have Petrus, Paulus, Laurentius, Sustus (*i.e.* Xystus), Epolitus, and Cyprianus represented. On a fragment of a glass, which was found in a cemetery outside Rome in the last century, Timotheus and Hippolytus are still visible, but the glass appears to have had six or seven figures.[2]

Another Hippolytus already mentioned is known only from the *Acts of S. Aurea* or Chryse, in which he appears as a subordinate character. These *Acts*, which formerly were accessible only in Latin in Mombritius, were edited in the year 1795 by Magistris in Greek also; and it is apparent that the Greek text, although written in a very barbarous style, is the original. An Emperor Claudius and a Præfect or

---

[1] In MAMACHI, *Origg. et Antiqq. Christ.* II. p. 73, from Aringhi II. p. 256.
[2] VETTORI, *Dissert. Philolog.*, Romæ 1751, p. 13. [See also BURGON, *Letters from Rome.* In Letter xx. the above remarks are largely confirmed. "S. Peter and S. Paul recur perpetually." Laurentius, Timoteus, and Sustus are all noticed as occurring more than once in a group of objects taken at random. Those unable to consult Padre GARRUCCI's great work, *Veteri Ornati di Figure in oro,* may find much interesting matter in the article GLASS, in SMITH and CHEETHAM's *Dictionary of Christian Antiquities.* "The apostles most frequently represented (on more than seventy glasses) are St. Peter and St. Paul." " St. Agnes occurs more than a dozen times, St. Lawrence seven times, and St. Hippolytus four times."]

"vicarius urbis," Ulpius Romulus, appear here as the persecutors. In the *Acts*, the first Claudius appears to be meant, for they make Censorinus say, "Christ in our days hath come down into the world."[1] The editor, who defends the genuineness of this document very thoroughly and carefully, naturally supposes that it was the second emperor of this name, Claudius Gothicus, although none of the *Acts* have numbered him among the persecutors; for even his faith is not strong enough to transfer this history into the days of the Apostles, when there was at Rome, at the very most, only the first beginnings of a Christian community; moreover, in that case, his whole hypothesis of the Hippolytus in question, who in his eyes is the Father, would fall through. The heroine of the history is an Imperial Princess Aurea; the *Vicarius* Ulpius causes her not merely to be racked at Ostia, but also to be tortured with burning torches applied to her bare flesh, and to be in other ways abused, yet exhorts her withal to marry and take a husband worthy of her high extraction. She is then scourged, and at last thrown into the sea with a stone round her neck. The holy Nonus, however, who is also called Hippolytus, draws her corpse out of the water, buries her before the gates of Ostia, then reproaches Romulus, and is by his command bound hand and foot and drowned in a pit near the town walls of Portus; whereupon, for the space of an hour, voices as of children were heard to cry, "Thanks be to God." In every line of the document, the rough hand of a romancing Greek betrays itself, who has invented this history as so many from the sixth century onwards were invented, all made after the same model; and one can but lament that *Baronius* allowed himself to be taken in by this clumsy production. Certainly, he has made a very arbitrary

---

[1] Ἐν τοῖς ἡμετέροις καίροις, p. 46, ed. Magistris.

use of it; he transposes, namely, without having the slightest historical ground for so doing, the persons and their fate from the time of Claudius to that of the Emperor Alexander, and thereupon produces in the Roman martyrology on the 22d of August Bishop Hippolytus of Portus Romanus, who was flung into a pit and drowned under Alexander; then, on the 24th of August, S. Aurea, whose corpse the blessed Nonus buried, without noticing thereby that this Nonus is the same Hippolytus whom he has made Bishop of Portus, and whom he considers as identical with the celebrated Father.[1] Neither in the Greek nor in the Latin text of the *Acts* is there, however, a trace that this Hippolytus is to be regarded as a Bishop. He is once called ὁ μακάριος Ἱππόλυτος ὁ πρεσβύτερος, which the Latin text, with wilful misinterpretation, renders *senex*, probably in order to designate the Hippolytus who occurs here as the older, remembering the younger Hippolytus, well known among the Greeks as a Doctor of the Church and Bishop of Rome. About the name of Nonnus or Nunnus, as it is read in some martyrologies, people have given themselves unnecessary trouble. Baronius believes that it represents a

[1] To justify this notice respecting Hippolytus inserted in the martyrology, he says in the Annals (Ad Ann. 229, sec. 6): *Videns sanctissimum virum sub eodem persecutore, quo et Callistus Pontifex passus est, et eodem quo ille interitu martyrium consummasse, nam et ille in puteum mersus fuit.* More damning evidence of carelessness and caprice he could scarcely have given. He borrows from *Acts*, which expressly name an Emperor Claudius as persecutor, makes him into the Emperor Alexander Severus,—that is, just the one who, according to the unanimous evidence of antiquity, was the mildest and most kindly disposed towards the Christians of all the Emperors; and then appeals to the *Acts of Callistus*, of whose utter worthlessness he must himself have been aware. What the *Acts of S. Aurea* and their account of Hippolytus are worth, SACCARELLI says (*Hist. Eccles.* iii. p. 265, Romæ 1773), bluntly enough: *Inter apocrypha tum Hippolyti cum S. Aureæ acta recensenda esse dubitari vix potest.* The edition of the Greek *Acts* has made this still more clear, but at the same time has the advantage that it now enables one to show whence some of the later Greeks derived the idea of making Hippolytus Bishop of Portus.

monk or ascetic; Magistris, on the other hand, thinks that Hippolytus was so called because he was ninety years old. According to the Greek text, he was originally called Nonus,—a common Roman name, like Decimus or Octavius,—but then, probably as the narrator would have us understand, received the name of Hippolytus ($\mu\epsilon\tau o\nu o\mu a\sigma\theta\epsilon i\varsigma$) first on his acceptance of Christianity. In the West, this name has given occasion to the confusion of Hippolytus with a Bishop Nonnus, who lived in the fifth century at the time of the Council of Chalcedon, and who occurs in the history of the Fathers of the desert as the converter of S. Pelagia. It is on this confusion that the *Acts* under the name of Hippolytus are based, of which the Bollandist CUPER[1] gives some portion, and which he euphemistically designates as "interpolated," whereas they are manifestly pure invention. They narrate that after the death of Pelagia, S. Hippolytus, who was also called Nonnus, a man by whose preaching Alexandria was converted, determined to visit the graves of the apostles in Rome, etc. etc. But this legend appears in the strangest muddle and strangest colours in S. Peter Damian. According to him,[2] S. Nonus, who was also called Hippolytus, first of all converted thirty thousand Saracens to the faith, and then S. Pelagia from unchastity to piety, composed several commentaries on the Bible,[3] then finally left his bishopric, retired from Antioch, where he was born, and went to Rome; here he buried the corpse of S. Aurea, who was drowned at Ostia, and was then himself thrown into a pit filled with water near the mouth of the Tiber, by the command of Ulpius, whereupon the Christians buried his body in the town of Portus. Here, then,

---

[1] *Acta SS. Aug.* IV., p. 506.
[2] *Epist. ad Nichol. P.*, ed. Paris, 1610, p. 28.
[3] *Sanctarum Expositionum libros.*

we have the third and the fifth century, the fictitious Presbyter of Antioch, the Father, and Bishop Nonnus all jumbled up together.

We must not, however, overlook the golden grain of truth which appears to lie concealed in this rubbish-heap of clumsy fictions. It cannot be doubted that the *Acts of S. Aurea* had a point of contact with history, at any rate in the names which occur in them; for in the *Depositio Martyrum* of the chronographer of 354, that important and authentically kept document of antiquity, we read on the 5th of September, *Aconti, in Porto, et Nonni et Herculani, et Taurini.* These four names are the threads which alone are able to conduct us through the labyrinth of later accounts and legendary decorations.

In the martyrology of S. Jerome, according to the recension in D'Achery, ACONTIUS and NONNUS in Portus stand on the 25th of July, in company with several other quite strange names; then, on the 5th of September, TAURINUS, HEROS, HERALIANUS (that is, HERCULANUS), and ARISTOSUS, likewise in Portus. Others, as Ado and Usuard, have HERCULANUS alone; Rabanus has TAURINUS and HERCULANUS.

But these names appear also with a very large company of martyrs who are said to have suffered in Ostia only, and not in Portus, and of whom, according to the remark of the Bollandist Stilting, HERCULANUS and TAURINUS were transferred to Portus in the calendars merely because they were buried there.[1] This is the company of S. Aurea, and of Bishop Quiriacus. The *Acts* of these martyrs exist in three or four versions. In one of them[2] the history is placed in the year 252, and the Emperor Gallus is the persecutor; the leading personage is a Præfect Censurinus, who being brought as a prisoner to Ostia, is there visited by the Priest

---

[1] *Acta Sanctorum*, II. Sept. p. 518.   [2] *Acta SS.*, II. Sept. p. 520.

Maximus, the Deacon Archelaus, and S. Aurea. Seventeen soldiers, his guards, and among them Taurinus and Herculanus, are converted by a miracle, and all of them at last beheaded,—Aurea with them. (Acontius and Nonnus do not occur here; in some calendars, *e.g.* in that of Lucca and that of Corbie, they have been specially placed on the 15th of July.) Taurinus and Herculanus are then buried in Portus, the rest in Ostia. Here Aurea is only a subordinate character; she merely stands sponsor at the baptism of the seventeen soldiers.

In the second version [1] Aurea is the leading personage, and the Emperor Claudius the persecutor. The history of Censurinus and the seventeen soldiers is the same; but Aurea is drowned with a stone round her neck, and buried by NONOSUS, who is also called YPOLYTUS, or, as it stands immediately afterwards, by Bishop HIPPOLYTUS, who is also named NONNUS, and he is then drowned in a pit. This Latin text comes nearest to the Greek one edited by Magistris; yet in the Greek text Nonus or Hippolytus is not designated as a Bishop, as is the case in the Latin; in neither is he brought into any connection with Portus. All occurs in or near Ostia; only his drowning takes place, according to the Greek text, by the wall of Portus; whereas in the Latin of the Bollandists, which otherwise agrees with the Greek, it merely says, *Ante muros urbis juxta alveum Tyberis*, which there must be understood of Ostia.

In a third text, which the Bollandists had before them, the martyrdom of S. Aurea and her fellow-sufferers is transferred into the time of the Emperor Alexander;[2] and at the same time Hippolytus, also named Nonnus, who interred her corpse, is made into *Episcopus Portuensis*.[3] This is therefore the Latin document, and

[1] *Acta SS.*, IV. Aug. p. 757. [2] *Acta SS.*, IV. Aug. p. 757. [3] *L.c.* p. 756.

indeed the only one in the West which makes Hippolytus Bishop of Portus. From the manner in which the Bollandists speak of it, the manuscript seems to be a somewhat late one, and I have no doubt that the transposition from the time of Claudius or Decius to that of Alexander was made only on behalf of Hippolytus, for the author might have known that a Bishop Hippolytus lived at this time. In another recension, which the Bollandists likewise had before them, Cyriacus (or Quiriacus), on the contrary, who otherwise appears as Bishop of Ostia, is made Bishop of Portus, and Hippolytus is named *Arabum Metropolitanus*. This is therefore the same account with regard to the latter as is found in Pope Gelasius, and probably flows from the same source, viz. Rufinus' translation of the *Ecclesiastical History* of Eusebius.

Hence it is always the same material which, after first one and then another of this company has been made the leading personage, is worked up into *Acts* with slight variations. We have some in which Censorinus, others in which Quiriacus or Cyriacus, others again in which Aurea is the leading personage; there were also short ones, in which Nonus or Hippolytus was the hero. The Bollandists[1] give the beginning of such *Acts;* they are the ones in which the strange confusion with the Bishop Nonnus, who converted S. Pelagia, occurs, and from which Peter Damian has borrowed material. In other points all here agree with the *Acts of S. Aurea;* that Hippolytus was Bishop of Ostia does not here occur. The later Greeks, among whom the *Acts of Censorinus* and *of Aurea* or Chryse were probably composed with a Latin original as the basis, have emended after their own fashion the personage Nonus or Hippolytus, who there occurs. They knew of only one Hippolytus, the Father, who,

[1] *L.c.* p. 506.

from his writings, was reckoned by them as Bishop of Rome. Hence in the Basilianic martyrology (of the tenth century) the confusion or blending of Nonus or Hippolytus, who is said to have buried S. Aurea, and himself to have been drowned near Portus, with the Father and Bishop of Rome has already taken place. That is to say, we are told that after the execution of S. Chryse (Aurea) and the rest, Pope Hippolytus, greatly moved at so great a massacre of the Christians, sharply rebuked the tyrant, who then in his wrath caused the Pope, with all his suite, consisting of Presbyters, Deacons, and one Bishop, to be first tortured and then thrown into the sea.

Now, if it be asked, What, then, is the historical worth and value of this story connected with the names of Censorinus, Aurea, Nonnus, or Hippolytus, etc., we can only confess our ignorance. The Bollandists also show themselves helpless here,—a helplessness which, it must be owned, re-occurs with them whenever they have to speak of the real Hippolytus, or one of the duplicates of him created by the confusion of the martyrologies. The one firm resting-place is assured, as already remarked, by the names which the Bucher catalogue or the chronographer of 354 has for the 5th of September. These three names, NONNUS, HERCULANUS, and TAURINUS, are (so to speak) the red thread which runs through the web of the *Acts*. But who can say whether all is not merely a fiction resting originally on these names, or whether there is still any matter of fact at the basis? Meanwhile thus much is at any rate clear, that this Nonnus, who is said in the *Acts* to have received the name of Hippolytus, has alone given occasion for bringing the Father Hippolytus into connection with the Roman Portus.

But it deserves to be remarked also, that in the

variations which occur in the different versions with regard to localities and persons, a certain amount of design is disclosed. According to the Greek text, the three clerics, Quiriacus, Maximus, and Archelaus, after their decapitation, were thrown into the sea, but the Presbyter Eusebius collected the corpses and buried them on the sea-shore near the town of Ostia. When in the Greek text it immediately goes on to say, "which he also buried close to the same (the town of Ostia) in the crypt on the Ostian way," either a word or two has fallen out, or this is a later interpolation. On the other hand, the author or translator of the Latin *Acts* knows nothing of the town of Ostia, but makes the bodies be buried close to Rome in the crypt on the Via Hostiensis.[1] For the relics with these names seem later on to have been brought from Ostia to Parma;[2] but people wished to have them in or near Rome also, and hence the variation in the Latin text. Fiorentini's martyrology of Jerome, however, agrees with the Greek text, for it has: *In Porto urbis Romæ natalis s. Ypoliti, qui dicitur Nonnus, cum sociis suis. In Hostia natalis ss. Quiriaci et Arcilai.* Both the Greek and the Latin text represent Taurinus and Herculanus as buried in the Roman Portus. Nonnus or Hippolytus in the Greek is a Presbyter, while the Latin translator renders ὁ πρεσβύτερος *senex*, manifestly because a Presbyter Hippolytus did not suit his purpose. For that the Greek text intends to designate not the man's age, but his ecclesiastical dignity, is clear from the mere fact that in these *Acts* three other Presbyters occur besides Hippolytus—viz. Maximus, Eusebius, and Cordius, who are always designated in the same way as Hippolytus, and to whom the work of burying is always assigned; thus Eusebius buries

---

[1] *Juxta urbem in crypta via Hostiense,* ap. Magistris, p. 57.
[2] As the Bollandists (vol. iv., August, p. 566) state.

Quiriacus, Archelaus, and the rest; Hippolytus buries Aurea; and Cordius (in the Latin text Concordius) has to bury Sabinian. The Latin translator shows the deliberate nature of his proceeding in this, moreover, that in the case of the others he renders ὁ πρεσβύτερος *presbyter*, and only in the case of Hippolytus renders it twice *senex*.

Baronius has discovered yet a *third* or *fourth* Hippolytus. He is said likewise to have died at Rome in the year 257, in the time of the Emperor Valerian. He lived an ascetic life outside the city in a cave, occupied in converting and preparing for baptism those heathen who came to him; and when at last his sister Paulina also and her husband Hadrias accepted baptism, they were condemned by the judge Secundianus to long torture and death, and gave up the ghost under the scourge. But the *Acts* of these martyrs in Baronius are far too unsafe and fable-like, as Pearson[1] has shown, for one to build much on them.

The confusion already attached to the name of Hippolytus was increased still more by the invention of a pretended PRESBYTER HIPPOLYTUS OF ANTIOCH, who, however, never existed at all, although he is mentioned in martyrologies, especially from the ninth century onwards. His commemoration is fixed for the 30th of January. All that is told of him is confined to the statement that he belonged to the Novatian schism, but before his death returned to the Church, —a statement first found in the martyrology of Ado, while in the small Roman martyrology and that of S. Jerome we read merely:[2] *Antiochiæ passio s. Hippolyti martyris.* Ado's addition about the Novatianism and conversion of the Priest, which he borrowed from Prudentius, or rather from sources influenced by him,

---

[1] *Annal. Cypr.* p. 59, ed. Brem.
[2] *Opp. s. Hieronymi*, Paris 1846, XI. p. 442.

was then copied by Usuard, Notker, and the later martyrologies. Baronius, indeed, thinks—while he undertakes to correct Prudentius by Ado, *i.e.* a narrator of the beginning of the fifth century by a compilator of the ninth!—that the Novatianism which the Spanish poet attributes to the Roman martyr of whom he sings is only a mistake transferred from the Presbyter of Antioch to the supposed Roman one. In reality, however, the state of the case is quite different. An Hippolytus of Antioch is entirely unknown to any Greek authorities; even in S. Chrysostom, who, being himself of Antioch, so constantly mentions things and persons in his native city, one finds no trace of him; still less in the Greek and Oriental *Menæa* and calendars. The older Latin martyrologies have, as is well known, no Oriental martyrs, or only one here and there; at any rate, the name of an Hippolytus of Antioch is not to be met with in any of the martyrologies which have come down to us before the eighth century. The genuine martyrology does not contain him; he first occurs in the copies, which have later additions.[1] All statements respecting him, therefore, go back to the so-called martyrology of Jerome, a compilation which notoriously is not the work of that Doctor of the Church, and which we know only in the condition in which it was in the eighth century, and thus with no lack of mistakes, confusions, and reduplications. But how did this fictitious Presbyter of Antioch first get into this compilation? From the chronicle of Eusebius, translated by Jerome, which unmistakably formed the basis of the martyrology, and whose short notice of Hippolytus gave occasion to the error.

And here we may remark that the two errors which

[1] See the martyrology in Bede's *Ecclesiastical History*, edited by SMITH, Cambridge 1722, fol.

have attached themselves to the name of Hippolytus, —the one that the Father was Bishop in Arabia, the other that there was a Presbyter of this name in the middle of the third century at Antioch,—flowed from one and the same source, viz. from the mistakes to which the juxtaposition of Hippolytus with Geminus and Beryllus gave occasion. In the chronicle of Jerome, which since the fifth century has been so universally used and copied, we read under the year 230, *Geminus Presbyter Antiochenus, et Hippolytus, et Beryllus Episcopus Arabiæ Bostrenus, clari scriptores habentur*, and word for word the same in the chronicle of Prosper.[1] Here, then, it was perplexing that in the case of the first and third names place and dignity were stated, but in the case of the second, and that such a celebrated name, all further information was wanting. It was very tempting to leave Geminus, who in any case was not further known, to himself, and to appropriate the *Presbyter Antiochenus* to Hippolytus, especially when the *et* had slipped out from the manuscript. Accordingly not one of the martyrologies has inserted Geminus, and thus has arisen the Presbyter Hippolytus of Antioch, who is utterly unknown to the Greeks, and out of whom also Ado, by transferring to him the well-known narrative of Prudentius, made a Novatianist. Or else Hippolytus, whom people were now unwilling to leave so utterly ἀπάτωρ, ἀμήτωρ, ἀγενεαλόγητος, as he is in Eusebius and Jerome, was made into a bishop of Bostra in Arabia. The translation of Eusebius' *Ecclesiastical History* by Rufinus gave occasion to this. In Eusebius[2] we read: Ἐπίσκοπος δ' οὗτος (Βήρυλλος) ἦν τῶν κατὰ Βόστραν· ὡσαύτως τε καὶ Ἱππόλυτος, ἑτέρας που καὶ αὐτὸς προεστὼς ἐκκλησίας, which is rendered by Rufinus: *Episcopus fuit hic apud Bostram, Arabiæ urbem maximam. Erat nihilominus et Hippolytus, qui et*

[1] P. 598, ed. Roncallius.   [2] *H. E.* VI. 20.

ipse aliquanta scripta dereliquit, episcopus.[1] Hence it was quite to be expected that some would understand, from reading Eusebius through Rufinus, that Hippolytus likewise had been bishop of Bostra, and perhaps the successor of Beryllus; and we see that Gelasius was led astray in this manner, for Bostra is what he means by the designation "metropolis of Arabia."

Now, however, it is time to subject to a closer examination the poetical account which PRUDENTIUS, a Spaniard in the first part of the fifth century, sketches of the conversion and death of his Hippolytus, and to see what we can extract from it of historical value, and what relation his statements have to the results of our investigation thus far. These results are in brief the following:

1. A Roman Presbyter, Hippolytus, was banished to Sardinia in the year 235, along with Pope Pontian, and his corpse was afterwards buried in the Via Tiburtina.

2. The Roman officer Hippolytus, the guard and disciple of S. Lawrence, who was torn to pieces by horses, is a mythical personage, of whose existence and faith no historical testimony is extant.

3. The Hippolytus of Portus, who is said to have been drowned there, is an invention.

4. The Presbyter Hippolytus of Antioch got into the martyrologies only by mistake, and never existed.

According to the account of the Spanish poet, Hippolytus was a Roman Presbyter who had at first taken part in the Novatian schism. When persecution again broke out, he (having meanwhile returned to the Church and to his rightful Bishop) was taken prisoner with others to Ostia on account of his faith, to receive his sentence from the Præfect of the city, who then

[1] See Magistris, p. 367.

was staying there. On the way thither he exhorted the Christians who accompanied him to have nothing to do with the schism of Novatian. As his name reminded the Præfect of the son of Theseus and his tragical end, he condemned him to a similar death. The old Presbyter was forthwith bound by the feet to a team of wild horses, and soon the faithful could do no more than collect the mangled limbs of the corpse.

The historical good faith and exactness of Prudentius, especially in depicting a non-Spanish martyr, cannot be rated very highly,—partly because the very form of his work and the necessities of poetical selection and decoration could not but lead him into great licences, partly because he has demonstrably fallen into gross errors. Thus it has befallen him to be led astray by a romance about Cyprian of Antioch and Justina, composed in the middle of the fourth century, and to represent the Bishop of Carthage before his conversion as a sorcerer and charlatan. In his hymn on S. Lawrence, he makes Pope Xystus be crucified, and S. Lawrence stand weeping at the foot of the cross, whereas the expression of S. Cyprian leaves no room for doubt that Xystus was beheaded.[1] His account of

[1] It is true that Tillemont himself assumes that we must give the preference to the statement of Prudentius, that Xystus was crucified, although the Roman tradition, as it is still preserved in the martyrologies and in the *Pontifical Book* (ed. VIGNOLI, i. 53), makes him be beheaded, and hence it is established that the expression *animadversus* used by Cyprian must be taken in the usual sense. It appears to me as decisive that the edict of Valerian ordered simply the execution of the Bishops and Priests, and that one has only to take into consideration the mode of proceeding which was observed in the condemnation and execution of S. Cyprian to find it utterly incredible that at the same time the most horrible and shameful of all deaths, that of crucifixion, was inflicted on the Bishop of Rome. In like manner, the hymn of Prudentius on the martyrdom of S. Agnes is not historical, although in the case of a saint who was reverenced at so early a period and so very widely, and who did not suffer until the Diocletian persecution, one might have at least expected a simple historical representation. But Prudentius gives us here again also to understand that he had no other historical foundation and authority than the tomb of S. Agnes

Hippolytus has been now pronounced by most moderns to be untenable, especially since Baronius charged him with having thrown everything into utter confusion, and transferred features which belonged to three different persons to one Roman priest, of whom he knew really nothing definite. The Novatianism he borrowed from a presbyter who at that time suffered martyrdom at Antioch; the manner of death, by a similar mistake, was borrowed from the companion of S. Lawrence of like name, and appropriated to the Roman Presbyter; and lastly, the place of death, Portus, was by a third error transferred from Bishop Hippolytus to this very same Presbyter. No doubt Baronius himself, as need scarcely be remarked any more, has proceeded on suppositions which historically are quite untenable, although what he maintains has since then been often enough repeated, even so late as by Paciaudi and Magistris. On the other hand, Ruinart, Tillemont, and Saccarelli, have accepted the historical correctness of the poem in its main features, and Orsi has admitted the narrative without hesitation into his ecclesiastical history.[1]

Prudentius narrates that the sight of the grave, and of the picture executed on the wall over the grave, attracted his attention to the history of Hippolytus.

and the story which was current among the people—*e.g.* v. 10. *Aiunt* jugali vix habilem toro, etc.; v. 57. Sunt qui rogatam *retulerint* preces fudisse Christo.

[1] Great pains to rescue the trustworthiness of Prudentius in this case also have been taken by the author of a treatise which appeared in Pesaro in the year 1771, SADARPHI, *Osservazioni sopra il Martirio di s. Ippolito Vescovo di Porto, descritto dal Poeta Prudenzio.* He tries to show that Prudentius has by no means made any confusion, as is commonly supposed, but that rather his account is quite historical, and treats of the great Father of the Church, who really in the end became a Novatianist, and then was torn to pieces by horses under Valerian,—all on the weakest grounds. After him MAGISTRIS has come back to the hypothesis that the Spaniard has confused together three persons of the name of Hippolytus, and that the Father was drowned.

He seems, therefore, to have taken his materials not from any written document whatever, but merely from a tradition existing among the Christians there, and from their narrations; consequently, with the exception of the statement about the Novatianism of the martyr and his recantation, all really historical features are wanting. The main thing is the description of the fresco, then the depicting of the crypt and of the great crowds of people at the celebration of his festival. The rest is only the usual background in pictures of martyrdoms. When, at the moment of his saint's being dragged over stock and stone, he puts the last words in his mouth: " These (the steeds) are dragging my limbs on after them; drag Thou, O Christ, my soul to Thyself!"—this is manifestly only a fancy of the poet's, and not by any means a happy one.

First of all let us consider the mode of his death. That a hundred and fifty years after the supposed event a very sensational fresco depicted the matter in this way, cannot be allowed as historical evidence. We know from other cases that already in the fourth century, popular legend, or even (as in the story of Cyprian and Justina) conscious fiction, was at work, inventing, or decorating and altering, histories of martyrs. And in the present case, the improbable nature of the mode of death certainly falls heavily into the balance. In the whole course of persecutions of the Christians—that of Diocletian even included—no second instance occurs in which so extraordinary a mode of execution is employed. The thing is still less credible when one considers place, persons, and circumstances. It is the Præfect of Rome, who has an old man brought to him at Ostia, and being reminded by his name of the fable respecting the son of Theseus, forthwith, in the exercise of the cruellest caprice and scorn, condemns the man to a kind of death which was utterly foreign to the laws and customs of the Roman Empire. One might certainly quote the execution of S. Lawrence, which took place in the year 258, as an instance of an extraordinary and un-Roman mode of death. The case, however, is very different. The punishment of the latter was an act of revenge and disappointed avarice, and yet so far in accordance with law, as by the decree of Decius torture was really to be applied in various forms, increasing in severity, in order to induce the Christians to apostatize. This was done with S. Lawrence; for he was first scourged and then tortured by the roasting fire, and died in consequence of this punishment, perhaps against the wish and expectation of the Præfect. In the case of the Hippolytus of Prudentius, on the other hand, the mode of proceeding must have been quite different. There is no mention of any attempt to induce him to apostatize in obedience to Roman law; but he is condemned to the most horrible death immediately on his confessing that he is a Christian.

I go still further. I maintain that, supposing one places the narrative of Prudentius in the time of Gallus or in the persecution under Valerian, it is still inconceivable that the matter can have taken place as he depicts it. Seeing that under Caracalla all inhabitants of the empire had received the *civitas*, a Præfect would dare still less even than before (every one being now a free citizen of Rome) to employ modes of death not provided by law, but dictated merely by cruelty or wantonness. The usual form of capital punishment was decapitation; besides this, the law provided for severer cases only the additional punishments of crucifixion, being thrown to the beasts in the amphitheatre, and burning. The last punishment was threatened specially against those who practised witchcraft;[1] and

---
[1] JULII PAULLI, R. S. l. v., t. 22, sec. 17.

as this was a usual charge brought against Christians, we see how in the Decian persecution many (as Cronion and Macarius at Alexandria) died at the stake. Exceptions occur only in those neighbourhoods where popular custom brought with it a peculiar mode of capital punishment, and where the authorities sometimes allowed that the execution of a Christian should take place in this form. Hence in Asia Minor, where formerly it had been the custom to stone the enemies of the gods, Maximus was stoned in the year 251, and then in Lampsacus, Andrew and Paul.[1] The other executions of Christians at this time took place by the sword. And I think that to every one acquainted with history, with Roman law and custom, and with the genuine *Acts* of the martyrs, it must (the more he weighs the matter) seem incredible that the Præfect of Rome caused a Christian, whether Presbyter or soldier, to be torn to pieces by horses.

But it is further surprising that Prudentius only adopts half of the legend, as we know it, only what relates to the mode of death, while he knows nothing of the Roman officer baptized by S. Lawrence, but makes Hippolytus into a schismatical presbyter. And yet he knew also the history of S. Lawrence, which is the subject of another long hymn of his, well enough. Probably the legend of the Roman soldier and neophyte Hippolytus was already in the mouth of the people; but Prudentius (who expressly gives the 13th of August as the day for commemorating his saint, and therefore in his description without doubt means the crypt in the Ager Veranus on the Via Tiburtina) had, on inquiry, preferred another older and better founded tradition, which was still extant at that time, viz. that the person buried there had been a Presbyter, who, after being a schismatic, had, before his death, returned

[1] Ruinart, p. 147.

once more to the unity of the Church. As he had no written authorities, but only statements made by word of mouth before him, he is wanting in exact marks of time. He might know that a cruel execution could not be placed in the time of Alexander Severus, favourably disposed as he was to the Christians, and indeed not in the period between 211 and 235 at all. Accordingly he put the history forward into the time of Gallus, and thereby the nature of the schism was given, in which Hippolytus was said to have taken part. It must have been that of Novatian. Nothing was then known of any other, and in the time of Gallus there was not even the trace of another existing in Rome. Here, then, we have fresh reason for considering the narrative of the Spaniard, not as simple history, but as a fiction based upon misunderstood facts. The earlier history of the Novatian schism, and of the persons involved in it, is known to us with tolerable exactness through Cyprian's correspondence with Rome. We see that it was always the confessors on his side, on whose reputation with the Christian populace Novatian supported himself. He cited them with much parade, and gave it as a proof of the goodness and justice of his cause that they had followed him from the first. Had, then, so remarkable and striking a case occurred at that time as that which Prudentius narrates; had a Roman Priest, immediately before his glorious martyrdom, returned once more to the Catholic communion, and exhorted the people to leave Novatian, we should certainly meet with a notice of it in Cyprian's correspondence. No doubt one might still make the attempt to rescue the statement of Prudentius, by putting it forward into the time of Valerian's persecution, that is, to the year 258 or 259. On the other hand, however, other difficulties would arise, and in particular the mode of Hyppolytus' death would then become still more incredible; for it is certain that Valerian wished the punishment of decapitation to be inflicted on Bishops and Priests. In distant Spain, the more severe punishment of the stake might possibly find place in the execution of Bishop Fructuosus; but for all that, it is inconceivable that, immediately after so distinctly-worded a rescript of the Emperor to the Roman Senate, the Præfect of the city should have acted with such refined cruelty in varying and intensifying the modes of death as Prudentius represents: "Nail him to the cross; fling this one bound into the flames; the rest on rotten boats sink in the sea; and the old Priest there shall be tied to the feet of wild steeds, and by them be torn to pieces." That is not history,—at any rate, not history of a scene in the time of Valerian. It is poetical painting, applied a hundred and fifty years after the event, to material taken merely from the legend in the mouths of the people.

I have no hesitation in seeking the origination of the legend of a Christian martyr Hippolytus, who was torn to pieces by horses, in a picture which may have existed close to the church of S. Lawrence. It was natural, in an age in which the pagan legends of Greece had already become strange to the lower classes in Rome, while at the same time their imagination was excited by the history of the martyrs, that a representation of the death of the Athenian king's son should be interpreted as depicting a Christian martyrdom. That the misinterpretation of pictures had a great share in the completion and decoration of Christian legends, cannot fail to be recognised. I will mention only a couple of instances. Nothing is more frequent in the *Acts* of the martyrs than the narration, how at the death of the saint the soul flew out of the body in the form of a white dove. Prudentius has this legend already in his history of S. Eulalia.¹ The same thing occurs in the *Acts* of S. Potitus² and Quintinus,³ in the history of S. Reparata,⁴ in the *Acts* of S. Devota,⁵ of S. Felix of Trèves, and many others. Now the figure of a dove, as Buonarroti⁶ and Aringhi remark, is found very frequently on the oldest Christian monuments, and the frequent occurrence of a white dove as a symbol of the soul freeing itself from the body in pictures which represent the death or martyrdom of a saint, has produced that legend.⁷ In the same way, numerous legends of saints, who are said to have freed a neighbourhood from a murderous dragon, have arisen.⁸ Papebrock⁹ remarked long ago that almost all the first bishops of Italian towns, or other convertors of the heathen, are said to have slain, or spell-bound, or driven into the sea, a huge snake or dragon with the sign of the cross. In the lives of the Oriental saints also the slain dragon is a usual occurrence. Not unfrequently it is also stated that the saint bound the dragon with his scarf or handkerchief, and sometimes the narrators appeal forthwith to a picture representing the saint

---

[1] Hymn ix. v. 161, Peristeph.

[2] *Acta Sanctorum*, Januar. I. p. 764.

[3] Surius on the 31st of October.   [4] *Rom. Martyrol.* VIII. id. Octobr.

[5] *Acta SS.*, Januar. I. p. 771.

[6] *Osserv. sopra alcuni frammenti di vasi antichi*, Firenze 1716, p. 125.

[7] [In the early monuments of the catacombs the dove is, as a rule, easily distinguished from other birds; but on the very earliest tombs birds assignable to no species are found, with or without the palm-branch, obviously as symbols of the released soul flying to heaven. Compare Ps. cxxiv. 7, lv. 6, and the analogy of the Psyche-butterfly. Similarly *caged* birds perhaps represent the soul in the prison-house of the flesh. See *Dictionary of Christian Antiquities*, articles BIRD and DOVE.]

[8] [The serpent from the earliest ages has been a symbol of both good and evil, the dragon only of evil, the griffin only of good. There may be exceptions, but this rule appears to hold in most cases. See article CHERUB in SMITH's *Dictionary of the Bible*, and articles DRAGON, GRIFFIN, SERPENT, in the *Dictionary of Christian Antiquities*; also MRS. JAMESON's *Sacred and Legendary Art*, p. xxxvi.]

[9] *Acta SS.* II. Martii, p. 118

with the dragon.[1] To represent Satan, whose temptations the saint overcame, in the figure[2] of a dragon, was a primeval custom with the Christians. Constantine caused him to be so painted in the vestibule of his palace, pierced through with a lance; and later on also, people were fond of representing the victory over idolatry in the figure of a captive dragon. Hence, therefore, that legend.

In the picture drawn by Prudentius we meet with one or two other features which, having reference to the ecclesiastical position of the martyr, and not to be put down to poetical decoration, are consequently of importance for our purpose, viz. the evolution of the true historical Hippolytus. He calls him expressly a Presbyter, but represents his relation to the Christian people in such a way as is really suitable only to a Bishop and the originator of a schismatical separation, not to a mere subordinate party to the same. Hippolytus is here the ecclesiastical head of a congregation which trusts him absolutely, and which has become involved in the schism first through him.[3] The heathen attendants of the Præfect call out to him that Hippolytus is the leader of the host of those who worship Christ, and that if only he were suddenly plucked away, the populace would turn again to the Roman gods. Without doubt, Prudentius would represent his hero as one of those belonging to the city of Rome, and his congregation as a Roman one; although he makes the condemnation take place in or near Ostia, whither the Præfect had gone that very day, in order to carry out the imperial edict there also. Had his Hippolytus been Presbyter or Bishop in Ostia or Portus, his con-

---

[1] So, for example, in the *Vita S. Pavacii*, ap. Bolland. ad 24 Jul., vol. v. p. 541: *Quia picta erat in domo episcopali in nostra urbe constituta.*

[2] EUSEB. *vit. Const.* lib. 3, cap. 3.

[3] *Seque ducem recti spretis aufractibus idem*
Præbuit, erroris qui prius autor erat.

gregation, to whom while still alive he was so dear, would assuredly not have allowed his bones to be carried to a strange city,—to Rome,[1]—but would have kept them near themselves. But in Rome Novatian was still living—according to the account of Socrates,[2] he did not lose his life until the persecution under Valerian—and in Rome there certainly were not several congregations of Novatianists, each with its own head, but only *one*, of which Novatian himself or his successor was the leader. We are therefore thrown back to an earlier time and an earlier Roman schism than that of Novatian, to a schism the author of which must have been Hippolytus himself. If it is objected that this contradicts the statement of Prudentius, who repeatedly calls the schism *Novati*, I reply that the whole account of the Spanish poet in all its features is such as cannot for one moment be regarded as historical; confusions or anachronisms, and combinations of different traditions, must be admitted. The alternative, accordingly, presents itself thus: Either this Hippolytus was a Novatianist, in which case he cannot have been what the narrator makes him, the leader of a separate congregation, the schismatical seducer of a whole Christian populace; or he was really in such an ecclesiastical position at Rome, in which case he was no Novatianist, but belongs to an earlier time, and the division brought about by his means was a different one. The reasons for the adoption of the second alternative are manifestly *overwhelming*. To this must be added, that Prudentius may well have had special reason for making his martyr a converted Novatianist. At that time, as we learn from Pacian's writings, the Novatianist sect still existed in the poet's home in North

---

[1] *Ostia linquunt,
Roma placet, sanctos quæ teneat cineres.*
[2] *Hist. Eccles.*, lib. iv. cap. 28.

Spain; and hence the wish to set before the opponents of the Church there so weighty an authority, and an example so worthy of imitation, may well have contributed to the idea of designating the schism, from which the Roman martyr again turned, as that of Novatian.

What is there, then, in the poem of Prudentius that we can make use of as historical material that will bear criticism? His martyr is that Hippolytus whose commemorative festival was celebrated on the 13th of August; he lived in Rome, was the originator of a schism, or, at any rate, he presided over a separate church communion, but returned to the Church before his death. With regard to the mode of death depicted by him, I believe that the legend about the Roman officer, whom S. Lawrence converted, was at that time already extant in Rome. He is said to have been dragged to death by horses; but Prudentius, who had learnt in some way that the martyr celebrated on the 13th August was no Roman soldier, but a Presbyter or Bishop, transferred the manner of death described in the legend and in the picture to him.

But was not the genuine historical Hippolytus a martyr? Jerome and Theodoret call him so expressly, and the later Greeks likewise. And he was one, yet not by a bloody, violent death, but in the same manner in which, according to his own statement, Callistus became a martyr,—by exile. Whoever suffered at all on account of the faith was, in the wider sense of the term, reckoned among the martyrs; so early as Cyprian we have the declaration that those who died in prison were martyrs;[1] and, only to mention one instance, Eusebius of Vercelli, who died a natural death, is called by S. Ambrose, and in the Roman martyrology, a martyr.

Mommsen has maintained, in his treatise on the

[1] Epist. 37, ed. Rigalt.

chronographer of 354, that in the list of the Popes, and oldest and most trustworthy which we possess, the part reaching down to 231 is probably the work of Hippolytus and borrowed from his chronicle; that Hippolytus gave merely a list of names, with a statement of the length of their episcopate, while the consulships and contemporaneous Emperors were added by a later hand, and not always correctly. The latter is certainly correct; but the former, viz. that Hippolytus is the original source, I consider as very improbable.[1] It appears to me rather as if the list had come originally from a Latin, and not from a Greek source. *Firstly*, in the catalogue Cletus and Anacletus are cited as two Popes; but this Cletus is unknown to all Fathers of the Greek tongue, and even to all Latins,—Optatus, Augustine, Jerome, Rufinus; had he already stood in Hippolytus' chronicle, which, as Mommsen remarks, was much used and copied, he would have been mentioned more frequently in the lists of the Popes, and would have been reckoned along with them in enumerating them. But the distinction between a Cletus and Anacletus rests on two witnesses only, viz. our Liberian catalogue and the author of the poem against Marcion. A tradition of the Roman Church cannot be brought to tell in favour of it, for in the oldest document, the Roman Canon for the Mass, only one is mentioned. But the authority of the Liberian catalogue cannot be rated very high for the period down to 230, for (and this is the *second* reason, which seems to me to be at the same time decisive against Mommsen's conjecture that the catalogue is borrowed from the *Chronicon* of Hippolytus) three Popes are wanting in it,—Anicetus (150–153), Eleutherus (171–185), and Zephyrinus (198–217).[2]

---

[1] [On this point Dr. Döllinger has changed his opinion. See Appendix, A.]
[2] There exist only two manuscripts of this catalogue,—the one at Vienna and the one at Brussels; ECCARD (*Corp. Hist.* I. p. 25) has given an

All the more important and trustworthy, on the other hand, is the second part of the catalogue, which begins with Pontianus, as Tillemont and others have already recognised, and as Mommsen confirms. This second part is the work of another, who adds single notes to the names of the Popes, having reference to the persecutions and schism. The very first historical note is one of very great importance for our purpose. It states :[1]—

Eo tempore (a. 235) *Pontianus episcopus et Yppolytus presbyter exoles sunt deportati in Sardinia in insula nociva Severo et Quintino cons. In eadem insula discinctus est IV. kl. Oct. et loco ejus ordinatus est Antheros XI. kl. Dec. cons. ss.* (235).

I have no doubt that this Hippolytus is no other than the celebrated Father, who accordingly was at any rate a Roman Presbyter. He was banished simultaneously with Pontian to Sardinia; if both of them

---

exact transcript of the first, BUCHER, and from him DUCANGE (*Ad Chron. Pasch.*, ed. Bonn, II. p. 198) of the second. In both of them the three Popes are wanting. In MOMMSEN they stand in the text, but are characterized as insertions by different type. The Bollandists also had printed it before (*Acta Sanctorum*, April. I.), with the completions inserted by themselves. Only, I do not know why Mommsen says (p. 583): The list contains at least one undoubted error as to facts, viz. it places Anicetus before Pius; whereas, from contemporaneous evidence, it is perfectly certain that Anicetus followed Pius. But Anicetus is wanting altogether; it is the second list, reaching down to Felix IV. and the *Pontifical Book* (cf. SCHELSTRATE, I. p. 414), which have this mistake. ["In reference to the first Roman bishops, the consentient statements of the Greeks, Irenæus, Eusebius, and Epiphanius, are infinitely more trustworthy than the Latin accounts." Of the latter there are three recensions,—the Roman in the Liberian catalogue, the African of Optatus and S. Augustine (derived from the Liberian), and the Gallican of Victorinus. The Canon of the Roman Mass agrees with the Greek diptychs—Linus, Cletus (=Anencletus), Clemens. Anacletus appears to be no name at all. The Greeks always have Anencletus, equivalent in meaning to Innocentius. See DÖLLINGER'S *First Age of the Church*, Bk. III. chap. i. pp. 298–300, English translation, 2d ed. 1867.]

[1] MOMMSEN, *Ueber den Chronographen vom Jahre* 354, Leipzig 1850, p. 635.

suffered this banishment merely as Christians and ecclesiastical dignitaries, then no doubt Hippolytus was selected out of the already very numerous Roman clergy, and sent into exile with the Pope, because next to him he was the most considerable person in the Roman Church. Now, seeing that no persecution took place under Alexander Severus, but the Christians were rather protected, and to a certain extent favoured, we must suppose that this was one of the first persecuting measures of the new Emperor Maximin. Banishment to Sardinia was pretty nearly equivalent to sentence of death, for the neighbourhood to which exiles were brought was so unhealthy that they soon died, and the place was chosen in Rome for that very reason, in order that those whom people wished to get out of the way might there find a grave. Maximin persecuted in the first place the friends and servants of Alexander, among whom were several Christians; and hence one may suppose that Pontian also and Hippolytus were banished for this reason. But the time was somewhat short for this. Alexander was murdered at Mainz (according to Clinton) on the 10th of February, or (according to Tillemont) not until the 18th of March, 235. But Maximin, during the whole of the year 235, was still fully occupied with the war in Germany; and Pontian must already have been some time in Sardinia when he resigned his office there on the 28th of September 235, whereupon (according to the statement of the catalogues of Popes in the sixth century) he died on the 30th of October of the same year, in consequence of the ill-treatment he received. Are we to suppose that Maximin made such haste to send an order from Germany for the deportation of the two men? To the rude Thracian who, first a goat-herd and then a soldier, had only just then been called with his legion from the banks of the Tigris to the banks of the Rhine, political reasons such as to determine him on a sudden persecution of the Christians, after so long a rest, were certainly not at all likely to occur. He who forthwith carried the war into the very heart of Germany, and above all, could boast that in the short space of two years he had waged more wars than any of the rest, who had, moreover, to suppress the conspiracy of Magnus and of Osrhoënic troops; he could not at the same time have busied himself with the internal circumstances of the city of Rome, and with the fate of a Bishop and a Priest. The catalogue of the Popes just mentioned says that the deportation took place through (that means, no doubt, *under*) Alexander. This Emperor, who at that time was in Germany, certainly did not order it himself, but the Præfect of the city may very well have done so; and Binius long ago made the conjecture[1] that it may have been done not on religious grounds, but on account of some other charge brought against them by the heathen. If we consider the condition of the Christians in Rome, as it appears from the description given by Hippolytus in the *Philosophumena*, it becomes very probable that the schism which had arisen there through the separation of Hippolytus from Callistus, and which continued even after the death of the latter, involved collisions and party contests, and that violent outbreaks were not wanting, to which the dispute as to the possession of the places of worship was sufficient to give occasion. Thus, then, it was likely enough that the Præfect thought to put an end to the disturbances by banishing the leaders of the two parties,—Pontianus (as the successor of Callistus) and Hippolytus. Again, in the year 309, as we learn from an epitaph composed by Pope Damasus, Pope Marcellus was banished by the Emperor Maxentius, not on account of his religion, but because his strictness

---

[1] In BIANCHINI, in his edition of *Anastasius*, II. p. 181.

about the discipline of penance in the case of those who had lapsed in persecution, had caused dissension and bloody fights in Rome.¹

This of course is only conjecture, and it may well have been that both men were exiled to Sardinia simply on account of their religion. But the expression *discinctus*, used by the old chronographer, tells us a fact which is calculated to throw some light over what is otherwise an obscure circumstance. For it is established by Hippolytus' own narrative, that, in consequence of the quarrel between him and Callistus, a schism took place in the Church of Rome; and further, that this division continued for some time longer after the death of Callistus. How was this schism, of which only fifteen years later, when the Novatianist dissensions broke out, not a trace is any longer visible, adjusted? The chronographer says that Pontianus resigned his office, for that is the meaning (according to Pagi's² declaration also) of *discinctus*, and Anteros was elected in his place. If we add to this the further fact that the bodies of both men, after they had died in Sardinia, were brought to Rome, and there solemnly

---

¹ S. DAMASI *Opera*, ed. Sarazanius, Paris 1672, p. 173.

² *Critica in Annales Baronii*, I. p. 217, ed. Antwerp. In military language it means "cashiered;" ecclesiastical usage takes it in a similar sense; thus it stands in Gregory of Tours (lib. v. cap. 27) of the Bishops Salonius and Sagittarius, who were degraded in a Synod, that they were *ab episcopatu discincti;* and Sidonius Apollinaris (lib. v. epist. 7) in a similar sense, *Reverentiam clericis, cinctis jura, discinctis privilegia*. *Cincti* and *discincti* are here used of the judges still in office and of those who had retired into private life. Compare SAVARON'S notes *in loco*. Further material respecting the ecclesiastical use of *cinctus* and *discinctus* has been collected by DU SAUSSAY in the *Panoplia Sacerdotalis*, p. 40; here, of course, merely a voluntary resignation can be meant. Heuschen and Mommsen propose to read *defunctus* instead of *discinctus;* but the simple and clear *defunctus* would certainly not have been changed in the manuscripts into the more obscure *discinctus*. [JACOBI also, in the article HIPPOLYTUS in HERZOG'S *Real-Encyklopädie*, contends for *defunctus*, maintaining that *discinctus est* cannot mean "resigned," but must be taken passively, "was deposed," which is nonsense, for there was no one to depose him.]

interred *on one and the same day*, we may not without probability conclude that the resignation of Pontian was followed by that of Hippolytus, that they were reconciled to one another, and wished by means of a joint resignation to bring the schism to an end, which they also succeeded in doing.

We are now at the point when we must answer the question, so long a riddle, and, since the discovery of the *Philosophumena*, doubly interesting and important, but now capable of a certain solution, Where did Hippolytus, if he was a Bishop, have his see; and is the theory now once more maintained and supported by many arguments, that he was Bishop of the Roman Portus at the mouth of the Tiber, historically correct?

I believe that now, for the first time, the utter groundlessness of this supposition can be convincingly shown, and propose to conduct my proof in the following manner:—

In the *first* place, I shall show that Portus Romanus in the third century was not a town, while the neighbouring Ostia still continued to be a considerable town

Secondly, that in Portus there was no Bishop before the year 313 or 314.

Thirdly, that a Bishop Hippolytus of Portus was unknown in the whole West, and likewise in the East until the seventh century.

Fourthly, that the unanimous tradition of the Eastern Church designates Hippolytus as Bishop of Rome.

Fifthly, that the later Byzantines, the author of the *Chronicon Paschale*, George Syncellus, Anastasius, and Zonaras, were led astray by the (spurious) *Acts of Aurea*, so as to make Hippolytus Bishop of Portus.

Sixthly, that Hippolytus, according to his own words considered himself as the rightful Bishop of Rome o his time.

Seventhly, that Hippolytus could not simultaneously

be a member of the Roman presbytery and Bishop of Portus.

The theory that the Hippolytus was Bishop of Portus was in earlier times variously defended, but since the middle of the last century has been abandoned as untenable by most of the Catholic and Protestant scholars who have gone into the question thoroughly; until Herr Bunsen again undertook with great warmth to come forward in its behalf, in the main only because it seemed to him to suit certain pet notions of his, and also certain consequences which he might be able to draw from the history of Hippolytus.[1] On the Catholic side, the author of the *Histoire Litteraire de la France*,[2] Ceillier, the Benedictine De la Reux, Cardinal Orsi, and Saccarelli, have declared against it. On the Protestant side, among others, Härrell[3] and Neander.[4] Ceillier thinks he must have been a Bishop somewhere in the East. Orsi conjectures that he may have been a Bishop of the heathen without a fixed see, who wandered about to convert and found churches, like his contemporary Caius, according to the statement of Photius. Against this, however, it has been already noticed above that the whole hypothesis of the undefined episcopate of Caius rests on a miscomprehension. On the other side, two Roman ecclesiastics, Ruggeri and Magistris, have given themselves much trouble to reproduce with all possible completeness the proof

---

[1] However, Herr Bunsen could still appeal in recent times to Seinecke, author of a treatise on Hippolytus, in Illgen's *Zeitschrift*, Jahrg. 1843, H. 3, p. 57, and to Ideler's *Chronologie*, vol. ii. p. 213. [The theory is maintained by MILMAN, *Latin Christianity*, I. p. 44, 4th ed., and also apparently by ROBERTSON, *History of the Christian Church*, I. p. 120, 2d ed.]

[2] Tome I. p. 363.

[3] In his *Commentatio Hist. Crit. de Hippolyto*, Götting. 1838, p. 13.

[4] "Neither the later accounts, which place his bishopric in Arabia, nor the others, which place it in the neighbourhood of Rome, can be taken into consideration," says Neander, *Geschichte der Christ. Kirche*, Zweite Ausgabe, I. 1175.

that Hippolytus was Bishop of Portus. The first wrote his treatise at the suggestion of Cardinal Ottoboni, Bishop of Portus, who was concerned that such a light should not be taken away from the Church from which he derived his title. His conclusion is, that the Hippolytus who composed the ecclesiastical treatises was certainly the Bishop of Portus, but there was contemporaneously with him another Hippolytus in Rome who was a soldier; both suffered martyrdom in the same way, killed by wild horses, and were interred in the same place. Incredible as this seems, the editor of the Greek *Acts of S. Aurea*, Simon de Magistris,[1] has carried the credulity which swallows camels still further. His Hippolytus was not only Bishop of Portus, but also of a considerable part of the city of Rome. The city of Rome, that is to say according to him, fell in the third century into two episcopal dioceses, of which the one embraced the part of the city lying east

---

[1] *Acta Martyrum ad Ostia Tiberina sub Claudio Gothico, notis ac Dissertationibus Illustrata*, Romæ 1795, fol. The greater part of the volume (pp. 61–434) is taken up with the *dissertatio de vita et scriptis Hippolyti Mart. Episcopi Portuensis*. The book is really a literary curiosity; the author, who cannot be denied to be a man of great reading, draws right through 'a *posse ad esse*,—this or that *may* very possibly have been the case,—which is quite sufficient for him to take the supposed fact forthwith into his fantastic and romantic history of Hippolytus, which he has put together out of the most wanton fictions. He makes him be born in 173 and be drowned in 269, *i.e.* almost a hundred years old, in order that his death may fall within the time of Claudius II., and the credibility of the *Acts* edited by himself be maintained. For the same purpose, we are told also in a separate treatise, that under Claudius II. a persecution of the Christians took place, although not a single fact even in the slightest degree tenable can be quoted in support of this. Hippolytus, as Magistris has discovered, went from Rome to Alexandria in order to avoid the sight of the secular games which had been instituted by command of the Emperor Philip; moreover, was on confidential terms of intimacy with this Emperor and his wife Severa. In Egypt, he induced Origen to submit to Pope Fabrianus, and actually, as the legend quite correctly states, converted thirty thousand Saracens, etc. etc. Had the author not brought together his learned apparatus with such pains, one might sometimes doubt whether he was really in earnest with his dreams.

of the Tiber, and the other the island of the Tiber and the district lying west of it, and belonged to the Bishop of Portus. Magistris knows further[1] that it was Pope Cornelius (in the year 251) who first created the new bishopric in Portus and handed it over to Hippolytus; thus at the same time dividing the city of Rome between Hippolytus and himself. All this is decorated with yet other hitherto unsuspected facts, and we are then assured that the unanimity of the Greek and Latin Church in reference to the Portus episcopate of Hippolytus is quite wonderful.[2] The proof of this is with him easy enough. For the Latin Church, Anastasius must answer, because he was Roman *Apocrisiarius* at Constantinople; for the Greek Church, all those are counted as witnesses who call Hippolytus a Roman Bishop; for by that, he says, they only meant to say that he was Bishop of Portus. Portus was, that is to say six or eight hundred years later, one of the seven suburban churches. Cardinal Humbert, Bishop of one such church, viz. of Sylva Candida, in the eleventh century (when the body of cardinals with the cardinal-bishops was already formed) called himself a Bishop of the Roman Church, and at the time of Urban II. (about the year 1090) some of these Bishops were called *Episcopi urbis*. Such a mode of arguing only tempts one to ask why, when he so liberally presents the Bishop of Portus with a considerable portion of the city of Rome, does he not rather deduce from this the fact, which has hitherto been so awkward and hard to explain for all modern writers, that the Orientals designate Hippolytus as a Roman Bishop? Why has he not said simply, The difference between the statement of the Orientals and mine is only this, that they make him

---

[1] *L.c.* p. 364.

[2] *Cæterum invitis quantumlibet censoribus magni nominis mirifica est consensio*, etc., *l.c.* p. 365.

Bishop of the whole city of Rome, while, according to my theory, he was only Bishop of a good part of Rome, and along with it of the seaport-town of Portus as well?

1. IN THE THIRD CENTURY, PORTUS ROMANUS WAS NOT A TOWN, AND OSTIA WAS STILL A CONSIDERABLE TOWN.

That Portus Romanus was neither a town nor an episcopal see before the beginning of the fourth century can, I believe, be maintained with an amount of probability bordering on certainty.

It has been usual of late to represent the relation between Ostia and Portus thus: After the Emperor Claudius laid out the newer and better harbour on the right arm of the Tiber, a flourishing place of the name of Portus soon sprang up about it, and Ostia, whose harbour became more and more blocked with sand, sank, and maintained itself only by its saltworks.[1] According to this, therefore, one must suppose that soon after the second century, while Ostia sunk to a borough of no importance, Portus rose to be a flourishing seaport-town. This, however, according to ancient testimony, was not the case. In the second, third, and fourth centuries it is Ostia which still continues to appear as an important town, while Portus as a *town* is not mentioned at all. Pliny, in his *Natural History*, speaks always of Ostia only. Minucius Felix at the beginning of the third century describes Ostia as *civitas amœnissima*. The Emperor Tacitus, in the year 275, presents a hundred columns of Numidian marble, not to Portus but to Ostia;[2] and Ammianus Marcellus, as late as the year 359, tells us of the

---

[1] So MANNERT, *Alte Geographie*, Bk. IX.; FORBIGER, *Handbuch der alten Geographie*, III. 707, and others.

[2] VOPISCI, *Tacitus Imp.*, cap. 10, p. 107, ed. Lips. 1774; AMM. MARCELL. XIX. 10, 4, p. 142, ed. Erfurdt.

excitement which arose in Rome when the corn fleet could not enter the harbour of Claudius on account of contrary winds; but the sacrifice with which the heathen Præfect Tertullus endeavoured to propitiate the Dioscuri, was offered not in the supposed town about the harbour, but in or near Ostia. Forbiger cites as proof of his seaport-town of Portus, nothing but an inscription of the year 353, in which the old corporation of custom-house officers of Ostia or Portus (that is, no doubt, of both places[1]), which together formed only one guild, is mentioned. In another inscription, of the year 193, it is the corporation of ships'-carpenters of Ostia, which erects a monument to a tribune of the shipbuilders of Portus as their *patronus;* the latter seem, therefore, by no means to have formed an independent corporation, like that of Ostia. Volpi, in his continuation of Corradini's work on old Latium,[2] has given us everything which was still to be found in the neighbourhood of the former harbour in the way of antiquarian remains; but all this reduces itself to the notice that there was a corporation of boatmen (*lenuncularii*) in Portus, and the names of a couple of harbour officials. Again, the gleanings which Fea made on the spot in the year 1801,[3] give no results such as to show the existence of a seaport-town of Portus. All that has any town-like appearance relates to Ostia, as the inscription of Lucilius Gamala noticed by Fea, which mentions the temple erected by him.[4] In the *Codex Theodosianus*, again, one finds no trace that Portus was a town; only the sailors there, corn-measurers, and sack-carriers are noticed.[5] Once more,

---

[1] *Susceptorum Ostiensium sive Portuensium antiquissimum Corpus*, in ORELLI, 3184, 3140.

[2] *Vetus Latium profanum*, Patavii 1734, VI. p. 150 *et seqq.*

[3] FEA, *Relazione di un viaggio ad Ostia*, etc., Roma 1802.

[4] In VOLPI, *l.c.* p. 154. The *Coloni ostienses* are meant.

[5] *Cod. Theodos.* V. p. 201, ed. Ritter.

the statement of Æthicus, a Christian writer of the fourth century, that the Tiber forms an island between the port of Rome and the town of Ostia (*inter portum urbis et Ostiam civitatem*), shows plainly that he knew nothing of a seaport-town of Portus, and that the only real town there was that of Ostia.[1] In short, the supposed seaport-town is an unknown quantity, until at last in the sixth century, in Justinian's time, Procopius says expressly that the borough of Portus had a strong wall, while Ostia was open.[2]

II. THERE WAS NO BISHOP OF PORTUS BEFORE 313.

It is then, in itself, very improbable that in the third century a harbour, where only sailors and porters seem to have lived, was the seat of a special Bishop. But we have also very definite reasons for supposing that not until the fourth century, after the cessation of the persecution of Diocletian, was a bishopric founded here. Ostia was an episcopal see earlier than Portus, and hence, according to the testimony of S. Augustine, the Bishop of Ostia had always the privilege of consecrating the Bishop of Rome; but even of a bishopric of Ostia there is no certain trace to be found before the year 313. In that year a Synod of three Gallic and fifteen Italian Bishops was held at Rome under Miltiades, Bishop of Rome, on account of the African schism. One sees that it is the Bishops from the immediate neighbourhood of Rome who were summoned by preference; there were present the Bishops of Terracina, Præneste, Tres Tabernæ, and Ostia;[3] therefore still no

---

[1] *Cosmograph.* p. 716, in Gronov's edition of Mela.

[2] [See article OSTIA in SMITH's *Dictionary of Greek and Roman Geography*, which harmonizes with these conclusions. BURN, one of the latest writers on the topography, in his *Rome and the Campagna* throws no light on this question.]

[3] OPTATUS, *de Schism. Don.* I. 23, p. 23, ed. Du Pin.

Bishop of Portus. Not till the following year, at the Synod of Arles, does a Bishop of Portus for the first time appear; and here, again, the manner and order of the signatures is of importance for the question of the age of the bishopric. For while the Gallic, Italian, and Spanish Bishops always add to the name of their see *de civitate*, the Bishop of Portus is the only one who signs himself *Gregorius episcopus, de loco qui est in Portu Romano*. Here, manifestly, *locus* is used in the sense of *vicus* or *pagus*, in opposition to *civitas*,[1] and hence it is certain that Portus was still not a town. Further, let us notice the order of the subscriptions: first come the Bishops from Italy, then the Gallic, British, and Spanish; next the African, and quite the last—separate, therefore, from the Italian—the Bishops of Portus and Centumcellæ, and the two Presbyters sent from Ostia,[2] no doubt because these churches situated quite close to Rome were the youngest, and had only just been created. We may then, with great probability at least, place the institution of a bishopric at Portus in the year 313 or 314.

III. A BISHOP HIPPOLYTUS OF PORTUS WAS NOT KNOWN EITHER IN EAST OR WEST BEFORE THE SEVENTH CENTURY.

Who, then, made the Father Hippolytus Bishop of Portus? No one before the seventh century, and then it was done not in the West, but in the East. Here, first of all, let us establish what hitherto has by no means been noted as it deserves, that precisely where we should necessarily first have expected to find a

---

[1] As in CICERO, *Epist. ad Attic.* VII. ep. 3: *Magis reprehendendus sum, quod Piresea scripserim, quam quod* in *addiderim, non enim hoc ut oppido præposui, sed ut loco.*

[2] *Conciliorum Galliæ collectio*, I. p. 106, Paris 1789.

notice of the fact, viz. in the writers and collections and monuments of the West, there not a trace of an Hippolytus who was Bishop of Portus is to be found. The martyrology of S. Jerome in Fiorentini's edition has on August 23d : *In Porto urbis Romæ natalis s. Hypolyti, qui dicitur Nonnus* (in the additions to Bede, *Nonus;* in the Ottoboni martyrology, *Nunnus*), *cum sociis suis.* This is manifestly the Hippolytus who occurs in the *Acts of S. Aurea,* with whom the Father and Bishop, even supposing that the other is to be accounted an historical person at all, has nothing in common but the name. In Ado and Usuard we read : *In Portu Rom. sancti Yppoliti; Quiriaci et Archelai.* The two last are transferred by the martyrology first mentioned to Ostia; here, by a frequently occurring mistake, they are transferred with Hippolytus to Portus. No doubt one finds in the martyrology of S. Jerome, and in those who follow him, mention of a Bishop Hippolytus, but he is never designated Bishop of Portus, and indeed the place where he *was* Bishop, or where he died, is not mentioned. Instead of it, however, one finds an addition which certainly allows one to conclude that the collector meant the famous teacher. The words are : *Hippolyti episcopi, de antiquis.* Dusollier[1] and Fiorentini[2] explain this correctly : *de priscis ecclesiæ doctoribus* or *episcopis.* In the martyrology of S. Jerome this addition occurs more often[3] in the case of Bishops

---

[1] In the Notes to Usuard, p. 70.

[2] In Fiorentini on the 29th of January we have : *In Tuscia Constantini, Epoliti Episcopi de antiquis.* In the text which D'Achery, and, after him, Vallarsi, have put forth, it runs: *In Tursia, Constanti, Hippolyti episcopi de antiquis.* Tursia, of course, is only a copyist's error for Tuscia. Constantius was Bishop of Arezzo. But the interpunctuation, as in Fiorentini, is the right one; Tuscia must not be made to refer to Hippolytus, to whom people knew of no place to assign. In one manuscript of the martyrology we find accordingly on the 29th of January : *In Africa Victoris, Honorati, et alibi Hippolyti episcopi de antiquis.* See Fiorentini's Notes, p. 289.

[3] For instance, of Maximin of Trèves. A Greek, Cyril of Scythopolis,

and clergy of the first two centuries. So that in the West no trace whatever of a Bishop of Portus bearing the name of Hippolytus can be found; for the well shown in later times, in which Hippolytus was said to have been drowned, as also the church dedicated to him there, have reference manifestly to the Hippolytus in the *Acts of S. Aurea*, who was not a Bishop.

The fact that Eusebius and Theodoret had no knowledge of a bishopric of Portus of which Hippolytus was Bishop, and the still more definite confession of Jerome that he had not been able to discover of what see this Father was Bishop,—these things have still greater weight than the general silence of the whole West. How can it be explained that to Jerome, who had stayed so long in Rome,—who, through his relation to Pope Damasus, possessed such exact knowledge of the state of affairs there,—the episcopate of Hippolytus in Portus was, in spite of all this, unknown? The Bollandists[1] admit that this reason is of decisive importance, and that it is impossible to withstand the distinct declaration of Jerome with regard to Portus as the episcopal see of Hippolytus; they propose, therefore, as an hypothesis, which, however, they are quite ready to give up, the supposition that Hippolytus was Bishop in Arabia, that he set out for Rome, was seized by the heathen in Portus, and executed on account of his faith. We need not stop to consider this suggestion, which has only shown the difficulty of thinking of anything tenable; but Herr Bunsen's attempts at explanation must be looked at more closely. Against the negative testimony of Eusebius he urges (p. 150): Eusebius, no doubt, had read in Hippolytus' work that

---

expresses the same by the designation τὸν παλαιὸν καὶ γνώριμον τῶν ἀποστολῶν. The last is of course incorrect, but it is based upon the fact that a portion of the *Apostolic Constitutions* bore the name of Hippolytus.

[1] IV., Aug. p. 150.

he was Bishop of Portus, but he considered it a mistake, an oversight, a slip of the pen; for he could not conceive that there was a special Bishop for the port of Rome. Let us connect with this the passage on p. 159: "That Portus was a special episcopal see, separate from the neighbouring and almost adjoining Ostia, may easily be explained by its importance and its unique character; inasmuch as it, at any rate since Trajan's time, was the actual seaport of Rome, and the place where all foreigners stayed whom commerce brought from over the sea to the banks of the Tiber. All foreign religious rites seem to have been instituted at Portus; for it can scarcely be a mere accident that among its ruins a pompous inscription of the time of Alexander Severus was found, which must have belonged to a monument erected by a servitor (νεωκόρος, ædituus) of the temple of Serapis at Portus. This inscription has been published by Spon."

Here, again, we have a characteristic proof of Bunsenian criticism.

First, if Portus was such an important place, how is it possible that Eusebius, the most learned man of the fourth century, did not know it? or why should he have thought the existence of a bishopric there inconceivable, and of necessity a mistake? The journey to Rome brought those who came from the East, and not merely those engaged in trade, by way of Portus, and it is scarcely conceivable that a man like the Bishop of Cæsarea, who took part in the most important events of his time, should not have been quite familiar with the name of the Roman Portus and its relation to the capital.

Secondly, *all* foreign rites, we are told, were instituted in Portus; and how is this proved? By an inscription which, if it could prove anything at all for the Roman Portus, would only show that *one* foreign cultus, viz. that of Serapis, existed there. However, it is not in the least true that this inscription was found among the ruins of the Roman Portus, as Herr Bunsen maintains, but, according to the statement of Spon, who was the first to give it to the world, was found in the small seaside town of Cannes, in Provence (*in oppido s. Cannati*), and from thence was brought by Herr von Peirese to Aix. That the stone bearing the inscription was first taken from the banks of the Tiber to France no one will easily believe; and the *portus* mentioned in the inscription is accordingly the harbour of Cannes.[1]

The authority of Jerome is thus set aside by Herr Bunsen. He is first set down as a "quarrelsome and somewhat ill-tempered theological writer, who troubled himself very little about such historical information respecting ancient times, in which he took no very special delight;" and then he proceeds to say: "I do not doubt that he could easily have found out what place Eusebius meant by the diocese and abode of Hippolytus, for in this article he mentions some works of Hippolytus not named by Eusebius. But why should he give himself the trouble? The passionate attack of Hippolytus on Callistus not merely as a liar and deceiver, but also as a heretic, was a vexatious thing. The passage quoted above, then, only means, *non mi recordo*" (p. 150).

These are things which really scarcely admit of a serious answer. The charge of a dislike for the teaching of the Fathers of the second and third centuries is in the case of Jerome the purest imagination. Every one acquainted with the literature of the primitive

---

[1] SPONII *Miscellanea eruditæ antiquitatis*, Lugd. 1685, sect. 10, n. 22. The *Itinerarium Antonini* mentions a *Portus Æmines*, which appears to have been situated in the neighbourhood.

Church knows that it is precisely in Jerome that we find a more exact knowledge of the more ancient teachers of the Church, and that we are indebted to him for more information about their teaching and writings than to any other of the Latin Fathers. That Jerome, merely out of vexation at Hippolytus' attack on Callistus, would not trouble himself further about the see of the former, will seem utterly incredible to those who remember the sharp censures and bitter reproaches with which Jerome more than once visited the Roman clergy, not excluding the Pope. When a man like him says, I have not been able to discover the name of the town, it is mere wanton violation of the simplest historical justice to accuse him of lying,— for that is what Herr Bunsen's passage amounts to. The state of the case is rather this: S. Jerome experienced what his contemporary Prudentius had experienced; at the time of these men the true history of Hippolytus was already so overburdened and obscured with the legends which had attached themselves to this name, that it was not possible to find one's way aright, and even the truth was held to be invention or mistake. Probably he had seen in single treatises of Hippolytus, or elsewhere, that the author was designated Bishop of Rome; but he, who certainly knew the succession of the Bishops of Rome well enough, knew well that among them no Hippolytus occurred; but as no other statement respecting the episcopal see of the man (for that of some later Greeks, that it was Portus, was not in existence yet), there remained nothing else for him to do but to confess his ignorance as he has done.

Herr Bunsen maintains further: "Cyril and Zonaras, in their historical works, give just the same designation to Hippolytus." With regard to Cyril, this is again incorrect. He can only have meant Cyril of Scythopolis, a passage of whom he found in Fabricius.¹ But he does not say a word about Hippolytus having been Bishop of Portus.

Immediately afterwards Herr Bunsen says: "The Byzantine historian Nicephorus, son of Callistus (about 1320), who treats of Hippolytus very thoroughly, calls him a Roman Bishop, which, although inexact, admits of being reduced to the true state of the case, and to his current designation among the later Greek writers, who give him the name of *Papa* (*i.e.* Bishop) or Nonnus (which means the same, or *Abbot*)."

Again a tissue of errors.

First, what is the meaning of this?—the designation "Roman Bishop" admits of being reduced to the true state of the case. The one statement, Hippolytus was Bishop of Portus, and the other, he was Bishop of Rome, simply contradict one another; just as it would be a contradiction to make a Bishop of Seleucia be a Bishop of Antioch, because Seleucia is about the same distance from Antioch that Portus is from Rome. Either the designation "Roman Bishop" of itself expresses the true state of the case,—and then there is no need for it first to be reduced to do so,—or it does not express it, which is the opinion of Herr Bunsen; and it simply rests on an error, of which at any rate some other explanation must be sought than an interchange brought about by the mere contiguity of Rome and Portus.

The statement that the later Greeks gave S. Hippolytus the appellation of *Papa* is correct, but it is incorrect that this only meant *Bishop*. They did this at a time when it was already the general custom to give this title of honour to the two oldest Patriarchs only—those of Rome and of Alexandria. And here I must contradict the statement, which is certainly a

¹ *Opera Hippol.* I. x.

very common one and very widely spread, that in the earlier centuries the title of Papa was given to all bishops without distinction. In the West, in Africa, Gaul, etc., this was no doubt the case; but by no means in the East, or in the Greek-speaking part of the Church. From the third century onwards we see the title given in the first place only to Bishops of Alexandria; Dionysius calls his predecessor Heraclas, and Arius calls Bishop Alexander *Papa*.[1] Later on, the title was given to Bishops of Rome also.[2]

The statement of Herr Bunsen, that the name Nonnus signifies a Bishop or an Abbot, is again pure imagination. Only the first is here of any value; but the word nowhere occurs in this signification. The first who makes use of it is Jerome, and with him it means "holy" or "chaste;" later on, in the Rule of S. Benedict, it is a title which the younger monks are to give to the older.

The testimony of Pope Gelasius appears to me negatively to be of very great weight. Is it conceivable that this Pope, at the end of the fifth century, would have made Hippolytus Bishop of Bostra, if there had been at that time any statement or testimony as to his having been Bishop of Portus in the neighbourhood of Rome? Either at that time no martyr whatever was still honoured in Portus under the name of Hippolytus, or it was known that this martyr was other than the ancient theologian and Father. How the Pope came erroneously to make Hippolytus Bishop of the metro-

---

[1] [Cf. DÖLLINGER'S *Fables respecting the Popes*, p. 112, English edition.]

[2] Dionys. Alex. ap. Euseb. *H. E.* VII. 7; Arius ap. Theodoret, *H. E.* I. 5. In the year 1143, NILUS DOXOPATRIUS (in the *Notitia patriarchatuum* in LEMOYNE, *varia sacra*, p. 233) notes it already as an ancient custom that the title of *Papa* was given only to the Patriarchs of Rome and of Alexandria. Yet I remember a citation in the *Bibliotheca Græca* of Fabricius, in which the title *Papa* was given to a bishop, but am not able now to lay my hand upon the passage.

polis of Arabia we can explain quite easily, with the help of a passage in Rufinus—always supposing that we start from the position that he was not Bishop of Portus. But if this last be accepted as a fact, then the error of transferring to Arabia a man whose name was still fresh in people's memory in the immediate neighbourhood, becomes quite incomprehensible.

Herr Bunsen endeavours to set aside the weight of Pope Gelasius' statement in the following manner:— "The title," he says, "which the passage quoted by Gelasius bears in the manuscript, is in any case not by Gelasius, but by some barbarian hand, as the style shows — *Hippolyti episcopi (epi) et martyris Arabum metropolis in memoria hæresium*. These words are neither sense nor grammar."

And pray why not? What is there senseless in the heading—Hippolytus, Bishop and martyr of the metropolis of Arabia (*i.e.* of Bostra)? Nor can I see what fault there is to find with the grammar of the words. And that Gelasius quotes a passage which is to be found in the little treatise against Noëtus, as taken from the *memoria hæresium*, is very easy to explain. Very probably he had the *Syntagma* described by Photius before him, to which the essay against Noëtus was appended, as if it belonged to it. I see here an error of fact respecting the Arabian bishopric, which Gelasius, as we have seen, has in common with another writer; but nowhere do I see the extraordinary barbarism of which Herr Bunsen speaks, and not the least reason for calling in the altering hand of a copyist as a help.

Herr Bunsen has certainly cited one witness for the statement that Hippolytus was Bishop of Portus, on whom, no doubt, some weight might have been laid, if only this supposed testimony did not proceed from a somewhat stupid mistake. He quotes, that is to say, from the *Chronicon Paschale* the celebrated martyr,

Peter of Alexandria, who (about the year 309 or earlier) calls Hippolytus so. A single careful look into this *Chronicon* would have shown him that it was not Peter, but the much later author of the *Chronicon*, who cites a passage of Hippolytus with this designation. This compiler, to strengthen himself in his controversy with a Quartodeciman, and in support of his own view of Easter, quotes successively Peter, Athanasius, Hippolytus, Apollinaris, and Clement of Alexandria. Herr Bunsen could not fall into this error, unless he took what stands between the quotation from Peter and the quotation from Hippolytus as being also the words of Peter. But he cannot possibly have read them in this way, otherwise it would have been clear to him at once that Peter could not about the year 308 have spoken, as here, of the ἁγία ἔνδοξος δεσποίνη ἡμῶν θεοτόκος καὶ ἀειπαρθένος καὶ κατὰ ἀληθείαν θεοτόκος Μαρία, and could not have appealed to Constantine and the Council of Nicæa.

IV. EASTERN TRADITION UNIVERSALLY STYLES HIPPOLYTUS BISHOP OF ROME.

The tradition that Hippolytus was Bishop of Rome is accredited by so many witnesses in the Greek and other Oriental churches, that it cannot be set aside by the supposition of a mere misunderstanding; on the contrary, a deeper reason must be supposed and sought. And I here produce these witnesses in order; all the more because, if I mistake not, from the nature of them one can draw a tolerably certain conclusion as to the source from whence their statement has been taken.

The Presbyter Eustratius, who lived at Constantinople about the year 582, cites this Father as Ἱππόλυτος ὁ μάρτυρ καὶ ἐπίσκοπος Ῥώμης.[1]

---

[1] *Opp.* HIPP., ed. Fabricius, II. 32.

In the beginning of the seventh century he is quoted by two contemporary writers, Leontius of Constantinople and Anastasius Sinaita, and at the beginning of the eighth century by Germanus of Constantinople, as Bishop of Rome. Leontius enumerates as the Anti-Nicene Fathers (διδάσκαλοι καὶ πάτρες), Ignatius, Irenæus, Justinus, the two Bishops of Rome, Clement and Hippolytus, Dionysius the Areopagite, Gregory Thaumaturgus, and Peter of Alexandria.[1]

S. John of Damascus quotes in his Eclogues two fragments of Hippolytus with this same designation.[2] Likewise in the eighth century George Syncellus, in his chronography, quotes him with the following title: Ἐκ τῶν παραδόσεων τοῦ μακαρίου ἀποστόλου καὶ ἀρχιεπισκόπου Ῥώμης Ἱππολύτου καὶ ἱερομάρτυρος.[3] In later times Theophylact and Cedrenus know him only as Bishop of Rome.[4] Specially noteworthy is it that in the Greek *Catenæ*, which give fragments from his exegetical writings, he is throughout quoted as Bishop of Rome. So in a *Catena* on the *Psalms*, edited by Corderius,[5] and in another one in manuscript at Florence, so also again in the *Catena*[6] on the four greater prophets, also at Florence, in which explanations of Daniel by Ἱππόλυτος ἐπίσκοπος Ῥώμης are contained.[7] The *Catena* on the *Pentateuch*, which Montfaucon saw in Venice,[8] calls him the Roman Hippolytus; so also the *Catenæ* which are

---

[1] LEONT. *de sectis*, p. 503 ; ANASTAS. SINAIT. *Hodegus*, p. 356; GERMANI *theoria rer. eccles.* in the *Biblioth. Patrum Græco-lat.*, Paris 1624, II. p. 148. In the headings of fragments in Fabricius also, *Opp.* HIPPOL. pp. 273, 282, 283, he is called Bishop of Rome.

[2] JOH. DAM. *opp.* ed. Lequien, II. p. 787.

[3] SYNCELL., ed. Bonn, p. 597. The translator makes this into *Archiepiscopi et in agro Romano martyris*.

[4] THEOPHY. *in Matth. Opp.* III. p. 586. CEDREN. I. 434, ed. Bonn.

[5] III. p. 551.

[6] Bandini, *Catalogus cod. Græc. Bibl. Laurent.* p. 36 : Tertius est Hippolytus, episcopus Romæ, etc.

[7] *Ibid.* p. 21.   [8] *Diar. Ital.* p. 443.

at Venice;[1] and in like manner the *Catena* on *Genesis* and *Exodus* edited by Lippomani, and the Florentine one on the *Pentateuch*.[2] In the *Catena* on the *Apocalypse* he is called πρόεδρος Ῥώμης. In the collection of Leontius and Johannes a passage from his explanation of *Genesis* is quoted, once more with the statement that his bishopric was Rome.[3]

One may consider it as the rule in Greek manuscripts, that when any more exact designation is added to his name, Hippolytus is given as Bishop of Rome. So in manuscript 177 in the Turin Library, where there are a couple of passages from his writings;[4] again in manuscript 128 in the Nani collection at Venice, where a λόγος τοῦ ἐν ἁγίοις πατρὸς ἡμῶν καὶ ἱερομάρτυρος Ἱππολύτου πάπα Ῥώμης exists along with his treatise περὶ συντελείας τοῦ κόσμου and περὶ τοῦ ἀντιχρίστου.[5] In Codex 295 of the Munich Library, folio 119, we have: Ἱππολύτου ἐπισκόπου Ῥώμης ὑπόθεσις διηγήσεως εἰς τοὺς ψαλμούς.

The general tradition of the Eastern churches, that Hippolytus was Bishop of Rome, is confirmed by the calendars and menologies of these churches, which herein exhibit a marvellous agreement. In some of them he is called simply *Papa*, because among the later Greeks it was the custom to apply this title only to the two most ancient Patriarchs, those of Rome and of Alexandria. The ordinary Greek menology mentions him on the 30th of January as Papa of Rome; the Basilian, which places the day of his commemoration on the 29th of January, calls him simply Papa.[6] The *synaxarium*

---

[1] Theupoli *Græca s. Marci Bibliotheca*, pp. 17, 18.   [2] Ed. 1547, p. 292.
[3] *Ser. vet. nov. coll.*, ed. Maius, Rom. 1833, VII. pp. 84 and 144. The editor calls it in a note, *frequens error Græcorum*.
[4] Pasini, *Cod. Taurin.* I. p. 263.
[5] *Græci Codd. apud Nanios asservati*, Bonon. 1784, p. 298.
[6] Assemani, *Kalend. eccl. univ.* VI. p. 109. Neale's *History of the Eastern Church*, Lond. 1850, I. p. 770: Hippolytus, Pope of Rome, M. 30th of January.

of the tenth century in the Laurentinà at Florence,[1] which in its list of saints mentions of the Bishops of Rome besides him only Marcellus, Sylvester, and Leo, places him on the 8th of January as Bishop of Rome. So also the Syrian, Coptic, and Abyssinian Church knows and honours him as Bishop of Rome. Under the influence of the Arabic language his name has been metamorphosed in Syria and Egypt into the more native-sounding Abulides.[2] The further Oriental development of the legend has attached itself to the drawing of a S. Hippolytus near Portus from the *Acts of S. Aurea*, viz. that he was thrown into the sea, and that his corpse came up again from the sea and was thrown up on the shore ; which certainly would have been a very natural occurrence, but yet has given occasion to a special festival. Thus it stands in the Monophysite Coptic martyrology (translated from the Arabic by Assemani)[3] on the 5th of February: *Requies s. Patris Hippolyti Papæ Romæ;* and on the 6th: *Manifestatio corporis s. Hippolyti Papæ Romæ, quod in profundum mare jussu Claudii imperatoris projectum fuerat.* Among Syrian writers, Dionysius Barsalibi mentions the Roman Bishop Hippolytus as one of the authorities[4] used by him; and in the *Liber vitæ*, the diptychs of the Jacobites at Aleppo, the following Bishops of Rome are enumerated among "holy fathers and orthodox teachers :" Linus, Anacletus, Clemens, Hippolytus, and Julius.[5]

How, then, can this universal and constant tradition

[1] BANDINI, *Catalog. Codd. Græc.* p. 131.

[2] LUDOLFI, *Fasti eccles. Æthiop.* Francof. 1681, p. 430. *Acta Sanctorum*, Bolland. ad 22 August, p. 505. Assemani, *Biblioth. Orient.* I. p. 15.

[3] *Bibliothecæ Mediceæ Codd. Oriental. Catalogus*, p. 175. With an unjustifiable, but by no means unfrequent amount of arbitrariness, Assemani gives: *Requies . . . H. Episcopi Portuensis, quem Papam Romæ appellant Orientales.*

[4] ASSEMANI, *Bibl. Orient.* II. p. 158.

[5] ASSEMANI, *Catal. Codd. Vatican. Syriac.* II. p. 276.

of the whole East be explained? It is not merely the Byzantine Greeks with whom Hippolytus was accounted as Bishop of Rome; the Monophysite Churches also, who separated from the Byzantines as early as the fifth century, know him only as such, and no one who considers their rigid severance from the hated Melchites will think it conceivable that they borrowed the notion first from the Byzantines. It must therefore date with them from the time before the separation, *i.e.* from the fourth, or first half of the fifth century. That the Orientals, Greeks as well as Syrians, studied the writings of Hippolytus a good deal, especially the exegetical ones, we know well; that they took from these writings the fact of his Roman episcopate, seems to me to be the simplest explanation. Probably he had himself designated himself Bishop of Rome in the title or introduction to some of his writings. In the one greater work of his that we possess, he mentions, among many other things relating to himself personally, this also, that he held the rank of Bishop; in others he may very possibly have named the city in which he received this position. And if he omitted to do this himself, it certainly was done by his disciples and followers, who expressed their admiration for the man by erecting a statue to him, and of course were the less likely to omit stating his hierarchical dignity and claims in their copies of his works, inasmuch as these were much disputed, and for the most part were not recognised by his contemporaries.

V. THE SPURIOUS ACTS OF S. AUREA THE SOURCE OF THE TRADITION THAT HIPPOLYTUS WAS BISHOP OF PORTUS.

The source from which the theory came that Hippolytus was Bishop of Portus, and the time at which this theory first made its appearance, can be shown with tolerable exactness. The source is the spurious Greek *Acts of S. Chryse* or Aurea, and the time was the middle of the seventh century, when the Monophysite controversy occupied all minds in the East, and Hippolytus was appealed to as one of the most important authors in this dispute between the Catholics and the Monothelites. The first who makes him Bishop of Portus, and probably also the originator of the error, is Anastasius, *Apocrisiarius* of the Roman see at Constantinople, friend and fellow-sufferer of S. Maximus, like him a victim to Monothelite hatred, whose death falls within the year 666. He was a monk, and perhaps a born Greek, but spoke both languages; at any rate he passed a great part of his life in the Eastern Empire, especially in Constantinople, and was therefore considered by the Greeks also as one of themselves after his death.[1] He had disciples also in Constantinople, of whom two brothers in particular, Theodorus and Euprepius, are mentioned as stedfast opponents of Monothelitism. This Anastasius, in the title to the extracts which he made from the treatise of Hippolytus against Beron, designated Hippolytus as Bishop of Portus. The list of the ancient Bishops of Rome was well known to him, and he knew that there was no Hippolytus among them, and yet he found him designated as Bishop. Then he fancied that he found a solution of the problem in the *Acts of S. Chryse*, for there a martyr of this name was brought into connection with Portus. Possibly at that time there already existed the church dedicated to this martyr, to which afterwards, at the end of the eighth and in the ninth centuries, the Popes made frequent presents; in connection with which, however, we must remember that in the passages from the collection of Papal biographies relating to this, it is always only Hippolytus the martyr

[1] *Acta Sanctorum*, Bolland. August. III. pp. 112 *seqq.*

who is spoken of; the title of *Bishop* is never given him.¹

A contemporary of Anastasius was the compiler of the *Chronicon Paschale*, which reaches down to the year 628. He likewise lived, as we learn from his work, in Constantinople, and was most likely a monk engaged in study in his monastery, where the *Acts of S. Chryse* were certainly known; but it is also very conceivable that he knew Anastasius personally, and from conversations with him derived the statement that Hippolytus was Bishop of Portus.

Accordingly, these two are the first vouchers for the fable of Hippolytus' episcopate in Portus. Then follows Georgius,² Syncellus of the Patriarch Tarasius, and, therefore, likewise an inhabitant of Constantinople, who compiled his chronography in the first years of the ninth century; but, owing to his deriving materials from various sources, he mentions Hippolytus one time as Bishop of Portus, the other time as Archbishop of Rome, according to the usual Oriental mode of designating him.³ Then follow in the twelfth century Zonaras, and in the fourteenth Nicephorus Callisti, both of them inhabitants of the Byzantine capital. And hence one sees, first, that this statement never got

¹ See these passages collected in RUGGERI, p. 142.

² [The Syncellus was the confidential companion and often the destined successor of the Patriarch. Georgius is frequently quoted by his title Syncellus. His great and only known work is his *Chronographia from Adam to Diocletian.*]

³ Fabricius has allowed himself (*Opp.* Hippolyti, I. 43) to insert the word πόρτου in brackets along with 'Ρώμης in the second passage, as if it had merely slipped out by an oversight; the ἀρχιεπίσκοπος might have been sufficient to tell him that this was not possible here.

The Patriarch Nicephorus of Constantinople, who also quotes a couple of passages from Hippolytus' work on Beron—in his *Antirrhetica* (*Spicileg. Solesm.* ed. Pitra, p. 348)—cannot be named as a separate witness for Hippolytus' episcopate at Portus, for he has merely taken his passages from the collection of Anastasius, and therefore has also copied the title of the ancient Bishop along with them.

beyond Constantinople; and secondly, that with the greatest probability it may be traced back to a single inventor, either Anastasius or the monk who compiled the *Chronicon Paschale*. And here it deserves to be remarked, that among all the numerous Greek *Catenæ* which include fragments of Hippolytus' exegetical works, hitherto not a single one has been found which called him Bishop of Portus; all either mention merely his name without addition, or call him Bishop of Rome. It is, therefore, for the most part only chroniclers who always copied one from the other who mention the episcopate in Portus; and among them Syncellus probably is indebted for his notice to the *Chronicon Paschale*. In the place where he speaks of Hippolytus and his writings[1] he could not well designate him Bishop of Rome, for only a couple of lines before he had mentioned Callistus as such. Zonaras again stands on the shoulders of these predecessors, and in the case of the later Nicephorus Callisti there is at any rate no need to inquire further as to the source.

Is there, then, need of further proof that the whole statement is derived from the *Acts of S. Aurea*?

If Anastasius or one of the chronographers only had the Greek text of these *Acts* which *we* know before him, the designation of Hippolytus in them as Presbyter, which in earlier times was often used of Bishops, would have sufficed for making Hippolytus a Bishop, and Bishop of Portus; for that Hippolytus was a Bishop he knew easily enough, if he knew any particulars about him whatever. But we have seen that there existed a Latin text of those *Acts*, in which Hippolytus was already expressly made Bishop of Portus; it is quite possible that this was so also in another recension of the Greek text, and that the first

[1] SYNC. *Opp.* ed. Bonn. p. 674.

of those who cite Hippolytus as Bishop of Portus had this recension before him. How very much *Acts* of the martyrs of this kind were altered to suit convenience and local wants in regard to names, places, and single details, is shown in superabundance by examples; and, indeed, the different texts of the *Acts of S. Aurea* are a striking instance. But in what high repute these *Acts* stood in the Byzantine East, one sees from the *menologium* of the Emperor Basil,[1] in which the day for commemorating S. Chryse is placed on the 29th of January; and from the great Greek *menæa*, according to which her festival is kept on the 30th. Accordingly, the day for commemorating Hippolytus also is always put in Greek *menæa* and calendars on the 29th or 30th of January, for the Greeks know no other Hippolytus than the one who occurs in the *Acts of S. Aurea;* and the time of his martyrdom must therefore fall in the time of the Emperor Claudius.[2]

VI. HIPPOLYTUS, AS HIS OWN WORDS SHOW, CONSIDERED HIMSELF BISHOP OF ROME.

Since the appearance of the *Philosophumena* the key to the statement of the Greeks that Hippolytus was Bishop of Rome has been put into our hands. He gives it in this work plainly enough; we see, that is to say, from the facts mentioned by him, and the expressions which he uses, that it came to a formal schism between him and Callistus, Bishop of Rome; that he charged Callistus with holding heretical opinions in the doctrine of the Trinity, and with being a disturber of Church discipline; and that, being himself elected Bishop of Rome by his supporters, he occupied a

---

[1] In UGHELLI, *Ital. Sacra*, X. col. 333.
[2] So *e.g.* the *Ephemerides Græco-Moscæ* in the *Acta SS.* Maii. I. p. 10, and the note there.

position in Rome similar to that in which we find Novatian thirty years later.

Hippolytus was beyond doubt the most learned man of the Roman Church and of the West in general, and stood in great and deserved repute while Bishop Zephyrinus was still living. Callistus, to whom even in Zephyrinus' time Hippolytus had taken up a position of sharp antagonism, aspired, so he tells us, to the episcopal throne;[1] and, moreover, reached this goal when his predecessor and patron died. Hippolytus certainly avoids saying simply that Callistus became Bishop of Rome in the place of Zephyrinus by election; he prefers to say that his opponent thought that after Zephyrinus' death he had obtained that after which he had striven.[2] This election must at the outset have been undisputed, and Hippolytus himself must have recognised Callistus in his new dignity; for, according to his statement, it was fear of him, Hippolytus, that moved Callistus, now Bishop, to repel Sabellius, and to exclude him from communion with him as a heretic. Hippolytus was therefore at that time still an influential man and a theologian of repute in the Roman community—the community of Callistus—and had devoted friends and followers who, like him, still belonged to the head community. Separated from communion with Callistus he cannot yet have been, for the exclusion of Sabellius, we are told, took place out of fear of him (δεδοικὼς ἐμέ); he had therefore still his place among the Roman clergy. Now begins the first contest, the dogmatic significance of which we will examine later on; here we are only concerned with the course it took externally. Callistus charges Hippolytus and his followers with Ditheism, while Hippolytus describes the Trinitarian doctrine of Callistus as an offensive heresy, a mixture of the doctrines of Sabellius with those of

[1] P. 118. [2] Νομίζων τετυχηκέναι οὗ ἐθηρᾶτο.

Theodotus, or a hovering between the two; and then, omitting certain intermediate links, and suppressing certain facts which he leaves us to supply, he shows us the Christendom of the city of Rome in a condition in which on the one side stands the school of Callistus, and on the other the Church of Hippolytus, so that a complete separation has already taken place. He designates the congregation of which Callistus was head, a διδασκαλεῖον, a σχολή, quite in accordance with the language of his teacher Irenæus and the other ecclesiastical teachers of that time. Thus the Bishop of Lyons speaks of the *school* of Valentinus; he says of Tatian, that in separating from the Church he had set up a *didaskaleion* of his own.[1] Hippolytus himself, in his earlier treatise, had already used the same expression of the sect founded by Noëtus.[2] Hippolytus, on the other hand, is now head of the Church; he is (as he says of himself in the introduction) the successor of the Apostles, clad with the dignity and grace of the high-priesthood and of the ministry, guardian of the Church; he excludes several persons from the Church, and these then go over to the "*school*" of Callistus.[3]

The course of events then was as follows:—

1. After the death of Zephyrinus, Callistus, his confidential adviser and his right hand, is elected Bishop of Rome.

2. Callistus withdraws from communion with Sabellius as a heretic, from fear of the learned Roman Presbyter Hippolytus, as the latter thinks.

3. Bishop Callistus and this Presbyter mutually

---

[1] *Adv. hær.* I. 31, p. 106, ed. GRABE.

[2] Ὃς εἰς τοσοῦτο φυσίωμα ἠνέχθη, ὡς διδασκαλεῖον συστῆσαι. *Contra hæresin Noëti: Script. eccl. opusc.* ed. ROUTH, I. p. 46 [50 in 3d ed.].

[3] P. 3.: ὧν (ἀποστόλων) ἡμεῖς διάδοχοι τυγχάνοντες, τῆς τε αὐτῆς χάριτος μετέχοντες, ἀρχιερατείας τε καὶ διδασκαλίας καὶ φρουροὶ τῆς ἐκκλησίας λελογισμένοι.

charge one another with heretical doctrine in reference to the Trinity.

4. It comes to a formal separation, in which it is not clear whether Callistus endeavoured to get rid of his opponent by degrading him and excommunicating him, or whether Hippolytus, supported probably by Bishops from outside, was the aggressor; at any rate, he allowed himself to be elected Bishop of Rome by his followers in the place of Callistus, who had been proclaimed a heretic.

5. Callistus, however, retains the majority of the Roman Christians in his communion, and most of the non-Roman Churches also declare for him; he and his following, therefore, call themselves the "Catholic Church." Accordingly, Callistus and his party throw in the teeth of the Hippolytians that their congregation is only a small handful, while they pride themselves on the number of his followers.[1]

6. Hippolytus and his followers are zealous for the more strict form of Church discipline, while Callistus proceeds according to the milder one, and promises to absolve and receive back into communion even such as have committed grievous sins. Hippolytus ascribes to this laxer system of penance the fact that the great majority remains in the communion of Callistus, or seeks it.

7. Even after the death of Callistus the schism continues, or, as Hippolytus expresses it, the school of Callistus remains, and retains the practice introduced by him, and his tradition with regard to the lax system of penance; the members of it were called by their opponents Callistians.

In this way, then, the riddle over which so many scholars have hitherto toiled in vain is solved — the question of Hippolytus' episcopate. He was really what

[1] $\pi\lambda\eta\theta\acute{u}\nu o\nu\tau\alpha\iota\ \gamma\alpha\upsilon\rho\iota\acute{\omega}\mu\epsilon\nu o\iota\ \grave{\epsilon}\pi\grave{\iota}\ \check{o}\chi\lambda o\iota\varsigma$, p. 291.

the Orientals say of him, Bishop of Rome, but he was so owing to a separation from his Bishop Callistus, whom he opposed, just as thirty years later Novatian came forward as the rival of Cornelius; only that the latter schism began immediately after the election, whereas that of Hippolytus, if one weighs his words exactly, cannot have commenced until some time after the promotion of Callistus. This schism cannot have spread far, although it occurred in Rome, *i.e.* in the centre of the Church, from whence a schism could with speed and ease be kindled in other parts of the Church. Had the schism commenced immediately after the election, so that Callistus and Hippolytus had contended as rival Bishops from the outset—as afterwards in the case of Cornelius and Novatian—things might very well have taken a different form, and Hippolytus might have found recognition in many Churches speaking the Greek language. That this last was not the case may be concluded—

1. From the fact that all Greek lists of the Popes, no less than the Latin one, mention Callistus only, and know nothing of Hippolytus.

2. From the silence of Eusebius, which in this case was not intentional, although this historian gladly passed over schisms and divisions which had left behind no visible results in his own time. But that he here mentions nothing primarily because the existence of this schism was unknown to him, is implied in the manner in which he confesses that he does not know what see Hippolytus held.

It will be seen later on, however, that the schism did nevertheless leave some traces behind it, which become clear now for the first time, owing to our having a more exact knowledge of the matter through the report of Hippolytus.

VII. HIPPOLYTUS COULD NOT BE AT ONCE PRESBYTER OF ROME AND BISHOP OF PORTUS.

Herr Bunsen, as we know, holds fast with the utmost tenacity to the fable of Hippolytus' episcopate in Portus; but seeing that it is plain from the narrative in the *Philosophumena*, that Hippolytus was permanently resident in Rome, and there took an official ecclesiastical position, Herr Bunsen has thought of an hypothesis which is to secure still further advantages for him in reference to his views. For Hippolytus, according to him, was Bishop in Portus and Presbyter in Rome; the two, says Herr Bunsen, were quite consistent with one another. One must therefore suppose that Hippolytus was always on the move, and spent a good portion of his time in wandering backwards and forwards between Portus and Rome; and here we have, at any rate, still to conceive what becomes rather a hard task for the imagination, how Hippolytus helped himself in the difficulty into which the collision between his episcopal functions in Portus and his business as a Presbyter in Rome must often have brought him; for to get a vicar to represent one was a custom not yet existing in the Church at that time.

Herr Bunsen assures us (p. 152) : " One who is quite ignorant of the earliest history of the episcopal power, and of the Roman Church in particular, may find something surprising in the circumstance that a Roman cleric under Severus and Alexander should be called a Presbyter as a member of the clergy of the city of Rome, and at the same time have the direction of the Church at Portus, for which there was nothing else but the old title of 'Bishop.' For that was the title of one who in any town 'stood at the head of a community'—in Ostia, in Tusculum, and the other suburban towns. And it is remarkable that they still have Bishops who at the same time are members of the presbytery of the city of Rome, and, together with certain Presbyters and Deacons of the same, constitute the ruling ecclesiastical magistracy of the Roman Church."

Then, further on, he says (p. 153): "That the old (Roman) parish Priests formed the ruling ecclesiastical magistracy of Rome, together with the Deacons of the districts as they were appointed to minister to the Christian poor and widows, is universally recognised; and it can scarcely be doubted that the suburban Bishops were united with this corporation as assistants of the metropolitan Bishop. We know their later constitution (dating from the eleventh century), according to which the seven suburban Bishops were declared regular assistants of the Pope as *Cardinales episcopi*—an utterly unintelligible arrangement, unless it was based upon their original connection with Rome; for Ostia and Portus at that time were a couple of miserable little places, and had been so for centuries."

I know not whether there are any persons who are so much overawed by the assurance of his tone, and the added threat of being rebuked as ignorant, as to take these theories of Herr Bunsen as genuine coin. My readers know already that Herr Bunsen's knowledge of ecclesiastical history does not impose upon me; and I will therefore at once declare, without circumlocution, that all that is here said is baseless invention.

Only let us clearly grasp the question with which we are here concerned. Hippolytus is said to have been at once Bishop of Portus and a Roman Presbyter, and in the latter capacity—that is, "as member of the ruling ecclesiastical magistracy of Rome"—to have taken up the position of antagonism to Bishop Callistus described by himself. I say that, according to the constitution then existing, this was impossible. A Presbyter of the Roman Church could not at the same time have been Bishop of another Church; such a cumulation of inconsistent ecclesiastical offices, in which the duty of residence enjoined by the Church could not possibly have been fulfilled, never occurred at that time, and, if any one had attempted it, would not have been allowed. Portus was, according to Herr Bunsen's own statement, twenty English miles distant from Rome; it was therefore, at the outset, physically impossible that he could have satisfied the requirements of his double office in two places so far apart from one another. The number of Roman Presbyters corresponded to the number of the basilicas there, and the congregations connected with these. We know from Optatus that towards the end of the persecution under Diocletian, about the year 311 perhaps, there were some forty basilicas in Rome; and in the year 251 the Roman Church had, according to the testimony of its Bishop Cornelius, six and forty Presbyters. How these Presbyters had their own churches and congregations, we see from the words of S. Athanasius, in the passage in which he speaks of the Synod which had pronounced him innocent; this Synod was held in the church in which the Presbyter Viton was wont to have his congregations.[1] Hippolytus had, therefore, as Roman Presbyter in an ecclesiastical community which in the year 251 was already so great that it was able to support fifteen hundred widows and "oppressed" (θλιβουμένους),[2] a congregation of his own by which he was fully occupied; and now we are told that along with this he held a bishopric also, twenty English miles distant, the care of which he must therefore have left

---

[1] Ἔνθα Βίτων ὁ πρεσβύτερος συνῆγεν. *Apol.* 2, *adv. Arian, Opp.* p. 140, ed. Bened.

[2] See the letter of Pope Cornelius in Eusebius, *H. E.* VI. 43.

to others, and which he can only have visited occasionally on expeditions from Rome.

Herr Bunsen supposes that the suburban Bishops were already in Hippolytus' time connected with the corporation of the Roman parish Priests (and so belonged to the clergy of Rome); for the later arrangement since the eleventh century, according to which the seven suburban Bishops were declared regular assistants of the Pope as *Cardinales episcopi*, is *utterly unintelligible*, unless it was based upon their original connection with Rome (p. 155).

Stated briefly, this argument runs: Because the seven suburban Bishops in the eleventh century were placed in regular connection with the Roman Church, and were reckoned among the clergy, such a connection must have existed also at the beginning of the third century.

Without waiting to dissect this logic any further, we may oppose the following series of facts to Herr Bunsen's theory, which is not supported by a single fact:—

1. The seven suburban Bishops—that is, the Bishops of Ostia, Portus, Albanum, Præneste, S. Rufina, Sabina, and Tusculum (or, at any rate, some of them)—for several centuries stood in no closer connection with Rome and the Roman clergy than other neighbouring Bishops of central Italy. They might sometimes, just when they chanced to be staying in Rome, take part in the service with the Bishop of Rome; that was, however, nothing peculiar to them, but was done in the case of foreign Bishops generally.[1]

2. The seven Bishops appear for the first time as

---

[1] So says INNOCENT I. in the letter to Decentius, Bishop of Eugubium, in the year 416: *Sæpe dilectionem tuam ad urbem venisse ac nobiscum in ecclesiâ convenisse.* Here *convenire*, as GIORGI (*de Liturg. Rom. Pontif.* III. p. 3) remarks, is equivalent to *concelebrare*.

connected together, and in special and lasting union with the Roman Church, in the year 769, when Stephen III. ordered that the seven Cardinal-Bishops, as *Hebdomadarii*—that is, changing each week—should have Mass every Sunday in the church of the Redeemer, that is, the Lateran Church, at the altar of S. Peter, and should there sing the *Gloria*. Baronius has already remarked, that here for the first time the Cardinal-Bishops of later times made their appearance. But not until the eleventh century do the designations *Romani episcopi, episcopi urbis, collaterales,* and the like, occur. At that time, about the year 769, and still earlier, since the war with the Goths, the sees of these Bishops were partly reduced to deserts, partly sunk to miserable villages; and hence most if not all of them were accustomed to live in Rome, and thus formed their liturgical nexus with the Lateran. Not even yet, however, were they reckoned among the Roman clergy; indeed, not till a considerable time later.[1]

3. In earlier times only one standing relation is found between some of these Bishops and the Roman Church; this was, that the Bishop of Ostia consecrated the Bishop of Rome, while the Bishop of Albanum and Portus said the prayers used on the occasion.[2] That was, therefore, a relation such as subsisted everywhere between suffragan Bishops and metropolitans.

4. These suburban Bishops took no closer participation in the affairs of the Roman Church; not one of them is mentioned as taking part in the proceedings on important occasions; it is always only the Presbyters and Deacons of Rome who appear as active. We can lay all the greater weight on this negative proof, because from the third century onwards in each cen-

---

[1] [See article CARDINAL, in SMITH and CHEETHAM's *Dictionary of Christian Antiquities.*]

[2] *Liber Diurn.* p. 24.

tury, moments occur in which the internal history of the Roman Church is preserved in a specially distinct way. These are in particular the schism between Cornelius and Novatian; in the following century, the intrusion of Felix into the place of the banished Liberius,[1] and the double election of Ursinus and Damasus which arose out of that; further, at the end of the fifth century the Byzantine attempt to drive out Symmachus by setting up Laurentius, and a hundred years later, the distinctly-known pontificate of Gregory the Great. In the Novatianist quarrel a great number of persons are named, especially confessors and Presbyters; not one of the suburban Bishops is mentioned. Cornelius reports that he assembled the presbytery, and that in addition to them five Bishops also came; they were strangers, sixty such having shortly before attended a Synod at Rome. In the confusion which followed on the death of Liberius we see only Presbyters and Deacons acting; a single suburban Bishop—the Bishop of Tibur—is named, but only as the consecrator of Ursinus.[2] In the collection of biographies of the Popes, the *Liber Pontificalis*, down to the end of the eighth century, only a single Bishop of Portus is mentioned,—John, who went to Constantinople to the Council there as ambassador, not of the Pope, but of the Synod of Western Bishops held at Rome in the year 680.[3] Not one of the Bishops of Ostia is mentioned in this same period; only here and there are they named as consecrators of the Pope. No Bishop of Tusculum is named before the year 680; Bishops of Præneste, Sabina, and Albanum occur only in subscriptions to councils; only of one Bishop of

---

[1] [See DÖLLINGER'S *Fables respecting the Popes*, p. 181, English translation.]

[2] Marcellini et Faustini, *præf. ad libell. prec.*

[3] *Liber Pontificalis*, ed. VIGNOLI, I. p. 285.

S. Rufina, Valentius, is the particular fact mentioned that Pope Vigilius took him with him on his journey, and sent him back to Rome, together with the Presbyter and *Vicedominus* Amplicatus, to take care of the Lateran church, and to superintend the clergy.[1]

5. In the subscriptions of the Synods held at Rome, the names of the suburban Bishops appear scattered among those of the other Italian Bishops, according to their seniority by consecration; thus, for instance, in the list of names of the Roman Synod of the year 465, the Bishop of Portus comes after the Bishop of Avignon and before the Bishop of Aquaviva.

6. The formularies of the Roman Church, which the *Liber Diurnus* contains from the time between 685 and 752, show likewise that the suburban Bishops were not yet considered as belonging to the Roman Church; that in more important affairs—the government during a vacancy, the election of a new Pope, etc. etc.—they were not yet in any way summoned to take part. In the letters which were sent to Ravenna during the vacancy of the see, it is the Arch-presbyter, the Arch-deacon, and the *Primicerius* of the *Notarii*, who conduct the correspondence;[2] where the whole Roman clergy is spoken of, or where the letter is written in its name, we always find only: *Presbyteri, diaconi, et familiaris universus clerus.*[3]

7. It is remarkable that among the ambassadors which the Bishops of Rome sent to Councils or to other countries on account of ecclesiastical affairs, a suburban

---

[1] See UGHELLI, *Italica Sacra*, I., and *Lib. Pontif.* I. p. 218.

[2] *Liber Diurnus*, ed. GARNER, pp. 23 seqq. [*Primicerius* (one whose name stood *first* on the *waxen* tablets) *notariorum* means chief of the secretaries, chancellor.]

[3] One Bishop also is mentioned, p. 18, but only as bearer of the letter notifying the election of the Pope to the Exarch; the letter itself, however, is signed in the name of the clergy by the Arch-presbyter, and in the name of the laity by the Consul.

Bishop never occurs. This would be utterly incomprehensible if these Bishops stood in a closer connection with the Roman Church. Constantly Bishops were taken for these legations, and naturally almost always Italian ones; thus, Liberius sent Vincentius, Bishop of Capua, and Marcellus, a Bishop of Campania, to the Emperor Constantius, and soon after Lucifer of Cagliari and Eusebius of Vercelli. But not until the eighth century, and then not till the year 769, do we find Bishops of the suburban churches as ambassadors, —as Andrew of Præneste, who was sent in 772 to King Desiderius, and Gregory of Ostia, who in 787 went as legate to England. At the first greater Council of the West, that of Arles in the year 314, we remark, quite at the beginning among the signatures, two Roman Presbyters and two Deacons as legates of the Pope, and last of all among the Bishops, the Bishops of Portus and of Centumcellæ, and two Presbyters from Ostia.

8. Even in the time in which these Bishops already conducted the weekly service in the Lateran church, they were still regarded as strangers, not as belonging to the Roman clergy; and hence declared incapable of attaining to the Papal dignity, to which only Roman Presbyters and Deacons were eligible, as also was expressly ordered in the Lateran synod of the year 769.[1] At the end of the ninth century it happened for the first time that one of these Bishops, Formosus, Bishop of Portus, was raised to the Roman chair; but thereupon a violent storm burst, and it is well known to what ill-treatment Stephen VI., the successor of Formosus, subjected his corpse in consequence. And here it deserves to be noticed that the defenders of Formosus, Auxilius and the unnamed author of the *Invectiva*,[2] attempt to base their defence, *not* upon the

---

[1] So still also in the *Ordo Rom.* IX., in MABILLON, II. p. 92.
[2] In Bianchini's edition of Anastasius, IV. p. lxx.

plea that although Bishop of Portus he yet belonged to the clergy of the Roman Church, but upon earlier instances of episcopal translations, and on the fact that forcible pressure had been put upon him by the Roman clergy and by the people.[1]

And now the reader may measure the extent and solidity of Bunsen's knowledge of history, when on p. 226 he reads the following: "According to the thirty-third Apostolical Canon, the Bishops of the suburban towns, including Portus, formed at this time an integral part of the Roman presbytery, the later so-called College of Cardinals. I think, moreover, that above I have made it more than probable that the origin of this arrangement can only be explained by the position which these towns, and specially Portus, occupied in the second and third century. This corporation consisted, therefore, of the parish Priests and suburban Bishops, exactly like the College of Cardinals at the present time; only that the Deacons of the Roman Church at that time manifestly occupied a more subordinate position than their later namesakes, the Cardinal-deacons." The thirty-third Apostolical Canon, on which this fiction of a presbytery composed partially of Bishops is built, is concerned with the relationship of suffragan Bishops to their metropolitan, and says in so many words: The Bishops of every country must recognise him who is first among them as such, regard him as their head, and do nothing without his sanction.[2] Did Herr Bunsen really under-

[1] BIANCHINI and CENNI have given themselves much trouble to make it seem probable that the Bishops of the suburban churches stood in liturgical connection with the Lateran church at a still earlier date,—as early as the time of Damasus, and chiefly since the time of Simplicius (see *Anastasii Vitæ Pontiff.* ed. Bianchini, III. p. 176; *Concil. Lateran.* ed. Cenni, præf. p. 84). But as they are neither of them in a position to produce any facts for this theory, we need not pursue it further.

[2] [The canon, sometimes numbered thirty-four or thirty-five instead of thirty-three, runs thus: "The Bishops of every country ought to know who

stand the canon to mean that provincial Bishops everywhere were to belong to the presbytery of the metropolitan church, and therefore that in one church there should be Presbyters, and in another Bishops ?[1]

is the chief among them, and to esteem him as their head, and not do anything without his sanction; but each ought to manage only the affairs that belong to his own diocese, and the places subject to it. But let him not do anything without the consent of all; for by this means there will be unanimity, and God will be glorified by Christ in the Holy Spirit."]

[1] [JACOBI in HERZOG entirely agrees with this seventh point, that Bunsen's theory of Hippolytus being Bishop of Portus, and at the same time a member of the Roman presbytery, " would be utterly at variance with the constitution of the Church in the third century."]

CHAPTER III.

THE HISTORY OF CALLISTUS.

THE ACCUSATIONS OF HIPPOLYTUS AGAINST HIM.

THE history of Callistus, Bishop of Rome, has been hitherto almost entirely unknown. The want of material has nevertheless not withheld a Roman Canon in the middle of the last century, viz. Pietro Moretti, from writing a whole folio volume about Callistus.[1] But he has not succeeded in establishing a single tenable fact of any importance; he has given a new edition of the *Acts of Callistus* from a manuscript in the archives of the Church of S. Maria in Trastevere, and accompanied it with an abundance of almost utterly worthless notes. These *Acts* are a fiction from beginning to end, and every attempt to find anything sound and serviceable in them must fail. The gentle friend of the Christians, Alexander Severus, is here represented as a bloodthirsty persecutor; among other things, he puts forth an edict that every Roman who is found at home one Wednesday, instead of appearing on the Capitol, is forthwith to be put to death. A good many monstrosities of the same kind occur. These false *Acts* are certainly tolerably old, for an extract from them exists in the martyrology of Bede; probably they were composed in the seventh

---

[1] *De S. Callisto Papa et M., ejusque Basilica S. Mariæ trans Tiberim nuncupata, disquisitiones duæ critico-historicæ, duobus, tomis exhibitæ.* Romæ, 1752, fol.

century, on the occasion of the translation of the bones of Callistus.

We are compelled, therefore, to take the history of Callistus simply from the report of his opponent Hippolytus; and we are unable to confront the circumstances related by him with any facts known from other sources. Without doubt, Hippolytus had not the conscious intention of slandering Callistus; he did not invent the transactions and fate of this remarkable man. Of many things he was an eye-witness, and others—very likely the greater portion—he has narrated as they were reported to him by his followers, who, like him, saw in Callistus a heretic rightly deposed from his bishopric. The statement respecting Cornelius, Bishop of Rome, which the deputies of Novatian publicly read before the Bishops and faithful assembled at Carthage, but to which they declined to listen, may have had a good deal of similarity with this description of his predecessor. At any rate, it is here indispensably necessary to separate so far as possible the bare simple fact from the colouring which the prejudiced reporter is at pains to give it, and from the motives which he suggests.

Under the Emperor Commodus (180-192) there lived in Rome a Christian, Callistus, who was the slave of Carpophorus, himself a Christian, and an official in the imperial palace. He committed to his slave's keeping a considerable sum, with a view to his setting up as a money-changer. Callistus drove his trade in the fish-market—the *piscina publica;* and as Carpophorus appeared as security, other Christians, and widows also, deposited money with him. He was unlucky, however, and lost everything. Fear of his master, who declared that he would bring him to account, drove him to flight; he was just in the act of leaving Portus on board a ship, when Carpophorus appeared in the port in pursuit.

At the sight of him Callistus sprang into the sea, was pulled out by the sailors, handed over to his master, brought back to Rome, and as a punishment sent to the tread-mill.

That a Christian should cause a fellow-believer to be sent to the *pistrinum*, tells more against the character of the master than of the slave. How slaves were treated in the *pistrinum*, is shown by the description of a contemporary: "Ye gods! what men I saw there, their whole skin cut about with the lashes of the whip, and marked as if with paint; their gashed backs hung over with the tatters of their jackets rather than covered; some of them wore only a small girdle round their loins; in all of them their naked body could be seen through their rags. They were branded on their foreheads, their heads were half shorn, on their feet they wore iron rings; their pallor was hideous; their eyelids were as it were eaten away by the smoke and vapour of the dark atmosphere, so that they scarcely had the use of their eyes any more."[1]

After some time certain Christians applied to Carpophorus on behalf of the unhappy man, to let him out of the slaves' prison; Callistus, they said, assured them that he had money still standing out in certain quarters. Carpophorus took him out of the *pistrinum*, but had him watched. Thereupon the Jews carried Callistus before the tribunal of Fuscianus, Præfect of the city, on the charge that, giving himself out to be a Christian, he had disturbed them in their synagogue. Carpophorus demanded him back as his own debtor and slave, with the (untrue) assurance that he was not a Christian. Fuscianus, however, believed the Jews, who declared that Carpophorus wished in this way merely to withdraw him from punishment, and pressed upon the Præfect all the more strongly to do them justice.

[1] APULEII *Metamorph.* 9 ed. Oudendorp. p. 616.

Callistus was accordingly scourged, and transported to Sardinia, to penal servitude in the mines there.

These events fall in a time in which most probably Hippolytus was not yet in Rome, but was with S. Irenæus at Lyons. He had it on hearsay. Here already party-passion has saved us from any of decoration and invidious innuendo. In the statement that Callistus, when he caught sight of Carpophorus in pursuit of him, jumped into the sea, one naturally thinks that he did this in order to escape; Hippolytus, however, maintains that he did it because he wished to drown himself. After this first unsuccessful attempt at suicide, Callistus is said again to have sought death, but this time an honourable one: he will die as a martyr, or at least with the confession that he is a Christian, and on account of a transaction to which religious zeal may have driven him. Whence did Hippolytus know that the poor slave only sought an opportunity of dying decently? Callistus himself of course did not say so; people must have insinuated this as to what happened to him, and Carpophorus may very well have been the first to bring this charge against him in his bitterness. It is manifest that the later numerous opponents of Callistus must have had every interest to present his scourging and condemnation to work in the mines in as unfavourable a light as possible, in order to diminish the honour of his martyrdom. How Tertullian endeavours to represent what Praxeas had suffered for the Christian faith as quite inconsiderable![1] But what, then, did Callistus really do? As money-changer he had had transactions with the Jews, and wished now to collect his debts from them. As he could accomplish nothing with the individuals, he placed himself one Sabbath at the entrance of their synagogue, or perhaps even went into their synagogue (from

---

[1] *Ob solum et simplex et breve carceris tædium.* Adv. Prax. c. 1.

the words of Hippolytus this is not clear[1]), and demanded the repayment of his loan in a noisy way. The Jews thought that they had an easy game with a believer, who had the threefold ill-luck of being a slave, penniless, and a Christian; at once they made the fact of his having dunned his debtors on a Sabbath, and in front of or in the synagogue, into a charge of an attack on their religious liberty, and hence, instead of paying him, they beat and abused him, and hurried him before the tribunal of Fuscianus, the Præfect of the city. Now his master appears against him, and lies to the Præfect; Callistus is not a Christian at all, but is merely seeking death. If this representation of Hippolytus is correct, Carpophorus knowingly told an untruth, for he had before mentioned that Carpophorus had trusted Callistus with sums of money, because he was a Christian. The poor slave succumbed of course under the double charge of his master and the wealthy Jews; he is first scourged as a punishment for disturbing the worship of the Jews, and is then sent as a Christian to the mines in Sardinia, where there were at that time many other Christians no doubt still remaining from the time of the Emperor Marcus Aurelius.

Now, is any weight whatever to be laid upon the statement of Hippolytus, that Callistus' only object was death? In the first place, was it in the least degree

---

[1] The word used by Hippolytus to designate the disturbance caused by his opponent in the synagogue is a strange one. The Jews were κατασταστιασθέντες ὑπ' αὐτοῦ, and he makes them say before the court, ἐκώλυε καταστασιάζων ἡμῶν. All the passages which the new *Thesaurus* of Stephen cites under this word, give the meaning: to oppress, do violence to, drive out of the city by means of a riot or political faction, to use violence and tumult against a magistracy. Here is a single unarmed slave, who is accused by the whole Jewish synagogue of "using violence" against them. The matter was no doubt just the other way; Callistus demands his money, and thereupon the Jews fall on him, and beat and abuse him.

probable that the Præfect would have him forthwith executed, merely because he had disturbed the Jews in their synagogue? If it really was his earnest desire to be condemned to death, he must have done some act of violence in a heathen temple, or at the festival of some heathen gods. Secondly, if Callistus had really imagined that his attempt to disturb the Jews would involve his execution, he must have expected that it would have been accomplished, not in a simple way with the sword, but by the horrible death of crucifixion; for this was at that time the usual[1] way in which slaves were executed. But who will believe that a man in his senses would intentionally have purposed such a mode of death for himself?

Marcia, the mistress of Commodus, was kindly disposed towards the Christians, and after some time sent the eunuch Hyacinth, who was also a Christian Presbyter, to Sardinia, to set free the Roman martyrs there, of whom Victor, the Bishop of Rome, had handed in a list. In this list Callistus was not placed; but he fell at Hyacinth's feet, and besought him with tears nevertheless to free him along with the rest; and Hyacinth compassionately induced the governor, by appealing to the influence of Marcia, to set free Callistus also. On his return to Rome he appears still to have had an enemy in his master Carpophorus, although now according to law he was free.[2] When Hippolytus maintains

---

[1] I merely recall the well-known passage in the *Miles gloriosus* of PLAUTUS: *Scio crucem futuram mihi sepulcrum*; *ibi majores mei siti sunt, pater, avus, proavus, abavus;* the frequently (*e.g.* TACITUS, *Hist.* iv. 11; VULCATIUS, *Avid. Cass.* c. 5; CAPITOLINUS, *Macrin.* c. 12) occurring expression, *servile supplicium;* and JUVENAL'S *Pone crucem servo*, etc. etc.

[2] For when a slave was condemned by the civil power to penal servitude, he became thereby a bondsman of punishment, belonged to his master no longer, and hence, if he was pardoned, was free. So a rescript of the Emperor Antoninus determined: *Quia semel domini esse desierat, servus pœnæ factus, non esse cum in potestatem domini postea reddendum.* D. 48, t. 19, l. 8, sec. 12.

that Bishop Victor regretted the freeing of Callistus, and kept silence about it merely out of good nature, the fact mentioned directly afterwards, that he allowed him support month by month, does not very well agree with this statement.

The earlier history of the man reaches down to the death of Victor, with regard to which period Hippolytus reports what he heard afterwards, for he probably did not come to Rome until the time of Zephyrinus. One sees that Callistus passed through a hard school of suffering, and he must have been a very depraved creature if he, Christian as he was, did not come out of it chastened.

A new act in the life-drama of Callistus commences with the promotion of Zephyrinus. Unfortunately, Hippolytus' account here becomes very fragmentary, and consequently obscure. The Bishop calls him from Antium to Rome, avails himself of his help, holds him in great honour (to his own misfortune, says Hippolytus), hands over to his charge the great cemetery, which later on received its name from this overseer (whereas it has hitherto been erroneously supposed that it was called so because Callistus was the original maker of it), and entrusted to him the direction and supervision of the clergy. Had Callistus been a layman up to this time? Who ordained him? Did Zephyrinus know him before his own promotion? Did he now become a Presbyter? On all these points the narrator, in whom one here remarks some embarrassment, gives no explanation. He merely tells us that Callistus was always with Zephyrinus, flattering the Bishop, and always saying what was agreeable to him; and thus had known how to make him serviceable for his purposes. Zephyrinus is depicted as an uneducated man, ignorant of ecclesiastical law, covetous, and gladly receiving gifts. This last reproach is easily explained, without our being compelled to suppose any vice in the character of the Bishop, when we remember that in the time of Zephyrinus the Church of Rome had to meet her great needs entirely out of voluntary offerings; that the Bishop had to provide for the maintenance of two hundred clergy and Church servants, and of fifteen hundred and eighty poor;[1] and that besides this, considerable sums had to be spent for the support of distant churches which were in difficulties.

If the history of Callistus is to be made connected and intelligible, the account given by Hippolytus cannot be acquitted of a certain amount of misrepresentation, dictated by his own or other persons' strong feeling, and at the same time suppression of important facts. For, first of all, it is hard to comprehend, according to his representation, how the covetous Zephyrinus came to give so considerable a position to a poor slave who lived upon the alms of the Church, and to commit to him the direction of the (lower) clergy, *i.e.* pretty much the later so-called office of Archdeacon.[2] Secondly, if Callistus was such a doubtful character, and his earlier history so scandalous, how did it happen that the Roman clergy allowed this man to be thrust into so influential a position,—that the Roman presbytery, which, as we learn from Cyprian's correspondence, formed so strong and vigorous a corporation, and on the occurrence of a vacancy in the see held the reins of Church government with a strong hand,—without whose consent and assistance even the Bishop was not accustomed to do anything of importance,—that this corporation, at that time certainly most vigilant and jealous of its honour, did not oppose the promotion of

[1] These are the numbers which Cornelius gives in the year 251, in Eusebius, VI. 43.

[2] [*I.e.* as we find it in the West. In the East an Archdeacon seems to have differed from other Deacons in little more than mere precedence. In the West this *officiorum primatus* came to be only second to the episcopate.]

Callistus? Manifestly, Callistus won not only the favour of Zephyrinus, but also the good-will and confidence of the Roman clergy—of the majority at least; —for otherwise he would not after Zephyrinus' death have been elected Bishop of Rome without opposition. I say without opposition; for had such occurred from any important quarter, *Hippolytus would certainly not have suppressed the circumstance.* When a man succeeds in raising himself from the most oppressed and despised position, that of a slave severely punished by his master, to the dignity of a Bishop,—and that in the capital of the world, in a Church of fifty thousand souls,[1] and from a clergy of two hundred persons,—this man can be no mere adventurer, no crafty and adroit juggler, as Hippolytus calls him. Ignorance, want of scientific culture, are not among the reproaches which his opponent brings against him; and the cunning, the juggler-like adroitness which he lays to his charge, very likely appeared in the eyes of others as the intellectual superiority of a man who, endued by nature with the χάρισμα κυβερνήσεως, finds in himself the confidence and in others the trust which carries him upwards to the highest step attainable by him. Hippolytus cannot bring himself simply to say that Callistus became Bishop of Rome after the death of Zephyrinus; if we did not know it otherwise, we should have to guess it merely from the circumstances mentioned by him; he merely says that Callistus, after Zephyrinus' death, believed that he had attained the goal at which he had aimed.

But we will look more closely into the single charges against the way in which Callistus conducted his

[1] The Roman community may very well have been as strong as this, when, from the number of clergy and of poor receiving support, one calculates the number of laity out of whose free contributions so much had to be supplied.

episcopal office, in order to see, after deducting the rhetorical flourishes and numerous exaggerations which have their root in bitterness, what may chance to remain over as actual fact.[1]

I. FIRST CHARGE: GENERAL FORGIVENESS OF SINS.

In the front place comes the complaint that Callistus was the first who set forth the principle of unlimited forgiveness of sins. The motive which Hippolytus attributes to him, of wishing thereby to give Christians freer scope for gratifying their passions and sensuality, we can leave alone, or set it to the account of party polemics. The fact itself is doubtless correct, and enriches our knowledge of the course of development which the discipline of penance had taken. But two factors must first of all be weighed and stated as an integrant part of the account. The first is, that according to Hippolytus' own asseveration the arrangements of Callistus in Rome were not merely transitory, but lasting; that they were maintained even after his death. At the time of the composition of our work they were still in force (that is, about the year 230). In the twenty years which elapsed from that point to the time when, through Cyprian's correspondence, we again are offered exact knowledge of Roman discipline, no considerable alteration, no retrograde movement towards the former more strict practice, can have taken place. Far too distinctly do the Roman Presbyters in the year 251 appeal to the fact, that the strictness of

---

[1] [JACOBI in HERZOG pronounces this defence of Callistus still more partial than the attacks of Hippolytus. The examination of the separate charges which follows is a sufficient answer to such a judgment. MILMAN, who had committed himself to a belief in Hippolytus before the appearance of Dr. Döllinger's work, does not in his later editions admit more than that Hippolytus' picture is " possibly somewhat darkened by polemic hostility ; " he thinks it " has an air of minute truthfulness " ! (p. 55, 4th edition).]

their Church, and her requisitions with regard to public penance, are not new, but the old unbroken tradition.[1]

Secondly: *the power of a Bishop, and even of a Bishop of Rome, was at that time the very reverse of absolute;* being limited in its exercise by consideration for the feeling and will of the clergy, especially the presbytery, and even of the laity. This was especially the case with regard to such changes as were calculated to introduce a new discipline contrary to what had existed before. No one who knows the life of the Church at that time will believe that Callistus introduced a practice previously unknown in Rome *against the will of his presbytery.*

The predecessor of Callistus, Zephyrinus, had mitigated the strict penance-discipline, by declaring that those who had been guilty of adultery or unchastity might again be admitted to communion after performing public penance. Against this "peremptory edict of the Pontifex Maximus, the Bishop of Bishops, the apostolical Papa,"[2] Tertullian directed his Montanist

---

[1] *Nec hoc nobis nunc nuper consilium cogitatum est, nec hæc apud nos adversus improbos modo supervenerunt repentina subsidia, sed antiqua hæc apud nos severitas, antiqua fides, disciplina legitur antiqua.* Epist. 31, Ap. Cyprian.

[2] These titles he gives in passing to the Bishop, whose ordinance he disputes. Cardinal ORSI and MORCELLI, and on the Protestant side MÜNTER (*Primordia Eccles. Afric.* p. 45), will not admit that Tertullian means the Bishop of Rome; a Bishop of Carthage must have been the author of the edict, they maintain; while NEANDER (*Antignosticus*, IIte Ausgabe, p. 263) declares for the ordinary opinion, that Tertullian had the Bishop of Rome in his eye. Münter and Morcelli give no reason for their view; the latter probably follows the authority of Orsi. But Orsi in both his works—the earlier one, *Dissert. Hist. de capitalium criminum absolutione,* pp. 98 *seqq.,* and the later one, *Istoria Eccles.,* Ferrara 1749, III. p. 12—has not grasped Tertullian's line of thought correctly; he fancies, that is to say, that Tertullian is asking the Bishop, whose edict he opposes, on what then he bases his authority to issue such a one; no doubt on the passage Matt. xvi. 18, where Christ gives to Peter the power of binding and loosing. The Bishop fancies, therefore, that by these words the power of loosing is committed to him also, *i.e.* to the whole Church united with Peter. Now, says Orsi, if Tertullian had addressed these words to Zephyrinus, he would

treatise on chastity. This was accordingly a mitigation which had reference merely to one kind of sin; while for others—for those, namely, which fell under the category of idolatry, apostasy, and murder—the strictness of full and unqualified exclusion from communion hitherto enforced was still to continue. What occurred forty years later in consequence of the Decian persecution, leads one to conjecture that after Zephyrinus a further movement in the discipline of penance, a progressive mitigation, must have taken place. The general pressure of those who had just shown themselves weak under persecution, and had fallen away in Rome as well as in Carthage, shows at once that Church discipline no longer stood at the point which Tertullian's treatise on purity exhibits; that the principle of not shutting out

---

not have said, "Thou imaginest that to thee also, that is, to every Church united with Peter (*ad omnem ecclesiam Petri propinquam*), this power has been committed;" but he would have said, "To thee, who boastest that thou dost sit on the seat of Peter, and to thy Church founded by him." The Cardinal has here overlooked that Tertullian is not asking for the basis of the authority by which the Bishop put forth an edict extending to other Churches and Bishops also,—this question is quite beyond the scope of the whole book. Tertullian is rather disputing the right of the Church, or of any single church, to absolve an adulterer, *i.e.* to admit him again to a communion. If the Church did not possess such a right, and her appeal to the power of the keys committed to Peter was illusory, then of course the right of the Bishop of Rome to put forth such an edict at once fell to the ground, for the Bishop could then allow neither to himself nor to the other Churches what exceeded the divinely-fixed limits of the Church's power generally. The power of loosing, Tertullian thinks, was not given to Peter in his ecclesiastical dignity as an Apostle and Bishop, but only personally as a *homo spiritualis;* and only such spiritual persons or organs of the Paraclete (of whom Peter was one, but are now only to be found in the Montanist communion) can absolve from sin. Had Tertullian, consistently with his principles, been able to concede to the Catholics that the Church in general possesses a power of absolving from every kind of sin, he would still have continued to have denied the opportuneness of the edict in question, but not its lawfulness and validity. But he did *not* admit that the Church which was united with the chair of S. Peter, the Church which merely has the multitude of Bishops (*ecclesia numerus episcoporum*), possesses this power; hence an edict respecting the exercise of a power which, according to him, did not exist, fell to the ground of itself.

those guilty of grievous sins for ever from communion was already further extended than in the edict of Zephyrinus, which referred only to the sin of unchastity. In the letters which the Roman clergy wrote to Cyprian in the year 250, the earlier discipline is already tacitly given up, and no longer thought of; the clergy will not decide until the episcopal see is again filled, although they have had long consultations on the subject in conjunction with many Bishops; but it appears that no one is of the opinion that those who have sinned most grievously should be turned out for all time, without hope of forgiveness. Novatian, the author of the first letter, will have the active discipline and strictness of the Roman Church maintained only thus far, that full forgiveness and re-admission are not granted to the fallen at once and on the spot, while new cases of apostasy were continually occurring; he merely blames "the far too great impatience and intolerable hastiness" with which the fallen demanded communion; it is not right, he thinks, by dispensing with penance, to grant them immediately and all at once the medicine of re-admission to communion.[1] This was already the view in Rome before the two Synods which Cyprian in Carthage and Cornelius in Rome held on this question. On the other hand, according to the testimony of Tertullian, discipline in Zephyrinus' time was still so strict, that baptized persons, who had fallen into the sin of idolatry, or of an attempt on another's life, were admitted among the penitents of the Church certainly, but without hope of re-admission to communion.[2]

[1] *Non intercepta pœnitentia . . . properata nimis remedia communicationum præstare; non momentaneam neque præproperam desiderare medicinam*, are his expressions. *Ep.* 31 *inter Cyprianicas.*

[2] That this was the case, the following passage from Tertullian leaves no doubt: *Adsistit idolatores, adsistit homicida, in medio eorum adsistit et mœchus. Pariter de pœnitentiæ officio sedent in sacco et cinere inhorrescunt,*

The further mitigation which, as we now learn from Hippolytus, was brought into practice by Callistus, falls, therefore, into the intermediate period between the years 219 and 249. What did this Bishop enact with regard to the discipline of penance?

In the *first* place he declared, that henceforth forgiveness of sins should be extended to *all*, and consequently even to the most grievous and hitherto excepted offences, viz. those belonging to the category of idolatry and murder;[1] or, as Hippolytus expresses it, the Church of Callistus offered communion to every one without distinction (ἀκρίτως), of course under the conditions universally binding in the Church, the undertaking and completing of the penance. Had Callistus gone so far as to re-admit sinners even without penance, Hippolytus would doubtless have emphasized this in the strongest way, as something quite unheard of in the Church before. But no one acquainted with the condition of things in the Church at that time will think that possible for a moment.

Accordingly, the reproaches which Tertullian had made against the Church on account of its illogical procedure were now set aside. The adulterer, so the advocate of Montanism had urged, you re-admit to communion, while others, who sit with him on the same penitential seat, and whose offence sometimes might be more deserving of indulgence, have no hope of being received again.

To every one the door of the Church was now opened, and the principle to which even Cyprian afterwards

---

eodem fletu gemiscunt, eisdem precibus ambiunt, eisdem genibus exorant, eandem invocant matrem. Quid agis mollissima et humanissima disciplina? Aut omnibus eis hoc esse debebis (beati enim pacifici), aut si non omnibus, nostra esse. Idolatrem quidem et homicidam semel damnas, mœchum vero de medio excipis? Idolatræ successorem, homicidæ antecessorem utriusque collegam?

[1] Λέγου πᾶσιν ὑπ' αὐτοῦ ἀφίεσθαι ἁμαρτίας, p. 290.

gave utterance was admitted—that as all must be admitted to penance, so must the hope of re-admission into the Church be granted to all.

What Callistus enacted was, however, by no means an entire innovation. This milder discipline was new only in the West; in some Eastern Churches it was certainly in existence some time earlier. Bishop Dionysius of Corinth, a contemporary of Soter, Bishop of Rome, wrote as early as the year 169 to the churches in Pontus, especially to that of Amastris, that they ought to receive all who in any way had been renegade or heretical, or had committed any crime whatever, if they turned to the Church again.[1] Accordingly, Dionysius would not hear of any sin involving the perpetual excommunication of the sinner; and his view or demand is exactly the same as that to which Callistus gave utterance fifty years later. On the other hand, the Roman see after Zephyrinus did not at once get its milder practice adopted throughout the West. We know from Cyprian that a number of African Bishops of the time immediately preceding him still held fast to the life-long excommunication of those who had fallen into the sin of unchastity, in spite of the edict of Zephyrinus. We see that the Spanish Church in the beginning of the fourth century held to the principle of making perpetual excommunication the penalty for certain sins, especially grievous ones; this appears from the canons of Elvira [c. 315 A.D.].[2] And Hippolytus himself appears to have held the first indulgence granted by Zephyrinus to be open to

---

[1] Euseb. *H. E.* 4, 23: Τοὺς ἐξ οἵας δ᾽οὖν ἀποπτώσεως, εἴτε πλημμελείας, εἴτε μὴν αἱρετικῆς πλάνης ἐπιστρέφοντας.

[2] [The practice was by no means uniform. The Council of Ancyra (c. 314 A.D.) limits the penalty to be inflicted for the very sins for which the Council of Elvira decreed final excommunication. It appears that perpetual exclusion was at no period the universal discipline of the Church for any sins.]

exception; for it is on that, and not on dogma alone, that the complaint which he makes against him is grounded, "that he is a novice in ecclesiastical laws and limitations." In reality, the principle of granting forgiveness to all, or of offering hope of re-admission to all, as Callistus established it, was only the natural consequence of the mitigation decreed by Zephyrinus in favour of a particular kind of sin.

II. SECOND CHARGE: RECEPTION OF EXCOMMUNICATED PERSONS.

But Callistus went further, *i.e.* he showed the application of his general principle to particular cases and categories. He declared accordingly, in the *second* place, that all who hitherto had belonged to some Christian sect or separated community, and now turned to the Catholic Church, should forthwith be received, without being put to open penance for sins which they might have committed in the former communion. That is what Hippolytus says when he makes Callistus declare, "the sin shall not be reckoned against him."[1] Let us here distinguish what Hippolytus lumps together in a general expression. Persons who turned to the Catholic Church from an heretical sect or a schismatical community were either from the outset (*i.e.* by birth or by their first conversion from Paganism) members of such a sect, or they had left the Catholic Church and wished now to return to it again. The Church was always wont to make a great distinction between these two classes; the latter had been renegades, the former for the most part were only unwillingly astray. S. Augustine repeatedly calls attention to the fact that the Church treats the one quite differently from the others.[2]

---

[1] Οὐ λογίζεται αὐτῷ ἡ ἁμαρτία, p. 290.
[2] Epist. 48, *Opp.* ed. Bened. 1700, II. 191; *De unico bapt.* c. 12, *Opp.* IX. 365.

That in the case of those who now for the first time became true believers, and therefore desired to be received into her bosom, the Church did not begin by reckoning about the past, did not inquire what sins they had previously committed in their heresy, whether they had already done penance for them, and the like; —this was as natural as it was just. Heathens and Jews were treated in the same manner. The Church was wont to punish only those sins which were committed in her communion, not those which fell in the "time of ignorance." When, then, Hippolytus states that, in consequence of the ordinance of Callistus, his society (his διδασκαλεῖον he calls the Catholic Church) was increased by many, who in the agony of their conscience sought for tranquillity or forgiveness, and who at the same time had been turned out of many heretical sects,—this is perfectly intelligible. Here we may remind ourselves how strong sectarianism was in Rome: and hence cases no doubt occurred in which persons had already wandered from one of these sects to another, yet without finding the wished-for certainty and peace, and at last joined the great Catholic Church, which willingly opened its gates to them. And here one could only wonder that Hippolytus mentions this in a fault-finding tone, did not what he says plainly disclose his dissatisfaction at the greatness of the "school of Callistus," compared with the probably small handful of those who belonged to his own communion. But—he continues—Callistus has even received some who have been condemned by us and expelled from the Church. Hippolytus here again chooses his words with deliberation; he will not say too much. "We (Hippolytus, Bishop of Rome, and his Presbyters) had condemned these persons (ἐπὶ καταγνώσει), and expelled them from the communion of *the* Church." The followers of Hippolytus constitute *the Church* absolutely, for the communion of Callistus is merely a διδασκαλεῖον, a conventicle, a school,—that we know; but why these persons were condemned we do not learn. Did they take offence at the doctrine of Hippolytus? Or did they think, perhaps, that he had done wrong in separating from Callistus? *If they had been expelled for grosser offences, he would no doubt have mentioned it.*

However, these persons had probably some time before left the communion of Callistus along with Hippolytus and his party, and now penitently returned to it again. Nevertheless Callistus received them also, contrary to the procedure otherwise usual in the case of renegades, without first subjecting them to a penance. This was wise, and probably contributed essentially to the result, that a few years later the whole schism disappeared without leaving a trace behind. When a dispute and a bewilderment arises suddenly in a Church, and in consequence of this a separation into two congregations, it would show want of tact and of judgment to apply principles usually enforced against heretics to the separatists who showed an inclination to return; for this would make the schism permanent: rather one ought to build a bridge for them and receive them with open arms. Thus Callistus acted; and just so did Pope Cornelius afterwards deal with the confessors seduced by Novatian, one of whom, the Presbyter Maximus, he even re-admitted to his priestly rank;[1] and in the same way the Catholic Bishops in Africa made the return to unity easier for the Donatists.

III. THIRD CHARGE: PROTECTION OF IMMORAL BISHOPS.

Third accusation. Callistus taught (ἐδογμάτισεν) that if a Bishop sins, even though it be a sin unto death, he is not to be degraded.

---
[1] Ep. 46 *inter Cyprianicas*.

We may here remark at the outset, that the Bishop of Rome certainly did not lay down with such unqualified generality that which his opponent makes him maintain. So clever and adroit a man as he was, according to Hippolytus' description of him, assuredly did not involve himself in contest, the issue of which might at last have been simply ruinous to his own authority, merely in order to keep a good-for-nothing Bishop in office. And what means had he at his disposal in that time of (on the whole) always severe discipline, and in the face of the jealousy with which Christians watched the moral reputation of their community in the eyes of the heathen, to protect and maintain a criminal Bishop against the voice of the other Bishops of the province, against the will of the clergy of the diocese, and against the contempt of the community? Thirty years afterwards, Stephanus, Bishop of Rome, was appealed to by the two Spanish Bishops, Basilides and Martial, who had shown themselves weak and faithless under persecution, and had been deposed in consequence, and he reinstated them in their Churches. The Spanish Churches were divided in consequence (new Bishops having meanwhile been consecrated in the place of the deprived), and appealed to the Bishops of Africa for help; and these declared that Stephanus had allowed himself to be deceived, and that the deposition of the two *libellatici* and the consecration of the new Bishops in their place was to be maintained. We see that although men recognised the right of the Pope to receive appeals from Bishops, and even to cancel a sentence of deposition, yet resistance was offered to him, and the resistance was strengthened by a call for the intervention of other Churches, when people were convinced of the justice and necessity of the deposition. Manifestly it was deposed Bishops who appealed to the higher authority of Callistus; he interested himself on their behalf, and declared in particular cases that not every offence was in itself a sufficient reason for deposing a Bishop.

But, says his opponent, Callistus declared that even a mortal sin was no reason for deposing a Bishop. That is very likely correct, and apparently it hangs together with his theory of mitigation. The strictness or mildness of discipline in the treatment of sinning Bishops and clerics kept equal pace with that observed towards the laity; if the latter was more indulgent, the procedure against the clergy must also assume a more gentle form. Only let us distinguish first with regard to the sins, and secondly with regard to the scale of ecclesiastical punishments.

1. The idea of a sin "unto death" was a very indefinite one, and Hippolytus himself, with his more rigorous view, might well reckon many sins as deadly which other Bishops did not regard as damnable and unpardonable, even in the case of a Bishop. In the Apostolical Canons—in the 24th Canon, only unchastity, perjury, and theft, and in the 26th Canon, actual ill-treatment of a Christian or of a heathen, are cited as the offences which ought to cause the deposition of a Bishop. But in a time in which the principles as well as the practice of ecclesiastical penance were still as strict as Callistus found them, it is certain that the circle of offences which were to involve a Bishop's deposition had become much more widely extended. Was it, for instance, to be sufficient reason for an accusation against a Bishop, and for his deposition, that he had once through excess caused scandal, or had struck his slave in anger? And how many cases occurred in which, even although no bloody persecution demanded a victim, yet, owing to the difficult relation of a Bishop to the heathen magistrates and to his own community, he stumbled or fell, which

gave the stricter part of his enemies opportunity to accuse him of a sin "unto death," and to move for his deposition?

The contemporary of Callistus, Tertullian, reckons among deadly sins which must be atoned for by public penance, these: being a spectator at public games and gladiatorial contests, taking part in a heathen banquet, hasty or rash swearing, breaking one's word, and the like.[1] If, then, the usual practice was followed, according to which a Bishop was to be deposed in those cases in which a layman would be excommunicated and put to public penance, then the deposition of Bishops must have become tolerably frequent, whereby the Church, her harmony and fixed order, suffered manifold injuries, and the loss certainly was greater than the advantage expected on the other hand from the exercise of the stricter discipline. If there existed in a Church a faction hostilely disposed to the Bishop—and how easily such a one was formed is shown by the instances at Carthage and Rome, the setting up of the anti-bishop Fortunatus against Cyprian, and of Novatian against Cornelius—then there certainly never was any want of an offence which might be laid to the charge of the Bishop as a sin "unto death," and be used as a pretext for his deposition. Callistus had, therefore, certainly very substantial reasons for coming forward as the protector of the Bishops, and for insisting that depositions should be less frequent, and not be inflicted

---

[1] *De pudic.* c. 7, *Opp.* ed. Oehler, I. 805. He says of such offences: *Perit igitur et fidelis elapsus in spectaculum quadrigarii furoris et gladiatorii cruoris et scenicæ fœditatis et xysticæ vanitatis, aut si in lusus, in convivia sæcularis solemnitatis, in officium, in ministerium alienæ idololatriæ aliquas artes adhibuit curiositatis, si in verbum ancipitis negationis aut blasphemiæ impegit. Ob tale quid extra gregem datus est, vel et ipse forte ira, tumore, æmulatione, quod denique sæpe fit, denegatione castigationis abrupit.* This cannot be said of the Montanist community only; it must have held good of the Catholics also, otherwise Tertullian would not have been able, as he does, to base his argument on this practice.

for every real or supposed deadly sin. He had all the more reason for this, inasmuch as he was the founder of a generally milder discipline, and was urged on by the logic of the thing itself to allow place for modification in the procedure against really culpable Bishops also. S. Basil testifies that it was an old rule in the Church, that those who had been deprived of their ecclesiastical office were not to be visited with any other punishment,[1] and consequently not with ecclesiastical penance as well; and in fact the Apostolical Canons show that the same offence was visited in the case of a cleric with deposition (καθαιρείσθω), in the case of a layman with excommunication and penance (ἀφοριζέσθω).[2] As long, therefore, as Church discipline was very strict, and certain offences involved life-long excommunication, others less, but always public penance, so long must the procedure against Bishops have been harder also, and their deposition more frequent. A Bishop could not continue in office when it was known in the community that he had committed the very sin for which some of themselves had been deprived of communion, and were now in the class of penitents. Accordingly the exercise of a milder discipline introduced by Callistus, by the establishment of the principle that every penitent sinner must be received again into communion, must have produced a double change, in which the second was quite the natural consequence of the first. In the first place, the cases in which public penance was inflicted must have become more rare. When murderers, adulterers, men who had denied Christ and offered to idols, after lasting penance, were seen again in the ranks of the faithful, and at the altar receiving the Eucharist, it was scarcely possible

---

[1] *Epist.* 188, *Opp.* ed. II., Garner, Paris. 1839, III. p. 393.

[2] *E.g. Can.* 64, 65. [The principle being οὐκ ἐκδικήσει δὶς ἐπὶ τὸ αὐτό, Nahum i. 9.]

any longer to inflict public penance on those who had been present at a heathen play, or had struck a man in a tumult of passion; place must be allowed for the milder punishment of a merely temporary suspension from receiving the Eucharist, without ecclesiastical penance, as already is found in the *Apostolical Canons*.[1] But at the same time also it could no longer be tolerated that a Bishop should be deposed for an offence which in the case of the laity no longer involved any public ecclesiastical punishment, or at any rate no heavy one. It was certainly not the meaning of Callistus that a Bishop, if he transgressed, should go wholly unpunished. Deposition was the more severe punishment; all the more so, because it was perpetual and irrevocable. But the milder one (the application of which Callistus, without doubt, thought fitting, where deposition would have seemed unjust), mere temporary suspension, occurs already in the *Apostolical Canons*, especially in the fifth: a Bishop, Presbyter, or Deacon, who out of false religiousness puts away his wife, shall be suspended (ἀφοριζέσθω); but if he persists, let him be visited with deposition (καθαιρείσθω).

IV. FOURTH CHARGE: ORDINATION OF DIGAMISTS.

A *fourth* charge which Hippolytus raises against Callistus is, that under him men who had already been married twice or thrice were ordained Bishops, Priests, or Deacons. The principle of the Church not to admit to the higher orders persons who have married again, is based notoriously upon the precept of S. Paul

---

[1] *E.g. Can.* 9. [If any Bishop, or Presbyter, or Deacon, or any of the priesthood, does not communicate, when the oblation is over let him state the reason, and if it be just, let him be forgiven; but if he refuse, let him be *suspended*, as becoming a cause of harm to the people and raising suspicion against him that offered (as being one that offered not rightly). The concluding words are wanting in some of the best Greek MSS.]

the Apostle.[1] That the Apostle, in requiring that a Bishop should be the husband of one wife, and likewise, in the parallel case of a Widow, that she must be the wife of one husband, refers not to simultaneous but successive polygamy, is clear of itself to every unprejudiced person. The Church has always understood it so, and it is an exegesis external to the Church that has taken the trouble to obscure the question and attribute this meaning to the apostle,—that men living in polygamy might be members of the Christian community indeed, only they ought not to be chosen as Bishops;[2] and this in the Roman empire, where every simultaneous second marriage was null, and, according to the Prætor's edict, involved infamy, and was punished as adultery; so that the offence of polygamy, with which Justin Martyr reproaches the Jews of his time,[3] certainly only found tolerance when it was practised by stealth. In more recent times, however, that exegesis has become somewhat less prejudiced, and SCHLEIERMACHER, HEYDENREICH, BAUR, DE WETTE, and GILBERT[4] have acknowledged that the apostle means to say that men who, after the death of their first wife, have taken a second or a third, are excluded from holding office in the Church.[5]

---

[1] 1 Tim. iii. 2; Titus i. 6.

[2] GROTIUS alone, whom one certainly must not reckon along with the mass of Protestant commentators, has the right explanation; with him also SALMASIUS, *De fœnere trapezit*, p. 51, and VITRINGA, *De Synagoga vet.* p. 665. In Germany, so far as one can see, HEDINGER was formerly the only one who was sufficiently free from prejudice to see and give utterance to the truth.

[3] *Dialog. cum Tryph. Opp.* ed. Otto, II. 442, 460.

[4] In KAUFFER's *Biblical Studies*, 1846, pp. 152 seqq.

[5] It should be stated that SCHLEIERMACHER, BAUR, and DE WETTE only came to a right understanding of the passage when they had determined to give up the Pastoral Epistles as the spurious productions of a later age. Most astonishing is this in the case of SCHLEIERMACHER, who declares only the First Epistle to Timothy to be supposititious, and then without hesitation maintains (*Werke; zur Theol.* II. 301): "Certainly every one who reads

In the first centuries there was no doubt about the meaning of the Apostle; his prohibition was always applied to those who had lived in successive polygamy. In the time of Callistus also it was the universal rule that, as Origen says, a Bishop, a Presbyter, a Deacon, and a Widow, should not have married a second time.[1] Tertullian appeals most frequently to this ecclesiastical rule, and what he says on the subject serves at the same time as confirmation of the statement that in the time of Callistus some exceptions really had been made to the otherwise dominant custom. In his earlier Montanist writings he affirms the fact, that not only among the Montanists, but in the whole Church and universally, digamists were not admitted to ordination; he remarks that, as he remembers well, some were even deposed again, and that because it was not found

this letter impartially, and has no other object in view than to bring it into harmony with itself, will here certainly find a prohibition of second marriages, not generally, but only for those who aim at office in the Church. Now this is manifestly not Pauline," etc. But as the same requirement is found, Titus i. 6, and this epistle is genuine according to Schleiermacher's theory, the self-made difficulty is set aside in the following way: "The words μιᾶς γυναικὸς ἀνήρ, Titus i. 6, we have not the least reason for understanding in any other sense than that of actual polygamy; and every one must agree with Theodoret, p. 653, that Paul nowhere else condemns second marriages, and the whole description here does not give us the least right to suppose that he further required in the ἐπίσκοπος an additional and peculiar sanctity." Against this arbitrary mode of proceeding, which, moreover, assumes in the face of all history that polygamy existed in the first Christian communities, BAUR has now most justly protested (*Die sogenannten Pastoralbriefe des Apostel Paulus*, p. 117), but only in order to win a new basis for the supposition that the three Pastoral Epistles are not Pauline. "If one," he says, "is to consider the μιᾶς γυναικὸς ἀνήρ as not Pauline in only one of these letters, this is evidence—seeing how all things dovetail into one another here, and each letter merely gives again its own contribution to the common subject—against the Pauline origin of these three letters. This repeated inculcation of monogamy points as strongly as any of the other criteria by which we have to investigate the origin of these letters to the second century." So also DE WETTE (*Exegetisches Handbuch*, Zweiten Bandes, fünfter Theil, p. 8). In his opinion, the precept is "altogether too positive."

[1] *In Lucam hom.* 17, *Opp.* ed. De la Rue, III. 953.

out until afterwards that they had married again as widowers; and he thinks that from this precept he can show the laity that they also are bound to forego second marriage, because the clergy must be taken out of the laity, and because it is unseemly to demand a blessing on a second marriage from priests who themselves have only married once.[1]

But in his last, or one of his last writings,[2] Tertullian maintains that among the *Psychici* (the Catholics) some were found even among the Bishops who had married twice; who thus, therefore, set the Apostle at defiance, and did not blush when that passage from the Epistle to Timothy was read in their presence. It is not to be overlooked that the zealous Montanist here speaks of cases which can only have happened a short time before; for in the earlier treatise he had borne witness to the opposite of such indulgence or falling asleep of discipline, viz. a strictness to the extent of deposition as the dominant condition. These cases consequently must have occurred in the time which elapsed between the composition of the latter treatise, the *Exhortation to Chastity*, and the publication of the book *On Monogamy*. When, then, Hippolytus expressly says that under Callistus people first began to make those who had married twice or three times Bishops, or Presbyters, or Deacons, we have a confirmation of the statement of Tertullian, and at the same time a date; the cases belong to the time between 218 and 222, and the treatise *On Monogamy* was accordingly written about the year 221, or somewhat later. It is no doubt probable that Tertullian had Bishops of the African Church primarily in his eye, for immediately before he accuses an African Bishop tolerably plainly of adultery, and holds him up to shame before the *Psychici*. But Hip-

---

[1] *De Exhortat. cast.* c. 7, p. 747, ed. Oehler.
[2] *De Monogamia*, c. 12, p. 782, ed. Oehler.

polytus also may very well have been thinking of the African Church in making his charge, for the last accusation which he brings forward manifestly tells principally against this Church, which at that time was in communion with Callistus, and not with him. Among those who have most recently occupied themselves with fixing the chronology of the writings of Tertullian, HESSELBERG [1] places the treatise in question in the period after the year 212, because there is no basis for a more exact statement. MORCELLI [2] places even the treatise *On the Crown* in the year 237, and does not make the activity of Tertullian as an author end until 239. It is sufficient for our purpose that there is no reason for putting back the treatise *On Monogamy* to the period before 218. But as regards the relation of Callistus to the consecration of those Bishops who had married again, Hippolytus will not lay to his charge a direct participation and immediate complicity in this transgression of the Apostle's precept. He distinguishes well by his manner of expression what Callistus *himself* had done and taught from that which was done *under him* merely (ἐπὶ τούτου)—that is, in any part of the Church in communion with him, and calling itself the Catholic Church, and so certainly with his tacit consent or toleration. As such he reckons the cases mentioned.

Meanwhile let us follow the history of this impediment of second marriage further; we meet here a dispute calculated to throw light upon the facts used by

[1] *Tertullian's Leben und Schriften*, Dorpat 1848, p. 135. UHLHORN in his dissertation, *Fundamenta Chronologiæ Tertullianeæ*, Götting. 1852, has placed the treatise *De Monogamia* in the year 205, without any external ground whatever, but merely for so subjective a reason as that on p. 51, the treatise *De Monog.*, along with those *De Jejun.* and *De Pudic.*, is very sharp and violent; whereas age disposes men to be for the most part somewhat more gentle, and the like. Did he remember Luther and his last writings? [or Jerome's attack on Vigilantius?]

[2] *Africa Christiana*, II. 97.

Tertullian and Hippolytus for the accusation they make. In the *Apostolical Constitutions*, 6, 17, and in the 17th *Apostolical Canon*, it is declared that one who has married a second time cannot be received into the order of clergy; yet the canon adds the condition, if he did not take his first as well as his second wife until after baptism. This has always remained the principle of the Greek Church, only he was looked upon as impeded by digamy who had married again *as a Christian*. If he had concluded the second marriage before baptism, it was supposed that the stain of incontinency involved in second marriage was taken away by the washing of baptism, and that consequently no impediment stood in the way of his entering into the clerical order. In the Latin Church both theory and practice were different. Here it was merely affirmed that the cleric must be the most perfect example possible to his congregation; that, if he had married twice, he became useless as a preacher of continence. Therefore the Popes, especially Siricius and Innocent I., and before them S. Ambrose, then S. Augustine and others, insisted that even those who had taken the one wife before baptism, but the other as Christians, must remain excluded from clerical office. Men who married widows were placed in the same category. The Synods in Gaul, Spain, and Africa drew up their canons about second marriages on the same principles. The Bishops at Valence,[1] in the year 374, ordered that at the ordination of a cleric, the difference whether he had married again before or after baptism could not be recognised.[2] The Synod of Agde decreed, in the year 506, that Presbyters and Deacons who, in spite of their second

---

[1] [There is a special treatise on this Synod by Dr. Herbst, Professor at Tübingen, in the *Tübing. Theol. Quartalschr.* 1827, p. 665.]

[2] C. 1, *Canones Apostolorum et Conciliorum*, ed. Bruns. II. iii. 146; I. 148.

marriage, had been ordained contrary to ecclesiastical law, should not exercise their ecclesiastical functions any longer;[1] and the Synod at Carthage, in the year 398, even deprived a Bishop, who should knowingly ordain a digamist, of his power of ordination. Meanwhile the Oriental view of second marriages came more than once into conflict with that of the West. Thus the Bishops of Illyricum, in the year 414, stated in a letter to Pope Innocent,[2] that with them a man who had had and lost a wife as a catechumen, but had taken another after baptism, would not be regarded as a digamist, for the first marriage was taken away with the rest of his sins by baptism. This view the Pope expressly contested,—that which was good and innocent in itself, such as marriage, could not be done away by baptism; he asked whether, then, the children of such a marriage were to become illegitimate through the father's baptism. Even S. Jerome adopted the standpoint of the Orientals. His friend Oceanus maintained that a Spanish Bishop, Carterius (against whom no other charge lay than that after the death of his wife, married before baptism, he had married again as a baptized Christian), had been ordained contrary to the apostolical precept. Jerome,[3] on the contrary, defended the ordination of this man, whose case did not fall under the ecclesiastical idea of digamy, and declared (certainly with exaggeration) that the world was full of such ordinations. Yet, when Rufinus attacked him on the point, he moderated his declaration to this,—that there were some Bishops in the Church

---

[1] [It also decreed that married Priests and Deacons should abstain from their wives. Its tone was therefore rigorist. It was assembled *ex permissu domini nostri gloriosissimi magnificentissimique regis*, meaning Alaric, the Arian King of the Goths; the Pope (Symmachus) is merely mentioned in giving the year.]

[2] *Epistolæ Pontiff. Rom.* ed. Coustant, p. 831.

[3] Ep. 69, *Opp.* ed. Paris, 1846, I. 654.

who found themselves in the same position as Carterius; and submitted that he had merely given his opinion in answer to a question, without at all claiming that it must hold good.[1] In the West, later on, we find only Gennadius of Marseilles on the side of Jerome; he states the rule of the Church in this way,—that he who has been twice married after baptism cannot be ordained;[2] in opposition to which Pope Leo, in his letter to the African Bishops of the year 446, still required universally that no one who had previously concluded a second marriage might remain in the priesthood.[3] In the East, however, Theodore of Mopsuestia endeavoured to alter the dominant custom. What determined him to do so was, as he stated, the conviction that very often a corrupt use, detrimental to the Church, was made of the old rule; and seeing that no one else of his time stood in such reputation in the whole East as a theologian and exponent of Scripture, no one else had so many devoted pupils as Theodore. He seems really to have made a great impression, and to have induced several Bishops to disregard the ancient canon.

Theodore states[4] that in his time it often happened that a man who was living a continent life, but had had a second wife, was refused holy orders; while another, who had lived a dissolute life, but had only been married once, was admitted without hesitation. But supposing a man had married a second time before baptism, he was baptized and then ordained, just as if baptism could undo the past, and cause that the man had not really lived with two wives; and besides all this, that people thought they had done a good thing,

---

[1] *Apol. adv. Rufin.* I. c. 32, *Opp.* II. 424.
[2] *De Eccles. dogm.* c. 72, ed. Elmenhorst, p. 38.
[3] *Opp.* ed. Ballerini, I. 674.
[4] *Catena in S. Pauli epist. ad Timoth. etc.*, ed. Cramer, Oxon. 1843, p. 23.

CHARGE IV.—ORDINATION OF DIGAMISTS.

when they received a man who hitherto had lived as he pleased, and moreover had given no proof of virtue or holiness, into the ranks of the clergy immediately after baptism. By this procedure the whole legislation of the Apostle S. Paul respecting the qualifications of a Bishop, and the testimony as to his previous life, was made of no effect. That the wife of the one remained alive, while that of the other died after a short time, and so made room for a second, was an accident, and the first was no better than the second on that account. The intention of the Apostle was not that the election to the episcopate should be made in reference to such accidents,—that one who had lived with two wives in succession in unstained matrimony should be rejected, while another, who had only had one wife, but at the same time had lived a dissolute life, should be ordained immediately after baptism.

Theodore then makes the declaration which "some" had already set forth before him, and which Theodoret borrowed from him afterwards almost word from word:[1] that at that time many Jews still lived in polygamy; others having wives had sinned with slaves or concubines; it was these whom the Apostle had excluded from orders. Theodoret adds that he cares nothing about the custom which prevailed in the great majority of cases, based upon another interpretation. The collector, however, remarks at the end, that this interpretation flatly contradicts ecclesiastical tradition and all Synods.

In the case of Theodoret a personal and party interest was added to the reputation of his master. One of his friends and fellow-combatants, the Comes

---

[1] THEODORET, *Opp.* ed. Noesselt, III. 653. [The passage is quoted by Alford on 1 Tim. iii. 2. He agrees with those who reject Theodoret's interpretation as improbable. " Still we must not lose sight of the circumstance that the earlier commentators were unanimous for this view."]

Irenæus, as zealous an opponent of Cyril as Theodoret himself, had been consecrated Bishop of Tyre by John of Antioch, in spite of his second marriage. After some years came an order from the Emperor to depose him, first because he was a Nestorian, but also on account of the circumstance of his second marriage; and Theodoret then wrote to the Patriarch that, in order to justify his consecration of Irenæus, he must turn to account the fact that in disregarding the second marriage of Irenæus he had followed the example of his predecessors; for Alexander of Antioch and Acacius of Beræa had ordained the twice-married Diogenus, and Praulius of Jerusalem had consecrated Domninus to be Bishop of Cæsarea under similar circumstances; moreover, Proclus at Constantinople, the chief ecclesiastics of the diocese of Pontus, and all the Bishops of Palestine, had approved the consecration of Irenæus.[1] Nevertheless these representations remained without effect, and Irenæus was compelled to give place to another. We see, however, that Theodoret, in a still higher degree than Theodore, had a strong practical interest in putting forth an interpretation of the Apostle's precept; at which, if it were the unbiassed opinion of an exponent of Scripture otherwise so thorough, one must fairly marvel.

Now if we return from this digression to the charge which Hippolytus and Tertullian brought against the Catholic Church of their time, it appears most probable that already in their time the difference was made between second marriage before and after baptism; and that several were made Bishops in spite of their double marriages, because it was thought this stain might be overlooked, as something belonging to the heathen period of their life; while the more strict and logical were of opinion that, according to the Apostle's

[1] *Ep.* 110, *Opp.* IV. 1180.

words, those also were to be excluded from office in the Church who had concluded one or both of their marriages before baptism. Still it is also quite conceivable that in some Churches, owing to the want of men properly qualified in other ways, it was thought allowable temporarily to set aside the Apostle's prohibition, and ordain men who had married again; just as afterwards the Synod of Neocæsarea declared in its twelfth canon, that, owing to the want of proper men (διὰ σπάνιν ἀνθρώπων), even *clinici* might be received into the presbytery.[1]

V. FIFTH CHARGE: ALLOWING CLERGY TO MARRY.

At first sight one cannot but regard the *fifth* charge as more serious and important. Callistus, according to the accusation of his opponent, ordered that if a cleric married he was to remain among the clergy, just as if he had committed no offence.

Here again a remark already made is once more confirmed. Hippolytus delights in expressing the things with which he reproaches his rival in the widest and most comprehensive form, yet in such a way that he says nothing really untrue, and always leaves it open to the reader to understand what has been said in a

---

[1] [The Council made another reasonable exception. The ground for regarding with disfavour those who had received clinical baptism was the suspicion of unchristian motives in the recipients, viz. of having "continued in sin" until the last moment. The Council decreed that if such persons cancelled this suspicion by conspicuous faith and zeal afterwards, they might be ordained. See ROBERTSON's *History of the Christian Church*, I. p. 167, 2d ed. The exact words of the canon are, διὰ τὴν μετὰ ταῦτα αὐτοῦ σπουδὴν καὶ πίστιν. HEFELE agrees with "all commentators, except Aubespine," that this canon speaks of those who *by their own fault* have deferred baptism till they were dangerously ill. Aubespine would refer it to those catechumens who fell ill before the time of their baptism arrived, and were baptized without the usual amount of instruction. The 47th Canon of Laodicea disproves this view. See HEFELE, *History of the Christian Councils*, vol. i. p. 229, English translation.]

narrower or wider sense. If one takes the words εἰ δὲ καί τις ἐν κλήρῳ ὢν γαμοίη quite in a general sense as they lie before us, then it follows that Callistus introduced or tolerated something *of which there is not another instance in the whole primitive*[1] *Church*. But if we look more closely, the matter stands quite differently. In Rome somewhat later there were on the one side forty-six Presbyters, and on the other a hundred and eight clergy of lower rank, namely, fourteen Deacons and Sub-deacons, forty-two Acolyths, fifty-two Lectores and other ministers; all these were included among "the clergy." Did then Callistus say, that even if a Priest took it into his head to marry, he was to be left quietly in possession of his place? Or did he declare that when one of the host of Lectores, Acolyths, Ostiarii, one of the Sub-deacons, or even perhaps a Deacon, takes a wife, he may continue to remain among the clergy? That Hippolytus only charges him with the latter declaration, cannot fail to be acknowledged by every unprejudiced person who weighs these words and their position. Immediately before, where the subject was the ordination of those who had married again, the author is very cautious not to speak generally of "clergy," for it might be supposed that these twice-married persons were to be admitted merely to the lower offices of the Church, and thus the whole point of the reproach would be lost; he therefore carefully enumerates Bishops, Presbyters, and Deacons. As soon, however, as the subject is marriage after ordination, he does not say that Callistus allowed clergy of these same orders (τῶν αὐτῶν βαθμῶν or τῆς αὐτῆς τάξεως) to marry; he does not say that Bishops, Presbyters, and Deacons, according to Callistus' will and pleasure,

---

[1] [For this apparently strong statement, that there is absolutely no example of marriage after ordination, the convincing authority of HEFELE is quoted, *Beiträge*, i. p. 123.]

CHARGE V.—ALLOWING CLERGY TO MARRY. 141

could marry and yet remain in office; but merely that if any one among the clergy married, etc. etc. Thus the expression ἐν κλήρῳ ὄντες, clergy, is here used rather on purpose to distinguish them from those of the higher orders in the Church, the Bishops, Presbyters, and Deacons mentioned immediately before; and this is the ordinary ecclesiastical use of the terms, of frequent occurrence in the canons also. In the 55th *Apostolical Canon* we read, if a *cleric* insults a Presbyter or a Deacon, he is to be deposed.[1] In the canons of the Synod of Laodicea, the κληρικοί, as ministers of lower grade, are regularly distinguished from the ἱερατικοί, *i.e.* Presbyters and Deacons.[2] A Bishop also, who was pretty nearly Hippolytus' contemporary, Cyprian, uses the expression sometimes of the lower ministers in the Church, as when he states that it is fitting to write to the Roman Church through *clerici,* and therefore he has ordained Saturus to be Lector and Optatus to be Hypodiaconus. And Ambrosius, like Hippolytus here, places the *clerici* in contradistinction to the Bishop and Presbyters.[3]

But it might be urged, the lower clergy were allowed to marry in any case; how could Hippolytus reckon this against Callistus as something extraordinary? With regard to that, we must remember that in the first five centuries by no means a fixed and similar discipline for the whole Church was reached on this

---

[1] εἴ τις κληρικὸς ὑβρίζει πρεσβύτερον ἢ διάκονον, ἀφοριζέσθω. The Nicene Synod in its third canon uses the same mode of expression as Hippolytus: Ἀπηγόρευσεν καθόλου ἡ μεγάλη σύνοδος, μήτε ἐπισκόπῳ μήτε πρεσβυτέρῳ μήτε διακόνῳ μήτε ὅλως τινὶ τῶν ἐν τῷ κλήρῳ ἐξεῖναι συνείσακτον ἔχειν.

[2] *Can.* 27, 30. 41, 42, 54, 55. [See also the 24th Canon. HEFELE agrees with this, dissenting from Van Espen's explanation that ἱερατικοί includes *all* who hold any office in the Church, the rest referring to unordained acolyths and sacristans.]

[3] *Sed prius cognoscamus non solum hoc apostolum de de episcopo et presbytero statuisse, sed etiam Patres in concilio Nicæni tractatus edidisse, neque* clericum *quemquam debere esse, qui secunda conjugia sortitus sit. Epist.* 63, c. 64, *Opp.* ed. Bened. I. p. 1037.

point. The Synod of Chalcedon says in its 14th Canon, *only in some Churches* is it allowed that Lectores and Cantores marry; and hence the 27th *Apostolical Canon*,[1] which gives ministers of these two grades liberty to marry, represents merely the practice of these Churches, while others even in the East continued to require celibacy from such clerics. The Acolyths, who formed a higher grade in the East than the two grades just mentioned, and sometimes a very numerous one (as in the Roman Church, where there were at that time forty-two of them), are not mentioned in the Apostolical nor in the Chalcedonian Canon, because this order was never introduced into the Greek Church. Now, as celibacy from the first was on the whole *more strictly observed in the West than in the East*, so one may with certainty suppose that in many Churches the Acolyths also were admonished to remain unmarried, especially where it was more strictly the rule that those of the higher grades should be taken from the lower orders, and therefore that Deacons and Presbyters should first have been Acolyths.

The Hypodiaconi also—without doubt they still bore this Greek name at that time in Rome, as also later in Cyprian's time in Africa—belonged no doubt to the *clerici*, whom Callistus allowed to marry. The discipline of the various Churches was still for a long time diverse with regard to these *clerici*, partly on account of the diversity of the business with the discharge of which they were entrusted. In the African Church, at least from the year 419 onwards, complete continency was imposed on the Sub-deacons also, because they handled the sacred mysteries (the Eucharist).[2] On the other

---

[1] [This canon is pronounced both by Hefele and Drey to be ante-Nicene, and Hefele thinks it a "faithful interpreter of the ancient practice of the Church."]

[2] GREGORII M. *Epp.* L. I. ep. 34, 42. *Codex. eccl. Afr.* c. 25, p. 163,

CHARGE V.—ALLOWING CLERGY TO MARRY.

hand, according to the order of Pope Siricius of the year 385, a Sub-deacon was still allowed to marry,—but on this condition, that, in order to be promoted in the ministry and become a Deacon, he must first qualify himself by continency;[1] so that if he married, he could never become a Deacon at all. And later on, Leo the Great took it for granted as known that the Sub-deacons also must abstain from marriage, which certainly was a rule not yet observed a hundred and fifty years later even in the Sicilian Church, closely united as that was with Rome.[2] In Africa, according to a canon of the third Synod of Carthage,[3] the young Lectores were required, when they came to man's estate, either to marry, in which case they could attain to no higher grade in the ministry, or else to take a vow of continence. Thus they obtained Acolyths and Sub-deacons, who were all unmarried, and of course were unable to marry afterwards. In the Eastern Church also in the time of S. Epiphanius it was the rule, at any rate in Cyprus and in the Patriarchate of Antioch, to choose as Hypodiaconi only unmarried men, or those who voluntarily separated from their wives.[4]

It is evident, therefore, that if discipline was still so diverse and variable in the fourth and fifth centuries, Callistus might well depart from the practice of his immediate predecessor, and allow *clerici,* viz. Hypodiaconi, Acolyths, and others of lower grade, to marry. And in fact we find in the canons of the Synod of

---

ed. Bruns.: *Ut subdiaconi, qui sacra mysteria contrectant . . . ab uxoribus se contineant, ut tanquam non habentes videantur esse.*

[1] *Epist. Pontiff. Rom.* ed. Coustant, p. 633.
[2] *Epist.* 14, *Opp.* I. 687, ed. Ballerin.
[3] C. 19, p. 126, ed. Bruns.
[4] They were taken, he says, Ἐκ παρθένων,—ἐκ μοναζόντων, ἐξ ἐγκρατευομένων τῶν ἰδίων γυναικῶν, ἢ χηρευσάντων ἀπὸ μονογαμίας. EPIPH. *Expos. fid.* c. 21, p. 1104, ed. Petav.; cf. *Hæres.* 59, n. 4, p. 456. Here also he mentions the Hypodiaconi as included among the classes of clergy who were bound to celibacy.

Ancyra (314), that a certain right of dispensation reaching to a still higher grade was allowed to the Bishops.[1] If a *Deacon*, it is there said, has declared at his ordination that marriage is necessary for him, then in case of his marriage he is to remain in his ministry, *because he has received leave from the bishop.* The general rule of the Church required, therefore, in Galatia also, that Deacons should live unmarried; but the Bishop could allow exceptions, and if he had ordained the cleric in spite of his avowal, this was *ipso facto* a dispensation. There is no question about Presbyters; in their case it was always understood that under any circumstances they remained single. Can it be that Callistus also allowed the marriage of a Deacon in the spirit of this canon, which of course was made a century later? Even if Hippolytus did not plainly give one to understand it so by the language he uses, I should without hesitation conclude that his reproach must have reference, not to the three higher grades, but to the *clerus* below the Bishops, Presbyters, and Deacons.

According to the view of Hippolytus, if Callistus had been more strict with the clergy who married, he ought to have deposed them, τῆς τάξεως μετατίθεσθαι, as it stands in the first canon of the Synod of Neocæsarea (314) with regard to married Presbyters. Instead of that, Callistus declared that they should "remain among the clergy,"—as if they had committed no sin, adds Hippolytus. But it made a great difference whether a man remained merely among the clergy, that is, in possession of his rank and of the means of subsistence hitherto apportioned to him, or remained also in the *ministry*, ἐν τῇ ὑπηρεσίᾳ, as the Synod of Ancyra secured for married Deacons. If a cleric was merely suspended from exercising ecclesiastical functions, this was the mildest form of ecclesiastical censure; it was applied

[1] *Can.* 10, p. 68, ed. Bruns.

CHARGE V.—ALLOWING CLERGY TO MARRY.

by the same Synod of Ancyra[1] to those Priests and Deacons who had at first yielded under persecution, but then had showed themselves stedfast. These were to remain in possession of their rank or position, but abstain from their functions; the Deacons, however, only from those connected with the Holy Sacrifice.[2] In the alternative, therefore, whether a Hypodiaconus or even a Deacon who married was to be deposed or merely suspended, *i.e.* precluded from exercising his functions, when Callistus decided for the latter, the rigorous Hippolytus might well take offence at it, since he always eagerly raked together whatever might cast a shadow on the man and his administration. But outside his narrow circle the conduct of the Bishop was no doubt regarded very differently. *Our authority's own statement, that the immediate successors of Callistus did not abolish the arrangements of their predecessor, but maintained them,*[3] says plainly enough that they and their clergy saw in these regulations only opportune and (on the whole) beneficial alterations.

Callistus justified his conduct by appealing to texts of Scripture, as his opponent reports, who of course sees in this only a misuse of God's word. These texts were Romans xiv. 4, Matthew xiii. 30; and the ark of Noah, with its clean and unclean beasts, was designated by him as a type of the Church. In this Callistus did what those who defended the Church against the misty rigour of the sects before and after him always did. Cyprian[4] spoke in the same way as Callistus respecting

---

[1] *Can.* 1, 2, p. 66. [It was for this weakness under persecution that the Spanish Bishops, Martial and Basilides, were deposed, and a Synod under Cyprian, A.D. 254, confirmed the sentence.]

[2] The Presbyters: τῆς μὲν τιμῆς τῆς κατὰ τὴν καθέδραν μετέχειν, προσφέρειν δὲ αὐτοὺς ἢ ὁμιλεῖν ἢ ὅλως λειτουργεῖν τι τῶν ἱερατικῶν λειτουργίων μὴ ἐξεῖναι. The Deacons: τὴν μὲν ἄλλην τιμὴν ἔχειν, πεπαῦσθαι δὲ αὐτοὺς πάσης τῆς ἱερᾶς λειτουργίας, τῆς τε τοῦ ἄρτου ἢ ποτήριον ἀναφέρειν ἢ κηρύσσειν.

[3] Οὗ διαμένει τὸ διδασκαλεῖον φυλάσσον τὰ ἔθη καὶ τὴν παράδοσιν, p. 291.

[4] *Epist.* 54, p. 99, ed. Odrem.

weeds in the Church, on account of which one ought not to separate from her. S. Augustine[1] several times uses Christ's words on the subject, "Let both grow together until the harvest," against the Donatists. The same Father applies the clean and unclean beasts being together in the ark to the good and bad existing in the Church.[2] Here, then, the Catholic orthodoxy of Hippolytus appears in a light which is very doubtful indeed. In the application which Callistus makes of the texts in question, he is found in agreement with the whole Church; while Hippolytus, who attacks him for it, and cites this also, like the rest of his charges, to palliate his separation from him, appears as a forerunner of Novatian and the Donatists. And we can find only a confirmation of this view in his report of the Montanists. As the peculiar feature of this sect, he mentions only their absolute submission to the pretended revelations of the Paraclete, communicated through certain women, and their innovations derived therefrom with regard to fasts and festivals.[3] Not a word about their limitation of the Church's power in the forgiveness of sins, or of their rejection of second marriage. That this silence is intentional is shown by the statement which immediately follows;—he wishes to write more particularly and exactly respecting the Montanists, because their heresy has been the occasion of mischief to many. That does not mean that many have been led astray by them; but apparently the meaning of Hippolytus is, that from the rigorism of the sect based upon the Montanist prophecy, many had taken occasion to throw themselves into the opposite extreme, to open the doors of Church communion far too wide, to offer communion to all without proper

---

[1] *E.g. Epist. contra Donatistas, Opp.* IX. pp. 251, 254, ed. Bened. Antwerp.
[2] *Contra Faust.* XII. 15, *Opp.* VIII. 168. P. 276.

distinction;[1] with all which he charges the Callistians, that is, the Church of Rome, even after the death of Callistus.

[The contrast between the East and the West with regard to the celibacy of the clergy becomes prominent at the Council of Elvira (c. 315), which forbade married Bishops, Priests, and Deacons from cohabiting with their wives,—a regulation which the Council of Nicæa abstained from making, in deference to the advice of Paphnutius, himself a celibate and confessor. The Council of Ancyra allowing Deacons to marry even after ordination, if they had declared their intention beforehand, is another example of the comparative freedom of the East; while the rigour of the West is again expressed more than once at Carthage and elsewhere. This contrast appears very strikingly in the estimate of the relative guilt of clerical marriage and fornication. The Council of Neo-Cæsarea punishes the former with less severity: that of Orleans places the two on a level,—*si quis* pellici VEL uxori *se jungat!* See article CELIBACY, in the *Dictionary of Christian Antiquities.*]

VI. SIXTH CHARGE: ALLOWING LADIES TO MARRY WITH THE LOWER ORDERS AND SLAVES.

Sixth accusation. Callistus allowed Christian women, who were unmarried and still young and strong, to marry according to their own choice, whether a poor freeman or a slave, and thus to conclude a marriage not recognised by Roman law.[2] The result of this con-

---

[1] Πᾶσιν ἀκρίτως προσφέρων (προσφέρον) τὴν κοινωνίαν, p. 291.

[2] Καὶ γὰρ καὶ γυναιξὶν ἐπέτρεψεν εἰ ἄνανδροι εἶεν καὶ ἡλικίᾳ τε τε καίοντα ἐναξία ἡ ἑαυτῶν ἀξίαν ἢν μὴ βούλοιντο καθαίρειν. Διὰ τοῦτο νομίμως γαμηθῆναι ἔχει ἕνα ὃν ἂν αἱρήσωνται σύγκοιτον, κ.τ.λ. For this somewhat corrupt passage three emendations have already been proposed. MILLER proposes to insert ἁμαρτεῖν after ἐπέτρεψεν, and to write: ἡλικίᾳ καίοιντο αἱ

cession was, that some of these women, who on account of their connections or of their wealth would not be accounted the mothers of children whose father was a slave or poor, availed themselves of criminal means of preventing the birth of their offspring.[1]

Nowhere does Hippolytus so expose himself, nowhere does he show his passionateness, amounting to blindness, so completely as here. "See," he cries in the most vehement passion, "to what godlessness this enemy of law has come, in that he teaches at once unchastity and murder!" Truly, it is not against

ἐν ἀξίᾳ, τὴν ἑαυτῶν ἀξίαν ἦν (or εἰ) μὴ βούλοιντο καθαίρειν. Here the insertion of ἁμαρτεῖν is too violent and arbitrary. But the alteration proposed by BUNSEN is no better: καὶ γὰρ καὶ γυναιξὶν ἐν ἀξίᾳ ἐπέτρεψεν, εἰ ἄνανδροι εἶεν καὶ ἡλικίᾳ γε ἐκκαίουντο, τηρεῖν ἑαυτῶν ἀξίαν ἦν μὴ βούλοιντο καθαίρειν. This τηρεῖν ἀξίαν certainly did not lie in the meaning of Hippolytus; with ἐπέτρεψεν we should much rather have to expect a word implying sharp rebuke. Still more unsatisfactory, and on grammatical grounds alone untenable, is the proposal of WORDSWORTH: καὶ γὰρ καὶ γυναιξὶν ἐπέτρεψεν, εἰ ἄνανδροι εἶεν, καὶ ἡλικιώτῃ καίοιντο ἀναξίῳ, ἢ ἑαυτῶν ἀξίαν μὴ βούλοιντο καθαίρειν, διὰ τοῦτο νομίμως γαμηθῆναι ἐκείνῳ ὃν ἂν ἀφήρωνται σύγκοιτον. Here ἡλικιώτῃ καίοιντο must at once be rejected, for one says καίεσθαί τινος. (HERMESIANAX, ap. *Athenæum*, 13, p. 598 A.) It appears to me that the alteration of a few letters is sufficient to restore the passage, and give it the right sense. I propose: καὶ γὰρ καὶ γυναιξὶν ἐπέτρεψεν, εἰ ἄνανδροι εἶεν καὶ ἡλικίᾳ καίονται (or καίοιντο), ἀναξίᾳ, τὴν ἑαυτῶν ἀξίαν ἦν μὴ βούλοιντο καθαίρειν, i.e. to women who were husbandless and still of an age to desire to marry, he allowed what was unseemly, supposing they were unwilling to resign their position in society. [ROEPER reads ἡλικίᾳ . . . . ἀναξίου, i.e. in the bloom of youth were in love with one unworthy of their affection. See note in the translation of the work in CLARK's *Ante-Nicene Library*, p. 344.]

[1] For this, says Hippolytus, they used partly bandages, in which they wound round and pressed tight their persons (περιδεσμεῖσθαι), partly drugs. In Rome there was a class of women, the midwives, or *veneficæ*, or *maleficæ*, who, as Juvenal (VI. 597) expresses it, made a trade of infanticide, and for a sum of money contracted to produce abortion: *Quæ steriles facit, atque homines in ventre necandos conducit.*

Of the drugs which were used for the purpose, Pliny speaks, *H. N.* XX. 21; XXVII. 5, 9. [That this crime was a common one among the Romans is notorious. It was punished by the primitive Church with penance for life. The Council of Ancyra (314) limited this to ten years, the Council of Serida (324) to seven years, even when the crime was preceded by adultery.]

CHARGE VI.—ALLOWING IMPROPER MARRIAGES.

Callistus that the indignation of the critical reader is directed, but against his adversary; and we can only comprehend how a man like Hippolytus could be so forgetful of all fairness, if we put ourselves in his place. As the head of a schismatical society, he was surrounded by a circle of devoted followers, who, themselves under the dominion of blustering party-spirit, reported to him everything which took place on the other side, already tinged with the malice of party warfare. In his mortification at finding that the large majority were on the side of Callistus, while his own community remained a small handful, or perhaps was continually melting away, he appears to have been accustomed to see in every step of the Bishop opposed to him only a hostile demonstration, and a means of increasing his following and strengthening his position; so that (an evil intention being taken for granted) even those regulations which, in the position of the Bishop and the existing situation of the Church, were reasonable and entirely lawful, appeared to him as direct invitations to commit grievous sin. Happily, however, he has always himself mingled the antidote with the poison; and we need nothing more than his own words, in which he formulates the charge, to free the sober truth, the simple matter of fact, from the invidious dress in which he clothes it.

Callistus is said, by permitting unequal marriages, to have given occasion to unchastity and infanticide. Let us hold our informer fast to his first accusation. He himself says Callistus declared that Christian women could *lawfully marry* (νομίμως γαμηθῆναι) with slaves or freemen, even if they were not married according to (Roman) law (μὴ νόμῳ γεγαμημένην). The Pope then set up a legal form of marriage, viz. the ecclesiastical, in opposition to the other—the pagan civil form. He declared that the Church did not deem herself bound by the conditions which Roman civil legislation set forth respecting the form of entering into a perfectly legal marriage (*nuptiæ justæ*)—conditions to which the civil authorities themselves attached no absolutely decisive force. That Callistus held such a union, under mere ecclesiastical sanction, as perpetual and indissoluble, need scarcely be stated; Hippolytus does not say for one moment that the women who contracted these unions dissolved them again according to fancy and convenience, as they might have done with perfect ease, according to Roman law and prevailing custom. Had such cases occurred, he would certainly not have failed to mention the fact. He only speaks of misdeeds committed to hinder childbirth,—misdeeds which were only too common even in marriages which were formally quite legal. How could he then represent the declaration of Callistus, that the Church did not regard inequality of rank as a hindrance to entering into an ecclesiastical marriage, as inciting or leading to unchastity (μοιχεία)?[1] Callistus doubtless said: For the very purpose of preventing women who are still in the flower of their age from succumbing to the temptation to incontinence, entrance into the state of matrimony must be made easier for them, just as the Apostle also wills that the younger widows should marry again. But Hippolytus appears to have belonged to the rigorists on the question of the state of matrimony, as on that of penance. Had any one asked him whether Christian

[1] Wordsworth, p. 269, translates μοιχεία "adultery," which is correct in itself, although it is not easy to see how Hippolytus could have seen in the permission granted by Callistus an incitation to that sin. This could only have had meaning if many of these women had taken advantage of the circumstance of their marriage not being formally legal, to dissolve the union again and marry some one else. But, in the first place, Hippolytus would have stated this definitely; and secondly, the severance of even a formally quite rightly concluded marriage was in Rome a matter of such ease and of such daily occurrence, that for a wife who was inclined to be divorced, it was a matter of comparative indifference whether her marriage had been concluded with the observance of the legal conditions or without it.

maidens ought rather to marry a heathen of their own rank or a believer of a lower rank, he would probably have answered, neither the one nor the other; and if no Christian of equal birth offers himself, then let them acknowledge the will of God, who calls them to serve him in single continence. His point of view might seem to have come nearest to that of Pinytus, Bishop of Cnossus, who, according to the expression of Dionysius of Corinth,[1] laid upon the necks of the brethren the heavy yoke of continency, *i.e.* wished to compel a large number of the laity[2] to remain unmarried. Only from so extravagantly rigorous and ascetic point of view could Hippolytus have reproached Callistus thus, that his granting the Church's blessing to unequal marriages was equivalent to an invitation to unchastity. If we give to the view which lies at the bottom of his charge the most favourable meaning, it must have run somewhat in this strain: Some of the women who have made use of the permission of Callistus have proved afterwards, by their pains to destroy the fruit of their marriage, that no nobler motive—not the desire to lead a life dedicated to the service of God at the side of a believing husband—not the longing for the joys of motherhood—but only lust, induced them to enter into that bond; seeing, then, that their marriage is devoid of the higher religious character, it is only a varnished harlotry, a εὐπρεπὴς μοιχεία, as Athenagoras says of second marriage; and Callistus is open to the reproach of having lent a hand and given occasion to such conduct, which, without the permission granted by him, would at any rate not have been so frequent.

But how easy it was for the Pope to justify himself,—how the blame and abuse of Hippolytus must rather

---

[1] EUSEBIUS, *Eccles. Hist.* IV. 23.

[2] Not clergy, as some have supposed; Dionysius would not have designated these simply as οἱ ἀδελφοί.

be turned into approbation and praise of this measure in the eyes of impartial and fairly-judging persons,—is seen plainly enough as soon as we take into consideration the theory and practice as to the nature of matrimony at that time, in connection with the moral condition of Rome.

In the time of the Emperors, the contraction of a matrimonial union was no longer accompanied by any legal or religious formality. The old stricter form of marriage by *confarreatio* or *coëmptio* (by means of which the transfer of the wife into the *manus* (power) of the husband was effected) was obsolete, and only that freer form of marriage was concluded in which the mutual consent, declared in any form of words, or even only by the mere fact, to live in matrimonial union with one another, was all that was essential. There was no thought of any authoritative leave to enter into the married state; a solemnization before witnesses or public officials was required just as little. No doubt there were many usages which might be observed at marriages, *e.g.* a declaration of the husband before assembled friends, a solemn introduction of the bride into the husband's house; but all that was not necessary, and was more often omitted. To the essence of the marriage belonged only that which was proved by the very fact of the union, the matrimonial intention (*affectio maritalis*), or the voluntary entry of a man and woman into a matrimonial union; the physical completion of the marriage was not at all considered essential as a point of law.[1] In doubtful cases, the mere fact of living together with a free-born person was decisive.[2]

It is necessary to consider this state of things in order to judge of the position which the Christian

---

[1] According to the rule of Roman law, *Nuptias non concubitus sed consensus facit. Dig.* 35, t. 1, l. 15.

[2] *Dig.* 23, t. 2, l. 24; 25, t. 7, l. 3.

Church assumed, and was obliged to assume, in reference to the Roman condition of marriage. In modern States, the entry into marriage, the validity of the bond, is always attached to some definite act performed under public authority; the Church or (in countries where civil marriage has been introduced) the magistrate is the tyer of the marriage bond. Nothing that the parties might do before this act is binding, and no subsequent act on their side can remove the binding force of that function. Not so in Rome. He who wished to conclude a marriage had need of the State neither in its civil nor in its religious capacity. Only the consent of a father to the marriage of a child still under his power was necessary. In itself, the need of seeking, in the intervention of an objective authority, a security and guarantee for the sanctity and permanence of the matrimonial relationship over and above the changeable wills of the individuals, is founded in human nature and in the nature of the union itself. But with the Romans, since the later times of the Republic, fickleness and caprice as to separating and marrying again had become so general and so prevalent, that every external method of tightening the marriage tie appeared to be impertinent,—a burdensome limitation of a liberty which had become a dominant custom.

But by Roman law a series of conditions were set forth, under which the union between man and wife became a valid marriage, recognised in all its consequences, both legally and politically. The effects, however, of the impediments to marriage created by these laws were very various. There were conditions, the absence of which not only made the marriage invalid, but even involved actual punishment and the violent interference of the civil power, *e.g.* the condition of celibacy; every attempt at bigamy was null and void, and was punished as adultery.[1] So also the prohibition of marriage between the nearest blood-relations. Other impediments involved merely the punishment of infamy, as the second marriage of a widow before the legal time of mourning had expired. Lastly, those which were based upon inequality of rank had merely the effect that the union, so long as the inequality continued, was not accounted as real marriage in the eyes of the law and of the State, although as a matter of fact it was tolerated, and was merely accompanied by the legal disadvantage that the parties could not leave one another anything in their wills.[2]

Of what kind, then, were the impediments based on inequality of rank, which Callistus met by making it possible for Christians to conclude such marriages with ecclesiastical sanction?

First of all, it must be observed that only a few years before the promotion of Callistus, an important and far-reaching change in Roman rights of marriage had taken place. The Emperor Caracalla, in giving to all inhabitants of the Roman Empire the rights of *civitas*, thereby gave to an immense number of *peregrini* the right of *connubium* with Romans. Hitherto, persons not possessing the Roman rights of citizenship could conclude only such a marriage with those who had the *civitas* as was valid according to the *jus gentium*, but invalid according to Roman law; the consequence of which was, that the children took the position not of the father, but of the mother.[3]

Subsequently to Caracalla's enactment, the circle of

---

[1] C. l. 2, *de incest. nupt.* C. l. 18, *ad leg. Jul. de adulter.*

[2] Strictly speaking, persons who lived in such a union not recognised as marriage by the State would, according to the Julian law (GAIUS, II. 111, 144, 280), be liable to the punishment of the unmarried, *i.e.* they would have to be regarded as incapable of acquiring anything in the way of a bequest. It is, however, very doubtful whether this was really the case.

[3] ULPIAN, III. 8.

those unions which the law did not recognise as true marriages with full rights, was drawn much smaller. There still remained prohibited—*firstly*, marriages between a freeman and a slave, or between a freewoman and a slave; for slaves generally (inasmuch as according to the Roman view they had no personality) were incapable of entering into a real matrimonial relationship, either among themselves or with free persons.[1] A union of this kind was, with respect to the parties, merely a *contubernium*, *i.e.* a relationship existing as a fact, but valid only according to natural law. *Secondly*, senators, their sons and daughters, and the descendants of their sons, could not conclude a valid marriage either with "honourless" or with freed persons. These marriages, which had been already forbidden by the Julian and Papian law, were declared null and void first under Marcus Aurelius and Commodus. Only that portion of the law which had reference to daughters of a senatorial family is of importance for our inquiry. The object of the prohibition, as one sees at the first glance, and as is expressly added, was to secure the dignity of senatorial families; so that Roman law takes account only of the rank-relations of the women restricted thereby. This led to the astonishing but perfectly logical anomaly, that the daughter of a senator who married a free-born person of lower position, and thereby certainly concluded a legal marriage, lost her rank as *femina clarissima*;[2] whereas, had she wedded a freedman, she would have retained her rank, because the law altogether ignored this marriage of hers, and therefore assigned to it no effect whatever. Supposing, however, that she had prostituted herself as a common harlot, and thereby already lost her rank,

---

[1] Ulp. V. 5. PAUL. *Rect. Sent.* II. 19, 6.

[2] D. I., t. 9, l. 8 (Ulpian). To this the expression of Hippolytus refers, τὴν ἑαυτῶν ἀξίαν καθαίρειν.

then she could enter into a valid marriage with a freedman.[1] And hence the further enactment, that if the father of a daughter who had married a freedman should be expelled from the Senate, she did not thereby become the legally recognised wife of her husband; for, adds Papinian very significantly, the rank belonging to the children cannot be taken away on account of their father's crime.[2] That the union of a senator's daughter with a freedman is a transgression of the law, that she has on her side made herself guilty of a crime, does not enter into the meaning of the legislator. And in truth she has not transgressed the law; it does not lie within her power to transgress it, for in fact it is not prohibitive, but declaratory; it merely enacts that such a union has not the validity and force of legal marriage; supposing that she ever enters into such a relationship, in the eyes of the law she is accounted as unmarried.[3] Her sons were *spurii*. But even this was no real disadvantage to them; they could still obtain offices,—they could, for example, be *Decuriones*. On the whole, it is plain that women of rank who married freedmen were judged from the standpoint of Roman law by the analogy of concubinage, which was formally allowed and sanctioned by the Julian and Papian law, as a union of men with women of a lower grade without legal consequences, but otherwise partook entirely of the character of a marriage.

The Christian Church found itself from the outset, without taking account of this action of Callistus, in direct, although for some time longer quiet and secret, opposition to the Roman law of marriage. Cases not

---

[1] D. 23, t. 2, l. 47.

[2] D. 23, t. 2, l. 34, sec. 3.

[3] True, that (D. 24, t. 1, l. 3) gifts which parties in such a union wished to make to one another were declared null and void, *ne melior sit conditio eorum, qui deliquerunt*. But the *deliquerunt* is clearly not to be taken in a strict sense.

unfrequently occurred in which she was compelled to make it the duty of her children not merely to abstain from making any use of what the law allowed, as in the case of divorce, but even to oppose the will and purpose of the law. We will mention only a couple of instances. If a free-born man who had a freedwoman as his wife became a senator, then according to the Papian law his marriage was to be dissolved and his wife divorced,—a law which lasted until the sixth century, when Justinian abolished it as a crying hardship. Suppose a Christian came into this position, what else could the Church declare but that here the divine law took precedence of the earthly, that the man was bound in conscience to retain his wife? Further, until the reign of the Emperor Marcus Aurelius, a father whose children, although married, were still in his *potestas*, could annul his child's marriage, even against the latter's will. Under Marcus Aurelius there was merely added as a condition that he must have grave reason for dissolving the marriage of his son or daughter; but the question as to the gravity of the cause was decided by himself; and the law had nothing further to say than to advise that one should try and induce the father not to make too hard a use of his paternal power. Here again, therefore, there was an irreconcilable conflict between the utterly heathen rights of the *patria potestas* (which had never been recognised by Christianity to this extent) and the indissolubility of the marriage-tie enjoined by the Christian religion. The Church was here obliged, in opposition to the law, to make the duty of the wife superior to that of the daughter.[1]

---

[1] D. 34, t. 30, l. 1. Here it no doubt says: *Et certo jure utimur, ne bene concordantia matrimonia jure patriæ potestatis turbentur;* but *quod tamen sic erit adhibendum, ut patri persuadeatur, ne acerbi patriam potestatem exerceat.*

In the cases cited by Hippolytus, Callistus by no means came into the position of being obliged to go so far. What he did was merely this, that he granted ecclesiastical sanction to unions between believers, in cases in which the Roman law did not recognise the binding force of a legal marriage, but treated them after the analogy of concubinage, and indeed regarded them as mere *contubernia*; so that he raised them to true indissoluble marriages. How this ecclesiastical sanction was given to the marriage, we know from a contemporary. The man and his intended wife declared before the Bishop, Presbyters, and Deacons that they wished to marry, and asked for the services of the Church to that end; thereupon the marriage was concluded by the Bishop or Presbyter uniting the betrothed, was confirmed by offering of the Holy Sacrifice, and sealed by pronouncing of the blessing.[1] That was the νόμος, the established rule of the Church; and hence, as we have seen above, Hippolytus represents Callistus as opposing marriage according to the law (of the Church) to the want of a valid marriage according to heathen law.

A look into the circumstances of Rome and of the Roman population at that time shows us, moreover, how strong the special grounds were which the Bishop of Rome still had for making himself and his faithful independent of the known conditions of the Roman law of marriage. When Callistus ascended the chair of S. Peter, Rome, in the thirty-eight years which followed the death of the Emperor Marcus Aurelius, in the reigns of Commodus, Severus, and Caracalla, had become the scene of horrors and crimes which surpassed even the times of Caligula and Nero. The Syrian Elagabalus, by new discoveries in debauchery, by set-

---

[1] Quod ecclesia conciliat, confirmat oblatio, obsignat benedictio. TERTULL. *Ad Uxorem*, II. 8; Cf. *De Monogam.* I. 10.

CHARGE VI.—ALLOWING IMPROPER MARRIAGES. 159

ting a public example of everything that befouls and degrades human nature, was busily destroying every remaining fragment of modesty and morality, and Rome was now in a higher degree than ever the sink into which everything corrupt and corruptible flowed.[1] The object of the Papian law, to maintain the rank and honour of the senatorial families intact, must have had little value in the eyes of the Christians of that time; for this simple reason, because it was precisely in these families that family pride was most closely united with zeal for the maintenance of heathen rites and the suppression of the ever more and more threatening Christian faith; and these, therefore, held on to idolatry with the most dogged perseverance, even after all around had become Christian. And in what condition were the senate and patrician families at that time? As early as the time of Marcus Aurelius, Vetrasinus was able to say to the Emperor, that he saw many men Prætors who had fought with him (as gladiators) in the arena.[2] Then Commodus caused freedmen to be admitted into the senate and among the patricians.[3] Then followed the wholesale executions of the followers of Albinus, carried out by Severus, and these fell chiefly on the senators and high officials — on one occasion two-and-forty.[4] His son Caracalla appeared to have made it his special business to demolish the senate, so great was the number of those who were executed as supporters of his murdered brother Geta, and also afterwards; or else were deprived of their property by various means.[5] The thus attenuated senate was then filled up by Elagabalus by the simple process of admitting new

---

[1] TACITUS' expression, *Annal.* XIV. 20. [*Quod usquam corrumpi et corrumpere queat.*]

[2] JUL. CAPITOL. *Vita M. Anton.* 12.

[3] *Vita Commod.* 6.

[4] DIO, l. 75, c. 8, p. 1262, ed. Reimar. SPARTIANI *Vita Sever.* c. 12.

[5] SPARTIANI *Vita Caracallæ*, c. 4. DIO, l. 77, p. 1290 *seqq.* ed. Reimar.

senators merely for money, without reference to age, property, or family.[1] One must therefore say that, in the condition into which the later Emperors vied with one another in bringing the senate, the Papian law, with its jealousy as to the honour of ancient and wealthy families, had already become an anachronism when Callistus declared that he would grant ecclesiastical sanction to the marriages of women of senatorial rank with those beneath them.

It is, however, surprising that Hippolytus names only two classes of persons to whom Callistus allowed marriage with ladies of rank, but never once mentions the third, against which the Papian law and the *senatus-consultum* under Marcus Aurelius were primarily directed,—namely, the freedmen. He names the freeborn citizens of inferior rank (εὐτελεῖς) and the slaves. The former of these are distinguished in later Roman legislation from the higher ranks merely in this,[2] that in punishments they were liable to condemnation to the mines, and sometimes also to cudgelling, whereas those of higher rank were sentenced to banishment to an island.[3] But marriages between the two were by no means forbidden; only of course a *clarissima* lost her rank and title by marrying a man of lower position. How, therefore, Hippolytus could find fault because Callistus allowed marriages which even according to Roman law had perfect legal validity, it is difficult to conceive. That a Christian woman, in order to marry a less wealthy fellow - Christian, willingly renounced a title and certain honourable distinctions, not even in Hippolytus' eyes could be penal; and one really does not know on what grounds he would have

---

[1] *In Senatum legit sine discrimine ætatis, census, generis, pecuniæ merito.* LAMPRID. c. 6.

[2] They are there called *tenues, tenuiores, humiliores,* in opposition to the *honestiores.* D. 49, t. 29.

[3] D. 48, t. 38. Cf. D. 50, t. 2, l. 2.

been able to refuse, if a Christian woman of his own congregation had asked him to marry her to a freeborn man of lower rank. Again, he cannot be supposed to have entertained the view that the Church ought not to recognise and bless a marriage until it had already been concluded in legal form, and had been entered in the public census-register. For the Romans had no necessary form of consent in general use, no process which was considered essential to the affirmation of the *consensus* or of the matrimonial intention; even the apportioning of a dowry, however usual, was not necessary.[1] Justinian, who still in the year 528 expressly declared that the mere intent to marry, and not the apportioning of a dowry, concluded a marriage, was the first to decree in his *Novels* that the marriages of senators and illustrious persons must be concluded by the drawing up of marriage-settlements;[2] but to all others he allowed the ancient liberty. Hence, moreover, there was no census-register in which one would be obliged to have the newly-concluded marriages entered. As, however, this has been frequently disputed, and is moreover of importance for determining the relation of the ecclesiastical to the civil law of marriage, the matter is worth briefly proving somewhat more exactly.

The Romans had public *Acta*, which appeared daily; and along with the events of the day, contained also proceedings in the law-courts, laws, and even domestic affairs, especially notices of births and marriages. These notices, however, were quite special; they proceeded for the most part only from the more distinguished families, and had no official character. It is certainly stated that Marcus Aurelius caused a com-

[1] So also as early as in the ordinance of Theodosius and Valentinian of the year 428. C. 5, 4, l. 22.
[2] *Nov.* 74, c. 4, sec 1.

pulsory registration of births[1] to be established for such notices, and from a passage in Julius Capitolinus it has been concluded that this institution already existed at the beginning of the third century.[2] But the silence of the Roman law-books, in places where one necessarily expects an official or judicial use of this State-register, leads rather to the conclusion that the institution of Marcus Aurelius soon fell into disuse again. The jurist Modestinus fifty years later mentions private entries of such things as legal proof of age; he knows nothing of the much more certain proof by means of public lists of births—a manifest sign that they did not exist. Of marriage-registers and lists of deaths there is absolutely not a trace to be found; cases of this kind, having reference to distinguished families, were mentioned in the *Acta*, which took the place of newspapers, merely as items of news. The passage which modern[3] scholars have quoted refers partly to these, partly to the special insertion of a name or of a fact in other public documents.

According to the statement of one lawyer,[4] a freedman who aimed at marrying his "patroness" could be condemned to the mines or the public works, according to the position of the latter. Yet the law could only interfere if the "patroness" was of higher rank.[5] According to this, the marriage of a senator's daughter with a freedman, whether her own or another's, would have been in any case legally invalid; while the marriage of another woman of higher rank with a

[1] παιδογραφίαι, D. 27, t. 1, l. 2. The Scholiast explains thus: 'Ως ὅταν οἱ πατέρες ἀπογράφωνται κατ' αὐτὸν τὸν καίρον, καθ' ὅν ἐγεννήθη τὰ τέκνα αὐτῶν.

[2] CAPITOLINI *Gordiani tres*, c. 4.

[3] Especially LE CLERC, *Des journaux chez les Romains*, pp. 186–198, 200–206; and DUREAU DE LA MALLE, in the *Mémoire sur la population libre de l'Italie* (*Mémoires de l'institut royal de France*, vol. x. pp. 480, 481).

[4] PAULI, *Sent.* II. t. 19.

[5] D. 23, t. 2, l. 13.

libertinus, could involve the punishment of the latter only when he was her own slave manumitted by herself, but otherwise was legally valid. That this latter point was the case, the *Novels* of the Emperor Leo and Anthemius say expressly: no previous law, it is there stated,[1] forbade marriages with freedmen, and so up to this period they are to be regarded as perfectly valid. Hence marriages of freedmen with their "patronesses" came to be not so very rare.[2] Besides, it was very easy to circumvent a prohibition of this kind; a mistress had merely to make over her slave to another person, on condition of his being manumitted, and then she was not his "patroness." But whether Callistus also allowed the blessing of the Church to marriages of high-born ladies with freedmen, we do not know, for Hippolytus does not mention this case; it is certainly probable, for the obvious reason that the Pope did not refuse the approbation of the Church to marriages with *slaves.* Now this in itself is at once very important, as the first onset which the Church made with a view to breaking down the brazen walls set up between slaves and freemen; and seeing that it is precisely on this account that Hippolytus directs the sharpest arrow of his censure against him, and that on this point contradictory views existed among Christians themselves, it lies within the scope of our discussion to contemplate the question more closely, and show on which side truth and right were in this matter.

There are then at the outset two questions which demand an answer.

1. What was the attitude which the Church at that time assumed towards slavery, especially in Rome?

---

[1] *Constit. novellæ,* ed. Hænel, p. 341.

[2] For instance, Claudius Hermas, in an epitaph, praises his wife as *patronam optimam, item conjugem fidelissimam.* ORELLI, *Inscr.* no. 3024; also 3029 and 4633; and MURATORI, *Inscr.* p. 1558, no. 9.

2. What was the position of unmarried Christian women of higher rank?

1. The overthrow of slavery, as it existed in the Roman Empire, was one of the greatest problems set before the Christian Church by the providence of God for solution,—a problem which was to be accomplished not so much by conscious and intentional efforts on the part of individual Christians or the Bishops, as by the silent, natural influence of Christian principles forcing their way into heathen society. It may well have been that the reach of these principles in reference to slavery was always clear to individual Church-teachers and Bishops. They perhaps did not take into consideration, whether an entire cessation of the system of bondage which appeared to have rooted itself so deeply in all existing arrangements was at all possible, or in what fashion social relations were to be formed after the abolition of an institution universally considered to be indispensable. But thus much at any rate was clear to all,—that things could not remain as they were, and that the Christian Church was called to raise these millions gradually out of the degradation into which Roman paganism had plunged them.

Under the Emperors many of the severities of the old law of slavery were diminished by legislation; and public protection—though certainly within very narrow limits—had taken the place of the old defencelessness of slaves, and the unrestrained power of masters over the life and death of their slaves. But this gain on the part of the latter was far more than outweighed by the aggravation of their condition, which was the inevitable consequence of the enormous increase in the wantonness, debauchery, and savage licentiousness of their masters. The more vicious the freemen were, the more were the slaves ill-treated and abused; everywhere they had to be at hand as the unresisting instruments of lust; on them, through them, by their aid, was wreaked whatever sensuality, cruelty, anger, revenge, or avarice suggested to their master. Hence the mere continuance of the existence of slavery was the inexhaustible source of an incalculable moral ruin. For it is only in this way that the corruption in the Roman Empire could have increased to such enormous power and universality,—that in the bosom of civil society there was a class of beings with human forms, human needs and passions, but exempt from all human rights and all moral obligations; who, instead of conscience and law, knew only the will of their masters. Both classes of society laboured as if rivals in mutual demoralization. The rulers lived in the school of those vices which a despotic power over other men, and unlimited freedom to abuse this power, ever produces and fosters. Even that portion of the free population which could not afford to keep slaves, shared in the curse of this institution; for agriculture and manufactures were for the most part left in the hands of slaves, so that idleness, effeminate indolence, coarse love of enjoyment, and emptiness of existence, with their natural sequence of vices, was the lot of these masses. But the slaves themselves, on whom it was continually impressed that they were not persons, but mere things,—that in general their sole *raison d'être* was to minister to the profit and pleasure, and humour the caprice of their masters,—had the faults peculiar to the oppressed. Lying, deceit, and theft are mentioned as the commonest vices among slaves. That a man had as many enemies as he had slaves, was almost a proverb. But Roman legislation itself by one single statement has declared the effect of slavery upon the slave more forcibly than the most detailed description could do. For a distinction was made between "novices" and slaves in service.¹ When a slave had been a year in service, he was no longer a "novice," but a *veterator*, a slave in service, and of much less value than one who was not yet in service; so that slave-dealers would fraudulently pass off a slave that had been in service for a "novice," in order to get a better price for him;² for, says Ulpian, it is taken for granted that a "novice" is more simple, tractable, and serviceable, while the other can scarcely be reformed or made fit for the service of his new master.³ Thus, according to Roman calculation, a year of slavery sufficed for the utter corruption of a man. Such was the fruit of those principles which were still in force even in the time of the Emperors: a slave has no rights;⁴ slavery in the eyes of the law is equivalent to death;⁵ everything is lawful against a slave;⁶ a master cannot be bound by any contract with a slave;⁷ there can be no obligation of any kind towards a slave;⁸ marriage in the case of a slave is a purely physical relation, a mere fiction, the reality of which lies only in the tolerance of the master; hence adultery is impossible in regard to slaves, and the laws about blood-relationship have no reference to them.⁹

Thereupon there arose a society in the Roman Empire, in whose bosom freemen and slaves were to be equals—the Church. This equality of religious and ecclesiastical rights the Church could give at once, and she did so; the rest must be the work of time. The amelioration of the slaves must be commenced with their moral and religious education; she taught them, as Origen[10] says, to acquire freedom of soul

---

[1] *Novitii* and *Veteratores*.   [2] D. 39, t. 4, l. 16, sec 3.
[3] D. 21, t. 1, l. 7.   [4] *Servile caput nullum jus habet.* D. 4, t. 5, l. 3.
[5] D. 35, t. 1, l. 59.   [6] SENECA, *De Clem.* I. 18.
[7] C. 2, t. 4, l. 13.   [8] D. 50, t. 17, l. 21.
[9] Dig. 38, t. 10, l. 10.   [10] *Adv. Celsum*, III. 54, p. 483, ed. De la Rue.

through the faith, and thus to attain to external freedom. Ecclesiastical offices were conferred upon slaves; a class of persons arose whose ascetic mode of life involved their dispensing with the services of slaves. By the third century, the Church, through its innate powers, had achieved such results that a Christian slave was certainly, on the average, nobler, better, and more capable of fulfilling the higher duties of the estate of marriage than a Roman senator or patrician, as the history of that period exhibits them to us. Hence it lay quite in the province and interests of the Church not merely to allow marriages between slaves and freeborn, but in many cases even to favour them. She was called to take the place of a mother to a class of beings who in the heathen state had not even a step-father. In Rome, the number of male slaves exceeded that of female about five-fold; so that most slaves found it at the outset impossible to enter into *contubernium* or a lasting marriage-relation with a female of their own condition, even when their master permitted them to do so,—and did not, like Cato,[1] prefer to forbid their marrying, and instead of it sell them the lawless gratification of their sexual impulses for money. Moreover, according to Tertullian's remark,[2] masters who were sticklers for civil purity of blood did not permit their slaves to marry outside their own body. Thus a condition of things had arisen which of itself would have sufficed in a short time to bring the Roman Empire to the dissolution of all social order and to inevitable ruin, had not the healing power of the Church intervened. On the one hand, the preference for celibacy was so widely spread among freemen, especially among those of higher rank, that even the vexatious enactments of the Papian law were powerless against it. Manifold artifices and fictions were invented for circumventing

[1] PLUTARCH, *Cato Maj.* c. 21.   [2] *Ad Uxorem*, II. 8.

them,—so great appeared to be the advantages of childlessness,[1] so oppressive the burden of a wife and sons. On the other hand, the tyranny of the law and of social arrangements had done everything to make an orderly marriage-relation either impossible or intolerable for that numerous portion of the population which was not free.

The quiet efforts of the Church to prepare the way at any rate for tearing down the wall of separation between freemen and slaves were, however, assisted in the time of the Emperors by many symptoms in the heathen world pointing in the same direction. For sometimes freemen, and even those of rank, descended to the level of slaves: this took place when they too fought as gladiators in the arena, and mixed with the slaves who fought there. And then, again, attempts became ever more frequent to raise slaves from their degradation to the higher position of the freemen by means of marriage. The legislation opposed these attempts only partially. The Claudian *senatus consultum* enacted in the year 52, that a free woman who entered into *contubernium* with another man's slave against the will of his master, should become the property of the master, together with all her possessions.[2] Accordingly, in all cases in which the consent of the master was obtained, or the lady was rich enough to buy the slave of him, these unions remained free; and an ordinance of Hadrian's provided that even the children of such a marriage, following the position of the mother, should be free, in spite of the slavery of the father.[3] On the other hand, the law made no attempt whatever to hinder unions, which beyond doubt were

---

[1] *In civitate nostra plus gratiæ orbitas confert, quam eripit.* SENECA, *ad Marciam*, c. 19. *Plerisque etiam singulos filios orbitatis præmia graves faciunt.* PLINII *Epist.* IV. 15. [TACIT. *Annal.* III. 25, 28.]

[2] TACIT. *Annal.* XII. 53; PAUL, S. R. II. 21; GAIUS, I. 91, 160; ULP. XI. 11.   [3] GAIUS, I. 84.

equally frequent, between free women and one of their own slaves. Of course these marriages were not legally valid, and of course the women who acted in this way fell into discredit, because they were generally (and in most cases with justice) supposed to have been influenced by unworthy motives; but still how often this took place in the time of Callistus is shown by Tertullian.[1] If the woman wished to make her marriage with her slave valid in the eyes of the law also, she had only to manumit him, and forthwith her *contubernium* became a legal marriage of itself, without further formality. It is true that a freedman who aspired to marriage with his "patroness" was threatened with punishment; but this was certainly not inflicted in cases where the only effect of the manumission was to turn an already existing *contubernium* into a legal marriage, or where the manumission took place simply with a view to the contemplated union. Accordingly, when in later times a law of Constantine forbade marriages between freedmen and slaves, it was the plea of the Julia who gave occasion to the Emperor Anthemius to issue his *Novels*,[2] that she had married not her slave, but her freedman, *i.e.* she had manumitted the slave whom she wished to marry for this purpose beforehand. And on this occasion the Emperor showed (what was stated above) that a law against the marriage of "patronesses" with their freedmen did not exist previously.

When, then, Callistus allowed ladies of rank and fortune to marry with one of their slaves, this was accomplished in one of two ways. Either the slave was first manumitted,—and then, according to Roman law, notwithstanding the disapprobation expressed here and there, this became a genuine and complete marriage,

---

[1] *Ad Uxorem*, II. 8.
[2] *Novellæ Constit. imperat.* ed. Hænel, Bonn. 1844, p. 342.

except in the case of senators' daughters, and on such marriages beyond a doubt the Church even before this used to set her seal of blessing; or else the slave remained for the time in his position,—and then in the eyes of the State this was a mere *contubernium*, which, however, the Roman Church, in her own sphere and in the eyes of the faithful, now raised to the dignity of a Christian marriage.

From the manner in which Hippolytus brings his charge, we must suppose that Callistus was the first, at any rate among Roman Bishops, who made it a rule to guarantee the blessing of the Church to these marriages between free women and slaves. This was not mere chance or caprice on his part, but was the result of the position of the Church. In the times of severe persecution under Marcus Aurelius and Severus, everything which might direct the attention of the heathen Government to the close organization of the Church, and to her character as an association strongly provocative of the political jealousy of the rulers, had to be avoided or concealed. And nothing was more calculated to awaken this jealousy than for the Roman jurists and administrators to learn that the Christians had their own law of marriage, their peculiar form of concluding marriages. Not until after Caracalla, when a time of lasting quiet and comparative security arose for the Christians, did the Church dare to introduce her principles of marriage publicly into life; and it was not otherwise than providentially that a man now ascended the chair of S. Peter who himself had drained the bitter cup of slavery to the dregs, who could say of himself—

"Knowing oppression myself, I know how to help the oppressèd."

2. But it was not merely the condition of the slaves, it was also that of the free-born Christian women of

whom the Bishop of Rome took account in his regulations. That among the men of higher rank the number of Christians at that time was still very small, is a well-known fact. Among the senators and State officials there were scarcely any believers; and if here and there there was one, he was an elderly rather than a young man. Far greater was the number of believing women among the upper classes. The consequence was, that a Christian maiden of good family could scarcely ever hope to find a Christian husband of her own station. A Christian woman had either to remain unmarried, or to take a pagan husband, or to unite with one who, though a Christian, belonged to the lower classes or was a slave. The overseers of the Church could not advise a Christian to ally herself with a heathen; rather they were compelled to disapprove of such a marriage most emphatically, for it was scarcely possible for a Christian wife in this case to keep herself pure from the taint of idolatry, and fulfil her religious duties undisturbed. To begin with, the entrance into marriage was commonly accompanied by pagan rites and ceremonies, in which no member of the Church could take part without being guilty of an act of apostasy.[1] In his second book, addressed to his wife, Tertullian graphically describes the disagreements, suspicions, and vexations which must embitter the life of a Christian woman married to a pagan husband, and fill her soul with sorrow and anxiety. Moreover, such marriages were very detrimental to the Christian community itself, because through their Christian wives the heathen could easily gain knowledge of the Christians' place of worship, their hours of meeting, the members of the community, and other things,—a knowledge of which they sometimes made terrible use

[1] Ideo non nubemus ethnicis, ne nos ad idolatriam usque deducant, a qua apud illos nuptiæ incipiunt.—TERTULL. *De Corona* 13, p. 451, ed. Oehler.

afterwards in times of persecution.[1] Accordingly, Tertullian would have all such marriages regarded as unchastity, and those persons who were "unequally yoked together with unbelievers" (2 Cor. vi. 14) expelled from the communion of the brethren; and Cyprian saw in such marriages of Christian women one of the causes of the Decian persecution.[2] Tertullian accordingly makes it a reproach against the Christian women of his time, that while heathen women so frequently united themselves with men of lower position or with slaves, merely to gratify their passions or live with greater licence, they, on the contrary, refused to marry a poor believer.[3] We see that, in the question of unequal marriages, Tertullian at any rate would have declared for Callistus, and against Hippolytus.

But, says Hippolytus, some of these women have afterwards, in order to avoid being reckoned as mothers of slaves or beggars, had resort to criminal practices. One need not wonder that this was the case, but that Hippolytus should lay the blame of it on Callistus. Suppose, then, that the Bishop of Rome had refused the sanction of the Church to these unions, what would have been the result? Would these women who were capable of such crimes have lived a continent life in unstained virginity, merely for want of the Church's blessing? Assuredly not; they would then have contracted the same unions as free, unrestrained, and of course secret *contubernia*, perhaps even with heathen slaves; and then they would have had double reason for availing themselves of the same wicked means of concealing the consequences.

---

[1] *Hoc est igitur delictum, quod gentiles nostra noverunt, quod sub conscientia injustorum sumus*, etc.—*Ad Uxorem* 5, p. 689, ed. Oehler.

[2] TERTULL. *ad Uxorem*, II. 3. CYPRIAN, *De Lapsis*, p. 123, ed. Brem. In his estimation, *jungere cum infidelibus vinculum matrimonii* is *prostituere gentilibus membra Christi.*

[3] *Ibid.* c. 8, p. 695.

CHARGE VI.—ALLOWING IMPROPER MARRIAGES. 173

We must not forget that Rome is the scene of action, that the time is the period of Caracalla and Elagabalus, —that Rome of which Juvenal could say[1]—

"Et jacet aurato vix ulla puerpera lecto,"

—where Seneca could esteem it as a special virtue in his mother Helvia, that she had not, like others, prevented the hopes of maternity.[2] In that time of peace the number of Christians had rapidly increased, and the Church of the great capital of the world, the Cloaca of the nations, which already numbered there so many thousands of members, could not hope that the prevailing corruption would not press in through her boundaries,—that her children would all remain unscathed by the pestilential atmosphere of vice. In a city in which women had to be forbidden by a special law from fighting like the gladiators in the arena; in which a memorial with the names of three thousand guilty persons was presented to the Emperor Severus with regard to his law against adultery; in which the favourite of this Emperor, Plautianus, secretly caused a hundred persons of good family, and among them even such as were already fathers, to be made eunuchs, that they might attend his daughter on her marriage with Caracalla,[3]—in such a city there must have been Christian women also, who through numberless channels, and in very various ways, came in contact with the corruption which surrounded them, and fell victims to it. Hippolytus himself mentions Marcia, the concubine of the Emperor Commodus, who was a zealous Christian,[4] and to whose influence the Christians chiefly owed the peace which they enjoyed under Commodus.

[1] *Sat.* VI. 593. Still earlier OVID, *Nux*, 23: *Raraque in hoc ævo est, quæ velit esse parens.*

[2] *Cons. ad Helviam*, c. 16: *Nec intra viscera tua conceptas spes liberorum elisisti.*

[3] DIO CASS. LXXV. p. 1267, Reimar.

[4] He calls her the φιλόθεος παλλακὴ Κομμόδου, p. 287. In the *Apostolical*

In all probability she was in the communion of the Church, and was admitted to the sacraments; otherwise she would hardly have asked Bishop Victor for a list of the confessors banished to Sardinia, and have brought about their release. Therefore Victor no doubt regarded her relation to Commodus as one of marriage—as an *inæquale conjugium*, as concubinage was afterwards called in Roman law.[1] And indeed Commodus had divorced the Empress Crispina for adultery as early as the year 183, and had afterwards caused her to be executed; and although on account of her low birth he could not formally marry Marcia, yet he treated her quite as his wife,—so much so that he appears to have had no other wife besides her, and to have given her all the honours of an Empress, only that fire was not carried before her.[2] In the end, however, in order to save her own life and that of many others from the frenzied tyrant, she also was compelled to take part in the conspiracy which determined his assassination. Here we have a telling instance of the complications in which the Church was involved with regard to prevalent customs.

Callistus, therefore, might simply reply thus to the accusations of his adversary: If the thing is right and just in itself, it may not be discarded on account of the abuses connected with it in individual cases. Just as no man could make it a charge against a Bishop, that women whom he had admitted to baptism had become renegades again from fear or through being led astray, so can no blame fall upon me, because my purpose of giving a moral status by means of the

---

Constitutions, VIII. 32, p. 418, we read: Παλλακή τινος ἀπίστου δούλη, ἐκείνῳ μόνῳ σχολάζουσα, προσδεχέσθω· εἰ δὲ καὶ πρὸς ἄλλους ἀσελγαίνει, ἀποβαλλέσθω. Accordingly the Roman Church had good ground for allowing Marcia the right of communion: that she was unchaste in her life is not laid to her charge on any side.

[1] C. 5, t. 27, l. 3. [2] HERODIAN, p. 486, ed. Frcf. 1590.

Christian marriage-tie to women exposed to temptations, to crime, and to paganism, has here and there, owing to the fault of these women, been frustrated and turned to evil. On the contrary, I might, nay, was bound to presume that Christian women, whom we had at any rate supposed to have courage to confess their faith before the heathen world, would also have possessed moral strength and self-denial enough to confess themselves as wives and mothers before this world, and openly avow their marriage with a fellow-Christian of humble birth.

VII. SEVENTH CHARGE: COUNTENANCING SECOND BAPTISM.

Finally, Hippolytus lays this also to the charge of Callistus, and still more to that of the Church in communion with him, that under him *second baptisms* first began to be granted. In the case of the other accusations which he makes against his adversary, he represents him as the immediate actor or teacher; here, however, and in the censure respecting the ordination of persons twice married, he merely states that it took place *under* Callistus, *i.e.* in his time, in Churches which acknowledged him, and with his tacit consent. It is manifest that he here alludes to the re-baptizing of converted heretics; but it is also manifest that this repetition of baptism took place not in Rome, but elsewhere. In Rome itself this of course could only have taken place by order of the Pope, or by his express permission, if not by his own hand. And seeing that Stephen thirty years later appeals so decidedly to the tradition of his Church, and declares this re-baptizing of heretics to be an innovation; seeing also that Cyprian and his party never deny or call in question the constant tradition of the Roman Church, no uncertainty whatever can exist as to the fact that this practice did not prevail in the Roman Church under Callistus any more than at any other time. It is true that, immediately after mentioning this "audacity" of baptizing a second time,—an audacity never heard of till now,—Hippolytus says: "These things this most wonderful Callistus has introduced, and his school still continue to maintain his customs and his tradition;" still this refers merely to those ordinances which Callistus himself made.

Thus there are two interesting historical facts which Hippolytus here discloses to us: first, that he himself, and those who were on his side and were in communion with him, recognised the validity of baptism performed by heretics; secondly, that the practice of re-baptizing persons who had been baptized by heretics began first at this time (in the years 218–222) to be introduced as an innovation in certain parts of the Church. Hereby we obtain a more exact date also for the African Synod of seventy Bishops, at which Agrippinus of Carthage got the re-baptizing of converted heretics passed.[1] It was not held so early as 197, as Morcelli thought; nor yet in 215, as Walch would have it; but in the years immediately following, yet before 222. And when S. Augustine says that the ancient apostolic discipline was falsified first under Agrippinus;[2] when Vincentius declares that he was the first among all mankind to introduce re-baptism, against the rule of the universal Church, against the view of all other Bishops, against the custom and ordinances of their forefathers,[3] we thus obtain a confirmation of this charge. It is true that Tertullian before this, in his book *On Baptism*, written when he was still a Catholic, and therefore before 218, and

---

[1] CYPRIANI *Ep.* 71. [2] *De Baptismo*, II. 7.
[3] *Commonitor.* c. 9, p. 114, ed. Klüpfel.

earlier in a Greek treatise, had denied that heretics have power to confer valid baptism;[1] but here, to be exact, he means only those who did not baptize in the Church's way, who had a different God and Christ, *i.e.* in particular certain Gnostic sects. At the same time he puts forth general principles, from which the worthlessness of every kind of baptism performed outside the communion of the Church might be deduced; and it may well have been his influence and his treatise which helped to bring about the decision of the Synod under Agrippinus, although at the time of the Synod he was already a Montanist.

In the East it was apparently the Synod at Synnada in Phrygia, mentioned by the Alexandrian Dionysius, which, at the same time that Agrippinus held his Council, first decided to re-baptize heretics; and Tertullian no doubt wrote his treatise on this question in Greek, in order that it might be taken into consideration by the Orientals then disputing and debating on the point. FIRMILIAN does not mention this Synod; it must have been held before his time, and the fame of it had no doubt already died away in his neighbourhood. But when he declares that even before the Council of Iconium heretical baptism was treated in those provinces as null and void, this was doubtless the very practice which the Synod at Synnada had established. The Synod of Iconium, which ordered the repetition of baptism performed by heretics for the provinces of Galatia, Cappadocia, Cilicia, and the immediate neighbourhood, must have been held somewhat later than the African one, for Firmilian, who did not die till 269, took part in it as a Bishop. It

---

[1] *De Bapt.* 15. Ideoque nec baptismus unus, quia non idem; quem cum rite non habent, sine dubio non habent. [But Tertullian does not state that it was the Church's custom to re-baptize. He rather implies that it was not, saying that the question of heretical baptism requires reconsideration.]

may therefore have been held about 231, as Ceillier also supposes, not long after the Synod at Synnada, mentioned by Dionysius.

The late DR. VON DREY, in his investigations respecting *The Apostolical Constitutions and Canons* (p. 261), has taken up again the position already advanced by LAUNOY,[1] that the most ancient tradition of the Church is favourable to the theory and practice of Cyprian. Accordingly he reckons the forty-sixth and forty-seventh Canons among those which stood next to the veritable *Apostolical Canons*, and even maintains: "This (that there is no baptism outside the Church) was the opinion from the beginning; and hence we find the principle of the Canons before us, along with the reasons alleged, repeated in order *by all ancient ecclesiastical writers.*" This is a manifest exaggeration. Of known names in the first three centuries, Drey can mention only Clement of Alexandria besides those involved in the dispute; and the expression of this Father, that heretical baptism is not the proper and true water,[2] is too indefinite to tell with certainty for one side or the other. The *Apostolical Canons* and the *Constitutions* are here to be accounted only as one voice, and are based apparently upon the decisions of the Synods of Synnada and Iconium.[3] DIONYSIUS of Alexandria no doubt held the baptism of several heretical sects to be invalid, but not of all; and Jerome's statement respecting his view must be taken with limitations, for we know from Basil that he allowed

---

[1] III. Epistol. p. 581.

[2] Τὸ βάπτισμα τὸ αἱρετικὸν οὐκ οἰκεῖον καὶ γνήσιον ὕδωρ λογιζομένη. *Strom.* I. sec. 19, p. 375. [Clement does not say that this "foreign baptism" was renewed.]

[3] [Bishop Hefele agrees with Dr. Döllinger against Drey, that the 46th and 47th Apostolical Canons cannot be considered very ancient. "This opinion had before been enunciated by Peter de Marca, who argued justly, that if this Canon had been in existence at the period of the discussion upon bap-

the baptism of the Papuzians or Montanists to count as valid, although this was afterwards rejected by the first Synod at Constantinople. S. ATHANASIUS only once calls the validity of Arian baptism in question. CYRIL speaks quite generally, but appears to have had in his mind only the heretics existing at that time in the Church of Jerusalem, especially the Manicheans. OPTATUS would make a great difference on this point between heretics and schismatics; and BASIL finally wavered on the question—at any rate would not go so far as his predecessor Firmilian; declared the baptism of those sects which held erroneous doctrines about God as null and void; but was of opinion that the baptism of many heretics—as the Enkratites—might, with a view to the advantage of the Church, be treated as valid.[1] Such is the state of the case with the authorities quoted by Drey, and he might no doubt have added others, as ASTERIUS of Amasea and AMBROSE himself. But we see that the view which he designates as that of the Apostles and of the Church, that outside the Church there was neither baptism nor any other sacrament, was at no time generally diffused or prevalent in the Church. If we except Cyprian and Firmilian, none of the Fathers appealed to this principle; most of them have pronounced and acted against it. The Synods of Nicæa and Constantinople (325 and 381) made a distinction between heresies; and as, through the wide diffusion of Arianism, the question became a practical and a burning one, and innumerable persons

---

tism administered by heretics, that is, about the year 255, S. Cyprian and Firmilian would not have failed to quote it." Note on the 46th Apostolical Canon, *History of the Christian Councils*, vol. i. p. 477, English translation, 2d ed. Hefele also agrees that this charge against Callistus respecting re-baptism almost undoubtedly refers to Bishop Agrippinus and his Synod at Carthage, and that this Synod is therefore to be placed between 218 and 222. *Ibid.* p. 87.]

[1] BASILII *Ep. can. ad Amphiloch.*, *Opp.* ed. Paris 1839, III. 390.

would have had to be re-baptized had men acted on Drey's principle, they recognised in the whole East also the necessity of allowing Arian baptism to stand.

SUMMARY.

Now that we have looked more closely into the grounds for the charges which Hippolytus makes, partly against Callistus personally, partly against the Churches in communion with him, let us ask ourselves, What, after all, actually remains as well-grounded complaint in this ecclesiastical philippic?

We have the description of another Bishop of a great metropolis, who (just like Callistus) was accused simultaneously of heretical doctrine, of worldly and corrupt conduct, and of intentional disturbance of Church-discipline. This was Paul, Bishop of Antioch, who lived forty-five years later than Callistus. The makers of the charge are the assembled Bishops of the East, and their letter is addressed to Dionysius, Bishop of Rome, and Maximus, Bishop of Alexandria. It is instructive to compare these two descriptions with one another. In the one case all is concrete, palpable, clear matter of fact; the whole conduct of Paul, the condition of the Church of Antioch under his tyranny and ill-treatment, is made perfectly intelligible. In the other, on the contrary, in the description which Hippolytus draws of the administration of the Bishop of Rome, the greater part swims before us in misty sketches: instead of definite facts we have sometimes only sharp words; and the clearest thing in the diatribe is the effort of the writer to let the reader suspect the very worst possible, without saying what is positively untrue. In Antioch we see a man who, through his ill-gotten wealth, through the favour of Queen Zenobia and the influence of his temporal office, oppresses the

Church of which he is Bishop, and tyrannizes over clergy and people, so that no one dares to oppose him; he takes good-looking women about with him, has songs in his praise sung in the Church, surrounds himself with a body-guard, etc. etc. Only after contemplating this picture does it occur to us that Hippolytus, on the contrary, can produce really nothing against the personal character of Callistus. Had he known any offence of his, any stain on the life of Callistus since his promotion, *it is quite clear that he would not have spared him the mention of it.* But nothing of the kind occurs. His complaints are confined to this, that through bad Church-discipline and unseemly concessions, Callistus had been the first to lighten the yoke of Christ for men, and allowed them to gratify their passions. But that he set them an example, that he indulged in τὰ πρὸς τὰς ἡδονάς—the pleasures of sense—the description does not contain a single hint. While the Oriental Bishops charge Paulus with all particularity and detail of facts (which must have been notorious), that through avarice, robbery, pride, unchastity, and intemperance, he had been guilty of almost every deadly sin,—Hippolytus cannot lay a single personal sin to the charge of his opponent. We see, further, that the Church of Antioch only bore with the administration of their unworthy Bishop because it had been robbed of its freedom and suffered violence; so that even the great Synod of Oriental Bishops was unable to dispossess him, and was obliged to appeal to the arm of the heathen Emperor. But in the case of Callistus all this was quite different. He had no other support than the fidelity of his clergy and his congregation; and Hippolytus himself is obliged to admit that, in spite of the unauthorized innovations of which he is said to have been guilty, even well-meaning persons, because they saw in his communion the Catholic Church, went over to his side.[1]

Had Callistus, as Hippolytus represents, been a hypocrite and an eye-server of the Bishop, and that, too, of a selfish and avaricious Bishop, it would be quite inconceivable that, after the death of this Bishop, a free election—that is, the goodwill of the people, the favour and respect of the Presbytery—would have raised him to the episcopal see. What means could he have put in motion? Bribery? He was poor, and the number of those to be bribed would in any case have been far too great. The influence of powerful supporters? Those in power were at that time heathen, and, *had there been anything of that kind, Hippolytus would not have been silent about it.* The votes were given neither by few nor in secret, but by many and openly. But nevertheless Hippolytus has so described Callistus; and Hippolytus was a pious, and therefore no doubt also a truth-loving man. Yes, he has told what was reported to him; and when party spirit works together with personal bitterness, as here, then credulity, even in the case of pious men, will very soon master love of truth.[2]

[1] Τινὲς νομίζοντες εὖ πράττειν,—he manifestly distinguishes these from the ὄχλοι who joined themselves to the school of the party of Callistus, p. 291.

[2] [Dr. Salmon's remark may be quoted as very much in point here: "Men incapable of asserting anything they do not believe to be true, still differ widely from each other as to the amount of evidence which will induce them to make an assertion, and themselves believe it firmly. Hippolytus strikes me as one of those arbitrary and self-confident men who have unbounded faith in their own theories, and the confidence of those assertions is quite disproportionate to the evidence they can produce for them." *Hermathena*, 1873, p. 109.]

CHAPTER IV.

CONTROVERSY BETWEEN HIPPOLYTUS AND CALLISTUS
RESPECTING THE DOCTRINE OF THE TRINITY.

I. SABELLIANISM.

THE heresy afterwards called SABELLIAN or PATRI-
PASSIAN, arose at the end of the second century in
Asia Minor, was from thence transplanted to Rome,
and there, at the beginning of the third century, gradually developed through the discussions and controversies
which it excited among the Christians in Rome. The
originator of the doctrine was NOETUS of Smyrna,
whose active life must be placed probably in the last
years of the second century.[1] A disciple of Noëtus,
EPIGONUS, brought his doctrines (still in the time of
Victor, as it appears) to Rome. But seeing that Tertullian, who had good information, says that PRAXEAS
was the first to bring this doctrine from Asia to Rome;
and another witness,[2] equally contemporaneous and
living in Rome, agrees on this point with the African,

---

[1] After the definite statement of Hippolytus, the date given by Epiphanius must of course be given up as altogether incorrect—viz. that Noëtus
had come forward as a teacher about 130 years before (*Hæres.* 57, 1); as
he wrote in the year 375, this would take us back only to 245.

[2] The author of the *Libellus adversus hæreses*, in Tertullian's treatise *De
Præscriptione*. That he lived in Rome, I conclude from the fact that, besides well-known persons mentioned by all writers on heresy, he mentions
only such as first appeared in Rome—as Cerdo, Tatian, Blastus, and one
mentioned by no one else, Victorinus, who was also a Patripassian. [It
has been supposed by some that for Victorinus we should read Victor;
others propose Zephyrinus.]

in that he too designates Praxeas the introducer of the doctrine,—Praxeas must either have been working in Rome before Epigonus or contemporaneously with him; and Hippolytus has omitted to mention him, possibly because before his own arrival Epigonus had again left Rome and gone to Carthage;[1] moreover, had there recanted. This recantation and the departure of Praxeas had no perceptible effect at Rome. CLEOMENES, the disciple of Epigonus, stood, in the time of Bishop Zephyrinus (202-218), at the head of the Patripassian party. Of him Hippolytus says, that he also violated Church-discipline in his mode of life—*i.e.*, no doubt, that he had sanctioned Pagan licence, or at any rate such as the more strict Christians disapproved.

SABELLIUS joined himself to Cleomenes, and became his successor as head of the sect in Rome. Hippolytus states respecting him that for some time he wavered (probably in the last days of Zephyrinus); that he had taken the representations which Hippolytus made to him on account of his views in no unfriendly spirit, but had nevertheless ended in deciding for the doctrine of Cleomenes. For this Callistus is declared to have been to blame, for Hippolytus delights in representing him as the originator of all mischief. It would have been possible for him to have led Sabellius back to the path of the true faith, had he but made common cause with

---

[1] Tertullian says that this occurred before his own secession to Montanism, and therefore before the year 201. [Hagemann would account for the silence of Hippolytus respecting Praxeas by identifying him with Callistus, supposing Praxeas to be a nickname. Robertson mentions this strange theory without disapprobation. *History of the Christian Church*, I. 121, 2d ed. A more reasonable explanation of Hippolytus' silence is that Praxeas had very little success in Rome, or that the erroneous character of his teaching was not detected while he remained there. (NEWMAN, *The Arians of the Fourth Century*, p. 120, 3d ed.) This last hypothesis, however, seems to be contradicted by Tertullian (*adv. Praxeam*, i.), where he appears unwillingly to admit that the Bishop of Rome had actually extracted a recantation from Praxeas.]

Hippolytus, upheld his form of doctrine to Sabellius as the perfectly adequate expression of the Church's truth, and confirmed it with the weight of his authority. He is here speaking of the time when Callistus was not more than a Deacon or Priest in the Church of Rome; and certainly herein lies remarkable testimony, involuntarily given by an embittered adversary, to the intellectual importance of the man, in the statement that his authority was so great, his word in matters of dogma so weighty, that it would have been possible for him to have converted the leader of a long-standing heresy. But Callistus is said to have estranged Sabellius from the truth, by pretending to cherish a view not very far removed from the doctrine of Cleomenes. This means that from the course of events we are to understand as follows: Callistus agreed with Cleomenes in finding fault with the teaching of Hippolytus, although for different reasons. But Hippolytus, who knew but one alternative,—either my doctrine or that of Noëtus,—after his usual fashion, makes use of an expression which the reader can make to mean more or less as he likes. Callistus is declared to have said to Sabellius that he agrees with Cleomenes,—whether in respect to the whole doctrine of the Trinity, or only in the single point of rejecting the views of Hippolytus, the reader is left to conjecture. Meanwhile it is quite manifest, from the course of events and from the description of Callistus' doctrine, as Hippolytus himself gives it, that the first cannot have been the meaning of Callistus.

The few notices found here constitute all the positive knowledge we have respecting the personality of Sabellius, and the usual statements must now be corrected. He was a Libyan of Pentapolis. Now, seeing that the first mention of the Sabellian controversies known hitherto falls within the year 257, and that it was Dionysius of Antioch who was called upon by deputies and letters from both parties in Cyrenaica to declare himself on the question, some have assigned the appearance of Sabellius himself to this late date.[1] There is, however, no reason for so doing. Neither Dionysius nor Eusebius, who quotes the passage of his letter, mentions Sabellius himself; even Athanasius[2] only says that certain Bishops in the Pentapolis held Sabellian opinions at the time of Dionysius. This, therefore, was a movement which in all probability did not arise until after the death of Sabellius.

We can now see, further, that Hippolytus was the only source from which even in antiquity men's knowledge of the doctrine of Noëtus was derived: for Theodoret[3] copied his account, with but slight alteration of expression, from the tenth book of the *Philosophumena*, and it has long since been remarked that Epiphanius derived his from the little treatise of Hippolytus against Noëtus. Theodoret, however, through having only the synopsis in the tenth book before him, has allowed himself to be misled by the ambiguity of expression[4] which is found there into the erroneous statement that Epigonus was the author of this heresy, and Noëtus only a later reviver of it. Hence even S.

---

[1] KURTZ, *Handbuch der Kirchengeschichte*, 1853, I. 281, combines the new discoveries from Hippolytus with the account hitherto given, and says: "Thirty years later (than his appearance in Rome) we find him as a Presbyter at Ptolemais, again with an independent system," etc. Now it would certainly be very astonishing if a Roman heretic, excommunicated about 218, appeared thirty (or really forty) years later as a Presbyter in a distant part of Africa, and still holding fast to his errors. The whole, however, is an invention on the part of Herr Kurtz. That Sabellius was a Presbyter at Ptolemais is stated by no ancient author; and so resort must be had to the author or copier of so many gross blunders, Gregory Abulfaradsch. The statement of Zonaras in the twelfth century, that Sabellius was Bishop of Ptolemais, is utterly worthless.

[2] *De sententia Dionysii*, Opp. ed. Bened. I. 246.

[3] *Hæret. fab.* III. 3, Opp. ed. Noesselt, IV. 342.

[4] Εἰσηγήσατο—αἵρεσιν ἐξ Ἐπιγόνου τινὸς εἰς Κλεομένην χωρήσασαν, p. 329.

Augustine could tell nothing more definite about Noëtus and the Noëtians, not even whether the doctrine of Sabellius differed from that of Noëtus, and if so, how; and merely remarks that the names of Praxeans and Sabellians were common enough, but it was not often that any one knew anything of Noëtians.[1]

That Hippolytus considered the teaching of Sabellius as essentially identical with that of Noëtus, is clear. Had he known any considerable difference between the two, he would certainly have completed his enumeration of all the heresies known to him by a more exact account of the peculiarities of Sabellius' teaching,—all the more so because he had a perfectly accurate knowledge of his views through personal intercourse and manifold investigations. Instead of which he expressly describes the theory of Noëtus, Cleomenes, and Sabellius as similar. Callistus, he says, strengthened the heresy of Cleomenes; he endeavoured to win both parties to himself by crafty words, he spoke to the orthodox now in the sense of the true doctrine, and then in that of Sabellius,—and Sabellius himself was through him confirmed in the dogma of Cleomenes. Now, this certainly sounds somewhat astonishing: Callistus expounds the dogma of Sabellius to the orthodox, and praises the teaching of Cleomenes to Sabellius. Yet the idea manifestly is, that Sabellius, Cleomenes, and Noëtus in essential points held similar doctrine. Further on (290) we read again that Callistus, after having excommunicated Sabellius as a teacher of false doctrine, fell sometimes into the error of Sabellius, sometimes into that of Theodotus; and finally, in the synopsis we have the same statement repeated, merely with the variation that Noëtus is named instead of Sabellius.

There existed then in Rome a special school or sect

[1] *De Hæres.* 41.

of Patripassians, which had a succession of teachers,[1] and which doubtless maintained itself there long after this time, for Epiphanius says that Sabellians were spread in tolerably large numbers in Mesopotamia and in Rome.[2] The system of the school was as follows: The one supreme God is originally, or in so far as He is called Father, invisible, passionless, immortal, uncreate; but on the other side, as Son, by His own will and free self-limitation, He became man—was born of the Virgin, suffered and died,—and accordingly is called Son only for a certain time, and only in reference to that which He experienced upon earth. The Son, or Christ, is therefore the Father veiled in the flesh, and we must certainly say that it was the Father Himself who became man and suffered.

Hippolytus, Theodoret, and Epiphanius call this the teaching of Noëtus. Respecting that of Sabellius, the oldest and most important witness, the Roman Dionysius (who had known either Sabellius himself or his associates and disciples in Rome), affirms that he blasphemously declared the Son Himself to be the Father, and *vice versâ*;[3] and the contemporaneous Novatian, that he said Christ was the Father.[4] That was Noëtus' idea; and as more exact statements respecting the Sabellian system are found first in the Fathers of the fourth century, especially in Athanasius, it is now no longer possible to define exactly what Sabellius himself, or other later Monarchists, contributed to the further development of this view.

The most important point in which Sabellianism (as it is always described in later times) differs from the teaching of Noëtus, or from the notice which Hippoly-

---

[1] Αἵρεσιν ἕως νῦν ἐπὶ τοὺς διαδόχους διαμείνασαν, says Hippolytus, p. 329; and, p. 283, he calls them τοὺς νοητοὺς Νοητοῦ διαδόχους καὶ τῆς αἱρέσεως προστάτας.

[2] Ἐπὶ τὰ μέρη τῆς Ῥώμης, *Hæres*. 62, p. 513, ed. Paris.

[3] In ROUTH, *Reliquiæ sacræ*, III. 180.   [4] *De Trinit.* c. 12.

tus gives of it, is the placing of the Holy Spirit, and therewith the more definite setting forth of a Trinity, not in the divine essence, but in God's relations to the world and to mankind. It is a Supreme Being, manifesting Itself in time, not in three Persons, but merely in certain *prosopa* or forms, which in Itself, silent and at rest, comes forth from this rest and silence in successive characters as the Monad developed into the Trinity, and reveals Itself and works as Son and Holy Spirit. With Sabellius the Monad is also the Father. This is not a form distinct from the absolute Unity, separate in revelation or in activity,[1] but God in one Person, to Whom the Logos and the Holy Spirit are related merely as a man's thought and wisdom are related to his spirit.[2] In that the Logos, *i.e.* the Father, considered according to His intellectual activity, or the speaking Monad, appeared as man upon the earth, He became the Son; but, as a beam emitted from the sun

---

[1] That this was not the theory of Sabellius, as Schleiermacher and Baur suppose, is seen from the passage ATHANAS. c. Arian. IV. 25: Ὁ πατὴρ ὁ αὐτὸς μέν ἐστι· πλατύνεται δὲ εἰς υἱὸν καὶ πνεῦμα. Also GREGOR. NYSS. contra Ar. et Sabell., in the great collection of Majo VIII., II. p. 1: "The Sabellians would abolish the Hypostasis of the Son, αὐτὸν δὲ τὸν πατέρα ἕνα ὄντα δυσὶν ὀνόμασιν γεραίροντα οἰόμενοι, υἱοπάτορα προσαγορεύουσιν." AMMONIUS confirms this (caten. ad Joh. ed. Corder. p. 14): οὐ γὰρ υἱοπατορίαν ἡ ἐκκλησία δοξάζει, καθὰ μυθεύων ὁ Λίβυς εἶπε. Again, in the passage c. Arian, 4, 25, Opp. 1, 626, Athanasius understands Sabellius to mean that the Father was nothing else than the Monad: Εἰ τοίνυν ἡ μονὰς πλατυνθεῖσα, γέγονε τριάς, ἡ δὲ μονάς ἐστιν ὁ πατήρ, τριὰς δὲ πατὴρ υἱός, ἅγιον πνεῦμα, κ.τ.λ. Then he says: "If the Monad were held to be anything else than the Father, then one could not speak of an *extension* of the Monad; but one must say that the Monad is the efficient cause of the Three—Father, Son, and Spirit; so that we should have to distinguish four,—first the Monad, then the Father, etc." Had Sabellius really distinguished the Father from the Monad, one must suppose that he had essentially modified the teaching of Noëtus. As, however, this is not the case, we can recognise in what is called Sabellianism only a more carefully thought-out exposition of the Noëtian theory. [This passage, in which S. Athanasius is commonly supposed, as by Dr. Döllinger, to attribute these opinions to Sabellius, is referred by others to Marcellus of Ancyra.]

[2] Thus in the treatise c. Sabellii Gregales in ATHANASII Opp. II. 37 seqq.

(the Father), at the appointed time He returned to the same again, so that the Sonship is for the Divinity only a transient moment, entered upon for the appointed end of the redemption, and again extinguished after that purpose was accomplished. Accordingly, ancient writers say that when, according to Sabellius, the Father becomes the Son, He ceases to be the Father; and when He again becomes the Father, He has ceased to be the Son.[1] Hence, then, also their constant declaration, that with the Sabellians it was the Father Himself who became man, and was subject to suffering.[2] Noëtus, moreover, had taught that so long as the Father was not yet born, He was rightly called Father; but that when it pleased Him to submit to birth, then He became His own Son.[3] As, however, the faithful, in order to the perfecting of their salvation and healing, had still need of those further gifts which Scripture and the Church call the gifts of the Holy Spirit, yet a third Theophany was added to that of the Son, viz. that of the Holy Spirit, which likewise is something transitory, and in which the expansion of the Monad into the Triad is completed.

When, then, the Sabellians, in spite of the name of Patripassians, which they commonly bore in the West, nevertheless maintained that they did not mean to affirm that it was the Father who suffered,—this could only mean, either that God (in so far as He suffered in and through the Man Jesus) wills to be called not the Father, but the Son; or, that no real Incarnation, no personal, indissoluble union of the Godhead with the Manhood, took place in Christ. God, or the Father, merely manifested Himself, and worked in and through Christ, and therefore the suffering touched only the Man. In a word,—only by denying the Incarnation,

---

[1] EUGENII *Leg. ad S. Athan.* in MONTFAUCON, *Coll. nov.* II. 2.
[2] ATHANAS. *De Synodis* 7, *Opp.* I. 740.   [3] *Philosophumena*, p. 283.

as Paul of Samosata or Photinus did, could the Sabellians rebut the charge of Patripassianism.[1]

II. THE TRINITARIAN DOCTRINE OF HIPPOLYTUS.

Hippolytus proclaims himself the most uncompromising opponent of the Noëtians and of Sabellius. Repeatedly and complacently he calls attention to the fact that it was he who in Rome again and again spoke against them, and compelled them, even against their will (although it must be owned only for a transitory moment), to acknowledge the truth. But his own theology gave offence to the Roman Christians in the opposite direction, and drew on him the charge of Ditheism. We proceed, therefore, to a description of his doctrine, for which the work before us, as well as the treatise against Noëtus, may serve as an original authority. For the dogmatic agreement between the two is so remarkable, that it affords a new proof that Hippolytus is the author of the *Philosophumena*.

God, the one and only God, was originally alone, and had nothing contemporaneous with Himself. All existed (potentially) in Him, and He Himself was all. From the first He contained the Logos in Himself, as His still unsounding Voice, His not yet spoken Word, and together with Him the (yet unexpressed) idea of the universe which dwelt in Him.[2] This Logos, the

---

[1] [Paul of Samosata in his views was to a certain extent the opposite of Sabellius. The latter practically identified the Father and the Son; Paul drew far too broad a distinction between them. "He began, like Sabellius, by not distinguishing the Divine Persons,—regarding the Logos as an impersonal attribute of God. In Jesus he saw only a man penetrated by the Logos, who, though miraculously born of a virgin, was yet only a man, and not the God-man. . . . . . Thus, while on one side Paul approached Sabellianism, on the other he inclined towards the Subordinatianists of Alexandria." HEFELE, *Conciliengesch.* I. ii. sec. 9.]

[2] Ἐνδιάθετον τοῦ παντὸς λογισμόν. *Philosoph.* p. 334.

Intelligence, the Wisdom of God, without which He never was, went out from Him according to the counsels of God, *i.e.* when He willed and as He willed,[1] in the times determined beforehand by Him, as His First-begotten. God begat Him as Prince and Lord of the creation that was to be, as His Fellow-Counsellor and Workmaster. In going forth from Him that begat Him, He had also already the ideas conceived in the Substance of the Father as His voice within Himself, and by means of it, and in fulfilment of the command of His Father, He now created the world in its unity.[2] The Logos is therefore a Power proceeding from the whole, but the whole is the Father.[3] He—the Logos —is the Intelligence of the Father, and therefore His Substance;[4] whereas the world was created out of nothing. Thus another God stood by the side of the first, not as if there were two Gods, but as a light from the Light, water from the Fountain, the beam from the Sun. He was the perfect, only-begotten Logos of the Father, but not yet perfect Son; He became that first when He became man. Nevertheless, God already called Him the Son, because He was to be born.

In the second Hypostasis, therefore,—the Logos,— Hippolytus distinguishes three stages of development or periods. In the *first* He is still impersonal, still in

---

[1] Ὅτε ἠθέλησεν, καθὼς ἠθέλησεν. *C. Noët.* c. 10, p. 59, ed. Routh.

[2] Φωνὴν ἔχει ἐν ἑαυτῷ τὰς ἐν τῷ πατρικῷ ἐννοηθείσας ἰδέας, ὅθεν κελεύοντος πατρὸς γίνεσθαι κόσμον τὸ κατὰ ἓν Λόγος ἀπετελεῖτο ἀρέσκων θεῷ. WORDSWORTH here translates: "The Father bade that the world should be created *in its single species*." What that is intended to mean is not very clear. Hippolytus simply says in Platonic language: The Logos created the world according to the ideas conceived already in the Substance of the Father (before He came forth from the Father), and therefore according to a plurality, yet still as unity, or as a whole bound together and compounded into unity. *C. Noët.* c. 11, p. 62.

[3] Διὸ καὶ Θεὸς, οὐσία ὑπάρχων Θεοῦ. *Philosoph.* p. 336.

[4] Οὔτε γὰρ ἄσαρκος καὶ καθ' ἑαυτὸν ὁ Λόγος τέλειος ἦν υἱός, καίτοι τέλειος Λόγος ὢν μονογενής. *C. Noët.* c. 15, p. 69.

indistinguishable union with God, as the Divine Intelligence, potentially as the future personal Logos, and inherently as the holder of the Divine ideas, *i.e.* of the patterns, after which the universe was to be created. *Second* moment : God now becomes Father, by an act of His Will operating upon His Being. That is to say, at a time willed by Himself He calls His own Intelligence, in the fulness of His inherent powers—*i.e.* of the ideal universe contained within Him—to a separate hypostatic existence, places Him as another (ἕτερος) over against Himself; yet in such wise that the Logos is related to the Father only as a part which has acquired an existence of its own, or as the single Force, the creative Power to the undiminished whole,—as the beam to the Sun, from which it proceeded. The Logos having thus become hypostatic, in order to the manifestation of God in creation, then the *third* moment commences with the Incarnation, and it is here that He first completes Himself as the true and perfect Son; so that it is also through the Incarnation that the idea of the Divine Fatherhood is first completely realized.

Hippolytus has repeatedly been charged with ascribing no personality to the Holy Spirit;[1] and indeed, those who have already derived this impression from his earlier known writings, will believe that they find a remarkable confirmation of this in the newly-discovered work; for here, in the statement of doctrine in the tenth book, the Holy Spirit is altogether ignored. We read merely of the Logos, the Creation, and the Incarnation. Nevertheless, in the treatise against Noëtus, Hippolytus distinguishes the Holy Spirit as a separate Divine hypostasis very clearly; thus in the words—
" By means of the incarnate Logos we recognise the Father, we believe in the Son, and we adore the Holy

[1] *E.g.* MEIER, in his *Lehre von der Trinität*, Hamb. 1844, I. 88.

Ghost."[1] The Father, he says again, has put all things under Christ, excepting Himself and the Holy Spirit; thus there are three. The passing over all mention of the Holy Ghost in the dogmatic sketch at the close of the work loses all its strangeness as soon as one considers that this is an exhortation addressed to the heathen of that time,[2] who must receive only the exoteric part of the Christian doctrine. The doctrine of the Logos was considered to belong to this part, on account of its connection with Hellenic, and especially with Platonic, philosophical theories. The doctrine of the Holy Spirit, on the other hand, of His office in the Church and His gifts, is something so specifically Christian,—intelligible only to those who are already believers,—that it was necessarily treated as esoteric, and reserved for those discourses which were intended for the narrower circle of hearers. Accordingly, Hippolytus gave utterance on this subject in his treatise against Noëtus, which was intended for Christians only, but not in this exhortation, this λόγος πρὸς "Ελληνας; just as even in his account of the end and object of the Incarnation, he mentions only teaching, giving of commandments, and setting an example, but is silent about the esoterically Christian doctrine of the Atonement.

But, granting that Hippolytus is free from reproach on this side, on the other hand it is impossible not to admit that his doctrine of the Trinity in general, and of the Logos in particular, seems to be strongly tainted with the influences of Greek speculation, and that defective thought with him seriously affects the integrity and logical validity of the dogma. To those

---

[1] C. 12, p. 64; cf. c. 8, p. 59.

[2] The statement begins with (p. 333) an address to the Greeks, Chaldeans, Egyptians, and the whole race of mankind. Instead of μαθηταί, l. 54, we ought no doubt to read μάθετε.

in particular who at that time stood on the basis of the Church's simple faith and confession, and who had not passed through the school of heathen philosophy, this conception of the mystery, this distortion of it by the admixture of Platonic ideas, must have presented much that was strange, and even offensive and objectionable.

First, the Logos, as a Person distinct from the Father, existed, according to Hippolytus, undoubtedly before the beginning of time ($προαιώνιος$), but not from all eternity ($ἀΐδιος$); the former, because He came out from the bosom of the Divine nature before the creation, with which time first began; not the latter, because once He had no hypostatic existence, because although in substance He existed from all eternity in God, yet only as the impersonal Intelligence of God.

Secondly, the relation of the Logos to the Father is that of strict subordination; the Father commands, the Son hears and fulfils; the Father is the whole of the Godhead, to which the Son is related merely as a Force.

Thirdly, the Trinitarian relation is not original in the Divine nature, not founded in the very Being of God, but one that comes into existence through successive acts of the Divine *Will*. That, according to the theory of Hippolytus, the procession or individualization of the Holy Spirit also as a Person, must be conceived as something not original, but coming to pass later, for a definite end and object, Hippolytus himself has, it is true, nowhere said exactly; but from his doctrine of the generation of the Logos, there can be no doubt of it. That God set one of His attributes, His Intelligence and Wisdom, as a Person, as a Second beside Himself, has its explanation simply in the Divine Will. Hippolytus does not even hesitate to say that, as God had bestowed (personal) Divinity on the Logos, He could equally well, had He so willed it, have made man to be God.[1]

Fourthly, Hippolytus no doubt sets forth strongly that the Logos is God, and of the being of the Father, whereas the world was made out of nothing; but the representation—so foreign to primitive Christian tradition—that the Logos is the ἐνδιάθετος τοῦ παντὸς λογισμός, and therefore the κόσμος νοητός, the centre of the ideas of the universe, or the universe conceived ideally, conjoined with the other representation, according to which intelligence and wisdom in God are made to be the potential elements of the hypostasis of the Son, which must first be developed by a process of coming into being, and find its completion in the Incarnation,—all these particulars make the undeniable merit of Hippolytus, in holding fast the substantial equality of the Father and the Son, appear in a very dubious light.

It is unmistakable that Hippolytus, directly or indirectly, has borrowed the notions, and to some extent also the mode of expression, of PHILO. With him also the Divine Logos is first of all the impersonal Divine Intelligence, the thinking power in God, but at the same time also the ideal archetype of the universe, the κόσμος νοητός; wherefore he calls it also the seat and compass of the Divine ideas.[2] Moreover, with Philo also the Logos is at once the Divine wisdom, and this again the world of ideas, after which the actual world was

---

[1] Εἰ γὰρ Θεὸν ἠθέλησε ποιῆσαι, ἐδύνατο· ἔχεις τοῦ λόγου τὸ παράδειγμα. *Philosoph.* p. 336.

[2] *De mundi opif.* ed. Mangey, I. 4. He also calls it the archetypal seal (ἀρχέτυπος σφράγις), the idea of ideas. *Ibid.* pp. 4, 5. With the words of Hippolytus, that God begat the Logos as the ἐνδιάθετος τοῦ παντὸς λογισμός, compare the following passage from Philo: οὐδὲν ἂν ἕτερον εἴποι (τις) τὸν νοητὸν εἶναι κόσμον, ἢ Θεοῦ Λόγον ἤδη κοσμοποιοῦντος· οὐδὲ γὰρ ἡ νοητὴ πόλις ἕτερόν τι ἐστὶν ἢ ὁ τοῦ ἀρχιτέκτονος λογισμός, ἤδη τὴν αἰσθητὴν πόλιν τῇ νοητῇ κτίζειν διανοουμένου.

formed. Now, immediately before the creation of the world, this Logos became personal, God begat Him as His first-born Son, *i.e.* He separated His wisdom from His other attributes and powers, and made it an hypostasis.[1]

In Hippolytus, Philo's doctrine of the Logos appears in some points no doubt in a better form. He sets forth more distinctly that the Logos is of the being of God Himself; but the anomalies of the doctrine are not thereby removed, and in some respects are still more prominent in him than in Philo. It sounds strangely enough that Hippolytus should designate the primeval solitude of the Divine nature as nevertheless a company, in which God exists, because He had with Him His attributes,—Intelligence, Wisdom, Power,[2] Will; but it sounds not less paradoxical that the Logos, after having already before the Incarnation become a Person through the Divine Will, yet only through being born of the Virgin and of the Holy Spirit, becomes the Son,[3] or (as he expresses it) brings a Son into being for God (the Father). Things like these, put forth in a community such as the Roman was, could not fail to give very great offence.

The Church at that time was wont to be very tolerant of the attempts made by Christians of philosophic culture to explain the mystery of the Trinity by the help of Platonic or Platonising speculations, or to

---

[1] *De confus. ling.* I. 414 : Τοῦτον μὲν γὰρ πρεσβύτατον υἱὸν ὁ τῶν ὄντων ἀνέτειλε πατήρ, ὃν ἑτέρωθι πρωτόγονον ὠνόμασε. And also *Allegor.* II. i. 82 : Ἣν (σοφίαν τοῦ θεοῦ) ἄκραν καὶ πρωτίστην ἔτεμεν ἀπὸ τῶν ἑαυτοῦ δυνάμεων, ἐξ ἧς ποτίζει τὰς φιλοθέους ψυχάς. Hence he also calls his Logos τὸν πρεσβύτερον τῶν γένεσιν εἰληφότων (*De migr. Abr.* I. 437), and God τὴν τοῦ πρεσβυτάτου Λόγου πηγήν.

[2] *Contra Noët.* c. 10, p. 61 : Αὐτὸς δὲ μόνος ὢν πολὺς ἦν, οὔτε γὰρ ἄλογος, οὔτε ἄσοφος, οὔτε ἀδύνατος, οὔτε ἀβούλευτος ἦν, πάντα δὲ ἦν ἐν αὐτῷ, αὐτὸς δὲ ἦν τὸ πᾶν.

[3] *L.c.* c. 4, p. 52 : Οὕτως μυστήριον οἰκονομίας ἐκ πνεύματος ἁγίου ἦν οὗτος ὁ Λόγος καὶ παρθένου ἕνα υἱὸν Θεῷ ἀπεργασάμενος.

accommodate it to categories borrowed from them. If only the true Divinity of Christ, His Personality, and His becoming man were not called in question, people were not very strict about constructions of that kind. But the doctrine of Hippolytus partly went already beyond the limits of what might still be tolerated, partly was set forth by him (as we see from his own narrative) in dictatorial fashion as truth absolutely valid and necessary to be believed, all contradiction of it being stigmatized as heresy and blasphemy. And yet it was precisely his system which bore in it the germs of heresies that were developed later.

The doctrine that God called the Logos into personal existence by a decree, by an act of His Will, became later on a main prop of Arianism, a welcome weapon in their hands. Of course the Trinitarian self-determination of God must not be represented as a merely natural and necessary process. In God, in Whom is found nothing passive, no mere material substratum, Who is all movement and pure energy, we can conceive of no activity, not even when directed towards Himself, in which the Will also does not share. The Eternal Generation of the Son is at once necessary, grounded in the Divine Nature itself; and therefore without beginning, and also at the same time an act of volition (*voluntaria*), *i.e.* the Divine Will is one of the factors in the act of begetting. Not without volition does the Divine Essence become the Father and beget the Son; but this volition is not a single decree of God,—not something which must be first thought or determined, and then carried into effect; but it is the first, essential, eternal movement of the Divine Will operating on itself, and the condition of all external, *i.e.* of all creative acts.

When, however, Hippolytus represents the bringing forth of the Logos as a free action of the Divine Will, this is certainly something very different. Here we are told that God (who is conceived, so to speak, as a ready-made Personality), after having been for a long time alone, at last sent the Logos, which He had hitherto borne within Himself as one of His attributes, viz. His Intelligence, forth from Himself, endowed with a hypostatic existence, as another Being distinct from Himself. This, therefore, is not a necessary (because founded in the very being of God), not an eternal event, although prior to all time, but an accidental one, inasmuch as God might have left the Logos in His original impersonal condition. Thus it would have been possible for the Son not to have come to any real hypostatic existence, or (in other words) for God to have remained without a Son.

Hence it was that the Arians and Catholics contended so fiercely, the former for, the latter against the proposition, that the Father brought forth the Son by an act of His own free-will.[1] The Arians considered that they had won everything if this was conceded; therefore, said they, it was with full freedom of Will that God, after taking counsel with Himself whether he should call the Son into existence, brought Him forth. This Counsel and Will preceded the creation of the Son; so that He is not from all eternity, but has come into being; there was a time when He was not; He is not God as the Father is. As Epiphanius narrates, it was one of their dialectical artifices to place before the Catholics this alternative: God produced His Son either of free-will or not of free-will; if you

---

[1] Thus ARIUS: Θελήματι καὶ βουλῇ ὑπέστη, ap. Theodoret, *Hist. Eccl.* i. 4. And again EUSEBIUS OF CÆSAREA: κατὰ γνώμην καὶ προαίρεσιν βουληθεὶς ὁ θεός· ἐκ τῆς τοῦ πατρὸς βουλῆς καὶ δυνάμεως, *Demonst.* iv. 3. According to ASTERIUS, the main subject of the letter which EUSEBIUS OF NICOMEDIA, the leader of the Arians, sent to Paulinus, was—ἐπὶ τὴν βουλὴν τοῦ πατρὸς ἀνενεγκεῖν τοῦ υἱοῦ τὴν γέννησιν, καὶ μὴ πάθος ἀποφῆναι τοῦ υἱοῦ τὴν γυνήν. *Marcelliana*, ed. Rettberg, p. 21.

say, "not of free-will," then you subject the Godhead to compulsion; if you say, "of free-will," then you must allow that the Will was there before the Logos.[1] Ambrose and Epiphanius answered, that neither expression was admissible, for the matter concerned neither a decision of the Divine Will nor a compulsion of God, but an act of the Divine Nature, which, as such, falls under the idea neither of compulsion nor of freedom.[2]

It is Athanasius who lifts his voice most frequently against this favourite proposition of the Arians, because, as he says, by their appeal to the Will and Counsel of God they seduced many. The meaning of their tenet, that the Son came into being through the Will of the Father, was virtually the same as that of those who said that there was a time when the Son was not;[3] and he therefore calls upon them merely to utter this latter proposition openly, which they hesitated to do, and therefore concealed it under the phrase of the Son's being brought forth by the Divine Will. From what saint, he asks further, have you learnt the expression "out of the Will"?[4] Accordingly, he too solves the Arian dilemma by declaring that the Generation of the Son as an act of the Divine Nature goes far beyond an act of the Will.[5] Cyril of Alexandria also makes a distinction, which is here very much in point, between the concomitant and the antecedent Will of the Father; the former, but not the latter, is concerned in the Generation of the Son.[6]

The Council of Nicæa directed one of its anathemas against the Arian proposition, that before the nativity the Son was not,[7] and thereby touched the doctrine of

---

[1] Ancorat. n. 51.
[2] AMBROSIUS, *De fide*, iv. 9. *Opp.* ed. Bened. II. 540.
[3] Ἦν ποτε ὅτε οὐκ ἦν. *Orat. III. contra Arianos, Opp.* I. 608.
[4] *De decret. Nic. Syn., Opp.* I. 223.   [5] *Or.* III. p. 611.
[6] σύνδρομος θέλησις, but not προηγουμένη. *De Trinit.* II. p. 56.
[7] πρὶν γεννηθῆναι οὐκ ἦν.

Hippolytus, just so far as he would have been obliged to favour the Arian proposition. Or rather he would have insisted on the difference between an impersonal existence of the Logos, still indistinguishably contained in the bosom of the Divine Substance, and His later attainment of Personality,—*i.e.* he would have distinguished between the potential and actual existence of the Son.

Although Hippolytus was such a decided and ardent opponent of Sabellianism, his doctrine has, nevertheless, certain points of contact with it, especially in the form which Marcellus of Ancyra gave it later on. No doubt it is only partially and in an improper sense that the system of Marcellus can be called Sabellian. He denied the hypostatic pre-existence of the Son; his Logos is not generated, but existed from the beginning impersonally in God; but by an expansion of the hitherto undivided Monad, went from God into creative activity, or indeed as this activity (as λόγος ἐνεργός), or as creative Omnipotence coupled with Wisdom; still, however, without thereby becoming a distinct Person. This same Logos, by a second going out or self-expansion of the operative Divine power, assumed man's nature; *i.e.* He seized upon humanity, united Himself with it, and henceforth dwelt in it, but still without even yet forming a distinct hypostasis. Rather the Logos was the whole fulness of the Godhead working upon man: only the God-man Christ is personal, and only He is called the Son of God. Hence the Sonship first began at the Incarnation; and when all is fulfilled, the Logos withdraws from mankind and returns to the Father.[1]

This doctrine is of course very different from that of Hippolytus, especially in the fact that in Marcellus one

---

[1] See especially Euseb. *Contra Marcellum*, pp. 33–39, and *De Eccles. Theologia*, pp. 63, 81, 100, 125, ed. Colon.

never arrives at an actual hypostatizing of the Logos. The Logos is, and remains, impersonal, and His going out from the Father is merely an action of God lasting for a certain time, and exhibited first in the work of creation, and secondly in operation upon the Man Jesus. In Hippolytus, on the other hand, the Logos becomes personal first at the creation, and remains so henceforth to all eternity; but He becomes perfect as the Son of God first at the Incarnation; and here again there is a point of contact between Hippolytus and Marcellus. Moreover, Hippolytus assumes a relation of strict subordination; the Logos has only obediently to fulfil the commands of the Father; which is impossible according to Marcellus, for God cannot be obedient to Himself. The relation between the two systems may be expressed thus: in both, God and His Logos are the same until the Creation; a Son exists not as yet, and the Logos is merely an impersonal power in God, not distinguishable from Him; but from the Creation onwards the two systems separate,— Hippolytus makes the Logos go out from God, and become personal and perfect Himself in Christ as the Son; whereas Marcellus makes merely the power and activity which he calls Logos go out from God, *i.e.* become active externally, finish its operation, and finally return to God without surrendering a personality which it never had. In his system, Sabellianism and Hippolytusism are mixed.

In a Roman monument, to be more definitely noticed hereafter, we have an echo of the contest which was carried on in the bosom of the Roman Church at the opening of the third century respecting the doctrine of the Trinity. In it Hippolytus is designated as a *Valentinian*, and as such condemned and deposed. No doubt this statement is founded upon a charge that was really made, and when Callistus deposed and excommunicated him, he may very well have used the expression that his doctrine was in part Valentinian.[1]

The Universal Father, said the Valentinians, the *Bythus*, or Monad, was for innumerable ages alone with his *Ennoia* or *Sige*, buried in profound and silent rest; when at last he determined to come forth from this rest, and, breaking this silence, to manifest himself. Thereupon he caused the spirit of intelligence, *Nous* or *Monogenes*, to proceed from him as a substantial image of himself, while *Sige* or *Ennoia*, rendered fruitful by the Father of all, bore *Nous*, who alone was able to compass the glory of the Father.

This doctrine appears sufficiently similar to the *theologumenon* of Hippolytus, according to which God in like manner, after having been for a long time alone

[1] The Bishops at Philippopolis in the year 347, in order to show that the Westerns had no right to overthrow or retract the decisions of the Orientals against Marcellus and others, say in their epistle or decree that the Orientals had formerly confirmed the decisions of a Synod in Rome against Novatian, Sabellius, and Valentinus. *Nam in urbe Roma sub Novato, Sabellio, et Valentino hæreticis factum Concilium ab Orientalibus confirmatum est; et iterum in Oriente sub Paulo Samosatis quod statutum est, ab omnibus est signatum.* Ap. S. HILAR. *ex oper. hist. frag.* III. ii. 662, ed. Veron. That *sub* here is only a clumsy misrendering on the part of the Latin translator, and means "against," is clear. With regard to Novatian (always called Novatus by the Orientals), as early as the year 341 the Bishops at Antioch, in an exactly similar manner, appealed to the fact that their Church had never objected when this man was excommunicated. SOCRAT. *H. E.* ii. 15. With regard to the question whether Sabellius and Valentinus were also mentioned, the editor of Hilary says: *An in eadem civitate (Roma) specialibus synodis pariter damnati sint Sabellius et Valentinus, nullo alio veterum monumento certo scimus.* Some light is now thrown upon the matter, inasmuch as we know that Sabellius laboured in Rome, and there was excommunicated by Callistus. The name Valentinus appears to be the result of a confusion; according to this statement, his condemnation by a Synod must have taken place before the middle of the second century, which is not probable. But from the authority quoted above we learn that Hippolytus was excommunicated for *Valentinian* doctrine. May not this have led to the union of the name of Valentinus with that of Sabellius? It is probable enough that Callistus held a Synod at which both Sabellius and Hippolytus were condemned, and that this decision was confirmed by the Orientals.

with Himself, determined to send forth from Himself His hitherto silent *Nous*, and caused this to become a Person, whereupon the production of a world of spirits and material creatures followed. At a later age in the Church, the theory that it required a determination and act of will on the part of the Father to call the Logos into personal existence, was still called the peculiar tenet of Valentinus, as (for instance) is frequently done by Athanasius.[1]

III. THE CONTEST BETWEEN HIPPOLYTUS AND THE SABELLIANS.

Let us now follow the historical course of the contest as we find it in the certainly somewhat confused narrative of Hippolytus. Besides the Theodotians, who still existed as a body at that time in Rome, there were two other parties under Zephyrinus, who contended with one another respecting the Trinity—the school of Cleomenes and Sabellius on the one side, of Hippolytus and his followers on the other. Hippolytus boasted that it was he who had emphatically and frequently refuted the Noëtians, so that they had often acknowledged the truth under the pressure of his arguments; but then (it must be confessed) had returned to their own doctrine, or, as he expressed it, had wallowed in their old filth again. At the same time he accuses Bishop Zephyrinus of having, out of covetousness, allowed various persons to attend the instruction of Cleomenes, and of having gradually approximated to his doctrine;

---

[1] So *Or. contra Arian.* III., *Opp.* I. 613, where he argues against those who make the Logos to be generated by the Will of the Father; and adds: πλασάσθωσαν ἕτερον λόγον, καὶ τὰ Οὐαλεντίνου ζηλώσαντες, χριστὸν ἕτερον ὀνομασάτωσαν. And p. 614: πάντα κινοῦσι, καὶ τὴν Οὐαλεντίνου ἔννοιαν καὶ θέλησιν προβάλλονται, ἵνα μόνον διαστήσωσι τὸν υἱὸν ἀπὸ τοῦ πατρὸς καὶ μὴ εἴπωσιν ἴδιον αὐτὸν τοῦ πατρὸς εἶναι λόγον ἀλλὰ κτίσμα. And he exclaims yet again to them: ῎Η ἀσέβεια Οὐαλεντίνου σὺν ὑμῖν εἴη εἰς ἀπώλειαν.

and that to this the influence and help of Callistus had greatly contributed. The charge, that Zephyrinus favoured the Noëtians out of avarice, may be understood to mean that he was unwilling to rob the common chest of the sums which these persons brought to it, and of the contributions which they from time to time made, by excommunicating them. Thus, in Rome, the sum of 200 sesterces, which he had lately given, was returned to Marcion when he was expelled for ever.[1] The amount of historic truth probably reduces itself to this: that in the time of Zephyrinus the small Noëtian school had not yet developed into a sect, and that most of those who were this way inclined still wavered hesitatingly,—as could hardly be otherwise at a time when no decisions of the Church respecting the doctrine of the Trinity were extant, and as Hippolytus himself affirms. Zephyrinus might therefore hold it advisable not at once to visit those who attended the lectures of Cleomenes, or in way allowed their views to be influenced by his, with ecclesiastical censures, such as excommunication. And we may also ask whether Cleomenes had already formulated the new doctrine so definitely as Sabellius afterwards did,—whether he did not veil it under orthodox-sounding expressions?

It was Callistus who (according to the statement of Hippolytus) induced Zephyrinus "to be ever promoting dissension among the brethren,"—viz. respecting the doctrine of the Father and the Son,—a charge which, however, the narrator himself refutes; for we see from his account that the dissension was already there, without any help from Zephyrinus and Callistus; that the two parties, whose leaders were Cleomenes and Sabellius on the one side, and Hippolytus on the other, were fighting vigorously and perseveringly with one another. This Hippolytus himself, as has been said,

[1] TERTULL. *Præscript.* c. 39 [*adv. Marcion*, IV. 4].

sets forth; and the discontent, which he here clothes in the charge of troubling the peace of the Church, has its basis in the fact that Zephyrinus and Callistus did not make his party and view unconditionally their own, but, taking a middle course, said that both parties were partly wrong and partly (in so far as they blamed the other side) right. We have only to listen to what he says himself. Zephyrinus, advised by Callistus, came publicly before the congregation and made this confession: "I know but one God—Jesus Christ; and besides Him I know no one that was born and has suffered." That was the language of the Church of that age, and it was thus that the martyrs confessed their faith before the heathen judges. Thus spoke the Scillitanian martyrs [1] (about the year 203); Pionius also, and his companions in suffering at Smyrna.[2] Zephyrinus means that He Who was born and has suffered is no other than the God in Whom we believe; in other words: "I know not two Gods; one that remains for ever invisible and afar off, and one that, drawing near to men in the form of a man, was born and has suffered among them." And, to prevent Cleomenes and his party from explaining this in their own sense, Callistus came forward and said that it was not the Father who suffered and died, but the Son. This was a direct contradiction to the doctrine of Cleomenes and his "chorus," who expressly maintained that He Who was

[1] RUINART, *Acta MM.* p. 88, ed. Amstelod.

[2] *L.c.* pp. 143 *seqq.* Pionius, Theodora, and Sabina declare, in answer to the question, *Quem Deum colis? Deum omnipotentem qui fecit cœlum,* etc., *quem cognovimus per Verbum ejus Jesum Christum.* Then to the question, *Quem Deum colis?* Asclepiades answers, *Christum.* The judge replies, *Quid ergo? iste alter est?* Asclepiades, *Non; sed ipse quem et ipsi paulo ante confessi sunt.* When they were again asked at the altar, and again confessed that they believed in the God Who made the world, the judges ask, *Illum dicis, qui crucifixus est?* and Pionus answers, *Illum dico, quem pro salute orbis Pater misit.* So, again, SAPRICIUS declares (*Acta S. Nicephori,* p. 241) that the true God, Who created all things—the God of the Christians—is Christ.

nailed to the Cross had not concealed from those who could understand it that He was the Father Himself.¹ And when Hippolytus goes on to add that in this way Callistus ever kept the strife awake among the people, one ought much rather to think that only in this way was it possible, without detriment to the teaching of the Church, to arrive at an understanding. Without intending it, Hippolytus himself bears witness to the uprightness of Callistus' conduct. He says that in private conversation Callistus spoke to those who were on the side of truth (*i.e.* the doctrine of Hippolytus) as if he was of the same opinion as they, and then again instructed them in the doctrine of Sabellius.² This was (when we place ourselves at the standpoint and in

¹ πατέρα δὲ εἶναι καὶ τοῖς χωροῦσιν μὴ ἀποκρύψαντα. *Philosophumena*, p. 284.

² Καὶ τοῖς μὲν ἀλήθειαν λέγων ὅμοια φρονοῦσι ποτὲ καθ' ἡδίαν τὰ ὅμοια φρονεῖν ἠπάτα· πάλιν δ' αὐτοῖς τὰ Σαβελλίου ὁμοίως, ὃν καὶ αὐτὸν ἐξέστησε δυνάμενον (δυνάμενος) κατορθοῦν. Besides the emendation already suggested, we ought, instead of καθ' ἡδίαν, to read κατ' ἰδίαν=in private, in opposition to the Bishop's δημοσίᾳ, immediately following. The conjecture of Dr. Wordsworth, κατ' ἰδέαν, is the very reverse of happy; and the interpretation which he would put upon these words, *sub specie similia sentiendi*, would certainly not easily occur to any one on reading them. But a more important point is, that Dr. Wordsworth in his translation has allowed himself a deliberate alteration of the passage, in order to make the conduct of Callistus appear more hateful and treacherous than even Hippolytus intended us to understand; for Dr. Wordsworth renders it, "And at another time speaking with similar language (of duplicity) to those who held the doctrine of Sabellius." According to this rendering, Callistus must have conversed with the followers of Hippolytus only in the sense of their doctrine, and with the Noëtians again only in the very opposite sense; and consequently it would be impossible to acquit him of the charge of duplicity. But before one can bring out this meaning, one must first arbitrarily alter the text, and make it say something altogether different from what stands there. Dr. Wordsworth contents himself with approving in a note the conjecture of Herr Bunsen, who wishes instead of πάλιν δ' αὐτοῖς to read πάλιν δ' αὖ τοῖς. But this makes no sense; at least we must have another word added, *e.g.* φρονοῦσι after τὰ Σαβελλίου, and even then the sentence would still not answer the requirements of Dr. Wordsworth. But it is scarcely consistent to print the Greek text with its clear simple meaning, and then in the translation to make the author say something altogether different.

the position of the two men) quite natural on both sides,—that Callistus should act in this way, and that Hippolytus should take this view of his conduct. To the latter, every objection raised against his system in the interests of the Divine Unity savoured of Sabellianism, just as the Arians also in a later age argued against the defenders of the Nicene doctrine. Accordingly, if Callistus ever said to the followers of Hippolytus, "You are quite right in insisting that it is the Son Who suffered, and not the Father; Father and Son, although of the same nature, are still distinct;"—this meant that in this at least Hippolytus teaches in accordance with the truth. But suppose that Callistus said, "The Son or Logos is not one who came into existence; He did not become Son first at the Creation, still less at the Incarnation; what He is, He is from the first—from all eternity. The Father can never be conceived except as having the Son in inseparable union with and in Him; there was no need for a determination of the Divine Will to precede in order to give existence to the Logos,"—then Hippolytus and his "chorus" would cry, "Listen to the disciple of Noëtus, the follower of Sabellius! Now it is clear that the deceiver has tried to win us over and corrupt us by his apparent agreement with our doctrine."

Meanwhile Hippolytus himself is obliged to confess that Callistus had nearly the whole Roman community on his side, but manifestly only because he remained true to what had hitherto been the teaching of the Church. "Every one," he says, "favoured his hypocrisy,"— of course always excepting Cleomenes and his followers on the one side, and the party of Hippolytus on the other. "I alone," says Hippolytus, "who saw through his meaning, did not sanction his views, but refuted him and opposed him." Hippolytus v. Callistus—such was the match, and a very unequal one. On the one side, the most learned man of his age, beyond a doubt the most considerable person intellectually in the Roman community, a defender of the Christian faith against heathen philosophy, a disciple of the celebrated (in Rome also well known) Irenæus; on the other, a poor slave taken out of the House of Correction. Which of these two was the innovator? Had Hippolytus insisted on nothing but what had hitherto been taught in the Roman Church, while Callistus tried to overthrow the traditional doctrine, and introduce the novelties of Noëtus, it would be quite inconceivable that every one should favour the opponent of the traditional doctrine, while the defender of it was left to stand almost alone,—and this in an age and in a community in which people held so firmly to what was handed down from antiquity. It is true that Hippolytus lays all the blame on the πανουργία, the deceit and hypocrisy of Callistus, which he was the only one to see through. This hypocrisy went such lengths, that, although he often entered into discussions with all parties, he really never committed himself to any error by which Hippolytus could convict him; for, as Hippolytus himself admits, it was only his inner meaning and disposition, the νοήματα of the man (285), and not his words or public lectures, which were made to furnish Hippolytus with material for his attacks or suspicions. Which simply means this: "Callistus, it is true, has not said anything such as to enable me to point him out to Christians as a Patripassian and denier of the Personality of the Logos; but seeing that in certain points he has said that Sabellius was right (in opposition to me), he must, in his innermost convictions, have been a Patripassian and Noëtian."

Callistus no doubt went farther than this. He not only thought the doctrine of Hippolytus dangerous;

before the congregation (δημοσίᾳ, 289) he publicly charged him and his followers with being *Ditheists*. What he said in justification of this certainly very serious accusation can scarcely (seeing that we know what the doctrine of Hippolytus was) be doubtful. "You show us," he would have said, "a Logos who once did not exist: you think you can state the moment when God bethought Himself that He would no longer be alone, but that He would place another side by side with Himself as a companion, by making one of His attributes, viz. His reason, into a Person. God then is the Sovereign, and the other His Son, whom He has made to be what He is simply according to His own will and pleasure; for the Son might have been left by Him in His original impersonal, and therefore unconscious, existence, and must obey Him in all things. With you, therefore, the existence of the Son is such a mere accident, depending solely on the choice and caprice of the Father, that you even go so far as to say that, had He pleased, God might have made any individual man (or mankind) to be God instead of His Logos.[1] What is this Logos and Son, according to your idea, but a second God alongside of the first, a God *brought into existence*, like the θεοὶ γεννητοὶ of Plato?[2] Or how do you mean, with such a doctrine as that, to save the Unity of God? Perhaps by saying that the one commands and the other obeys? or that you understand the Logos to be the ideal world originally shut up in the bosom of the Father?[3] Is very much gained for the Unity of God by saying that between God and the Logos there is a community of power?[4] You hope, possibly, to secure the Divine Unity by maintaining that the Logos, as coming out of the Nature of

---

[1] *Philos.* p. 336.
[2] PLATO, *Pol.* VIII. p. 546 B.   *Timæus*, 40 D.   *Timæus Locrus*, 96 c.
[3] Ἐνδιάθετον τοῦ παντὸς λογισμόν, p. 334.   [4] *Contra Noët.* p. 59.

the Father, has the Nature of God.[1] But ask any philosophical idolater whether mere community of nature is sufficient to make several Gods into one. You know, of course, what the Greeks say of Athene, the goddess who sprang out of the breast or head of the Father. They call her now the Intelligence that pervades the universe,[2] just as you call the Logos the Idea (λογισμός) of the universe. They say that 'Zeus, who could find no one equal to himself in dignity through whom she might be produced, begat her himself, and therefore she alone is the true daughter of the Father. The Father is indeed the great Artificer and King; she is born from his head, from which nothing more lovely could be born than Athene. She is inseparable from him: she remains with the Father, as if she were grown together with him: in him she breathes, and is his assessor and the sharer of his counsels. She sits at his right hand: herself higher than an angel, she communicates to the angels the commands which she has first received from the Father.'[3] Would not one suppose that you had borrowed your description of the Logos from this speech of ÆLIUS ARISTIDES, which appeared some fifty years ago, merely changing the female into the male? This Athene is certainly of like nature with Zeus, coming out of his substance; but for all that, are they not two different divinities? She, too, is simply a deity brought into existence, who once was not, but had only a possible, a potential existence in the head of the great god; until he, taking counsel with himself, determined to allow her to go out from him as his reason or wisdom, now become a person, and place her side by side with himself."

---

[1] Διὸ καὶ Θεὸς, οὐάρχσία ὑπων Θεοῦ, *Philos.* p. 336.
[2] Φρόνησις διὰ πάντων διήκουσα. ATHENAGOR. *Legat.* c. 19.
[3] Ἀγγέλου μὲν γάρ ἐστι μείζων, ἤ γε τῶν ἀγγέλων ἄλλοις ἄλλα ἐπιτάττει πρώτη παρὰ τοῦ πατρὸς παραλαμβάνουσα. ARISTID. ed. Dindorf, I. 15.

Assuredly it is no wonder that the large majority of the Roman clergy and laity held with Callistus rather than with Hippolytus. On the death of Zephyrinus it was again manifest that it was Callistus and not Hippolytus in whom the people recognised their faith and the clergy their doctrine; for he, and not Hippolytus, who otherwise certainly had claim to be so, was elected Bishop. Zephyrinus had hitherto allowed Sabellius to remain in his communion, probably because he too regarded Sabellius as one who was hesitating, and might still be won over; whether he also tolerated the others who held similar views, is not clear. The new Bishop at once excommunicated him, because his doctrine was damnable; and Hippolytus gives two reasons which induced Callistus to do this: first, fear of himself, Hippolytus; second, fear that, if he did not do it, he would be accused in other Churches of being a heretic.

From this we see that Hippolytus was still in communion with the Church; that the schism did not at once begin on the election of Callistus by the counter-election of Hippolytus, but not till somewhat later. But Hippolytus here again mentions that Callistus publicly charged him and his followers of like views with being Ditheists.[1]

This must have occasioned the breach, the circumstances of which Hippolytus does not give us, but which the rest of his narrative and his mode of expression set forth in the clearest way. Persons whom

---

[1] Διὰ τὸ δημοσίᾳ ἡμῖν ὀνειδίζοντα εἰπεῖν δίθεοί ἐστέ. Wordsworth translates: Because he had before calumniated me in public, and said, "You are a Ditheist." Where is there any "before" in the Greek? Hippolytus speaks of what now took place, as the second part of the sentence, which mentions the exit of Sabellius in exactly the same construction, sufficiently shows. Moreover, δίθεοί ἐστέ is not, as Wordsworth appears to think, the colloquial plural. When Callistus said, "Ye are Ditheists," he cannot have meant Hippolytus only, but thereby designated a number of persons, a party, as such.

Callistus had declared publicly before the congregation to be Ditheists, could be allowed by him to remain in the Church only if they retracted their doctrine; and this in the case of Hippolytus was not to be thought of. Accordingly, it seems more probable that it was Callistus who excommunicated him and his followers, and that thereupon Hippolytus was elected Bishop by his party. That the great majority of Churches continued to recognise Callistus is indubitable, and it seems to the present writer that Hippolytus says as much himself. For immediately after mentioning that Callistus wished to secure himself in the eyes of other Churches from the discredit or charge of heterodoxy, he again notices the cunning adroitness of the man, and says that in time the crafty charlatan brought over many to his side. This cannot refer to the Christians in Rome, for Hippolytus had already mentioned that in Rome every one sided with Callistus, while he alone opposed him, so that he had no need there gradually to win over "many;" but it means the external Churches, of whom he was speaking a little while before. Without doubt Hippolytus on his side left no stone unturned to induce these Churches to recognise him: he described Callistus to them as an heretical Noëtian; and as his reputation at that time was already widely spread in the Church, he thus found himself in a better position than Callistus, who was certainly less well known outside Rome. On the other hand, Callistus of course had the majority of the clergy and people to bear testimony for him, and, moreover, was in possession. However, just as afterwards in the case of the Novatian schism many Churches refrained from recognising either side until they had obtained more accurate information, and until the suspicion against Cornelius was cleared up, so no doubt was the case here also; after a while (ἐπὶ χρόνῳ) the majority decided for Callistus, and of course Hippolytus attributed this to the deceit and knavish cunning of his rival.

Hippolytus further contends that Sabellius, after his excommunication, frequently charged Callistus with having departed from his former belief. This is very credible, and lies in the nature of the position in which Callistus found himself between two opposite and erroneous views respecting the Trinity. During the lifetime of Zephyrinus he had specially contended against those who, as his successor, the Roman Dionysius, says, violated the most sublime and sacred doctrine of the Church—that of the Monarchia—by dividing it into three Powers, or separate Hypostases, or Deities, and thereby destroying it; whereby, as Dionysius adds, they fell into an error diametrically opposite to that of Sabellius.[1] Hippolytus and his followers were the forerunners of these erroneous teachers, censured by Dionysius forty years later; for their theory respecting the Logos led to a "dividing (διαίρεσις) of the Sacred Monad." Callistus had here a common interest with Sabellius and the Noëtians, viz. the defence of the Divine Unity; he was obliged to make use of expressions and put forward statements which this party likewise employed, or at any rate could interpret in their own sense; his texts were the ones which they quoted also. But when he became Bishop, and now recognised the necessity of combating Sabellianism also, it was quite natural that the leader of this party should charge him with having formerly

---

[1] ATHANAS. *De decr. Nic. syn.* c. 26, p. 231, in ROUTH, III. 179. Hippolytus and Callistus disputed only about the relation between the Father and the Son; as yet nothing was said respecting the Holy Spirit, whose position and Personality would follow necessarily from that of the Son: if the Son was only a later-produced Being, called into existence by an act of the Father's will, the same would hold of the Holy Ghost. If, on the other hand, the eternal Personality of the Son was saved, the same would result for the third Hypostasis of the Trinity.

used very different language, in that he had emphatically preached the duty of defending the indivisible Unity of the Divine Monad against a system which severed the Logos from this Unity. What here happened to Callistus has happened to the Church itself, whenever it has had successively to combat opposite errors. Thus the Monophysites declared that formerly, in the contest with the Nestorians, the Church had used entirely Monophysite language, etc. etc.

IV. HIPPOLYTUS' CONTRADICTORY ACCOUNTS OF THE DOCTRINE OF CALLISTUS.

Hippolytus did not rest content with general accusations; he described the Trinitarian doctrine of Callistus more exactly as a new heresy invented by him, a heresy into which he had fallen, partly under the pressure of the charges of Sabellius, partly because he found it difficult to develop a doctrine different from that of Hippolytus; for he nevertheless felt that the charge of Ditheism, which he had once publicly made against his opponents, must be supported by a corresponding form of doctrine. But here at the very beginning we must observe that, according to the testimony of Hippolytus, the conduct of Callistus was in the main determined with a view to the doctrine and judgment of other Churches. If he excommunicated Sabellius in order to avoid a reputation among foreign Churches of favouring heresy, it is quite clear that he would not have invented a doctrine which he must have known would be rejected by the Churches collectively as heretical. A man who is scrupulous about even tolerating a false teacher, will certainly not be in the least likely to risk being himself stamped as a heresiarch by adopting and teaching the same doctrine in a slightly altered form. We will, however, consider more closely what Hippolytus says respecting the doctrine of Callistus.

One is at the outset astonished at the unmistakeable contradictions and inaccuracies with which Hippolytus has interspersed his twofold, though in both cases very short, description of Callistus' form of doctrine.

Firstly, Callistus is said to have taught that the Father and the Son are not merely one God, but one single Person; and immediately afterwards the reporter himself mentions that, "in order to avoid blasphemy against the Father,"[1] Callistus expressly declared that the two were not one Person. Therefore the statement about the single Person is merely a deduction, which Hippolytus wished to foist on his adversary.

Secondly, Callistus, as his opponent reports, taught that the visible, *i.e.* the man Jesus, was the Son, and that the Divine Pneuma dwelling in the man, or the Son, was the Father. If we compare the short report in the synopsis in the tenth book, the groundlessness of this charge is evident. For here Callistus teaches that the Son, or the Logos, is in His nature the one God and Creator of the universe, and therefore in His nature one with the Father. This Logos became

---

[1] Οὐ γὰρ θέλει λέγειν τὸν πατέρα πεπονθέναι καὶ ἓν εἶναι πρόσωπον ἐκφυγεῖν τὴν εἰς τὸν πατέρα βλασφημίαν ὁ ἀνόητος καὶ ποικίλος, κ.τ.λ. p. 289. ὥστε is to be supplied before ἐκφυγεῖν. Dr. Wordsworth incorrectly translates, "For he does not like to say that the Father suffered, and *was one Person*, because he shrinks from blasphemy against the Father;" instead of, "and that there is only one Person." Could Callistus possibly have supposed that it was blasphemy to say that the Father is one Person? In a previous passage we read: τὸν λόγον αὐτὸν εἶναι υἱὸν αὐτὸν καὶ πατέρα, ὀνόματι μὲν καλούμενον, ἓν δὲ ὄν, τὸ (ὄντα) πνεῦμα ἀδιαίρετον· οὐκ ἄλλο εἶναι πατέρα, ἄλλο δὲ υἱόν, κ.τ.λ. These last words Dr. Wordsworth renders thus: "and that the Father is not one, and the Son another (Person)," a manifest perversion of the sense. The substantive of ἄλλο in each case is the immediately preceding πνεῦμα. The Father and the Son are not two Pneumata, but only one, is the doctrine of the Church; the Father and the Son are only one single Person, is Sabellianism and heresy.

flesh. Accordingly, the man who even in the Godhead, regarded absolutely and without reference to the Incarnation, distinguished the Father from the Son, *at any rate in name*, who said that it was the Logos, or Son, Who became man,—he cannot at the same time have maintained that the distinction between the Father and the Son is that the Son is the visible man, the Father the indwelling Deity. According to him, the man is taken into the Sonship only by personal union with the Logos; therefore what Callistus said, and what Hippolytus in his irritation has misunderstood and perverted, would be this: Christ, Who in His manhood was visible on the earth, and one day will be so again, is the Son, but the Logos is at the same time essentially one with the Father, the Father dwells in Him; and thus, by the closest essential union with the Logos, the Father dwells also in Christ.

Thirdly, Does the assertion of Hippolytus, that Callistus maintained that the Son or Logos is distinguished from the Father only in name and not in reality, rest upon definite statements of Callistus, or is it merely a deduction drawn by Hippolytus himself? It seems to me clear that the latter is the case. Callistus no doubt said that there was no difference of nature between the Two; he certainly stated this with peculiar emphasis in opposition to Hippolytus, whose doctrine seemed to him necessarily to presuppose or to create a difference of this kind; but that the Father and the Son were distinguished *merely* in Name, he cannot have taught. For he says that the Logos is the One God, the Creator of the universe; and that this Logos is He Who is called the Son; that this Logos became flesh. Consequently, the relation in which God is the Logos or the Son is with him an original one; not (as with Hippolytus) one subsequently produced. While the Noëtians called it a strange and unheard-of thing that the Logos should be called the Son;[1] while Hippolytus taught that God had called His Logos Son only by anticipation, because He was to be born as a man, the unincarnate Logos being not yet truly and perfectly Son,[2]—Callistus notices the relation of the Father to the Son as one existing already in the Divine nature; it was the Logos, or the Son, Who became flesh. Hippolytus does not say here that, according to Callistus, God was called the Son in so far as He became man. But if God is already Logos and Son before the Creation and Incarnation, and independently of these externally manifested acts, then the name "Son" denotes a real and original relation in the Godhead; "Son" cannot be a mere name given to God at pleasure along with others, without expressing any actual fact whatever.

Fourthly, The doctrine of Callistus is said to be a compound of elements, taken half from that of Noëtus and Sabellius, half from that of Theodotus. But even from the partial and highly-coloured account of Hippolytus, one cannot recognise any Theodotian elements in the teaching of Callistus. According to the statement of our informer, Theodotus of Byzantium taught that Jesus was merely a man of extraordinary piety, on whom the Pneuma, named Christ, descended at his baptism in the Jordan, but without His thereby becoming God. According to Hippolytus' account, Callistus taught the opposite of all this: with him God the Logos became man in the Virgin's womb; a mere man Jesus never at any moment existed; and God did not descend upon a full-grown man, but took man's nature and made it Divine by uniting it with Himself.[3]

---

[1] HIPPOL. *Contra Noët.* p. 67.　　　　[2] *L.c.* p. 69.
[3] Τοῦτον τὸν Λόγον ἕνα εἶναι Θεὸν ὀνομάζει καὶ σεσαρκῶσθαι λέγει, p. 330.

After such proofs of incorrect conception and perversion of the truth under the influence of passion, we must go to work critically and inquiringly, and separate the doctrine of Callistus respecting the Trinity from the insinuations and deductions with which Hippolytus has interpolated it.

Callistus, as is clear from the narrative of Hippolytus, developed his theology only in opposition to Sabellius (whom he had excommunicated) on the one side, and to Hippolytus on the other; he wished to avoid Sabellius' confusion of the Father with the Son, and Hippolytus' ditheistic separation of the Logos from God. Accordingly, his teaching respecting the Godhead is as follows: There is One God or Divine Spirit (ἓν πνεῦμα), Who fills all things in heaven and earth with His Presence. This Divine Pneuma is the Father and the Son, Who are in nature the same; nevertheless these are not mere empty titles of the same God, nor yet designations of His different modes of revelation or forms of activity; had Callistus meant this, he must have said with the Noëtians, that God was called Father and Son according to the difference of time (κατὰ χρόνων τροπὴν). Hippolytus strongly charged the party of Cleomenes with this; had he been able to state the same of Callistus, he would certainly not have passed it over in silence.

When, therefore, Hippolytus further makes Callistus say that the same Logos is Son and also Father,[1] we must correct this statement, coloured as it is by the narrator, by a reference to the synopsis: "God is also the Son, but in nature One, for God is not another Pneuma different from the Logos, and the Logos is not different from God;"[2] and in the words

---

[1] Τὸν Λόγον αὐτὸν εἶναι υἱὸν, αὐτὸν καὶ πατέρα, p. 289.

[2] Πνεῦμα γὰρ ὁ Θεὸς οὐχ ἕτερόν ἐστι παρὰ τὸν Λόγον ἢ ὁ Λόγος παρὰ τὸν Θεόν, p. 330.

immediately preceding, it is plainly stated that the One God is Father, and at the same time Son or Logos.¹ The expression, then, which was put into the mouth of Callistus above, is much more likely to have run as follows:—The Logos or Son is not in the Divine nature distinct from the Father; Both are One God. It is remarkable here that Hippolytus once more quotes propositions which after all merely state the pure Catholic doctrine as the peculiar doctrine of Callistus. Thus in the synopsis, after having here also again attributed to his opponent the theory that there is only one single Prosopon,—a theory which, according to Hippolytus' own statement, Callistus rejected,—he continues: "Of this Logos, Callistus says that He is the One God and became flesh." No doubt this is all directed antithetically against Hippolytus; and therefore he quotes it as if it were something peculiar to Callistus. The Bishop of Rome wished to protest against two perilous features in the theology of Hippolytus: *firstly*, the identification of the Father with God to such an extent that the two conceptions exactly coincided, and the Logos came to stand as a later and accidentally-produced Being, merely near and external to the Godhead, as a ἕτερος, as Hippolytus said; *secondly*, as a corollary of the first, the supposition of a second inferior Divine Being, owing His existence to an act of the Father's Will, and destined only for obedience. Hence it is that Callistus so emphatically insists that "God is not another Pneuma beside the Logos;" hence it is that he adds, "for I will not speak of two Gods, but One." He was quite right in condemning the tendency of Hippolytus'

---

¹ That "Son" and "Logos" are synonymous in Callistus, is shown from this very passage by the connection between υἱός and λόγος; after saying that the Father and the Son are One God, in nature One, he adds: *for* God is not a different Pneuma from the Logos. Therefore Logos=Son.

teaching; he saw that in placing the Logos beside God, in making the Logos be produced out of God (Who had long since been existing complete and perfect in Himself) as a Being called into personal existence by an act of the Divine Will, Hippolytus rendered Ditheism or (if the Holy Spirit were included) Tritheism inevitable. Accordingly, Callistus declared, what the later Fathers of the Church also acknowledged, that the Father as such is not God, for otherwise of necessity there would be no longer any room in the Godhead for the Logos; the idea of the Godhead being already filled by the Father alone, and the Father being the whole or totality of the Godhead (τὸ δὲ πᾶν πατὴρ), the Logos could only appear as a second God side by side with the first.[1]

What Callistus further insists upon, and always in direct opposition to the views of Hippolytus, is the inseparable union and unity of the Father and the Son. Here he appeals to the words of Christ (S. John xiv. 11), "Believest thou not that I am in the Father, and the Father in me?" The Father dwells in the Son; being in Him, He took flesh, and by uniting it with Himself made it Divine.[2] This representation of the mutual indwelling (περιχώρησις) of the Divine Persons, which the Fathers since the Arian times have carefully developed, is very much to be noted in Callistus; properly considered, it alone is sufficient to show that he kept clear of all Sabellian confusion. "The Father, Who is or dwells in the Son;"—is it

---

[1] *Contra Noët.* c. 11, p. 62. On the other hand GREGORY OF NYSSA says (*Lib. de comm. notion.* I. p. 915): Οὐ γὰρ καθὸ τὴν ἑτερότητα (His distinct Personality) σώζει πατὴρ πρὸς υἱόν, κατὰ τοῦτο Θεὸς ὁ πατήρ· οὕτω γὰρ οὐκ ἂν Θεὸς ὁ υἱός· εἰ γὰρ ἐπεὶ πατὴρ ὁ πατήρ, διὰ τοῦτο καὶ Θεὸς ὁ πατήρ· ἐπεὶ μὴ πατὴρ ὁ υἱός, οὐ Θεὸς ὁ υἱός, κ.τ.λ. He might also have said, in that case the Son would be either not God, or a second God beside the first.

[2] Ὁ γὰρ ἐν αὐτῷ (υἱῷ) γενόμενος πατήρ, προσλαβόμενος τὴν σάρκα ἐθεοποίησεν ἑνώσας ἑαυτῷ, p. 289.

conceivable even that Sabellius or Noëtus should express themselves thus? Only those could do so who distinguished the Father and the Son as two Persons or subjects, and did not consider them to be merely successive and various ways in which God has revealed Himself.[1]

When, therefore, Callistus said that the Father, dwelling or existing in the Son, took man's nature, he presupposed the Incarnation of the Son *per se;* but at the same time wished to indicate the union of the Father with the Son as so intimate, that the Father became man at the same time with or in the Son, and therefore suffered also with the Son, on account of this impossibility of separation. Praxeas used the same expression with regard to the suffering,[2] but with him it has a different meaning; for with him God is the Son only in relation to the body or human substance. Therefore, in his case, "the Father suffered with the Son" means merely that the suffering, which in the first instance affected only the human body, reached the Godhead also, which formed the soul of this body. Callistus says, on the other hand: the Logos became flesh;[3] but the Father dwells in the Logos, and all that the Logos or the Son does and suffers, the Father does and suffers also; therefore the Father in and through the Son took part in the Incarnation and the Passion.

Without doubt it was precisely upon the Incarnation and Passion that Hippolytus had laid stress, in order to make it palpably necessary that, although the Logos was of the Substance of God, yet He must

---

[1] Thus CYRIL OF ALEXANDRIA also remarks, that the words of Christ, S. John xiv. 10, on the one side express the identity of the Godhead, and the oneness of nature in the Father and the Son; on the other side: διὰ τὸ ἕτερον ἐν ἑτέρῳ εἶναι, μὴ ἕν τι ὂν ἐν ἀριθμῷ νοηθῇ. *Thesaur. de Trin., Opp.* V. 109.

[2] *Compassus est Pater Filio.* TERTULL. *Adv. Prax.* c. 29.

[3] Τοῦτον τὸν λόγον . . . σεσαρκῶσθαι λέγει, p. 330.

be conceived as being subordinate to the Father or God, a Being nearer or nearest to God. For this reason it was thought that Callistus placed both, even in reference to the οἰκονομία, in such close connection; and he was thus brought to the view which the later Fathers (on the strength of this same passage, S. John xiv. 10) afterwards developed still further, that each Person imparts His properties to the other two Persons, and that the three Persons are so united as to do all things in common.[1]

Two remarks force themselves upon us here in considering this memorable contest in the Church of Rome. Hippolytus, as we have seen, charged the Churches in communion with Callistus with having introduced the practice of rebaptizing (*i.e.* heretics who went over to them). The African Church was the one specially intended. In the lively and uninterrupted intercourse between the Roman and African Churches, it is impossible that the latter had not taken careful notice of the continual disputes and divisions in the former, especially as these had reference to the most sacred dogma of the Christian faith. Owing to the appearance of Praxeas, who had tendered his recantation to the Church of Carthage, the Africans were already acquainted with these disputed points; and they were now compelled to declare for the one side or the other. That along with the communion of Callistus they also

---

[1] So especially JOHN OF DAMASCUS, III. 4 : καὶ οὗτός ἐστιν ὁ τρόπος τῆς ἀντιδόσεως, ἑκατέρας φύσεως ἀντιδιδούσης τῇ ἑτέρᾳ τὰ ἴδια, διὰ τὴν τῆς ὑποστάσεως ταυτότητα, καὶ τὴν εἰς ἄλληλα αὐτῶν περιχώρησιν. And in the following chapter he says that the Persons are united in their nature and natural *idiomata* : καὶ τῷ μὴ διΐστασθαι μηδὲ ἐκφοιτᾷν τῆς πατρικῆς ὑποστάσεως. GREGORY OF NYSSA expresses the union and entire community of activity still more strongly : οὔτε γὰρ χρόνῳ διαιρεῖται ἀλλήλων τὰ πρόσωπα τῆς θεότητος, οὔτε τόπῳ, οὐ βουλῇ, οὐκ ἐπιτηδεύματι, οὐκ ἐνεργείᾳ, οὐ πάθει, οὐδενὶ τῶν τοιούτων, οἱάπερ θεωρεῖται ἐπὶ τῶν ἀνθρώπων. De comm. not., Opp. ed. Paris 1638, II. p. 85. [See the *Report of the Reunion Conference at Bonn*, 1875, pp. 11-15, 68, 69, and *passim*; Pickering, 1876.]

accepted the doctrine with which he opposed Hippolytus, is clear. Are we, then, to believe that the African Churches changed their doctrine respecting the Trinity between one day and another, like a coat?

Again, if in the Church, which by its superior grandeur, antiquity, and dignity formed the centre of the whole Christian world, to which all directed their eyes, with which all held communion and intercourse,[1] —if in this Church a heresy denying the Divine Personality of Christ had been favoured under Zephyrinus, and become triumphant under Callistus, how are we to explain the fact that, although the dissension remained confined to Rome, yet outside Rome also, at any rate in the majority of Churches, Callistus and not Hippolytus was recognised? that in all lists of the Bishops of Rome, Greek as well as Latin, Callistus only is named, although he held fast to his doctrine till his death? Hippolytus says expressly that the *didascalia* of Callistus, his form of doctrine, was published throughout the world, *i.e.* the whole Church far and wide had become acquainted with the dissension between him and Callistus;[2] and that other Bishops and Churches neither could nor would remain neutral spectators, every one who has any idea of the primitive Church and its disposition knows. All who came to Rome from other Churches during the schism would be compelled at once to decide to which congregation they would belong,—whether they would receive the holy communion with the party of Hippolytus, or in one of the churches of Callistus. When Novatian's schism afterwards broke out in Rome, it forthwith blazed forth in the most different parts of the Church in Gaul, and again in the East; and not until the year 254 did Dionysius of Alexandria announce to Stephen,

---

[1] Irenæus, *Adv. hær.* III. 3, 2.   [2] P. 292.

Bishop of Rome, that the Churches in the East, hitherto divided by Novatianism, were once more in unity and peace. If, then, thirty years earlier, when Hippolytus separated from Callistus, the great majority of Bishops and Churches remained on the side of Callistus, because they held him to be orthodox, and recognised their own doctrine in his,—then all is easily explained. The schism lasted only till the time of Pontianus,—that is to say, for about fifteen or sixteen years,—and as Hippolytus himself to all appearance abandoned his separate position before his death, the schism died out without leaving a trace behind. Hippolytus' teaching respecting the Trinity contained nothing calculated to render it specially popular: it bore too much the character of a mere composition of discordant elements, and of a transitional stage that must lead to a further development, to find many who would care to plant it as the standard of a particular sect,—although at that time many, as to some extent Origen and perhaps also Tertullian, might feel themselves more akin to him than to Callistus.

But if, on the other hand, we were obliged (with Dr. Wordsworth) to suppose that Callistus was really a teacher of Sabellianism, while Hippolytus was regarded by contemporary Bishops and Christians as a defender of the Church's orthodoxy, then certainly everything becomes inexplicable. The matter causes great excitement in the whole Church, as Hippolytus says; Alcibiades, a Syrian, on hearing the fame of it, comes from Assamea to Rome; but after all nothing is done. No Synod is held; no serious attempt is made to bring the Bishop of Rome to a better mind, or to depose him. The "school" of Callistus maintains itself even after his death, and continues to hold fast his doctrine ($\pi\alpha\rho\acute{\alpha}\delta o\sigma\iota\varsigma$); and once more we meet no trace of other Churches ceasing to hold communion with its members.

And more than this. Some thirty years after the death of Callistus, NOVATIAN's book on the Trinity appears. Its author lived in Rome, writes there; mentions, moreover, the Sabellian heresy with disapproval in no measured terms, and controverts it in passing. But he describes it only briefly, by stating that it made Jesus Christ to be the Father; and he never gives the faintest indication that this false doctrine, or one closely akin to it, had been so powerful only a short time before in Rome, had been favoured by the Bishop, taught publicly by others, and had won the acceptance of the majority in the Roman Church: his arguments are directed towards a totally different quarter, viz. against those who made Christ a mere man. On the above supposition this would be all the more incomprehensible, inasmuch as Novatian really exhibits an unmistakable relationship to Hippolytus' form of teaching. With him also the Father is the one God; the Son has His divinity as a gift, a present, from the Father; He was once in the Father, and when it pleased the Father the Son went out from Him; the time of His production depended on His Father's Will; by His obedient subjection to this Will He exhibits the unity of God; and the power of the Godhead, sent out from the Father alone, and conferred upon the Son, gradually returns to the Father.[1] Thus with Novatian also the unity of God was rather postulated than really maintained, and one can understand how the Macedonians in Constantinople delighted in making use of this work.[2]

Let us now consider that between the time in which the supposed heretical "school" of Callistus was still

---

[1] NOVAT. *De regula fidei*, ed. Jackson, Lond. 1728, c. 22, p. 176; c. 31, pp. 238, 240.

[2] HIERONYMI, *Apol. contra Rufin.*, *Op.* IV. 416.

existing in Rome, and the appearance of this book, there lay at the very outside twenty years, and it will be transparent that the heresy which denied the Divine Personality cannot possibly have been dominant in Rome only a short time before. Novatian, in whose time the remembrance of that contest was certainly fresh and lively, would have devoted more pains and attention to a heresy which had been vanquished only a few years before, and, of course, only after recent contests and efforts; he would have mentioned persons and events; whereas he directs the point of his polemics altogether in the opposite direction.

V. A SIXTH CENTURY ACCOUNT OF THE DISPUTE BETWEEN HIPPOLYTUS AND CALLISTUS.

Let us now consider somewhat more closely that old report which has been already mentioned: hitherto unnoticed and uncomprehended, it has light thrown upon it for the first time by the narrative of Hippolytus. It was in the time of those disturbances and commotions which invaded the Roman Church at the beginning of the sixth century, when a strong party set up a rival to Pope Symmachus in the person of Laurentius, and the Arian king of the Goths, Theodoric, seized the opportunity of interfering in the internal affairs of the Roman Church, and making the Popes dependent on himself,—it was at this time that a member of the Roman clergy, whom Coustant, on account of his barbarous style, considers to be of Gothic origin, forged certain documents to support the proposition that the Pope cannot be judged by any earthly power, and at the same time do something for the position of Presbyters of Rome. The perpetrator of these forgeries incorporated one or two earlier events or legends in his work; thus, in the mythical Synod of Sinuessa, the legend, which had been in earlier times circulated by the Donatists, that in the persecution of Diocletian, Marcellinus, Bishop of Rome, had sacrificed to idols;[1] and again, in the Acts of a supposed Synod at Rome under Pope Sylvester, he has inserted a note referring to the dispute between Callistus and Hippolytus; for at his time a recollection of this still lived on somewhere in Rome, but so disfigured and fragmentary that neither the time at which the events occurred, nor the persons who took part in them, were any longer recognisable. Who Callistus (whom he makes to be condemned by Sylvester) was, he evidently did not know; but the accusation made against him he gives correctly—Sabellianism. That he in one place says that Callistus admitted only one Person in the Trinity, and in another that he had divided the Trinity, is only one of the signs of clumsiness and ignorance which recur throughout the whole document.[2] In the case of Hippolytus, also,

[1] [See Dr. DÖLLINGER'S *Fables respecting the Popes,* p. 79, Rivingtons, 1871, where the contents and origin of this very ancient ecclesiastical legend are critically examined.]

[2] The passage runs thus: *Cognitum loquor, et probo Calistum et Victorinum, qui arbitrio suo fecerunt creaturam, et Jovianum, qui in sua extollentia dicebat Pascha non venire die suo nec mense, sed X. Kalendas Maias custodire.* (Here, without doubt, the right reading is that given by Coustant in the note: *Calistum et Hippolytum, qui arbitrio suo fecerunt creaturam, et Victorinum, qui,* etc. This is required, moreover, by the introductory *Titulus canonum,* which runs: *De condemnatione Calisti, Victorini, Hippolyti.*) *Ego enim, sicut lex memorat, in vestro judicio commendo sermonem; ut introducantur hi tres quidem; primo arbitrio (f. arbitror) Calistum damnari; corroboretur examen. Qui se Calistus ita docuit Sabellianum, ut arbitrio suo sumat unam personam esse Trinitatis, non enim coæquante Patre et Filio et Spirito sancto. Victorinum itaque præcipue præsul regionis antistes* (Coustant thinks *præcipue damnandum*), *qui in sua ferocitate quidquid vellet affirmabat hominibus, et cyclos paschæ pronunciabat fallaces; ut hoc quod constituit X. Kalendas Maji custodiri, vestro sermone, sicut veritas habet, cassetur, et nostro judicio condemnetur, et filiorum nostrorum Augustorum præcurrat auctoritus condemnandum Victorinum episcopum. Et introierunt omnes, ut suo sermone damnarentur judicio. Damnavit autem Hippolytum diaconum Valentinianistam, et Calistum, qui in sua extollentia separabat Trinitatem, et Victorinum episcopum, qui ignorans lunæ rationem, sub arbitrio (arbitrii) sui tenacitate disrumpebat veritatem. Et præsentia*

he did not know that he was a Presbyter, and accordingly mentions him as a Deacon; why he makes him to be accused and condemned as a Valentinian, has been already discussed.

But who is Victorinus, who is condemned along with Callistus and Hippolytus, yet not on account of his teaching respecting the Trinity, but on account of an interference with the Easter-cycle? Coustant, to whom the other two names are quite strange,[1] thinks that in Victorinus he recognises Victorius of Aquitaine, who in 457 constructed an Easter-cycle which was afterwards much disputed. One must freely admit that the clumsy caprice of the author of these fictions renders it altogether credible that he has brought a man of the 5th century into conjunction with two personages of the second century. Probable, however, it is not, when one considers that at the time when this document was composed Victorius had been dead at the most forty years, and that therefore there must certainly have been persons still living in Rome who had known him; further, that the opposition to his cycle did not arise till a good deal later,—Victor of Capua first wrote against it in 550. Moreover, in this document, Victorinus appears, not as the author of a cycle of his own, but as the impugner of the cycle of others. It appears to me, therefore, much more natural to suppose that this Victorinus is the one mentioned by the author of the *Libellus* of heresies, and by no one else.[2] He must

episcoporum supradictorum, et presbyterorum aliorumque graduum damnavit Hippolytum, Victorinum, et Calistum, et dedit eis anathema, et damnavit eos extra urbes suas.

[1] *Ignota ecclesiasticis in monumentis nomina*, are his words, Appendix, p. 42. Baronius had long ago remarked (a. 324, n. 126): *Quisnam autem hic fuerit, qui damnatus in hoc Rom. concilio est, Victorinus, ignoratur; sicut Hippolytus et Callistus hæretici.*

[2] P. 168, ed. Routh: *Praxeas quidam hæresim introduxit, quam Victorinus corroborare curavit*, etc. [As already noticed, some would read Victor, others Zephyrinus, for Victorinus. But see p. 306.]

have been a contemporary of Hippolytus and Callistus, and have lived in Rome. I have already remarked that the *Libellus*, when it has anything peculiar, betrays its Roman origin; and the connection into which it brings Victorinus with Praxeas also argues Rome as the locality. He may have been connected with Cleomenes and Sabellius, and one of the προστάται of the Noëtian sect mentioned by Hippolytus: he seems to have maintained Patripassianism in a most coarse form, even to the extent of saying that the Father now sits at His own right hand. But in this place he is introduced merely as an impugner of the Easter-cycle, who maintained that Easter must be kept on the 22d of April. If my conjecture, that this Victorinus lived in Rome at the beginning of the third century, is correct, then beyond a doubt the cycle of Hippolytus is the one meant; for even if this cycle was not, as Isidore maintains, the very first that was constructed in the Church, it was at any rate at that time the only one in Rome and in the West, and was used as a basis still later even by Eusebius of Cæsarea. This, then, was the cycle which Victorinus attacked; but what he wished about the 22d of April (supposing that the text is right) is less clear. Did he wish that the Feast should not be a moveable one, but always be celebrated on the 22d day of the month of April? Or did he wish that, as the 21st of April was the extreme limit for Easter Sunday in the sixteen-years cycle of Hippolytus, Easter should be allowed to fall still later. In any case one may safely suppose that the dispute between him and Hippolytus was not respecting the Easter question alone, but also respecting the Trinity as well, although that is not here mentioned.

From the spurious so-called *Constitutum Sylvestri* the subject passed into the later lists of the Popes, but in a form scarcely recognisable. Arius and Photinus took the place of Hippolytus and Victorinus, although Sylvester could not know anything of the future heresy of Photinus. Callistus, however, or Calixtus, was retained.[1]

VI. THE PROBABLE END OF THE SCHISM.

That the division in the Roman Church, to which the dispute between Callistus and Hippolytus led, lasted till the time of Pontianus; that both leaders, Hippolytus and Pontianus, were banished to Sardinia in 235, and that there a reconciliation ensued through the resignation of both and the consequent election of Anteros in Rome, I have endeavoured thus far to establish. The statement that the successor of Anteros, Fabianus, caused the body of Pontianus to be brought back from Sardinia and solemnly buried in the cemetery of Callistus, is not indeed found in the chronographer of 354, but in the second Catalogue of the Popes, which reaches down to Felix IV., and was made in the sixth century. It is doubtless but a weak authority, for in other places it contains much that is fabulous, and its authorities are often fictions or impure sources. This statement, however, we may believe;[2] for in the deposition of martyrs as given by the chronographer of 364, it is stated that Pontianus was deposited in the cemetery of Callistus, as Hippolytus in the Tiburtina. The body of Pontianus, therefore, was brought back from Sardinia, and that this took place under Fabianus,

---

[1] See the texts of the Catalogue of the Popes in SCHELSTRATE, *Antiq. Eccl.* I. 446, 447. In the first we read: *Damnavit Calixtum et Arrium et Fotinum.* In the *Liber. Pontif.* ed Vignoli, I. 81: *Et damnavit iterum Arrium, Callistum et Photinum et Sabellium et sequaces eorum.*

[2] The date, however, deserves no credit (*die depositionis ejus ab XI. Kal. Decembris*), for this is manifestly a confusion; it is the date given by the chronographer of 354 and the *Liber Pontificalis* for the ordination of Anteros.

independently of evidence, is the most natural supposition. Now we know for certain that in the middle of the fourth century the *depositio* of the two, Pontianus and Hippolytus, although their resting-places were in totally different places, was celebrated on the same day, the 13th of August; and in the oldest collection of Roman liturgies that has come down to us, a *Natale Sanctorum Hippolyti et Pontiani*, with the special prayers for it in the Mass, is given on this very day.[1] Thus it becomes at least highly probable that Hippolytus also died in Sardinia, that his body was brought back to Rome with that of Pontianus, and that the burial of both took place on the same day, although in different places. That he was not buried with Pontianus in the cemetery of Callistus seems to have been because this spot was specially set apart as the resting-place of Bishops of Rome, as one sees from both the lists of depositions given by the chronographer; and people were unwilling to lend the appearance of a confirmation to the claims made by Hippolytus in his lifetime, by bringing him after his death into the company of lawful Bishops.

Thus in the 3d and 4th centuries the 13th of August was kept in memory of both men, and no doubt also in thankful remembrance of the happy conclusion of the schism. Soon after the beginning of the 5th century, however, this seems to have been changed. The

---

[1] [It is to be noted that *depositio*, though sometimes used of entombment, more commonly indicates the day of death, the day on which the soul *lays down* the burden of the flesh. Thus it would be an obvious synonym for *natale*, which commonly means the day of a saint's death. Another instance of these two words being used as synonymous occurs on March 21st, on which day the martyrology of Jerome has *Depositio Benedicti Abbatis*, while that of Bede has *Natale Benedicti Abbatis*. It appears that *depositio* is more usual of Bishops, *natale natalitium* of martyrs; and that no festival of a Bishop or other canonized person appears in any calendar before A.D. 400. SMITH and CHEETHAM, *Dict. of Christ. Ant.* articles CALENDAR and DEPOSITION.]

recollection of the true history of the two men had been lost all the more easily, inasmuch as the special prayers for the Mass on their festival spoke only quite generally of martyrs, without any special characteristics. And so Pontianus disappeared altogether from the liturgies, and Hippolytus, as we have seen, was brought by the myth into connection with S. Lawrence, who like him was buried in the Tiburtina. Prudentius gives us the legend of Hippolytus in a state of transition from history to inventive myth. His saint is, so to speak, half the converted and reconciled rigorist schismatic, half the mangled martyr of the later S. Lawrence legend. A similar relation is exhibited in the liturgical collection called the *Sacramentarium Leonianum*. Between the prayers belonging to the day kept in joint remembrance of Pontianus and Hippolytus a preface of later origin has been inserted, in which Pontianus is no longer remembered, and Hippolytus is known only as the Roman warrior converted by S. Lawrence. This mixture of dissimilar elements, some earlier and some later, need not surprise us; it is frequent in this collection. According to all appearances this *Sacramentarium* is, as the Ballerini[1] have remarked, the first larger collection of this kind, put together by some ecclesiastic in Rome towards the end of the 5th century. He took, it appears, what he found ready to hand in the different Roman churches, often mere fragments or isolated portions, and thus sometimes put together things that had no connection, or joined ancient and recent in one. Thus on the 14th of September, in the mass of SS. Cornelius and Cyprian, he has inserted a preface of S. Euphemia; and an *oratio* referring to Pope Simplicius has found its way into the Mass for the festival of S. Sylvester.

[1] *Opera S. Leonis*, II. præf. p. x.

The memory of Callistus has always been held in high honour in the Roman Church. The cemetery of which he had had the care,[1] the greatest and most celebrated of the Roman precincts, henceforward bore his name; and in the *depositio* of martyrs in the chronographer of 354, the oldest memorial of this kind in the Roman Church, he already has a place, and moreover, among the Bishops of Rome named here and in the *depositio* of the Bishops, he is the earliest. This is the more important, because, as Mommsen has remarked, the list apparently bears an official character, and the annotations begin with Callistus. His being placed among the martyrs is on account of his former banishment to Sardinia. In the older missals, the Gregorian in Muratori and the Lateran edited by Azevedo, he is not as yet designated as a martyr,—in the latter merely as a confessor, according to the distinction which arose afterwards.[2] The later martyrologies, it is true, mention him as a martyr, and to some extent give particulars of his martyrdom; but in this they draw their materials from spurious and utterly worthless *Acts*.

Hippolytus mentions further, that the "school" which retained the tendencies and doctrines of Callistus received the name of *Callistians*,—that is to say, the Roman Church remaining in communion with its

---

[1] [The earliest instance of the term cemetery is perhaps the passage in the *Philosophumena* (ix. 7) in which Hippolytus tells us that Zephyrinus "set" Callistus "over the cemetery"—εἰς τὸ κοιμητήριον κατέστησεν, an expression which shows that the term is already familiar among Christians. To pagans it was strange (though perhaps not "hardly intelligible"), as the phrase τὰ καλούμενα κοιμητήρια, occurring more than once in edicts respecting the Christians, indicates. *Dict. of Christ. Ant.* article CEMETERY.]

[2] *Vetus Missale Rom.*, Romæ 1754, p. 280: *Beato Callisto Confessore tuo et Pontifice suffragante.* The MS. which is the original of this missal is not earlier than the 11th century; but it is remarkable that the false *Acts* of Callistus, which were invented at a much earlier date, have exercised no influence upon it.

Bishop Callistus and his followers. It was from this that the comparatively small handful of Hippolytians had separated as forming the pure and spotless Church, which knew well how to discern with whom one ought to enter into communion, *i.e.* not with Callistians, nor with such as had been guilty of mortal sins; whereas those of the *didascaleion*, those of the school of Callistus, who "had the face to call themselves the Catholic Church," offered communion to all alike, if only they accepted the conditions of penance to be undergone, and similar doctrine.

It need scarcely be said that the name Callistians is found nowhere else; it was adopted only among the party of Hippolytus, which survived only for about fifteen years, and even in this period had no increase worth mentioning. The case is just similar to the name of *Cornelians*, which the Novatians afterwards gave to the Catholics;[1] and the designation of *Athanasians*, by means of which the Arians thought to degrade the confessors of the Nicene doctrine into a sect; or the appellation of Cyrillians, which was applied by the Nestorians to the Catholics.[2]

VII. HIPPOLYTUS' RELATION TO ORIGEN.

That ORIGEN and HIPPOLYTUS were closely related is what we might have expected. Origen, with his thirst for knowledge and his burning zeal for religion, was not the man to miss an opportunity of becoming personally acquainted with any of the few learned and intellectually eminent men which the Church of his day possessed, or of gaining instruction from intercourse with them. But, besides his master Clement, and per-

---

[1] EULOGIUS, ap. Photium, *cod.* 280, p. 1622.

[2] See the Acts of the Council of Ephesus, *Concil. coll.* ed. Labbé, III. p. 746.

haps Julius Africanus, Hippolytus was the only person who came into consideration as a learned theologian: to converse with him, the disciple of S. Irenæus, must have been singularly attractive to the younger Origen. The wish to have a close acquaintance with the Roman Church brought him to Rome in the time of Zephyrinus, somewhere about the year 217; the desire of making the acquaintance of Hippolytus, whose reputation was certainly already a wide one, may have helped to bring him. The Alexandrian, although still a young man of about thirty years of age,—he was born in 185,—was already a celebrated teacher himself; no less than seven of his pupils had suffered a martyr's death in the persecution of Severus. Now, seeing that in a homily in praise of our Lord, Hippolytus has mentioned the fact that Origen was then present, we may with good reason suppose that this took place at that time in Rome. Similarity of pursuits must have bound the two men still more closely together. Hippolytus was the first Christian theologian who attempted detailed explanations of books of the Old Testament. Origen directed a large portion of his life to the same object; and thus in the whole Church there certainly was no other man with whom it would have been of greater importance for Origen to remain in continual intercourse than the Roman Presbyter. Apparently it was from Hippolytus, or a disciple of his from Rome, that Origen obtained the information respecting the Elchasaites which he made public in a homily delivered before his congregation.

In Rome, Origen must have been a witness of the differences in which Hippolytus was already involved with Zephyrinus and Callistus. The subsequent events and the position taken by Hippolytus were certainly not unknown to him, and did not fail to arouse his sympathies. It seems to me all but certain that he sided with Hippolytus against Callistus. The following points may be noted.

Firstly, Origen (at any rate at his earlier period) shared the rigorist principles of Hippolytus respecting penance and the forgiveness of sins; indeed, he expresses himself in such a way that one easily recognises in it a criticism on Callistus or his followers.[1] "There are certain people who, I know not how, assume to themselves what transcends the power of a Bishop, possibly because they have no knowledge even of what a Bishop should know; they boast that they can forgive idolatry, can remit the sins of adultery and fornication, as if even sins unto death could be absolved through their prayer for such as commit such things."[2]

Secondly, Origen speaks with special dislike of Bishops of the large town, who in their proud exaltation would not allow even the best members of the Church to speak freely with them.[3] Now it is quite true that we do not find exactly this charge among those which Hippolytus heaps so liberally upon the head of Callistus; and it is quite likely that Origen may have had his own Bishop Demetrius primarily in view. But soon afterwards the Alexandrian speaks of Bishops and Priests to whom "the uppermost seats" (πρωτοκαθεδρίαι) were entrusted, and who made over whole Churches to unfit persons, who made improper men rulers (ἄρχοντας). This, then, comes very near to the

---

[1] *De orat.* 28, ed. de la Rue, I. 256.

[2] Later on, no doubt (in 248 or 249, when he wrote against Celsus, a work which, according to Eusebius, belongs to this time) he says nothing of a perpetual excommunication of grievous sinners, but testifies that it is the universal custom of the Church to receive the fallen again after long penance. *Contra Celsum*, 3. 51, *Op.* I. 481. Had he meanwhile changed his opinion? Or are we to suppose that, besides the sins described by him as pardonable, which he does not define more exactly (τοὺς ὑπ' ἀσελγείας ἤ τινος ἀτόπου νενικημένους), there are still the most grievous—idolatry, adultery, etc.—ever excluded from being pardonable?

[3] *Comm. in Matt.*, *Op.* III. 723.

complaints against Callistus mentioned above. On the death of Callistus, Origen was thirty-seven years old. One cannot of course build anything certain on this passage, for here again experiences which he had in Egypt, or in the eastern provinces, may have passed before his mind.

Thirdly, Origen's teaching respecting the Trinity certainly comes much nearer to the truth than that set forth by Hippolytus. With Origen the generation of the Son is eternal and everlasting, and he took great pains to lay due emphasis upon the personal pre-existence of the Logos (no doubt in close connection with his idea of a similarly eternal creation). But, nevertheless, his system of subordination betrayed him into saying things respecting the relation of the Son to the Father which bring him very near to the errors of Hippolytus, and which (after all softenings and apologies made for them by defenders of the great man in ancient and modern times[1]) still remain inadmissible. He places the Son far below the Father, who is the one Supreme God; he maintains that Christians rise even above the Son up to the Father. With him the Son is in fact not very God of the Substance of the Father; He has only a dependent divinity, requiring perpetual sustenance from the Fount-Head, the Father. The Son, he says, would not remain God if He did not remain in unbroken contemplation of the profundity of the Father.[2] The Father, who with Origen, as with Hippolytus, realizes in Himself the whole idea of the Godhead, imparts a portion of His Nature, that, viz. which is communicable; but retains the remainder, the inmost and highest attributes of the Divine Nature, for Himself. Through this communication, which is at once an act of the Divine Will (though not an arbitrary one), and also the hypostatizing of it, *i.e.* of the

[1] [See note at the end of this chapter.]   [2] *In Joh.* t. 2. 2, *Op.* IV. 51.

personified Will of the Father, the Son has His origin, and He again communicates what was given to Him to other beings. Origen says "gods;" he means the *numina* of the stars and the angels set over various nations. It is in this way, no doubt, that we can explain how he distinguished four classes of men in reference to their knowledge and veneration of the Deity. The first is of those who had the Supreme God of the universe as their God; the second is of those who did not advance beyond the Son of God, His Christ; the third, the star-worshippers; the fourth composed of those who pray to things which are not gods at all, *i.e.* the grossest idolaters.[1]

Now it is true that all this appears again less strongly expressed in many passages of this great and gifted man, who *in intellect, profundity, and penetrating insight was far superior to Hippolytus*. Origen would allow no division of the Divine Substance; he would certainly have answered the question, whether the Son has all divine perfection, in the affirmative. It is by a sort of doubling of the Divine Substance that he explains the existence of the Son; but for this very reason he also does not hesitate to speak of a δεύτερος Θεός, a second God; hence, again, the Father's self-consciousness is different from and higher than that of the Son, and he frequently makes use of the comparison that the Father is as much above the Son as the Son is above the world. And thus with him also the Son is the instrument of the Father, the latter being the Ruler, the former the subject fulfilling His commands.[2]

Origen, therefore, certainly avoided that grievous

---

[1] *L.c.* p. 52.

[2] Polemical zeal against Sabellianism, which partly influenced Hippolytus, has been adduced by way of excuse for Origen also, who is thought to have been seduced thereby too far in the opposite direction. Thus argues the anonymous apologist in Photius, cod. 117, p. 295, ed. Rothomag.

error of Hippolytus, that the Father once existed without the Son, the Son being produced afterwards by an arbitrary act of the Divine Will; but, nevertheless, the practical common sense of a Callistus, had he been better acquainted with his doctrine, would doubtless not have shrunk from charging him also with Ditheism, though of a more subtle and less patent kind. The excommunicated Hippolytus might have cried to Origen, as Abelard afterwards to Gilbert of La Porée:

"Tunc tua res agitur, paries cum proximus ardet."

In the year 231 or 232, when Origen had been condemned, deposed, and excommunicated by two Synods at Alexandria, a Synod was also held against him at Rome; therefore under Pontianus, at a time when the schism of Hippolytus still continued. "Rome assembled her Senate against him," says Jerome in a passage in his letter to Paula.[1] But when he adds that Origen was condemned not on account of new doctrines or heretical opinions, but because people found the splendour of his eloquence and learning intolerable, he is certainly not correct; his doctrine also was certainly in question. But one thing is surprising, that the case of a Presbyter belonging to another Church should be made the subject of discussion at a Roman Synod, specially summoned for the purpose. According to the usual practice, the simple adoption and ratification by the Bishop of Rome of the sentence pronounced at Alexandria would have sufficed; it must, therefore, have been that Origen himself had appealed to Rome. But a still more probable hypothesis is, that Origen in some way or other had taken part in the disputes in Rome, perhaps by siding with Hippolytus' party against Callistus and his successor, and that Pontianus had

---

[1] *Invectiv.* in Hieronymi Op., ed. Martianay, IV. 430.

consequently in a special Synod pronounced a condemnation of his doctrine as well as of his conduct. This probability is increased by the fact that Origen said nothing about this Roman condemnation at the time; and not until the time of Pontianus' successor, Fabianus (236–249), that is, several years later, when the Hippolytus schism was already at an end, did he put out a defence of himself.[1]

One more point may here be noticed. Firmilian of Cæsarea was the zealous pupil and devoted friend of Origen; he invited him to stay with him in Cappadocia, and again spent a considerable time with him in Palestine. The letter which he later on sent to Cyprian in the controversy about the baptism of heretics goes beyond all bounds, and is full of bitterness and animosity against Stephen and the Roman Church.[2] May not the attitude taken by this Church in the matter of Origen have been one main cause of this bitterness?

The historically very important question, whether among the Alexandrian Bishops Demetrius alone was an opponent of Origen, or whether Heraclas also contended against him and his doctrine, has for a long time been left undiscussed. It is accepted as ascertained that only Demetrius treated Origen as an enemy, and drove him out of Alexandria, and this not so much on account of his doctrine as on account of his foreign ordination and the well-known strange act of his youth. And yet there has been ready at hand evidence by no means unimportant to show that under Heraclas the controversy in Alexandria broke out afresh, and that this Bishop also raised himself against his former teacher and his doctrines.

[1] EUSEBIUS, vi. 26. HIERONYMI, *Epist.* 65, *ad Pammach.* c. 4.
[2] MOSHEIM calls it *Epistola fellis plena et præter modum acerba. Comm. de rebus Christ.* p. 539.

Theophilus, Bishop of Alexandria, had appealed[1] to the fact that Heraclas expelled Origen from the Presbytery and from communion, and compelled him to withdraw from Alexandria. This was stated in the synodal letter of a Council of Egyptian Bishops apparently held under Theophilus;[2] it is confirmed by the anonymous biographer of S. Pachomius;[3] and still more important is the confirmation implied in the statement of Eusebius, that Origen, shortly before the persecution under Maximinus, in the second year after the elevation of Heraclas, again migrated from Alexandria to Cæsarea in Palestine.[4]

But Eusebius and Jerome know nothing of a quarrel between Origen and Heraclas; and was it likely that the latter, who for thirty years had been the pupil of the great theologian,—he whom Origen himself had chosen as coadjutor in the catechetical school,—would as Bishop come forward as the enemy of his honoured master?

The silence of Eusebius, however, is not of the very slightest moment: as a zealous disciple of Origen, he

---

[1] This is shown by GENNADIUS, *De vir. ill.* c. 33.

[2] Quoted by Justinian in his letter to Mennas. Harduin. III. 263. In the same letter Peter of Alexandria is also quoted as mentioning the severe attacks which his predecessors, Demetrius and Heraclas, had endured at the hands of Origen, p. 258.

[3] *Acta S.S.* May 14, sec. 21, p. 20.

[4] This statement is not found in the *Ecclesiastical History* of Eusebius, where he would have been obliged to say something respecting the causes of this strange new wandering abroad, and this he preferred to leave unsaid; but it no doubt occurred in his chronicle; and that it was there in the Greek original also is shown by Syncellus, who has the same. See *Scriptor. vet. nova Coll.* ed. Maius, viii. 392. Modern writers who have written about Origen have taken no notice of it, apparently because they considered it erroneous. REDEPENNING maintains (*Origenes*, I. p. 413) that after his condemnation by Demetrius in 231 Origen never returned to Egypt, but remained in Palestine till the outbreak of the persecution under Maximinus. But is it not in itself probable that, after Demetrius was dead, and his own pupil and friend had become Bishop, he would return thither again?

suppresses everything calculated to bring into notice the opposition in matters of doctrine which Origen provoked. Accordingly, he says nothing about the Synod held by Demetrius or the sentence which it pronounced.

With regard to Jerome, he notices these circumstances only once or twice, and that quite casually. He does not mention Heraclas at all, excepting in his book on ecclesiastical writers. But that Heraclas, notwithstanding the ties by which he was bound to Origen, drove him out of Alexandria,—nay, more, that he would not allow him (as will presently be shown) to teach anywhere in Egypt,—all this shows how direct the antagonism was in which Origen had placed himself with regard to the doctrine of the Church, and with what earnestness his heterodoxy was opposed even during his lifetime.

This has been almost universally denied. TILLEMONT[1] thought that the enemies of Origen might very possibly have substituted the name of Heraclas for that of Demetrius, because the former was a much more important person in the Church than the latter. DE LA RUE[2] appeals simply to the relation of Heraclas to his teacher; this makes it quite incredible that he took any steps against him. MOSHEIM, NEANDER, and REDEPENNING have not thought it worth while so much as even to mention the question. SCHUITZER[3] considers the statement about the synodal letter incredible, for this simple reason (without seeking others), that it involves an error in chronology, for Heraclas was still Origen's assistant when Origen left Alexandria [no doubt the first time, but we have to do with a second departure of Origen from Alexandria]; but he nevertheless adds: "It is anyhow conceivable that Heraclas,

---

[1] *Mémoires*, III. 770.
[2] In the note to the *Origenianis* by Huet, *Opp. Orig.* IV. P. II. p. 93.
[3] *Origenes über die Grundlehren der Glaubenswissenschaft*, Einl. p. xlii.

out of official zeal or on other grounds, may have thought himself obliged to enforce the decisions of his predecessor Demetrius and his Synod even against his own friend." But Heraclas did not meddle with the decisions of his predecessor; he allowed Origen again to preach in Alexandria, and not until he again began to put forth his anomalous doctrines in these sermons also did he proceed against him. Further detail on the subject has been preserved to us by Photius, who was in possession of various original authorities in ecclesiastical history which are now lost, and for the history of Origen in particular had documents which have come down to us either only in fragments or not at all. His narrative runs thus:—

In the lectures which Origen delivered in Alexandria on Wednesdays and Fridays he used openly to introduce his heresy; for this Heraclas excommunicated him, and expelled him from Alexandria. With the intention of going to Syria, Origen came to Thmuis in Egypt, where the Bishop Ammonius allowed him to deliver a lecture in his church. Heraclas, hearing of this, went himself to Thmuis, deposed Ammonius, and made Philip (a younger man, but of repute among Christians) Bishop in his place. Later on, however, Heraclas, at the request of the congregation, restored Ammonius to the episcopal dignity, and entrusted the management of the see to the two—Ammonius and Philip. But as long as Ammonius lived, Philip never seated himself upon the episcopal throne, and whenever Ammonius addressed the congregation or celebrated the Holy Eucharist, he always stood behind him. Not until Ammonius died did he ascend the episcopal throne; and he became one of those Bishops who were distinguished for their excellence.[1]

[1] It is the ninth *Erotema* among the συναγωγαί καί ἀποδείξεις, which FONTANI has edited in his *Novæ eruditorum deliciæ*, Florentiæ 1785, I. pp.

This second expulsion of Origen falls, it appears, in the year 234 or 235, previous to his seeking protection from the Maximinian persecution with his friend Firmilian in Cappadocia. As Heraclas lived till 248, Origen did not return again to Egypt. It is true that Heraclas was succeeded by another of Origen's pupils, Dionysius; but Origen could not promise himself any greater tolerance from him than from his predecessor; and moreover, the Decian persecution followed soon afterwards, and in 253 this remarkable man died,—one who, notwithstanding the dangerous ferment which he

---

1–80. But as the text there has been mutilated in parts, one most important passage being omitted, I append it here from a MS. in the Royal Library at Munich, *cod. gr.* 68 :—

Πότε κατηρέθη ἐπίσκοπος καὶ πάλιν ἐδέχθη κανονικῇ εὐθύτητι, ἡ τοῦ ἰδίου λαοῦ παράκλησει·

Ἐν διαφόροις μὲν συνόδοις, καὶ ὑπὸ διαφόρων πάτρων τοῦτο πολλάκις ἐγένετο, ὥσπερ καὶ ἐπὶ τοῦ ἁγίου Ἀθανασίου γέγονε, καὶ ἐπὶ Μαρκέλλου ἐπισκόπου Ἀγκύρας, καὶ Μακαρίου καὶ ἑτέρων πολλῶν ὡς εἴρηται· παρακλήσει δὲ λαοῦ ζητοῦντος τὸν ἴδιον ποιμένα ἐγένετο ἐπὶ Ἡρακλᾶ τοῦ ἁγιωτάτου πατριάρχου Ἀλεξανδρείας, οὗ διάδοχος Διονύσιος, εἶτα Μάξιμος, καὶ μετ' αὐτὸν Θεωνᾶς, καὶ μετ' αὐτὸν ὁ ἅγιος ἱερομάρτυς Πέτρος. ἐγένετο δὲ τοιῶσδε· ἦν ἐν ταῖς ἡμέραις τοῦ αὐτοῦ ἁγιωτάτου Ἡρακλᾶ ἐν Ἀλεξανδρείᾳ Ὠριγένης ὁ καλούμενος ἀδαμάντιος, τὴν ἰδίαν φανερῶς ἐξηγούμενος αἵρεσιν, τετράδι καὶ παρασκευῇ· τοῦτον τοίνυν ὡς παραποιοῦντα τὴν ὑγιαίνουσαν διδασκαλίαν, καὶ παραχαράσσοντα τὴν ὀρθόδοξον πίστιν, ἐχώρισεν ὁ αὐτὸς ἅγιος Ἡρακλᾶς τῆς ἐκκλησίας καὶ ἐδίωξε τῆς Ἀλεξανδρείας. ὁ δ' αὐτὸς ἐκκήρυκτος Ὠριγένης, ἀπερχόμενος εἰς τὰς Συρίας [τὰς τῆς Συρίας πόλεις, Font.] κατήντησεν εἰς πόλιν ὀνομαζομένην Θμούην, ἐπίσκοπον ἔχουσαν ὀρθόδοξον ὀνόματι Ἀμμώνιον,[1] ὅς καὶ ἐπέτρεψε τῷ αὐτῷ Ὠριγένῃ ὁμιλῆσαι λόγον διδακτικὸν ἐν τῇ αὐτοῦ ἐκκλησίᾳ. τοῦτο δὲ ἀκούσας ὁ πάπας Ἡρακλᾶς ὁ εἰρημένος ἐξῆλθεν εἰς Θμούην, καὶ δι' αὐτὸ τοῦτο καθῄρησε τὸν Ἀμμώνιον, καὶ κατέστησεν ἀντ' αὐτοῦ ἐπίσκοπον Φίλιππον τινὰ νεώτερον μέγαν πολιτευτὴν ἐν τῷ χριστιανισμῷ. ὕστερον δὲ παρακληθεὶς ὑπὸ τοῦ λαοῦ τῆς αὐτῆς πόλεως ὁ πάπας Ἡρακλᾶς ἐδέξατο αὖθις ἐπίσκοπον τὸν Ἀμμώνιον, καὶ παρέδωκεν ἀμφοτέροις τῷ τε Ἀμμωνίῳ καὶ τῷ Φιλίππῳ τὴν ἐπισκοπὴν Θμούης. μετὰ δὲ τὸ ἀποστῆναι τὸν ἅγιον Ἡρακλᾶν ἐκεῖθεν ὁ μὲν Φίλιππος οὐδ' ὅλως ἐκάθισεν ἐπὶ τοῦ θρόνου, ἀλλ' ἐξηγουμένου τοῦ Ἀμμωνίου, γοῦν λειτουργοῦντος, ἱστάμενος διατέλει ὀπίσω αὐτοῦ πάσας τὰς ἡμέρας τῆς ζωῆς Ἀμμωνίου· κοιμηθέντος δ' αὐτοῦ [ὅτε δὲ ἐκοιμήθη ὁ Ἀμμώνιος, Font.], ὅτε ἐκάθισεν ἐπὶ τοῦ θρόνου ὁ Φίλιππος, καὶ ἐγένετο τῶν ἐπισήμων ἐν ἀρετῇ καὶ θαυμαζομένων, Font.] ἐπισκόπων.

---

[1] The passage, καὶ κατέστησεν to τὴν ἐπισκοπὴν Θμούην, is omitted in Fontani.

left behind him in the Church, yet was one of her noblest sons, a source of enlightenment to countless numbers both in his own age and afterwards.

The statement that Origen delivered his lectures on Wednesdays and Fridays is quite in accordance with the ancient custom of the Alexandrian Church. According to the testimony of Socrates,[1] on these two days portions of Holy Scripture were read aloud, and then expounded by the teachers (διδάσκαλοι).

The institution of two Bishops in the Church of Thmuis is the first instance of this kind in the primitive Church, and therefore noteworthy. It is true that as early as 212, Narcissus, Bishop of Jerusalem, had a colleague and coadjutor in Alexander; but here the circumstances were different. Alexander had to take the place of Narcissus, who was 120 years old, and could no longer perform his episcopal duties. Theotecnus, Bishop of Cæsarea, ordained Anatolius as his successor; and it was only on this account that for a short time they exercised the episcopal office together. The first instance similar to the one before us seems to be the one at Jerusalem, when Macarius at the request of the people kept back Maximus, whom he had already ordained as Bishop of Diopolis, as his official coadjutor; but here also the chief object was to secure a particular successor.[2] A complete analogy to the case in Thmuis is found in the circumstances which arose somewhat later in the African Church, when several Donatist Bishops with their congregations returned to the Church, and then exercised their office in the same place in common with the Catholic Bishop: the custom was that each should take the raised seat or episcopal throne in turn, which Philip would not do at Thmuis.[3]

---

[1] *Eccles. Hist.* V. c. 22. [2] Euseb. vi. 11, vii. 32; Sozomen, ii. 20.

[3] Hence the proposal of the Catholic Bishops at the Conference at

[NOTE.—Among modern defences of Origen, that of Dr. NEWMAN, in his *Arians of the Fourth Century*, must ever take a front place. It occurs at the end of his vindication of the "apparent liberality of the Alexandrian school" (chap. I. sec. iii.). It is a pleasure to help to make it still more widely known by quoting it entire. It is with the feeling that one is making a concession to literary and ecclesiastical etiquette that one calls Origen's enemy, Jerome, a saint; it is the fear of being guilty of a literary and ecclesiastical impertinence that alone withholds one from giving that title to Origen.

" Origen, in particular, that man of strong heart, who has paid for the unbridled freedom of his speculations on other subjects of theology by the multitude of grievous and unfair charges which burden his name with posterity, protests, *by the forcible argument of a life devoted to God's service*, against his alleged connection with the cold, disputatious spirit and the unprincipled, domineering ambition, which are the historical badges of the heretical party. Nay, it is a remarkable fact that it was he who discerned the heresy [1] outside the Church on its first rise, and actually gave the alarm,

Carthage : *Poterit quippe unusquisque nostrum, honoris sibi socio copulato, vicissim sedere eminentius, sicut peregrino episcopo juxta considente collega. Coll. Carth.* I. die, c. 16, Harduin, I. 1057.

[1] "The Word," says Origen, " being the Image of the invisible God, must Himself be invisible. Nay, I will maintain further, that as being the Image He is eternal, as the God whose Image He is. For when was that God, whom S. John calls Light, destitute of the Radiance of His incommunicable glory, so that a man may dare to ascribe a beginning of existence to the Son? . . . Let a man, who dares to say that the Son is not from eternity, consider well that is all one with saying Divine Wisdom had a beginning, or Reason, or Life." ATHAN. *De Decr. Nic.* sec. 27. *Vide* also his περὶ ἀρχῶν (if Rufinus may be trusted) for his denouncement of the still more characteristic Arianisms of the ἦν ὅτε οὐκ ἦν and the ἐξ οὐκ ὄντων. (On Origen's disadvantages, *vide* LUMPER, *Hist.* X. p. 406, etc.) [Contrast these statements both philosophically and theologically with Hippolytus' strange views respecting the Logos.]

sixty years before Arius' day. Here let it suffice to set down in his vindication the following facts, which may be left to the consideration of the reader:—First, that his habitual hatred of heresy and concern for heretics were such as to lead him, even when an orphan in a stranger's house, to withdraw from the praying and teaching of one of them celebrated for his eloquence, who was in favour with his patroness and other Christians of Alexandria; that all through his long life he was known throughout Christendom as the especial opponent of false doctrine in its various shapes; and that his pupils—Gregory, Athenodorus, and Dionysius—were principal actors in the arraignment of Paulus, the historical forerunner of Arius. Next, that his speculations, extravagant as they often were, *related to points not yet determined by the Church*, and consequently were really what he frequently professed them to be, inquiries. Further, that these speculations were for the most part ventured in matters of inferior importance, certainly not upon the sacred doctrines which Arius afterwards impugned, and in regard to which even his enemy Jerome allows him to be orthodox; that the opinions which brought him into disrepute in his lifetime concerned the creation of the world, the nature of the human soul, and the like; that his opinions, or rather speculations, on these subjects were imprudently made public by his friends; that his writings were incorrectly transcribed even in his lifetime, according to his own testimony; that after his death, Arian interpolations appear to have been made in some of his works now lost, upon which the subsequent Catholic testimony of his heterodoxy is grounded; that, on the other hand, in his extant works the doctrine of the Trinity is clearly avowed, and in particular our Lord's Divinity energetically and variously enforced; and lastly, that in matter of fact the Arian party does not seem to have claimed him, or appealed to him in self-defence, till thirty years after the first rise of the heresy, when the originators of it were already dead, although they had shown their inclination to shelter themselves behind celebrated names by the stress they laid on their connection with the martyr Lucian.[1] But if so much can be adduced in exculpation of Origen from any grave charge of heterodoxy, what accusation can be successfully maintained against his less suspected fellow-labourers in the polemical school? so that, in concluding this part of the subject, we may with full satisfaction adopt the judgment of Jerome: It may be that they erred in simplicity, or that they wrote in another sense, or that their writings were gradually corrupted by unskilful transcribers; or certainly before Arius, like 'the sickness that destroyeth in the noon-day,' was born in Alexandria, they made statements innocently and incautiously which are open to the misinterpretation of the perverse."

For Dr. Newman's opinion of Jerome, see *Historical Sketches*, III. p. 173 (*The Church of the Fathers*, 263).]

THE LATEST INVESTIGATIONS RESPECTING THE BOOK AND ITS CONTENTS.

While this treatise was in the press, further discussions respecting the subject of it appeared in London by WORDSWORTH, in a work specially devoted to the subject, in Paris by LE NORMANT, in Germany by GIESELER and BAUR. A critical view of the widely differing opinions set forth in these writings will at the same time afford an opportunity of taking up cer-

---

[1] HUET. *Origen*. lib. i., lib. ii. 4, sec. 1; BULL, *Defens. F. N.* ii. 9; WATERLAND'S *Works*, iii. p. 322; BALTUS, *Défense des Ss. Pères*, ii. 20; TILLEMONT, *Mem.* iii. p. 259; SOCRAT. *Hist.* iv. 26. ATHANASIUS notices the change in the Arian polemics, from mere disputation to an appeal to authority, in his *De Sent. Dionys.* sec. 1, written about A.D. 354.

tain points which have not been made sufficiently prominent in the preceding discussion, or require more definite treatment.

M. Le Normant[1] maintains, in opposition to a previously printed article by the Abbé Treppel, who declares himself for the opinion that Hippolytus is the author, that this view is untenable, for a Bishop of Portus could not have assumed the position in Rome which the author attributes to himself. On the other hand, everything fits in very well, if one supposes that the Origen named in the manuscript was really the author of the book, and the man who played in Rome the part depicted by himself. I do not contradict this view, because I am quite convinced that so distinguished and impartial a scholar as M. Le Normant, for whom I entertain feelings of sincere respect and friendship, as soon as he subjects the question to a fresh investigation, and weighs the facts put forward in this treatise, will give up the Origen hypothesis. He has rightly seen that the occurrences in the Church of Rome would be inexplicable if the chief personage were a Bishop of Portus. But that Hippolytus was not Bishop of Portus appears (to me, at least) capable of being proved to demonstration; and as soon as this stumbling-block is removed out of the way, everything falls into place and is explained at once.

Herr Baur, in two articles in the periodical edited by himself and Zeller,[2] has endeavoured to give still further grounds for the opinion previously started by Fessler, that the Roman Caius is the author of the *Philosophumena*. His grounds are:

Firstly, the author of the *Philosophumena*, according to his own declaration, was also the author of the treatise on the Universe. But, according to the state-

---

[1] *Le Correspondant*, Paris 1853, tom. 31, pp. 509–550.
[2] Jahrg. 1853, Heft 1 and 3.

ment of Photius, the author of the latter treatise acknowledged that he was also the author of the *Labyrinth;* accordingly the *Labyrinth* is no other than our *Philosophumena,* and that this work bore the title of the *Labyrinth* cannot be doubted, because—at the commencement of the tenth book the author *speaks of a labyrinth of heretics!*

But seeing that Theodoret quotes from the *Labyrinth* matter which is not to be found in the *Philosophumena,* Herr Baur helps himself out of the difficulty by supposing two treatises, both bearing the title of *Labyrinth,* and both composed by Caius. Theodoret, he says, calls the treatise used by himself the *Little Labyrinth;* and so there must have been another, from which this one was distinguished by the epithet $\sigma\mu\iota\kappa\rho\acute{o}s$, a supposition confirmed by the *Philosophumena,* in which the author refers to a former similar treatise of his, viz. of course, the *Little Labyrinth.*

Now, to begin with, it is extremely improbable that the title *Little Labyrinth* would be the designation of a smaller treatise in contradistinction to a larger one of like contents and like title. The expression is to be understood objectively, as Herr Baur himself allows, of the heretics spoken of in the treatise; and it would be altogether without point and senseless if the author of two treatises on heresies were to call the more detailed one the *Great Labyrinth,* or simply the *Labyrinth,* and the shorter one (*previously* written, be it observed) the *Little Labyrinth;* in which case the substantive in the title would refer to the subject-matter, and the adjective to the size of the work. The title is perfectly intelligible simply from what Theodoret states as the contents of the treatise, which discussed the Monarchians and their internal contradictions, especially with regard to their capricious alterations and interpolations in the text of Scripture. The author had shown that four of the Theodotian sect, viz. Theodorus, Asclepiades, Hermophilus, and Apollonides, had each of them produced a differently worded text of Holy Scripture by their additions and garblings.[1] On account of this confusion he called the whole sect a labyrinth; and because they formed only a small handful, and were unable to extend themselves in any direction, he called them the little labyrinth.

But further, it is impossible that the former treatise mentioned in the *Philosophumena* can be the little *Labyrinth* of Theodoret; for the former was directed against heretics in general, and contained a list of all the heresies known to the author; whereas the treatise mentioned by Theodoret is about the Theodotians only.[2]

Herr Baur says: "All that we learn from the treatise itself respecting the life of the author, which is so closely interwoven with the history of the Church of Rome, agrees, moreover, far better with a Presbyter living in Rome, such as Caius was, than with Hippolytus, about whom even respecting his locality nothing further is known." The argument is a circle; for that Caius was a Roman Presbyter is a conclusion depending upon the very question whether he wrote the two treatises, the one on the Universe and the *Labyrinth*. Eusebius and Jerome know nothing of his being a Roman Presbyter; no ancient writer calls him such; he is mentioned in no Martyrology. Photius is the first to make the assertion, but only in connection

---

[1] THEODORET, *Hæret. fab.* 2, 5, p. 332, ed. Schulze.

[2] Κατὰ τῆς τούτων αἱρέσεως ὁ σμικρὸς συνεγράφη Λαβύρινθος, *l. c.* 381. As Theodoret had this treatise before him, and mentions it in connection with no other heresy, there cannot well be a doubt that it was confined to a criticism of this sect. [JACOBI in HERZOG thinks that, in spite of Döllinger's arguments, Baur's theory of the two *Labyrinths* " has a good deal in its favour;" but he does not tell us what, merely saying that the fact of Hippolytus not giving this name to the two treatises is of no import. Against Döllinger, Baur, Bunsen, and perhaps Routh and Caspari, he doubts whether the treatise mentioned by Theodoret was by Hippolytus.]

with the treatise on the Universe, with respect to which he himself confesses that it is doubtful whether Caius or some one else is the author of it. It appears that the writer of the *Labyrinth* designated himself in this book as Presbyter and Bishop of the heathen, and at the same time gave Rome as his dwelling-place. But inasmuch as he therein states that the treatise on the Universe is also his, and Photius found on the margin of his copy of this treatise the assertion that Caius was the author of it, it was forthwith concluded that Caius was a Roman Presbyter and Bishop of the heathen. In reality, however, it was Hippolytus who thus designated himself.

In his second article Herr Baur endeavours to show that Theodoret already knew the *Philosophumena* under the name of Origen, and whenever he quoted it always mentioned Origen as his source; and that hence it follows that Hippolytus could not be the author, for Theodoret in certain passages mentions Origen and Hippolytus together as authors who had written against the same heresies.

Here, then, is the first and main question,—Was there anywhere in antiquity a work about heresies in general which was known under the name of Origen, and has Theodoret mentioned this work as one of his sources? To this we must answer, Firstly, no ancient writer knows or mentions any such work under the name of the great Alexandrian; only treatises against individual heretics (*e.g.* his Dialogue with the Valentinian Candidus) are mentioned. Secondly, Herr Baur no doubt would have us believe it to be perfectly clear that Theodoret cites such a work of Origen, for " he says himself in the introduction that he has collected the fables of the ancient heresies out of the ancient teachers of the Church, Justin, Irenæus, Clement (the author of the *Stromata*), Origen, Eusebius (both him of

Palestine and the Phœnician), Adamantinus, Rhodon, Titus, Diodorus, Georgius, and others, who had armed their tongues to repel lies. In the course of the work itself no one is so constantly mentioned (commonly in conjunction with several others of the writers just mentioned) as Origen. In all these passages Theodoret cannot refer merely to the occasional statements which are found in the extant treatises of Origen on heresies, but (*seeing that he mentions Origen in conjunction with those who have written special treatises on heresies*) *no other than such a special treatise by Origen;* and no such treatise exists, unless we suppose that Theodoret refers to our *Philosophumena*, already at that time ascribed by many to Origen. This is a prodigious error! Of the eleven writers named by Theodoret as his sources, only two are specially writers on heresies, viz. Justin and Irenæus; they alone have written on heresies in general in special works. With regard to Clement, Theodoret himself lets us know that he has primarily in view the *Stromata*, a work in which there is casual mention made of this or that heresy: no one knows anything of Clement's having written a special work on heresies generally. Eusebius of Cæsarea can just as little be credited with such a book; Theodoret refers to his *Ecclesiastical History* and certain others of his works. Eusebius of Emesa, according to Theodoret's own statement, wrote against Marcion and Manes, Rhodon against Marcion and Apelles. Adamantinus is named on account of his Dialogue against the Marcionites; Titus (of Bostra) on account of his work against the Manichæans. Diodorus controverted Photinus and Sabellius. In the whole of Christian antiquity a work on heresies in general is ascribed to none of these men. Accordingly Herr Baur ought to have drawn exactly the opposite conclusion, because Origen is named among authors who have left us only special treatises against particular heresies, or casual statements respecting sects and false teachers in larger works devoted to other subjects;—he also is named and made use of by Theodoret only on account of such special tracts and casual passages. That the *Philosophumena* already at that time (about the year 440) was ascribed by *many* to Origen, is so far from being the truth that one ought much rather to say by *nobody*.

Herr Baur endeavours further to show that when Theodoret mentions Origen in connection with a heresy, this also has a place in the *Philosophumena*, and comes to the conclusion that everything quoted by Theodoret out of this supposed treatise of Origen's agrees exactly with the *Philosophumena*. But Theodoret says expressly that Origen wrote *against* this or that erroneous teaching; whereas the author of the *Philosophumena* contents himself with a description of the doctrine, and an indication of the source in heathen philosophy from which it is derived, as, for instance, in the case of Hermogenes. Moreover, the agreement which Herr Baur maintains to exist is really in most cases quite fictitious, as in the case of Menander, of whom only the name is found in our work, and it is merely said that Saturnilus taught the same doctrine as Menander; and in the case of Severus, in connection with which the few lines in the *Philosophumena* respecting the Enkratites are made to furnish the basis for the statement of Theodoret that Origen refuted him. But how could it escape Herr Baur, that precisely in the case of those sects respecting which our work supplies more detailed information not found in other writers on heresy, Theodoret does not quote Origen? This is the fact in the case of the Naassens or Ophites, the Peratics, Noëtians, Sethians, and further of Justin and Monoimus, whom Theodoret does not once mention. On the whole, however, it is quite evident that he did not have the whole work before him, but only the Synopsis or the tenth book, and this apparently anonymously; which is also the reason why he does not mention Hippolytus along with those eleven writers at the commencement of his work. When he notices (3, 1) Hippolytus among those who have written against the Nicolaitans, he means by this not the few lines in our work which have reference to them, but either a special treatise, which Stephen Gobarus also had in view, or (what is more probable) his treatise on the Apocalypse.

On the other hand, Herr Baur is perfectly correct when he proceeds to show how groundless and arbitrary is Herr Bunsen's argument for Hippolytus, and (as he euphemistically expresses it) "is astonished at the audacity of this argument." But in consequence of this the "Hippolytus-hypothesis" is not in the smallest degree shaken; least of all has Herr Baur made it doubtful by his endeavours to attribute the book to Caius.

I turn now to Herr GIESELER, who has lately treated of the same subject in an essay[1] *On Hippolytus, the first Monarchians, and the Church of Rome in the first half of the third century.* That Hippolytus wrote the *Philosophumena* he considers as demonstrated, but maintains that the composition of the book falls in the later and Novatian period of his life. Taking the hymn of Prudentius as his authority, he makes Hippolytus join the Novatian party in 251, and thereupon go as the emissary of this party to the East: in Alexandria, Dionysius gives him a letter exhorting the Novatians to abandon the schism: after his return he is condemned to death in the Valerian persecution, returns once more to the Catholic Church, and then dies in the year 258 as a Catholic martyr, 73 years old.

[1] *Theologische Studien und Kritiken*, Jahrg. 1853, Heft 4, pp. 759–787.

This whole fable is built by Herr Gieseler upon very rotten foundations. On the historical credibility of the picture drawn by Prudentius, I have already said all that is necessary [p. 51]. Herr Gieseler seems to have found nothing to stagger him even in the mode of execution: that a Roman Prefect, in a fit of passionate caprice, should have an old man dragged to death by wild horses merely on account of his name, he accepts as credible; the Spanish poet, who put together his story in Rome 150 years later, under the influence of a picture and of the myth current in the mouth of the people, is for him a decisive authority; and in addition to that, he appeals twice to the Roman martyrology, viz. the later one drawn up by Baronius, which places the martyrdom of Hippolytus in the year 258, under the Emperor Valerian. Here he has merely omitted to notice that the Hippolytus of the martyrology (on the 13th of August) is an altogether different Hippolytus, viz. the Roman officer of the later version of the story of S. Lawrence; for which reason his nurse Concordia also, and the nineteen members of his family who all suffered death with him, are mentioned there immediately after him. Baronius himself, to whom is due all that relates to the different Hippolytuses in the martyrology, has in this (as he states in the notes [1]) proceeded on the assumption that Prudentius has amalgamated three different personages into one. A glance at the older martyrologies and other documents of the Roman Church would have sufficed to show Herr Gieseler that in the story of Hippolytus, Prudentius stands absolutely alone. Nowhere else is there a trace of the converted Novatianist, or of his martyrdom. Everywhere the only one known and named is the mythical officer, the disciple of S. Lawrence, who experienced that extraordinary mode of death.

[1] P. 363, ed. Venet. 1597.

Now just let us consider further, that for centuries the Novatianists formed a strong and numerous community in Rome, and that as late as 423 Pope Celestine took away from them several churches which they had in Rome.[1] Therefore in Rome the strife between the Novatianists and the Catholics was always burning; and the example of a celebrated teacher of the Church, who at the very beginning of the schism at first zealously served the Novatianist cause, then solemnly recanted, and exhorted those who had shared his views to return to the unity of the Church, and finally sealed all this with a glorious and extraordinary martyrdom, —this example must have been for the Catholics a powerful and victorious weapon; and the memory of Hippolytus and his history must, by sheer force of mere antagonism, have been kept always alive among them. Nevertheless, what we find is universal, absolute silence! Not one of those who wrote against the Novatianists mentions him,—neither Pacian nor Ambrose, who nevertheless (as Jerome tells us) made use of the exegetical writings of Hippolytus in composing his own.[2] Nor do the Novatianists ever pride themselves upon having so distinguished a teacher of the Church among the first founders of their community; otherwise there would certainly be some trace of it in Eulogius and elsewhere. And lastly, how are we to explain the fact, that in Cyprian's letters, in which the notabilities among the Novatianists are frequently spoken of, Hippolytus' name is never mentioned? Truly, if Herr Gieseler, in holding fast to the Novatianism of Hippolytus, can digest all these facts also, then—one must wonder at the strength of his faith.

---

[1] SOCRAT. 7, 10.

[2] *Nuper sanctus Ambrosius sic Hexameron illius (Origenis) compilavit, ut magis Hippolyti sententias Basiliique sequeretur.* Epist. 84, Opp. ed. Vallarsi, i. 529.

But besides all this, in order to make the hypothesis tenable, positive testimony must be got out of the way, —above all, that of Photius, that Hippolytus was a disciple of Irenæus. If, then, we place Hippolytus' intercourse with Irenæus in the later years of the Bishop of Lyons (say about the year 195), and if we suppose that Hippolytus was then 27 years old, his birth will fall about the year 168; and therefore in 235, the year of his death, according to the former reckoning, he was 67. But according to Herr Gieseler, he must have been torn to pieces by horses at the age of 90; and as late as 84, out of burning zeal for the cause of the schism, which he nevertheless afterwards abandoned, must have made the long and wearisome journey to the East and to Egypt. These are certainly incredible items; and consequently Herr Gieseler will not for a moment admit that Hippolytus was a disciple of S. Irenæus (p. 763): "One cannot pay any attention to the statement of Photius, for even earlier teachers of the Church, even a Eusebius and a Jerome, knew nothing about Hippolytus; and therefore Photius cannot have taken this statement from an older witness."

But *first*, the assertion that Eusebius and Jerome knew nothing about Hippolytus must be limited to this, that his position in Rome, and the circumstances in which he was there involved, were unknown to them. *Secondly*, there is no ground whatever for the assumption that Photius had no sources of information which Eusebius and Jerome had not seen before him; rather the opposite is certain. *Thirdly*, Hippolytus himself has proclaimed himself a disciple of Irenæus, for in his smaller treatise on heresies he remarks that he had compiled the refutation out of the lectures of Irenæus (ὁμιλοῦντος Εἰρηναίου), and had made a synopsis of his lectures. This cannot be understood, as Herr Gieseler appears to think, of the extant work of Irenæus; in which case one would have to do violence to the word ὁμιλεῖν, and take it in one knows not what unheard-of sense. Hippolytus, therefore, wrote down the substance of the lectures which Irenæus delivered upon heretics, and then incorporated it in his treatise.

But whence does Herr Gieseler derive his information respecting Hippolytus' journey to the East in the interests of Novatianism? He catches here at the straw of a name; all the rest is derived from the great treasure-house of possibilities. Hippolytus joined the Novatianist party, and this sent emissaries to various Churches; now, as he possessed a Greek culture, theological learning and reputation, he may very well have been sent also, and that to the East. He is said to have preached in Tyre before Origen, and from thence probably to have gone to Alexandria, where Dionysius gave him a letter destined to promote peace in Rome.

This house of cards, built up of possibilities and conjectures, which falls to the ground directly one applies to it the testimony of Photius and of Hippolytus himself respecting his relation to Irenæus, rests upon the statement of Eusebius, that Dionysius sent to Rome an ἐπιστολὴ διακονική, the bearer of which was a man of the name of Hippolytus. This expression means, according to Herr Gieseler, " an epistle in the interests of the Church, and in particular of peace in the Church, *i.e.* an exhortation to the Novatianists to desist from their schism." This manifestly very arbitrary explanation of διακονική is new; hitherto it has been supposed, and certainly very naturally, that the epistle was so called because it treated of the office and duties of a Deacon.[1] The sense which Herr Gieseler gives the word would in no way mark any peculiarity of the epistle in question,

---

[1] Rufinus translates it *de ministeriis;* Valois, *de officio diaconi.*

for all the numerous epistles of Dionysius mentioned by Eusebius were of course written in the interests of the Church, to contend against heresies, to compose ecclesiastical dissensions, and the like. But how could it ever have entered Dionysius' head to entrust to a zealous schismatic, who had come to the East for the sole purpose of beating up recruits for his sect, a letter which had for its object the exact opposite, viz. to put an end to this sect altogether? Had he wished that his epistle should not reach those for whom it was intended, he could not have found a better bearer.

That the Hippolytus named by Eusebius as the conveyer of an epistle from Dionysius was the celebrated Father, cannot (in Herr Gieseler's opinion) well be doubted, because—Eusebius fourteen chapters earlier "speaks of the latter, and mentions no other Hippolytus besides him." By the same logic one must argue that the Telesphorus, to whom in like manner Dionysius has addressed an epistle,[1] can be no other than Telesphorus the Bishop of Rome, because Eusebius has mentioned him in an earlier passage, and no other person of that name occurs in his writings. Probably Eusebius knew nothing further of this Hippolytus, but merely found him mentioned in this epistle of Dionysius, just as he mentions by name, without further designation, many other otherwise unknown persons to whom Dionysius addressed letters.

Up to this point Herr Gieseler has put forth this tissue of conjectures and arbitrary combinations under the more modest forms of expression, "it appears," "it may be readily accepted," and the like; now, however, p. 778, he suddenly changes the hypothesis into certainties, and continues his work of construction thus:—

"The Catholic Romans no doubt preserved the

[1] EUSEB. vii. 26.

memory of the Presbyter Hippolytus (for he could not be recognised by them as Bishop), who shortly before his martyrdom returned from the Novatianist party to the Church. But in the East, through his journey in the interests of Novatianism, Hippolytus had been known as a Bishop who had come from Rome, and before his later writings he himself called himself a Bishop. Accordingly, when a long time afterwards people in Rome inquired after Bishop Hippolytus, it is easily intelligible that nothing was known about him there, for no doubt it was soon forgotten that the Presbyter Hippolytus, so greatly revered as a martyr, had for a long time been a Novatianist Bishop. And hence it came to pass that Eusebius and Jerome, who certainly had set on foot investigations respecting Bishop Hippolytus, could learn nothing about him."

Herr Gieseler here forgets one further piece of forgetfulness, without which his hypothesis cannot stand, —the Orientals also must very soon have forgotten that Hippolytus had come to them *as a Novatianist*, and kindled or fed the flame of dissension and division in their Church. For, according to Herr Gieseler's own hypothesis, *that* is what he is supposed to have done. One ought surely to think that a thing of that kind is not easily forgotten. But the Romans also, notwithstanding that their recollection for such things was continually sharpened by the presence of Novatianists in Rome for more than two centuries, must very soon have lost all remembrance of Hippolytus' Novatianism; for, with the exception of Prudentius, not a single person in the whole West knows anything of it. Finally, Herr Gieseler goes on to tread in the footsteps of Herr Bunsen, and supposes that our work has been intentionally garbled in the tenth book; that is to say, that " a good deal that referred to the author's connection with the Novatianists has been omitted," etc.

Let us now proceed to cast a critical eye upon the manner in which Herr Gieseler disposes of the *progress and importance of the Trinitarian disputes in Rome.* According to him, at that time a definite Church doctrine on the subject of the Trinity did not as yet exist. There were, however, two views, according to which the supporters and opposers of the Montanist theory of prophetic gifts, Montanists and Antimontanists, were divided; the one party considered the Logos "as an inferior Deity, emanating in Time into activity from the Father," the other denied a personal distinction between the unrevealed and revealed Deity, *i.e.* the Person of the Logos. In short, Sabellianism prevailed among the Catholics.

Ab uno disce omnes, thinks Herr Gieseler. Praxeas, it is well known, was a Sabellian; but Praxeas was also Antimontanist; therefore at that time all Antimontanists, *i.e.* all members of the Catholic Church, were Sabellian. We shall scarcely have to dispute the conclusiveness of this argument; but we must nevertheless allow ourselves a little note of interrogation, in the shape of a couple of considerations.

First, hitherto we have been accustomed to think that it was precisely among a portion of the Montanists that those were found who denied a distinction of Persons in the Godhead; that is to say, that of the two parties into which the Montanists were very early divided respecting the doctrine of the Trinity, one, viz. the Æschinists, held and taught Sabellianism.[1] And this denial of a distinction of Persons must have become more and more general among the Montanists; for later Fathers, Jerome and Didymus, lay it to the charge of the Montanists generally, that with them Father, Son, and Spirit meant but one and the same,—so much

[1] *Libellus adversus hæreticos,* ed. Routh, p. 167. [They made Christ to be Father and Son in one.]

so that they had even altered the form of baptism; and hence at the Council of Constantinople in 381 their baptism was condemned as invalid.[1]

Secondly, as proof that Praxeas merely "adopted the Patripassian view common among the Anti-monarchians," Herr Gieseler advances the following: "It was easy for Praxeas, who was greatly venerated as a Confessor, to quiet the Bishop and Presbytery in Rome respecting the charges of the Montanist party." Almost every word here is incorrect. For first of all Tertullian says expressly that Praxeas was called to account for his doctrine before the ecclesiastical authorities, not in Rome, but in Carthage.[2] And as regards the easiness of the quieting, it has never yet occurred to any one to produce the demanding of a written recantation, and the taking a solemn promise never again in future to teach a doctrine hitherto maintained,—as a proof that those who made the demand were at bottom agreed with the person called to account. What more, then, could the Bishops and Presbytery have desired from Praxeas? But that this was really required and done, is palpable from the very words of Tertullian, quoted by Herr Gieseler himself.[3]

The well-known assertion of the Theodotians, that

---

[1] HIERONYMI, *Epist.* 41. DIDYM. *De Trinitate*, pp. 279, 382, 445. The latter, who interested himself greatly in this subject, says expressly that the Montanists τὸν αὐτὸν υἱοπατέρα ὁμοῦ καὶ παράκλητον νοοῦσιν, and (p. 279) the Phrygians (Montanists) were rebaptized διὰ τὸ μὴ εἰς τὰς τρεῖς ἁγίας ὑποστάσεις βαπτίζειν, ἀλλὰ πιστεύειν τὸν αὐτὸν εἶναι πατέρα καὶ υἱὸν καὶ ἅγιον πνεῦμα. THEODORET also remarks that a part of the Montanists taught the same doctrine as Sabellius and Noëtus. *Hær. fab.* 3. 2, *Opp.* III. 343, Schulze.

[2] *Fructificaverant avenæ Praxeanæ* hic quoque *super seminatæ, dormientibus multis.*—*Adv. Prax.* c. i. Seeing that Tertullian, as every one allows, wrote this at Carthage, it is quite evident that in what immediately follows Carthage is meant. This is admitted by Neander also. *Antignosticus*, 2d ed. p. 442.

[3] *Caverat Doctor de emendatione sua, et manet chirographum apud psychicos.*—*Adv. Prax.* c. i.

until the time of Zephyrinus their doctrine prevailed in Rome, is considered by Herr Gieseler as in the main perfectly true. Until the time of Victor, he says, the Church (not merely the Church of Rome, therefore) contented itself with general statements, with which the view of the Theodotians was as compatible as the other. But their view, as Hippolytus informs us, was, that Jesus was (His miraculous birth excepted) an ordinary man, who lived as other men, only with unusual saintliness; whereupon at His baptism in Jordan, the Spirit (or Christ) descended on Him in the form of a dove and illuminated Him. This doctrine, then, could before the time of Zephyrinus, or at any rate of Victor, be taught without contradiction in the Church, and specially in Rome! How foolish and dishonest, then, the appeal to the tradition and doctrine of the Roman Church must have appeared to the heretics against whom Irenæus wrote, when he held these before them as a decisive test! Was Christ a mere illuminated man—or was He God? We are asked to believe that during the whole of the second century this was still an undecided question in the Church; every one could teach on the question what he pleased; the heathen and catechumens, when they asked for a definite explanation, would be quieted with the direction that they might select the one view or the other, according to their fancy, or perhaps that the truth lay half-way between the two; if any persons liked to die for confessing the Divinity of Christ, that was their affair,—the Church itself left the question undecided.

Such was the state of things at that time in Herr Gieseler's Church! Certainly the Theodotians' love of truth appears to be rendered somewhat dubious by the definite statement of Hippolytus, that Victor, Bishop of Rome, whom they counted as one of themselves, excommunicated their master Theodotus. Herr

Gieseler, however, puts a note of interrogation, and thinks that "we must forego a certain decision respecting these different statements."

It was not, therefore, until the close of the second century, according to Herr Gieseler's view, that in the Church of Rome they got so far as that Christ was "decidedly recognised as a Divine Person." It follows that not until then could an Incarnation of God be spoken of, which hitherto had been assigned to the class of things indifferent, or even to the region of fiction. But now arose the question: *Who* then became man? the Father, or the Son, the Logos? This point could not come up until then, and here it was that, according to Herr Gieseler, the Montanist dissensions showed the best.

For Herr Gieseler knows that all decided Antimontanists (*i.e.* on the whole, all Catholics) were opposed to the doctrine of a Divine Generation, because thereby sensuous ideas were imported into the Godhead, and that in consequence they were all either Sabellian or Patripassian in their views. Such people had also, of course, as Antimontanists, "astoundingly lax principles of Church discipline."

If any one asks for proofs of these wonderful things, Herr Gieseler answers with "it seems to me," "we shall not go wrong if we," etc. (p. 768). And so—we shall not go wrong if we imagine that for a long time the whole ancient Church (with the exception of the Montanists and their friends) denied the existence of a plurality of Persons and the eternal Personality of the Logos, while it maintained the Incarnation of the Father. Callistus, whom Herr Gieseler of course conceives as grossly Patripassian, found himself, therefore, in a very numerous company. And if any one is not fully contented with the Gieseler construction of Roman affairs, and would like to ask for further facts and proofs for this Patripassian deluge, which, with the exception of a few Montanist oases, is said to have spread over the whole Church, and to have covered it for a couple of decades,—he must be set aside as difficult to satisfy, and shortsighted.

But now comes a new and strange historical phenomenon. The prevalence of Patripassianism in the Church is nevertheless but of short duration; these Sabellian floods soon to very great extent passed away; the antagonism of the whole body of Antimontanists to the idea of Divine Generation all at once disappeared; everywhere now it is taught that not the Father but the Son became man. *How* that now came to pass, under what influences and with what contests so wonderful a change, such a leap from one doctrine to its exact opposite, was brought about,—to know this would certainly be in the highest degree instructive and important; but from Herr Gieseler all that we learn about the matter is the following:—

" Meanwhile the general disposition tended more and more against the Monarchians, to the view that the Divine Person of Christ is distinct from the Father; and the Monarchian view became more and more generally to be regarded as heresy."

This statement seems to recommend itself by its simplicity; everything is happily explained into "dispositions" and "views;" and just as it sometimes happens to individuals suddenly to go over from one opinion to its exact opposite, just as our views are only too often dependent upon our disposition, so, if we place ourselves at Herr Gieseler's standpoint, and merely drive out thoroughly from our minds the obsolete and crack-brained notion that there must have been, or ever was, in the Church something stable and objective, a doctrine firmly handed down, we shall find it easy to see that such was the case in the Church. Already in the third century, and earlier, the Church had her "dispositions," which naturally, like all dispositions, tended now this way, now that, under the influence of external circumstances, or perhaps of unaccountable caprice. A little while ago she was in general Patripassianly disposed; some time afterwards she took another turn, one does not know why,—but enough she found it good forthwith to be Trinitarian in opinion, and to regard her hitherto cherished (Sabellian) view "more and more generally as heresy," as Herr Gieseler says, p. 772.

Thus, then, the dispute in Rome is placed in its proper light. Callistus appears as the representative and champion of the still prevailing "disposition and view," which was distinctly Patripassian. Hippolytus, on the other hand, is the forerunner of the disposition next to follow in the Church, and contends prophetically for a doctrine which is shortly to burst into prevalence, but for the present is still in very bad repute among all Antimontanists. Both, therefore, were right after their own fashion, the man of the present and the man of the future; the perverse thing was, that they regarded their dissension so earnestly and tragically, charging one another with blasphemy and heresy, instead of recognising that they were dealing simply with ephemeral dispositions and views, which, as mere products of a condition of things in itself changeable, were necessarily subject to change.

The crown is placed on this view of history by the further assurance, which agrees with the previous representation of "dispositions and views," that, although they no doubt contended hotly enough in Rome about Church doctrine and discipline, yet they had not yet been thoroughly in earnest, but remained together in a charmingly peaceful or (if you like) unpeaceful way in one ecclesiastical community; content to put up with sharp words, much in the same way as is common with quarrelsome married people, who cannot get on with one another, but yet are not willing to go the length of a separation. "Here it must not escape our notice," says Herr Gieseler, "that, violent as was the contest between the two parties which raged under Callistus, yet it never came to a schism. Both sides had their representatives in the Presbytery, and here there were frequent strifes; the stronger party excluded many sinners from communion, who were immediately received again by the opposite party; and Callistus emphatically made his episcopal authority felt over the Presbytery, but it never came to a separation into two communions. Callistus held the See only three years or less; the shortness of this period may have been the reason why the schism, for which certainly everything was ready, never actually broke out."

This condition of things, which other people cannot but consider as simply monstrous and inconceivable, appears in Herr Gieseler's eyes to present nothing even abnormal or unusual. In a century in which whole Churches divided and put an end to intercommunion about the time of keeping Easter, and the validity of heretical baptism; in a Church in which a few years later a division arose, which lasted for more than two hundred years, and spread over the whole of the rest of Christendom, merely about a single point in the discipline of penance;—in such a time and Church a party forms itself, directed against the teaching and authority of the Bishop, charges him openly with apostasy from Christian truth in the very chief and central doctrine of the whole religion, and accuses him of denying the Divine Personality of Christ, of breaking through the wholesome bounds of continence imposed by the Church, and admitting even the grossest sinners from the most corrupt motives, and of being a blasphemer. The Bishop, on the other hand, accuses them openly before the congregation of believing in two Gods. The one party excludes persons from the communion, who are forthwith received again by the other. And over and above all this, the Bishop—the very Bishop who thrust Sabellius out of the Church— leaves the Presbyter who leads his opponents in the quiet enjoyment of office, lets him administer the sacraments, and allows him to preach from the pulpit the doctrine branded by himself as Ditheism; which, however, does not at all prevent this Bishop from (as Herr Gieseler assures us) "*emphatically* making his episcopal authority felt over the Presbytery,"—over the Presbytery in which one party took upon itself despotically to exclude persons from communion, whom the side devoted to the Bishop immediately received back *into the same community*. So that, as it would seem, the Roman Church in the third century was like a house with two doors, in which one portion of the servants solemnly thrust out of the front door those of the inmates who do not please them, while the master with the rest of the servants stands ready at the back door to let in again immediately those who have been thrust out; whereupon the same master sits down with them again peaceably at table, without even the thought ever entering into his head of turning those disturbers of the peace and usurpers of his domestic authority themselves into the street.

It is quite true that Herr Gieseler makes a slight attempt to modify the monstrosity of his caricature of the ancient Roman Church, by the remark that this anarchical condition of things did not last long, because Callistus was Bishop only three years. On which one has only to remark that, first of all, he arbitrarily curtails the episcopate of Callistus,[1] and that, secondly,

[1] According to Dodwell's reckoning, Callistus reigned eight or nine years

Hippolytus himself cuts him off from even this poor refuge; for he testifies that at the time when his book was composed (and according to Herr Gieseler's own showing it must have been written a considerable time after the death of Callistus), the sect or school of the Callistians still subsisted, and held fast to the doctrine and discipline of their master.

With regard to the well-known statue of Hippolytus, Herr Gieseler maintains it to be "an historical impossibility" that as early as the third century the Christians in Rome had erected this statue to him: the truth rather is, that during the dispute with Alexandria about the Easter question, after 387, the Easter-cycle of Hippolytus was engraved on the seat of an old statue, which thereby was made into a statue of Hippolytus.

The impossibility is said to consist in this, that "statues of saintly persons remained until a much later age unknown to the Westerns." But there is no indication, and no reason which compels us to assume, that the statue, if it falls within the third century, was erected to Hippolytus as a saint. To the present writer it has always seemed very possible that the congregation of Hippolytus set up this monument of him immediately after his banishment to Sicily; and even if it was set up just after his death, it was assuredly not the saint whom people wished to honour, but the

(214-222); Baronius gives him six years; the chronographer of 354 makes him preside over the Church for five years (218-222). Supposing, then, that one takes from the first and last years only a half-year, there will still remain four full years. On the other hand, Herr Gieseler endeavours to lengthen the lives of Noëtus and Sabellius as much as possible. In the case of the former, he sees in the assertion of Epiphanius (whose inaccuracy in chronological statements has been long acknowledged by everybody) a necessity for making him appear in Asia as an heretical teacher as late as 245. Sabellius is declared to have once more laboured in spreading his doctrine at Ptolemais after the year 250, of which not a trace is to be found anywhere; for if the doctrine which was called Sabellian showed signs of life at that time at Ptolemais, we are still very far from having a proof that Sabellius himself was active there.

celebrated teacher, the most considerable theologian, notwithstanding his errors respecting the doctrine of the Trinity, that the Church of Rome up to that time had possessed.

How improbable it is that as late as the beginning of the fifth century there still survived such a knowledge of the Greek writings of Hippolytus, especially the smaller works, which had passed out of recollection even in Churches of the Greek tongue, has been already shown. About the Easter-canon Herr Gieseler himself quotes Ideler's words, that it was nothing better than a rude attempt, which only stood the test a few years; and hence the monument must have been erected very early, perhaps even under Alexander Severus. Eusebius of Cæsarea, in composing his own cycle, had made use of the canon of Hippolytus; from that time the latter had lost all further importance; and it is impossible to see what rational object the Romans of the fifth century could have intended to attain by immortalizing a canon composed two hundred years before, and long since utterly useless. The notion that it might have given weight to their pretentions in opposition to the Alexandrians, if they produced in stone a proof that two hundred years ago a Greek had lived in Rome capable of composing an Easter-cycle, is simply too ludicrous.

Herr Gieseler bases his hypothesis that the Antimontanists denied the Trinity and the Personality of the Logos, not on Praxeas only, but also on the so-called Alogi; and hence it may be worth while to subject to a critical examination the views hitherto put forth respecting this party, and the conclusions which have been drawn from the statements respecting them. One would perhaps not be wrong in thinking that this important point in ancient ecclesiastical history is one specially in need of revision.

Herr Gieseler says (p. 765): "It is well known that some of the Antimontanists went so far as to reject the whole idea of the Logos, together with the source of it, the Gospel of S. John." And (p. 769) he designates those the "most decided Antimontanists, who denied the genuineness of the Gospel of S. John, and of the Apocalypse, and the continuance of the *Charismata*." In connection with these statements, I shall endeavour to answer the following questions:—1. Were the Alogi really "the most decided Antimontanists?" 2. What were their reasons for rejecting the two writings of S. John, the Gospel and the Apocalypse? 3. Did they deny the doctrine of the Logos, and along with it the Divine Personality of Christ?

1. Epiphanius is the only writer to whom we are indebted for more definite information respecting those whom he called, with a sarcastic *double entendre*, Alogi; for the notice of them in Augustine is merely taken from the Synopsis of Epiphanius, and need not here detain us further; and the brief statement of Philastrius is only valuable as contemporary and independent testimony confirming Epiphanius; and Epiphanius says not a word from which we can deduce that there was a special opposition between these rejecters of S. John and the Montanists. On the contrary, he brings them at the very commencement into connection with the Phrygians or Montanists, the Quintillianists and Quartodecimans, both which sects are with him only variations of Montanism. It is true that, as far as the mere run of the words go, this connection has reference only to the circumstances of the time, but at the same time it seems to show that the Alogi belonged to the same family of sects. According to his report they had their seat only, or at any rate chiefly, at Thyatira in Lydia, where there was also a community belonging to the Phrygian sect close beside them. Both societies

laboured with such good success for the perversion of the Catholic believers resident there, that they brought the whole town to accept the Phrygian doctrine and sect; and the Catholic Church there for a hundred and twelve years was utterly extinguished.[1] The Alogi proceeded to make use of this fact as a weapon against the genuineness of the Apocalypse. The author of this book, they said, addresses in the second chapter a letter to the congregation at Thyatira, in which he presupposes the continuance of it until the coming of the Lord (v. 25); but at the present time there exists no congregation belonging to your Church in Thyatira; how can you then maintain that this book is the genuine prophetic writing of a divinely illuminated Apostle, when you yourselves must confess that the congregation whose continuance (as you suppose) he has there promised, viz. your own, has already perished?

The objection of the Alogi, then, has merely a meaning κατ' ἄνθρωπον. They could not have accounted

[1] MERKEL (*Umständlicher Beweis, dass die Apocalypse ein untergeschobenes Buch sei*, 1785, pp. 143 ff.), who is bent on showing that Epiphanius has altogether misunderstood and misrepresented the objection of the Alogi respecting the non-existence of the Church of Thyatira, an objection having reference to S. John's own time, says: "Had they (the Alogi) denied that in their time an orthodox Church existed at Thyatira, they would have excluded themselves from the number of orthodox members of the Church, and made themselves heretics, which they certainly would not have done if they were in their senses." No doubt; but that does not prove Merkel's point, that the Alogi could not have been speaking of their own time, but only of that of S. John. What it proves is this, that the Alogi did not count themselves as belonging to the Church whose disappearance from Thyatira they quoted. Certainly they did not say ἐκκλησία χριστιανῶν, but perhaps ψυχικῶν, or something of that kind. As Cerinthus was a contemporary of the Apostle, and lived in Asia Minor, the objection of the Alogi, had it been intended to refer to the time of S. John, would have had no sense: this EICHHORN (*Einleit. in's N. T.* II. 410) has already shown. For at any rate the Alogi could not mean that Cerinthus wrote the letter to a congregation at Thyatira which at his time did not exist, inventing the state of things there in the most clumsy way; which would have been equivalent to openly putting the mark of spuriousness on his own revelation with his own hand.

themselves as belonging to that Church which had now disappeared from Thyatira; for *they* were in Thyatira, and even if not a single member of the Catholic Church was any longer to be found there besides themselves, and they formed a small handful, *they* must have regarded themselves as the true continuation of the Church there. Hence they must certainly have formed a party estranged from the Catholic communion. Nor can their objection mean that at the time of the Apostle S. John there was no Christian Church at Thyatira, for that is contradicted first by the words οὐκ ἔνι νῦν ἐκκλησία, κ.τ.λ., and secondly by the whole answer of Epiphanius, which in that case would be utterly meaningless. For this Father replies to this effect: That precisely this perversion of the Catholics at Thyatira to Montanism confirms the prophetical authority of the Apocalypse; for in that the Seer speaks of a "woman Jezebel, which calleth herself a prophetess, to teach and to seduce my servants to commit fornication," he has in these very words foretold that the Christians there would be perverted by a heresy which (like the Phrygian) is wholly based upon the utterances of false prophetesses. Still, this lasted only 112 years,[1] and now (about the year 375) there is again a Catholic Church, already on the increase, in Thyatira.

[1] Epiphanius has here two notes of time; one, that the break in the Catholic Church at Thyatira lasted 112 years, *i.e.* from 263 to 375 about; the other, that the time of the Apostles, of S. John and their immediate disciples (καὶ τῶν καθεξῆς), embraces 93 years from the Ascension, *i.e.* lasted to the year 126, when Quadratus and Aristides put forth their *Apologies*. In this latter note of time, people have erroneously sought for the date of the apostasy of the faithful at Thyatira, which would create an inexplicable contradiction between this chronological statement and the other, and is at once refuted by the much later rise of Montanism. Epiphanius would fix the limits of the apostolic age merely to show that the apostasy of the Church of Thyatira prophesied by S. John did not take place until long after the apostolic period, and that thus the prophetic power of the author of the Apocalypse was established.

Thus the report of Epiphanius by no means represents the Alogi as opponents of the Montanists: the grounds on which, according to his representation, they disputed the genuineness of S. John's Gospel and the Apocalypse have nothing to do with the Montanist controversy; and in attributing the Apocalypse also to Cerinthus, they were influenced, not (as the latest theory supposes) by the passages of Revelation which seem to favour Chiliasm, of which Epiphanius says not a word, but rather by the connection of Revelation with the Gospel, in which they fancied they recognised the hand of Cerinthus, and also by the (to them) unintelligible symbols and visions, from which they were able to derive no really practical or edifying meaning, and no instruction of any kind. "What good," they said, "is the Apocalypse to me, with its seven angels and seven seals? What have I to do with the four angels at Euphrates, whom another angel must loose, and the host of horsemen with breastplates of fire and brimstone?"[1]

According to the representation of Epiphanius, the Alogi in Thyatira were the helpmates of the Montanists there, and with them brought about the secession of the whole city to the Phrygian sect. They (the Alogi), he says, who now deny that this event was (prophetically) revealed, then lent a helping hand to the overthrow (of the Catholic Church in Thyatira). No doubt the Alogi admitted that what occurs in the Apocalypse respecting the condition of the congregation at Thyatira had had its fulfilment,[2] *i.e.* that Cerinthus herein had before his eyes an occurrence which really took place in his time at Thyatira; but the interpretation of Epiphanius, viz. that by the seductress Jezebel the Montanist prophetesses were intended, they could of

---

[1] EPIPHAN. I. 456 *sqq.*, ed. Petav.
[2] Ὁμολογοῦσι γὰρ καὶ οὗτοι Θυατείροις ταῦτα πεπληρῶσθαι, p. 456.

course not allow. They were therefore an offshoot of the Phrygian family of sects, which was widely disseminated in that neighbourhood; separated from the main body, no doubt, not merely by the rejection of the two canonical books, but also in other points not well known to Epiphanius. Chiliasm would be one of these points; but of it one must observe that it seems to have been a question of very subordinate importance, at any rate with the Asiatic Montanists; for in the dispute between the Catholics and the Montanists it is not mentioned, but Tertullian merely reckons the kingdom of a thousand years in the Jerusalem descending from heaven among the things set forth by the new prophecy.[1]

Only in consequence of a violent alteration of the text of Epiphanius, which Merkel,[2] the opponent of the Apocalypse, was the first to devise, and which more

[1] *Adv. Marc.* III. 24.

[2] Ἐνοικησάντων γὰρ τούτων (the Alogi) ἐκεῖσε (in Thyatira) καὶ τῶν κατὰ Φρύγας (here οἱ μὲν is to be inserted), καὶ (this is to be left out) δίκην λύκων ἁρπαξάντων ταὶ διανοίας τῶν ἀκεραίων πιστῶν, μετήνεγκαν τὴν πᾶσαν πόλιν εἰς τὴν αὐτῶν αἵρεσιν, οἵ τε (δὲ) ἀρνούμενοι τὴν ἀποκάλυψιν τοῦ λόγου τούτου, εἰς ἀνατροπὴν κατ' ἐκείνου (ἐκεῖνο) καιροῦ ἐστρατεύοντο. These last words are to be punctuated thus: οἱ δὲ ἀρνούμενοι τὴν ἀποκάλυψιν, τοῦ λόγου τούτου εἰς ἀνατροπήν, κατ' ἐκεῖνο καιροῦ ἐστρατεύοντο. It is astonishing how so violent a change, devised merely to favour an hypothesis which it was wished to introduce into Church history, and without any support from any MS., could have found so much assent, and finally that of Lücke (*Vollst. Einleitung in die Offenbarung des Johannes*, zweite Aufl. 1852, p. 581). According to this metamorphosis of the text, ἁρπαξάντων is to go with λύκων, while in the unchanged text it refers simply to the Alogi and Phrygians, who like wolves had rent in pieces the faith of the guileless faithful. In the οἱ ἀρνούμενοι τὴν ἀποκάλυψιν τοῦ λόγου τούτου, the last words correspond to ἐπιλαμβάνονται τούτου τοῦ ῥητοῦ; the event just mentioned of the apostasy of Thyatira is meant. The Alogi, says Epiphanius, denied that this event had been foretold and made known; they, who by a strange irony of fate themselves had contributed to bring it about, εἰς ἀνατροπὴν (τῆς ἐκκλησίας) ἐστρατεύοντο. Instead of this simple meaning, which is required by the whole context, the words which naturally belong to one another are to be torn apart, τοῦ λόγου τούτου united in an unnatural construction with εἰς ἀνατροπήν; and these words are then made to mean, "You, Alogi, contended then, while the Montanists perverted the faithful in Thyatira, to the overthrow of this cause or doctrine (λόγου)," viz. of

recent writers have eagerly pounced upon, have people succeeded in transforming the Alogi into zealous opponents of the Phrygians, or Ultra-Antimontanists, as Neander expresses it. But even in the passage in Irenæus[1] which probably refers to the same society as that which Epiphanius calls Alogi, is there no confirmation of the opinion that these Alogi were Antimontanists, who, merely in order to deprive their opponents of the support which they found in the Fourth Gospel and the Apocalypse, denied that these were the writings of S. John. Irenæus says that there are men who, in order to deny the outpouring of the gift of the Holy Spirit in the Church, reject the Gospel of S. John, and with it the spirit of prophecy. These unhappy men would themselves be prophets [he says false prophets],[2] and deny the Church the gift of prophecy. And so, precisely because they wished to claim

Montanism. Which sets at defiance language, construction, and context. Seeing that just before this we have εἰς τὴν αὐτῶν αἵρεσιν, Epiphanius, if he had wished to speak of the efforts directed against this, would have written τῆς αὐτῆς αἱρέσεως, or τῆς αἱρέσεως ταύτης, or something similar, not the indefinite and ambiguous τοῦ λόγου τούτου. But further, Epiphanius says expressly that the perversion of Thyatira by the Phrygians was crowned with such complete success that the whole city accepted the heresy. He must mean, then, that this happened in spite of the efforts of the Alogi to overthrow Montanism, which efforts remained entirely without fruit. But in this case we should have expected some such word as μάτην or εἰκῇ to have been added; and moreover this is contradicted by the whole course of events in the matter. For if all Christians at Thyatira, as both sides (Epiphanius and the Alogi themselves) maintain, became Montanist, what then (one would like to know) became of the "most decided Antimontanists," the Alogi? Was this the sole result of their contest with Montanism, that they too were absorbed by it, and not until a later day their party again migrated to Thyatira, one knows not whence, and had to begin all over again? HEINICHEN (*De Alogis,* p. 95) observes rightly of this alteration of the text: *At hoc non est emendare sed corrumpere scriptores.*

[1] *Adv. hær.* iii. 11, p. 223, ed. Grabe.

[2] Here again, according to MERKEL'S proposal, immediately adopted by GIESELER, the text is to be altered, and instead of *pseudoprophetæ* we are to read *pseudoprophetas;* the sense being,—"They admit that there are false prophets (as if there were need to wait for any one to admit what every one at that time—no matter to what community he belonged—saw

for themselves a monopoly (so to speak) in the gift of prophecy, they disputed the possession of this gift by the Church from which they were excluded and separated. This was in accordance with the Montanist theory, which, firstly, would not allow to the *Psychici* the true *charisma* of prophecy; secondly, only accounted those visions and prophesyings to be divine which were experienced and made known in a state of ecstasy; and which further maintained that the true prophetic spirit ended and came to a close with Montanus and the two prophetesses Priscilla and Maximilla. And hence the anonymous opponent of the Montanists in Eusebius, and Epiphanius along with him, said that this very thing was an advantage on the side of the Church over the Phrygian sect, that the gift of prophesying remained ever with the Church; whereas, according to their own confession, it had already died out among the Phrygians.[1] That this sect gave as one of their reasons for rejecting the Gospel of S. John the promise of the Paraclete which it contains, as Irenæus reports of them, is very credible; for whatever distinguishes this Gospel from the others was accounted by them (and necessarily so) as a sign of its spuriousness; and hence the passages about the Paraclete in the 15th, 16th, and 17th chapters must all the more have excited their indignation, because this designation of the Holy Spirit is unknown to the other Evangelists and also to the apostolic epistles, while in the First Epistle of S. John not the Spirit, but Christ, is called the Paraclete. It

before his eyes), but true prophets shall not be found in the Church." One sees that this alteration also, weakening the words of Irenæus, has been devised merely to suit an hypothesis, and when BLEEK (*Beiträge zur Evang. kritik*, p. 209) calls MASSUET also a defender of it, he is quite incorrect. Strange that even Bleek supposes that the Alogi were first driven to reject S. John's Gospel by the misuse which the Montanist fanatics made of the writings of S. John; and yet of this misuse not a trace is anywhere to be found.

[1] EUSEB. v. 17. EPIPHAN. p. 403.

might perhaps be urged against this that it was precisely with these Montanists that the Paraclete has so important a position, and is designated as the proclaimer of the new revelation. But this is not the case until we come to Tertullian: Montanus always implied that it was God the Father who spoke through him, Priscilla claimed to be sent by Christ as His instrument, and Maximilla called herself "the Word, the Spirit, and the Power." Neither do the Antimontanist writers in Eusebius mention the Paraclete. But yet another reason might dispose Montanistly inclined persons to take offence at this Gospel precisely on account of these passages, viz. that the Paraclete of S. John is absolutely and essentially different from the prophetic spirit of the Phrygians, and utterly incompatible with it. The latter manifested itself in a few specially gifted and simultaneously living persons, who stood utterly alone and separate, without either predecessors or successors, and exhausted itself in them. Whereas the Paraclete of S. John was given to the whole Church, and is to remain with it inseparably throughout all time (xiv. 16, 17); He is the Spirit from Whom the Church has received the whole doctrine of salvation (not merely isolated additions, with increased strictness of discipline), and by Whom it is perpetually reminded of all that Christ taught (xiv. 26); Who was sent immediately after the departure of Christ, not first after a lapse of 130 years. It was not until the appearance of so audacious and reckless a method of exegesis as that of the now Montanist Tertullian, that an attempt was made to transform the Paraclete of the Fourth Gospel into the spirit of the Phrygian prophets. The earliest assertion of the Montanists, that their prophets were those whom the Lord had promised to send to His people,[1] refers, there-

---

[1] Euseb. v. 16.

fore, not to the Paraclete of S. John, but to the saying of Christ (S. Matt. xxiii. 34): "Behold, I send unto you prophets, and wise men, and scribes; and some of them ye shall kill and crucify," etc.

It follows, then, that the notion that the opponents of the Fourth Gospel described by Irenæus and Epiphanius, in blind Antimontanist zeal against the misuse which the Phrygian sect had made of the four or five passages relating to the Paraclete, denied the authenticity of the whole Gospel, and attributed it to Cerinthus, — this notion, on the first examination, appears utterly worthless and untenable, for Neander has already remarked that the use of these passages on the Paraclete could so easily be wrested from the Montanists—nay, that these passages could so easily be turned against them.[1] Much more probable is it that it was no other than a branch of the Phrygian sectarians who attacked the genuineness of the Fourth Gospel, in order to get rid of the troublesome objections abstracted from it,—the Catholic contrast of the Paraclete in S. John as the sun of the universe, illuminating the whole Church, and a continuous succession of teachers and prophets, in comparison with the Montanist prophets, who glimmered like a couple of stars in an otherwise dark night,—to get rid of the whole of this at one blow; although we must always remember that this reason alone would never have sufficed for the attempt to deprive of its authority an apostolical book, which had long had a firm hold on the mind of the Church in those parts.

That the Alogi denied the Divinity of Christ, and were Unitarians in the same or like manner as Theodotus and Artemon, has lately been frequently maintained, but not proved. The most plausible ground for it lies in the expression of Ephiphanius, that Theodotus

[1] *Kirchengeschichte*, I. 1005, first edition.

is a detached branch (ἀπόσπασμα) of the Alogist heresy. Nevertheless, the testimony of Epiphanius, as well as that of the independent Philastrius, is decisive, that with regard to Christ and the Blessed Trinity they were orthodox. Epiphanius repeatedly affirms, "They have the like faith with us;" "In all other things (*i.e.* except the rejection of the two writings of S. John) they appear to hold fast the holy and divine doctrine."[1]

The explanation of HEINICHEN[2] and others, that, with the exception of the article on the Divinity of Christ and the doctrine of the Trinity, the Alogi were orthodox, is manifestly inadmissible, for Epiphanius would certainly have expressly mentioned this exception. On that supposition, one cannot for a moment think that he would have spoken of any agreement whatever with the Church and with other dogmas in the case of those who denied the Divinity of Christ. He knew far too well that the dogma of the Divinity of Christ is the foundation and corner-stone of the doctrinal edifice of the Church, and that when this is thrown out, an agreement in the remaining important points would be no longer even possible, but only a deceptive appearance. But the Bishop might well say of a community whose sole difference consisted of Montanist tendencies in mere matters of discipline, that in other things it had one and the same belief as the Church. When, therefore, he used the above expression respecting Theodotus, all that was passing through his mind was that the Alogi, by their rejection of the Fourth Gospel, had thrown down the strongest Scriptural bulwark of the Divinity of Christ and of the Incarnation of the Logos, had prepared the way for Theodotus, and professed a relationship with his

---

[1] EPIPH. p. 424. Petan has incorrectly rendered the latter passage thus: *Ex quo deniceps sacrosanctam et divinam fidem redarguunt.*

[2] *De Alogis*, p. 24.

heresy. Parodoxical as it may sound, it was simply and solely in the interests (no doubt misunderstood) of dogmatic Christology that these people thought themselves bound to reject the Fourth Gospel as a production of the heretic Cerinthus.

2. That the spiritual Gospel, in its all-pervading difference from the Synoptics, excited the suspicion of a party in the second and third century by its unique character, in which the objective historical element—the description of the life and teaching of Jesus Christ—remains so entirely in the background,—this fact, when duly weighed, has nothing that need offend one. One must conceive the position of this party as one in which it saw the Fourth Gospel, not as a long-known book, hitherto in undisputed possession of apostolic authority, and forming part of the *paradosis* of the Church, but as a work only partially received as genuine, and with its claims in need of critical examination before being accepted. The book proclaims itself as a writing composed for a particular purpose, to furnish grounds for dogmatic belief (John xx. 30, 31); it omits most of the miracles and events recorded by the other Evangelists; it relates specially those discourses of Christ in which He speaks of His heavenly glory and power, and represents Himself as One who has come from heaven with divine knowledge and authority, and will soon return thither again; while the discourses of Christ in the other Evangelists refer more to His work and the Church which He is about to found, and contain ethical precepts and denunciations.

Cerinthus had already been active in Asia Minor, as the founder of a sect and spreader of a doctrine, when the Gospel of the Apostle appeared; hence his doctrine was already known and feared in certain circles, which now for the first time became aware of the existence of this Gospel. To them the very peculiarities of the new Gospel appeared to stand in close relationship with the teaching of Cerinthus. The Gospel says nothing about the miraculous conception and birth of Christ, the signs and wonders which attended His birth, the whole history of His youth, His public appearance as a boy in the temple; and leaps immediately from the Word become flesh to the baptism in Jordan and the descent of the Spirit. In all this they fancied they recognised the hand of Cerinthus, to whom Jesus is a mere man, born in the natural way of Joseph and Mary, whose whole youth was that of a (no doubt very good and pious, but still) ordinary man. Hence Cerinthus regarded the whole history of the birth and youth of Jesus as unimportant, or actually fictitious; and accordingly he made the history of Jesus as the Messiah commence with the meeting of Jesus and the Baptist, and what took place immediately before the baptism. In the assertion of the Evangelist that the turning of the water into wine at Cana was the first miracle wrought by Jesus, they detected the design of Cerinthus, who meant in this way to express that the carpenter's Son (as he called Him before the Logos or Christ descended upon Him at His baptism and abode upon Him) *could* have performed no miracle. No less designed appeared to them the silence about Christ's transfiguration on Mount Tabor; for, as Cerinthus admitted no real Incarnation or taking of the Manhood into the Godhead, but merely a temporal indwelling of the Logos in the Manhood, it appeared to favour his dogmatic interests that an event was passed over from which it was possible directly to infer a participation of the human Body in the glory of the Godhead inseparably united with His Person. The "prince of this world,"—an expression which occurs in no book of the New Testament excepting this Gospel, and here occurs thrice, but each time in such a connection that it is *possible* to understand by it some powerful being other than Satan,—this ruler of the world in the Gospel appeared to the Alogi to be the same as the one who in the Cerinthian system was subordinated to the Supreme God, Whom he did not know, as the Creator of the world and of man, and as the God of the Jews. Once more, the wonderful signs which accompanied the death of Jesus are omitted in this Gospel; and this again fits in with the Cerinthian system, according to which the Logos or Christ departed when Jesus was taken prisoner, and only the Man, left to Himself and stripped of all Divinity, was given over to suffering and death. What, then, would be the meaning of those wonderful phenomena, that sympathy and sorrow of the whole of Nature, as reported by the other Evangelists, at the death of a mere man? Lastly, the circumstance that a Gospel, otherwise so rich in didactic material, reports none of the discourses which Jesus held with His disciples during the forty days after His resurrection, might be easily explained by the Cerinthian doctrine that the risen Jesus was no longer the bearer of the Logos, or possessed of that higher illumination.

Let us suppose, what is not impossible, that a party of Cerinthians in Asia Minor, at the very beginning of the second century, got possession of the Fourth Gospel, triumphantly used and displayed it as the testimony of the beloved disciple in favour of their doctrine,—in a word, treated it just in the same way as the Valentinians did a little later,—and it will then be very intelligible how Catholic Christians, filled with suspicion against a book which had only just become known, thought that on further investigation they really did recognise the pretended traces of Cerinthian teaching, and then went on to compare it with the other Evangelists, and to allow the force of those apparent contradictions noticed by Epiphanius.[1]

3. Epiphanius says repeatedly that the Alogi rejected the Logos in the Gospel of S. John; *i.e.* starting from the fond notion that Cerinthus was the author of the Gospel, they thought that in the choice of the expression Logos to designate the Divine Redeemer they again recognised the hand of Cerinthus, who had brought his Logos-doctrine out of Egypt and taken it into his theory even before the Apostle S. John—that is, before the appearance of his Gospel. The Logos of Cerinthus is an Æon, generated and sent by the supreme unknown God, which descended upon Jesus at His baptism, taught and worked through Him, but at last before His passion again withdrew from Him.

That the doctrine of the Logos at the beginning of the Gospel gave offence to many, when it first became known in Asia Minor, cannot surprise us. Not one of the Apostles had hitherto made use of this expression; and precisely the circumstance that it already had a definite signification and technical stamp in the Judaic-Alexandrian theosophy (Philo), whence Cerinthus also had borrowed it, must have increased the offence caused by its being found at the beginning of the Gospel as

[1] HEINICHEN (pp. 37, 38) has not understood the objections of the Alogi to the Gospel of S. John, and hence thinks them so foolish and groundless that the Alogi could not have been determined by them to attack this Gospel, as mentioned by Epiphanius, but by a totally different reason, viz. their rejection of the dogma of the Divinity of Christ. To this utter misunderstanding also must be ascribed his explaining the assertion of the Alogi that Cerinthus was the author of the Fourth Gospel as a fable maliciously invented by Epiphanius (p. 42), although Philastrius makes the same statement. As a witness on the other side he quotes S. Augustine, who (as appears here) does not merely follow Epiphanius. Heinichen has not remarked that S. Augustine knew nothing but the Summary or *Anacephalæosis* of Epiphanius' history of sects; and the statement that Cerinthus was the author of the Fourth Gospel was not mentioned, simply because it is not contained in the Summary. On the whole, Heinichen's treatise, with its arbitrary treatment of historical evidence, has done more to confuse the history of the Alogi than to elucidate it.

the key to the whole. And thus it might easily happen that this very mark, stamped full on the forehead of the Gospel, would at once awaken misgivings in certain places whither the Gospel came without further credentials, inasmuch as they failed to recognise the Apostle's intention of counteracting the heretical misinterpretation of the Logos, and of giving to the doctrine that the Divine Word Himself became flesh apostolical sanction; and also fancied that they ought to oppose this expression and refuse it entrance into the Church. The Alogi, then, belonged to a circle in which the Fourth Gospel down to the time of the outbreak of the Montanist movement had found no admittance, so that they ended in joining the Phrygian schism, withdrew (from the middle of the second century onwards) from united action with the Catholic Church, and thus were able to maintain their barricade against the two writings of S. John down to the fourth century. But a belief in the divine dignity of Christ they had from the first derived from the universal tradition of the Church, from the Epistles of S. Paul, and other writings in the Canon. They knew that Christ in His higher nature is the Son of God (Rom. i. 3, 4), that being in the form of God He thought Himself equal to God (Phil. ii. 6), that in Him dwelleth all the fulness of the Godhead bodily (Col. ii. 9), etc. etc. Notwithstanding, then, the strong expressions which Epiphanius used respecting them once or twice, what he charges them with is always nothing more than this, that they would not accept the Logos; never that they disputed the dogma of the Divinity of Christ, or had altogether too low views respecting Him.[1]

---

[1] HEINICHEN gives himself much useless trouble to press more out of the words of Epiphanius, viz. a full denial of the Divinity of Christ, or Theodotianism. He quotes the passage (p. 434), Ποῖ τρέπεσθε, Κήρινθε, Ἐβίων, καὶ οἱ ἄλλοι; οὐκ ἐστὶν οὕτως ὡς νομίζετε, κ.τ.λ. Under the οἱ ἄλλοι he under-

To this it may be objected that the Alogi must have seen that the Logos in the prologue of the Gospel was altogether different from the Cerinthian Logos. On the other hand, it must be remembered that the Cerinthians understood the expression, "The Word was made flesh," in their sense of the mere temporary union and indwelling of the Logos in flesh, viz. in the Man Jesus; further, that Cerinthus, although he could not maintain a creation of the world by the Logos in the sense of the Apostle, because a lower Being—the God of the Jews—is with him the Creator of the visible universe, yet apparently, like Heracleon, supposed an activity of the Logos in the creation, or a dependence of the creating Æon on the higher Logos, which proceeded immediately from the Father; and so, equally with Heracleon, could say in the words of the prologue, all things, even the visible universe, were (in the last instance) made by the Logos.

I turn now to the book of Dr. CHR. WORDSWORTH, Canon of Westminster.[1] It treats only of the ninth book of the *Philosophumena*, and this merely so far as it narrates the contest of Hippolytus with Zephyrinus and Callistus. His purpose, however, is not so much to give a scientific explanation of this section of the work, to render the events intelligible, critically to

stands the Alogi, who are therefore named here as of like views with Cerinthus and Ebion. But he has overlooked the fact that S. John is here introduced by Epiphanius as speaking, and is here made to name those against whom, according to tradition, he wrote his Gospel; so that the later Alogi are of course excluded. The objection that Epiphanius would certainly not have omitted to urge the dogma of Christ's Divinity against the Alogi, had they denied it, he thinks to set aside (p. 81) with the answer that the Bishop would not have been able to accomplish anything with positive grounds against a party which denied the authenticity of the Gospel of S. John. As if the Epistles of S. Paul, etc. would not have supplied him with positive proofs in abundance!

[1] *S. Hippolytus and the Church of Rome in the earlier part of the third century. From the newly discovered Philosophumena.* London 1853.

separate in the statements of Hippolytus the objective historical contents from the subjective colouring which the personal sympathies of the author have manifestly mingled with the narrative, as to find a useful weapon for polemical purposes. The main object of the book is to show that the Roman See, in the first part of the third century, was tainted with heresy and vice,—a *cathedra pestilentiæ*,—and that the events of that time afford a decisive argument against the authority attributed to the Chair of S. Peter in the Roman Church. All questions connected with Hippolytus' work and narrative attract him just so far as they stand in conjunction with this object. It suits his purpose, therefore, that the condition of the Roman Church at that time should be painted in dark colours. She is considered to be wrapped in a thick black cloud of heresy and corruption, so that Hippolytus is the one bright spot in this darkness. The strong expressions and sharp sallies of Hippolytus do not content him; where they seem to him too tame, he helps them in his translation with more powerful touches. The impression which he has thereby produced upon members of his own Church has already been stated by an English Church newspaper[1] in the following words: "The one effect of Wordsworth's book upon us is, that it has *indefinitely strengthened the suspicion* which we could not help cherishing that the ninth book of the *Philosophumena* is *spurious*." Much of Dr. Wordsworth's book appears to this paper to be a "sermon against Papal aggression."

That the ninth book is spurious is, however, impossible; it belongs as an essential part to the whole work. But what is to the point in this criticism is this, that Dr. Wordsworth by his treatment of the subject and by his commentary has made Hippolytus'

[1] *The Guardian*, June 8, pp. 383, 384

narrative into an inextricable, self-contradictory jumble; and that the course of events in Rome, when grasped in this way, must seem to every one who knows the history of the early Church an insoluble riddle.

The first chapter is designed to show that Hippolytus was Bishop of Portus. Dr. Wordsworth does not attempt the difficult task of proving this for himself. He is content with quoting from an insignificant and scientifically worthless treatise of the Italian RUGGIERI, of which he speaks in terms of high praise: " beyond the possibility of a doubt," he has proved that Hippolytus is the disciple of Irenæus and the celebrated Father, Bishop of Portus. This tone of confidence induced me to read Ruggieri's treatise through once more with attention, to see whether some argument or proof of importance had not possibly escaped me; but I could discover nothing which in the least degree could shake the criticism of this treatise as given above. As, however, the subject is of sufficient importance, and the theory of Hippolytus' episcopate in Portus is maintained with such tenacity and unyielding persistence, it may be worth while to add a few further remarks on Ruggieri's book.

Ruggieri unconcernedly supposes that within a short period of time there were two martyrs of the name of Hippolytus,—the one Bishop of Portus, the other a Roman officer,—who both at the same place suffered the same extraordinary death of being dragged to death by wild horses. Both were buried in the same place, viz. the Ager Veranus, and both were commemorated on the same day; so that, in order to make the stupendous similarity complete, he had only to declare them to be twins! The degree of historical and critical ability which is displayed in such a supposition is not belied by the general course of the discussion. The numerous statements of Greek authorities, that Hippolytus was Bishop, Archbishop, or Papa of Rome, he appropriates with naïve self-complacency as so many indisputable testimonies for the episcopate of Hippolytus in Portus. The obvious fact that witnesses who gave him the title of Archbishop and Papa could not possibly have been thinking of a little seaport town, but must have meant nothing less than the Church of Rome, makes not the slightest impression on him. Accordingly he quotes the testimony of Leontius and Anastasius Sinaita, both of whom make Hippolytus Bishop of Rome. With regard to the latter, he says he does not care who Anastasius was, or when he lived; sufficient for him that he confirms his (Ruggieri's) opinion respecting the episcopate in Portus.[1] Leontius is treated in much the same way, and his *disertissimum testimonium*[2] plays a great part in the course of the discussion, and is held against all opposing testimony like a shield. After quoting a whole series of additional authorities for Hippolytus having been Papa or Bishop of Rome, he comes (p. 78) quite calmly to the conclusion that from this it is clear how universally ecclesiastical antiquity supplies testimony for Hippolytus' episcopate in Portus, and how weak and worthless the grounds are on which this is disputed. For, says he, Bishop of Rome means simply Bishop in the Roman province, Bishop of one of the suburbicarian churches. But, as the whole of South Italy and Sicily belonged to this province, the Orientals (according to Ruggieri's theory) might by their Bishop or Papa of Rome have just as well meant Bishop of Capua or of Syracuse as Bishop of Portus!

Ruggieri meanwhile attempts to prove that the Greeks called the suburbicarian province of the Roman See, Rome; and the Bishops of Rome, οἱ ἀπὸ

[1] *De Portuensi S. Hippolyti sede Dissertatio*, Romæ 1771, p. 71.
[2] *L.c.* pp. 70, 79.

'Ρώμης, or οἱ κατὰ 'Ρώμην. The first point, indeed, he merely states without producing anything whatever in its favour; the second would prove nothing to serve his purpose, for the Orientals call Hippolytus, not ἐπίσκοπος κατὰ 'Ρώμην, but simply Bishop or Papa 'Ρώμης. What, then, does he bring to establish his second assumption? The heading of the synodal letter from Sardica, which runs: "The Synod in Sardinia assembled from Rome, Spain, Gaul, Italy, Africa, Sardinia," etc. Here at once the position of Rome, and further the circumstance that Spain and Gaul are mentioned next to Rome and Italy, not until after them,—all this is clear evidence that here only the city of Rome is meant, from which the presiding Papal Legates had come to Sardica. His second and last proof is the decree of the Emperor Aurelian, that he, whom the Bishops in Italy and Rome (οἱ κατὰ τὴν Ἰταλίαν καὶ τὴν 'Ρωμαίων πόλιν ἐπίσκοποι) would recognise as Bishop of Antioch, should have possession of the episcopal house there. That means simply, the Bishop of Rome and the rest of the Italian Bishops. An ecclesiastical province called Italia, side by side with the Roman province, has never existed; when Italia is spoken of as an ecclesiastical whole, the Bishop of Rome is mentioned as its head,—thus Socrates [1] calls Liberius Bishop of Italia. So strong, however, is Dr. Wordsworth's trust in Ruggieri's authority, that he blindly copies all this from him (p. 10).

In similar fashion Ruggieri deals with the adverse testimony of Jerome and Gelasius. A word more about each. Jerome came as a very young man (about A.D. 350) to Rome, and prosecuted his studies there, remaining until 372, *i.e.* over 20 years. He narrates of himself that he diligently sought out the graves of the Apostles and Martyrs, and descended into the

[1] *Hist. Eccl.* iv. 11.

catacombs.[1] Later on, under Damasus, he spent four more years in Rome; and after all this, he assures us that he was unable to discover the place where Hippolytus had been Bishop, although he must often have witnessed the annual festival on the 13th of August described by Prudentius, and the streams of pilgrims meeting together from far and near in crowds at the grave of Hippolytus! One would have thought that such things were calculated to shake the firmest belief in the episcopate at Portus; but Ruggieri and his admirer and copier, Wordsworth, do not find here any really serious difficulty. We have already seen how Herr Bunsen tries to help himself here. Ruggieri thinks that Jerome was ignorant of some things which are now known, and quotes as proof of this one or two paltry trifles which do not deserve serious consideration, *e.g.* that he did not know that Caius was with S. Irenæus in Lyons (which, as a matter of fact, no one even now knows), and the like.

The authority of Gelasius is made innocuous with similar ease. In the sixteenth century, Baronius, owing to very defective patristic knowledge and critical power, doubted whether the book on the two natures of Christ was really by the Roman Bishop Gelasius. The subject has since then been accurately investigated, new sources of information have presented themselves, the decisive testimony of Fulgentius and that of Pope John II. have left room for no further doubt; and since then, all scholars capable of giving an opinion have declared themselves for the authenticity of the Roman Gelasius. What, then, does Ruggieri do? Tillemont had already said to him, "As Gelasius knew nothing of Hippolytus' having been Bishop of Portus, this is a proof of the groundlessness of this supposition." Ruggieri answers, that Baronius 200 years ago doubted

[1] *In Ezechiel*, c. 40.

whether the Roman Bishop Gelasius was the author of the book; he freely owns that he does not know how the matter stands, but that, at any rate, this is a complete refutation of Tillemont's argument![1] Even here Dr. Wordsworth treads in Ruggieri's footsteps. He must remark, he says (p. 64), that it is scarcely possible that Gelasius, Bishop of Rome, should not have known that Hippolytus, Bishop of Portus, was a suffragan of his See. Any reader would now expect Dr. Wordsworth to go on and draw the natural conclusion from this correct premise; therefore, that Hippolytus was Bishop of Portus is a fiction. Not at all; Dr. Wordsworth prefers—therefore it is very doubtful that the Roman Gelasius is the author of the book.

Dr. Wordsworth states further, that Ruggieri's book is to be regarded as an official document, in which the judgment of the Roman Church concerning S. Hippolytus is laid down.[2] That this is far from being the case, he might before this have seen from SACCARELLI, the most considerable Roman ecclesiastical historian who has written since Ruggieri. Saccarelli has so well seen through the weakness and worthlessness of Ruggieri's attempts at proof, that he again makes Hippolytus a Bishop in Arabia, who came to Rome and worked there.[3] In a recent Roman work, the

[1] For fear of being thought to do Ruggieri's logic an injustice, I quote his own words: *Quomodocunque sese res habent, hanc quæstionem viris doctioribus disentiendam relinquimus. Nobis tantummodo sufficiat probasse incertum adhuc esse num S. Gelasius P. hujus libelli auctor extiterit,* etc. *Quapropter Tillemontii argumentum penitus concidit,* etc.

[2] "It may be considered as embodying the judgment of the Roman Church concerning S. Hippolytus."

[3] *Historia Eccles. per Annos Digesta,* III. p. 265, Romæ 1773. Ruggieri's treatise appeared there two years earlier. Herr Gieseler acknowledges (p. 776) that in the fourth and fifth century, according to the testimony of Eusebius, Jerome, and Gelasius, there can have been no knowledge of a Bishop Hippolytus in Portus; but thinks it quite possible that the statement that he was Bishop there may have been contained in some MS. of one of his writings not discovered until a later age, but that it is also equally

question as to where this Father was Bishop is stated as a thing still unknown.¹

We have seen that the Presbyter ANASTASIUS, who found a writing of Hippolytus against Beron in Constantinople, and copied portions of it, is the first and most considerable authority for the episcopate of Hippolytus in the Roman Portus. According to his statement, the author was thus designated in the MS. which he copied. These fragments have for a long time aroused the greatest suspicion. Lately, however, a very powerful voice has been raised for their genuineness; DORNER, in his celebrated work,² supposes that the fragments are taken from the treatise of which that against Noëtus forms a part, and he makes them the basis of his account of the heresy of Beron and of the doctrine of Hippolytus respecting the Incarnation and the relation between the two Natures. Herr BUNSEN considers that Dorner has so completely refuted the arguments (HANELL's) against the genuineness of the fragments, that it seems unnecessary to waste a word on the subject. It appears to me, on the contrary, quite clear that these fragments, or the writing from which they are taken, must be spurious; the arguments which I shall presently advance for this opinion have, at any rate, not yet been refuted. I hold these fragments to be a forgery of the sixth or seventh century, a product of the Monophysite controversies; and I think

possible that people were led by the mere circumstance of his having been put to death at Portus to call him Bishop of this town. As regards the first possibility, it has perhaps been sufficiently answered by the remarks made above in the text; the second rests on the identity of the Father with Prudentius' martyr, which I hold to be a manifestly baseless supposition. The episcopate in Portus has its origin, as has been shown, in the fictitious *Acts of S. Aurea*.

¹ MORONI, *Dizionario di Erudizione Storico-Ecclesiastica*, tom. 36, p. 74, Venez. 1846.

² *Entwicklungs-geschichte der Lehre von der Person Christi*, zweite Aufl. I. 536 ff.

one has only to read the treatise against Noëtus and these fragments, one immediately after the other, to perceive at once that an utter difference of tone and of method in argument creates a broad chasm between the fragments and the treatise. Since the appearance of the *Philosophumena*, a more exact knowledge of Hippolytus' language and mode of description renders a decision of the question still easier, and the probability that the fragments are not by Hippolytus still greater. But, in particular, the following points, duly weighed, can scarcely leave a doubt as to their spuriousness.

1. While the theological terminology of Hippolytus, in the treatise against Noëtus and in the ninth book of the *Philosophumena*, appears to be still defective, and confined to a few words and formulæ which had already received a theological stamp, the author of the fragments can command an abundance of technical terms respecting the doctrine of the Incarnation, such as was only developed in the course of the Apollinarian, Nestorian, and Monophysite controversies; he wields this terminology with a certain ease and readiness, taking for granted that it is well known, whereas Hippolytus often seems to have some trouble to find the right expression.

2. In Hippolytus' treatise against Noëtus, a simple, homely tone prevails; the treatise is, in the main, a string of texts of Scripture. In the fragments the language is turgid, overladen with epithets; texts of Scripture, with the exception of one or two words, are not quoted.

3. In the fragments expressions are frequent which are foreign to Hippolytus' writings and his whole period, and betray a much later age, reminding one more of Synesius, the Areopagite writings, and the later Neoplatonists. The author speaks of a κίνησις ταυτουργός, of the θεότης τῇ σαρκὶ ταυτοπαθής, of a δύναμις

ὑπεραπείρος, a θέλησις ἀπειροδύναμος, an ἀγαθὸν ἀπειρόσθενες; he uses the words οὐσιώσας and ἐνουσιώσας, of which the first does not occur earlier than Athanasius, the second only in Hierocles, in the fifth century. Not less unlike Hippolytus sounds ἀνελλιποῦς ὑπάρχον θεότητος; and again, ἡ παντοκρατορικὴ, καὶ τῶν ὅλων ποιητικὴ τῆς ὅλης θεότητος ἐνέργεια. Here we have, at the same time, an instance of that redundance and fluency which is utterly foreign to the style of Hippolytus.

4. The technical expressions, μεταβολὴ ἰδιωμάτων, διαίρεσις προσωπική, φυσικὴ ὕπαρξις, and the like, exhibit the later development and stereotyped use of theological language produced by the controversies mentioned above, and are an anachronism when placed in the mouth of a writer at the beginning of the third century.

5. The author of the fragments speaks of the "inseparable union of the two Natures of Christ so as to form one *Hypostasis*," which plainly shows that he uses this expression in the sense of *Person*.[1] But for this Hippolytus uses the word *Prosopon*.[2] *Hypostasis* in the third, and to some extent in the fourth century also, is used for *Nature*; thus in Hippolytus' contemporaries, Irenæus, Origen, the Roman Dionysius, nay, even by the Council of Nicæa.[3] It was not until after the Alexandrian Synod of 362, which left it open to speak of one *Hypostasis* or of three, —*i.e.* to use the word in the sense of Nature, or in that

---

[1] Ἄρρητός τις καὶ ἄρρηκτος εἰς μίαν ὑπόστασιν ἀμφοτέρων γέγονεν ἕνωσις. Anastasius, in his rather bad translation, has, *in unam substantiam*, and does not see that he thus makes his author affirm precisely what he is opposing with all his might—Monophysitism, and that he makes him say the opposite of what he has said just before. Similarly (p. 226) he translates the passage that Christ worked both as God and Man, κατ' αὐτὴν τὴν ὄντως ἀληθῆ καὶ φυσικὴν ὕπαρξιν, "secundum eandam quæ veraciter vera est et naturalis substantia," instead of "secundum *ipsam*," etc., and thus again makes him teach the Monophysite doctrine.

[2] Both in the treatise against Noëtus and also in the *Philosophumena*.

[3] PETAVII, *Dogm. Theol. de Trin.* iv. 1; *De Incarn.* ii. 3.

of Person,—did the latter meaning become gradually prevalent in the East. That Hippolytus lived in Rome makes here no difference, for in the West also *Hypostasis* was used in the sense of Substance or Nature as late as the fourth century; the Council of Sardica, and that of Rome under Damasus, still spoke of one *Hypostasis* of Divine Persons. The later use of the word was first fixed by S. Basil.

6. The author of the fragments speaks not only of the πανάγια τοῦ θεοῦ σάρξ, but also of the πανάγια ἀειπαρθένος Μαρία. The epithet πανάγιος, used of the Blessed Virgin, does not occur till a good deal later. Hippolytus commonly says simply ἡ παρθένος, without any addition, and once ἡ μακάρια Μαρία; that he would ever have spoken of the "Flesh of God" is, to say the least, extremely improbable.

7. In the form of doctrine, also, the fragments are marvellously different from the genuine writings of Hippolytus. In the refutation of Noëtus, the object of the Incarnation is stated as being the rescue of fallen man, and the winning of immortality (ἀφθαρσία) for him. With this simple explanation, contrast that of the fragments:[1] Christ became man, and suffered "in order to ransom the whole race of mankind, which had been sold into death, and to lead them to immortal and blessed life; in order to secure the holy hosts of intelligent beings in the heavens and render them unchangeable by the mystery of His Incarnation, whose work is the binding together of the universe in Him;" or, as it is expressed in another passage, "in order to bind up the universe and render it unchangeable."[2] This idea is quite foreign to Hippolytus, and (so far as I know) is not found in any other ancient Father.[3] In

---

[1] P. 227, ed. Fabric.   [2] Διὰ τὸ δῆσαι πρὸς ἀτρεψίας τὸ πᾶν, p. 230.
[3] S. Augustine is the first to utter a somewhat kindred thought: *Ut Dei sapientia ad unitatem personæ suæ homine assumto . . . fieret et deorsum*

the address to the heathen,[1] he states as the object of the Incarnation of the Logos that Christ willed to be a law and pattern for mankind, and to show that God had made nothing evil, and that man's will is free.

8. If these fragments belong to the beginning of the third century, they contain a wonderful anticipation of that development of doctrine which otherwise was generally diffused and brought to maturity only by the contests of the fourth and fifth centuries, such as perhaps could not be found elsewhere. Petavius[2] has already remarked, that the words of Hippolytus (in these fragments) are in such clear opposition to the much later heresy (of the Monophysites) that a refutation of this error written so long beforehand is marvellous.

9. In addition to all this, we have the *external* evidence. The treatise is mentioned by no one earlier than the seventh century; Theodoret did not know of it, otherwise he would certainly have made use of it. No heretic named Beron is known; no one of the later writers on heresies mentions him; Hippolytus would undoubtedly have inserted him along with the others in the *Philosophumena* had he known of such a person. Is it likely that so extraordinary a heresy as that which Beron is said to have disseminated, that in Christ the two Natures were transfused one with another so as to be entirely commingled,—a doctrine which is quite

---

hominibus exemplo redeundi, et eis qui sursum sunt, angelis exemplum manendi (*De Consens. Evang.* i. 35). FULGENTIUS comes nearest to the conception of the author of the fragments: *Non alia (gratia) stantem angelum a ruina potuit custodire, nisi illa, quæ lapsum hominem post ruinam potuit reparare. Una est in utroque gratia operata; in hoc ut surgeret, in illo ne caderet* (*Ad Trasimundum Regem*, ii. 3, *Opp.* ed. Paris 1684, p. 90). Nothing similar is to be found in the Greek Fathers, except Origen. Cf. the saying of Cyril of Alexandria, that even the angels had their holiness only through Christ in the Holy Ghost (*De Ador.* I. 310).

[1] *Philosophumena*, p. 337.
[2] *De Incarnatione*, viii. 8; *Dogma. Theol.* v. 389, ed. Amstelod.

unique in the earlier centuries,[1]—should have entirely escaped the notice of every one,—of Eusebius, Epiphanius, and Philastrius? Let us remember how eager men were to be able to represent to the originators of an innovation in dogma, that their doctrine had already been taught and already condemned in the case of this or that ancient heretic. When, therefore, none of the numerous opponents of Monophysitism (until about 640) mention Beron, and Hippolytus' refutation of him, this can only be explained by the supposition that both the existence of Beron and the treatise of this Father were unknown to them. It is quite true that the treatise was quoted at the Roman Synod of 649; but it was beyond a doubt Anastasius who brought his selections thither, and supplied the passages which were quoted there.

If, then, the treatise from which these fragments are taken is spurious, there is at once an end of the possibility that the designation of Hippolytus in the heading as "martyr and Bishop of Portus, near Rome," originated in an earlier age. Whether Anastasius was the first to add this designation, or found it already in the MS., it belongs at the earliest to the seventh century or end of the sixth, and was derived (as has been shown) from the spurious *Acts of S. Chryse*. With the exception of Anastasius, the compiler of the *Chronicon Paschale*, or of the rhapsody of statements with regard to the time of Easter prefixed to it, is the only writer who calls Hippolytus Bishop of Portus on the strength of a quotation from one of his writings; but he makes use of the first treatise against heresies, the *Syntagma*, and we know from Photius that the author of this book

[1] No doubt TERTULLIAN (*Contra Prax.* 27) refuted the doctrine that in the Incarnation there was a change of one Nature into the other; but what a difference between the simple discussion of Tertullian and the artistically-conducted argumentation of the author of the fragments, who has a technical word ready for every conception that may arise!

was not so designated in it. Therefore this compiler also derived his statement either from Anastasius, or from the spurious work against Beron, or direct from the *Acts of S. Chryse*. The two others, Zonaras and Syncellus, do not come into consideration, for they quote no writings of Hippolytus, and fall within a much later age. And thus the fact that all others who have made use of Hippolytus' writings, or have quoted passages from him, invariably call him Bishop or Papa of Rome, appears all the mere striking and decisive.

The gross error of Herr Bunsen, that Peter, Bishop of Alexandria about 309, quoted Hippolytus as Bishop of the Roman Portus, has been faithfully copied by Dr. Wordsworth; after which he has a long and serious discussion as to why Hippolytus does not directly say that Callistus was Bishop of Rome. There is, he thinks, something almost mysterious in this apparent ambiguity of language, such as at first arouses suspicion, etc. etc. At last he comes to the conclusion that Hippolytus did not wish to profane the title of Bishop by giving it to the heretical Callistus. This mystery is of Dr. Wordsworth's own making. Nothing is more simple or natural, or more in accordance with the condition of things in the Church at that time, than that Hippolytus should refuse to call a man whom he regarded as an open heretic and spoiler of the Church, and from whose communion he had withdrawn, Bishop of Rome. It *would* have been mysterious and incomprehensible had he and his followers persisted in maintaining this position, without providing themselves with a proper Bishop according to their own views. But this they did; they constituted themselves under their Bishop Hippolytus the orthodox Church of Rome, as is quite plain from their calling those in communion with Callistus a sect or school, and from the statement that Callistus received those whom they excommunicated into his Church.

Dr. Wordsworth has here also allowed himself to be misled by Herr Bunsen. He says (p. 82) that Hippolytus appears in many respects to regard Callistus as "a professorial teacher" rather than a person of high authority in the Church; he calls his followers a "school," and never gives them the name of "Church." So also Herr Bunsen:[1] "Callistus *set up a school*, in which this doctrine (Sabellianism) was taught, as Hippolytus says, in opposition to the Catholic Church." Herr Bunsen seems inclined to suppose that Callistus was not himself Professor in this school, but caused others to lecture instead of him, and in accordance with his views on dogmatic theology, or perhaps only on the subject of the Trinity. Dr. Wordsworth, on the other hand, understands Hippolytus to mean that Callistus exercised the Professor's office in his own person in his school. A glance at Hippolytus' treatise against Noëtus would have shown what he meant by a "school" in opposition to the Church. He says there,[2] that *after Noëtus was thrust out of the Church* he was so arrogant as to form a *didascaleion* or school—*i.e.* instead of recanting, and thus regaining the communion he had lost, he set up a separate and heretical Church, composed of those who agreed with him. It need excite no surprise that Hippolytus leaps over some links in the chain of events in which he was entangled, and does not expressly narrate his expulsion, his formation of a separate communion, and election as Bishop. On the one side, a certain shyness restrained him in this,—a feeling that among the Christians of his time nothing was more hateful than the erecting

---

[1] *Hippolytus und seine Zeit*, I. 98.
[2] *Scriptor Eccl. Opuscula*, ed. Routh, I. 46. [ὅς εἰς τοσοῦτο φυσίωμα ἠνέχθη, ὡς διδασκαλεῖον συστῆσαι.]

of altar against altar, and rending the unity of the Church. On the other side, however, he wrote primarily for his followers, and then also for his contemporaries, who knew the state of things in Rome on the main point; for he himself says that the doctrine of Callistus, and of course also the events connected with it, had created great commotion in the whole Church. It was everywhere known that in the Roman Church there was a schism about the doctrine respecting the Father and the Son, and also about Church discipline, and that there were now two Churches there, each of which maintained that it was the Catholic Church. It was manifestly one of the reasons which induced him to publish a second treatise about heresies, that he intended at the same time to make this a vehicle for an official apology, and a polemical description of the relation in which he and his community stood or wished to stand towards other Churches and the rival Church in Rome. And thus in this apology, where one looks for a definite statement respecting the steps which immediately led to the establishment of a separation, one is reminded of the way in which the eloquent defender of Milo steers clear of the reef on which he and his client, had he simply related the catastrophe, might easily have been wrecked. Hippolytus leaves it uncertain and obscure to readers at a distance *when* exactly the formal separation took place,—whether already under Zephyrinus, or at his death, or not until the time of Callistus; he leaves us to conjecture whether Callistus was in undisputed possession of the episcopate when he separated from him, or whether Hippolytus was not perhaps the one elected first, and Callistus set up as rival Bishop afterwards. We, no doubt, with the knowledge of additional facts gained elsewhere, are in a position to state the course of events accurately enough; but to readers at a distance in that century, into whose hands this treatise came some time after the death of Callistus, it must have seemed doubtful whom the reproach of having been the originator of the division really touched; and the intention (more or less conscious) of leaving this doubtful guided Hippolytus' pen.

In order to clear up the "mystery" why Hippolytus did not give Callistus the title of Bishop, Dr. Wordsworth has recourse to a supposed Johannean school, from which Hippolytus is descended through Irenæus.[1] This school, he says, had principles of its own respecting the episcopal office, and the duty of being in communion with those who have the *charisma* of the apostolical succession, and with it also the true doctrine of the Church. These being the views of the whole Church, and containing nothing specially Johannean, Dr. Wordsworth proceeds to quote from the Apocalypse the words about men "which say they are apostles and are not," but are liars (ii. 2). In this simple fact, mentioned also in S. Paul's Epistles, that at that time there were false apostles without any commission from the Church, Dr. Wordsworth sees a special Johannean doctrine, which Irenæus and Hippolytus are said to have continued to teach. As evidence he quotes a well-known passage from the eighth book of the *Apostolical Constitutions*,[2] in which it is said that there are false prophets also, and "a Bishop who, being entangled in ignorance or wickedness, is no Bishop, but is falsely so called." Thus teaches, he adds, a disciple of S. Irenæus, and this disciple is—S. Hippolytus. The name is printed in large letters. Dr. Wordsworth believes that in these words Hippolytus alludes to events in Rome, and that the Bishop entangled in ignorance is Zephyrinus, while the wicked Bishop is Callistus.

[1] *S. Hippolytus and the Church of Rome*, pp. 87-90.
[2] *Constit.* viii. 2; *Patres Apost.* ed. Coteler, Amstelod 1724, II. 393.

Here his eagerness to seize whatever may serve his purpose has done him an ill turn On the strength of the statement on the Roman statue, that Hippolytus wrote a treatise with the title *Apostolic Tradition respecting the Charismata*, Fabricius incorporated a portion of the eighth book of the *Constitutions* with his collection of Hippolytus' writings, and it is from this that Dr. Wordsworth quotes. But the second chapter, from which this passage is taken, is not by Hippolytus, and cannot be by him. Grabe[1] has long since warned us that the compiler of the eighth book allowed himself the greatest liberty in dealing with the collection which bears Hippolytus' name, arbitrarily altering some things, and adding a good deal. In the second chapter, in immediate connection with the words quoted by Dr. Wordsworth, we read: "An Emperor who is unbelieving (or irreligious, δυσσεβής) is no longer an Emperor, but a tyrant; and a Bishop who," etc. This is manifestly written after Constantine, in an age when the Christian religion had already become the imperial religion; perhaps under Julian, or soon after his time: Hippolytus could not possibly so have expressed himself in his own time, when all Emperors without exception were δυσσεβεῖς. This, at the same time, determines that the second sentence about the Bishops likewise falls into the times of the fourth century.

The long discussion as to how it comes to pass that the occurrences in the Church of Rome at that time are mentioned by no ecclesiastical historian might have been disposed of in few words. We have no continuous history of the Church in general, nor of the Roman Church in particular, during that time, but merely lists of the Bishops in chronological order in

---

[1] *Spicileg. Patrum*, I. 285; and an *Essay upon two Arabick Manuscripts*, Oxford 1711, p. 25.

the chief churches, descriptions of various heresies, extracts from certain letters and writings of that time in Eusebius; and even he has made a practice of omitting internal disputes in the Church still continuing in his own time, when they did not lead to actual divisions and separations.

As an instance of Dr. Wordsworth's love of what is strained and far-fetched, we may notice his suggestion (p. 132) that the name Victorinus, who is mentioned as a Patripassian by the author of the treatise on heresies at the end of Tertullian's *Præscriptiones*, may have arisen through the hesitation of copyists between Victor and Zephyrinus, or by a composition of the two names, the true reading being Zephyrinus. And again, the remark (p. 132), that when the author of the *Labyrinth* in the history of Natalius speaks of the avarice causing the ruin of many, which made this confessor a renegade, he had in his mind Zephyrinus, whose vice was covetousness.

The bloody persecution of Christians under Decius Dr. Wordsworth represents as a severe judgment sent upon the whole Church on account of the heresies and views which, thirty years earlier, had prevailed in the Church of Rome. According to his view, therefore, the Christians in Africa, in Egypt, in Asia Minor, and Syria, who furnished the greatest number of martyrs in this persecution, had to suffer because thirty years previously a Bishop of Rome, long since dead, favoured Sabellianism in his congregation and administered Church discipline on lax principles; although Dr. Wordsworth himself says that this favouring of heresy ceased with the death of Callistus. This is a new application of *delirant reges, plectuntur Achivi*. As evidence, he quotes first the lamentations of Cyprian over the corruption which in his day (*i.e.* some twenty years later) and in the African Church had become diffused, and then the Novatian schism, which, as is well known, did not begin till 251.

With regard to the rest of the book, it may suffice to remark that Dr. Wordsworth treats all the evidently exaggerated charges of Hippolytus as if they were made with the calm precision of a public prosecutor, and as if his expressions were always to be taken in their most comprehensive sense.

Dr. Wordsworth leads us back to Herr Bunsen's work. He speaks with emphasis and indignation of Herr Bunsen's unscientific caprice, of the positiveness of his assertions, which all the while rest upon the weakest grounds, and yet touch the most essential articles of the Christian faith and life, or the most important questions in ecclesiastical history; his book, he says, teems with almost innumerable errors, and his object is to undermine the foundations of the Christian faith (pp. 58, 301). The same criticisms on Herr Bunsen have proceeded from other quarters in England, and that from the bosom of the very Church which he has prized so highly in this book, smothering it with adulation through the mouth of Hippolytus. The *Christian Remembrancer*, for instance, designates Herr Bunsen's whole description of the theology of Hippolytus' age a series of misrepresentations; it remarks[1] that he can never be trusted with regard to any one fact, and that in his aphorisms he puts forth a system of naturalism veiled in Christian terminology. Herr Bunsen's utterances cannot fail to produce this impression in England, when, for instance, he says distinctly that "the human soul is a part of the self-consciousness of God before all finite existence;" when he pronounces that to represent *revelation as an objective historical act* is false, and as untenable as it is unphilosophical and unintelligent, and adds that "this erroneous

[1] January 1853, pp. 218, 234, 238.

representation was all the more perplexing, inasmuch as it assumed for the revelation of the divine will and nature something *higher than the human mind,*" etc. Thereupon Herr Bunsen contrasts with this false conception of revelation, which assumes it to be an historical fact and a real personal intervention of God in the history of man, the true conception of it, thus: " Revelation is a revelation of God in the mind of man, and only by a figure is represented as if God Himself spoke in human language to man. It has two factors, which, as soon as they exist, work together. The one is the infinite factor, or the immediate revelation of eternal truth to the mind through the power which this mind possesses of perceiving it; for human perception is the correlative of divine manifestation. This infinite factor is of course *not historical;* it dwells in every individual soul, only in indefinite difference of degree. The second factor is the finite or external one. This medium of divine revelation is first of all a general one, the universe or nature; in a special sense, however, it is an historical manifestation of divine truth through the life and teaching of higher minds among men, of specially gifted individuals, who impart something of eternal truth to their brethren," etc. etc.

These things need no comment. In England they will be readily endorsed by the Anglo-German prophet, as Herr Bunsen calls him, Carlyle; and in Germany the *Rationalismus vulgaris* has already greeted Herr Bunsen as an equal helpmate and kindred spirit, who merely speaks a somewhat pleasanter language. A theological faculty has hastened to crown with the wreath of a doctor's degree the treasure stored up in this book of truths, which are to transform the world and build the Church of the future. But the theologians and orators of free congregations also, the friends of enlightenment, etc., with whose words Germany a little while ago was still ringing, will joyfully recognise in Herr Bunsen an ally and brother-in-arms in the war against hierarchy, Churches with clergy, creeds, incomprehensible (or uncomprehended) dogmas, etc. etc. The rest of us abstain from the thankless task of emptying out before the public the dust-bag which he has filled with all kinds of rubbish, with bits of stone and mortar, crammed together out of Fathers, canons, and liturgies, and of subjecting the whole to an examination. Just one or two specimens of the way in which he deals with Hippolytus and the Greek Fathers may here be subjoined:—

1. In Hippolytus' concluding address[1] we read: "Him (the Logos) alone the Father produced from that which is (ἐξ ὄντων); for the Father Himself was that which is." Herr Bunsen translates: "Him alone *of all things* the Father produced." The great difference between the words of Hippolytus and this interpretation is at once seen in the fact that Hippolytus here exactly expresses the doctrine of the Council of Nicæa, carefully directed against the Arians, who (as is well known) taught that the Son was created ἐξ οὐκ ὄντων, out of nothing; whereas Herr Bunsen makes Hippolytus express himself as he would have done had he been an Arian.

2. In a passage already mentioned of the same concluding address, Hippolytus says: "Had He (God) willed to make thee a God, He would have done it: *thou*[2] *hast the instance of the Logos;* but, inasmuch as He willed to have thee a man, He hath made thee a man." Herr Bunsen translates: "He could have done it, *for thou hast the image of the Logos.*" That παράδειγμα

---

[1] *Philosophumena*, p. 334 [Book X. chap. xxix. p. 395, Clark's *Ante-Nicene Library*.]
[2] Ἔχεις τοῦ Λόγου τὸ παράδειγμα.

does not mean an image, any lexicon would have told him.

3. Still stronger is the following. In the same passage Hippolytus thus exhorts: "Cherish not enmity one against another, ye men, and hesitate[1] not to turn again." In Herr Bunsen this runs, "Doubt not that you will exist again!" This reminds one of another essay in the art of translating given us on a former occasion by Herr Bunsen. The exhortation of S. Ignatius in the letter to Polycarp, "Flee[2] evil arts; nay, rather mention them not at all in public," becomes with Herr Bunsen, after he has "emended" the text after his own fashion, "Flee coquettes; rather have intercourse with older women!"

4. Herr Bunsen alters the text, also, when Hippolytus says anything that he does not like. In Hippolytus we read: "Christ[3] is the God over all, who commanded us to wash away their sins from men." To this Herr Bunsen objects that Hippolytus cannot have said that Christ is the Father, as the text has it (Hippolytus, however, does not say so, but, in agreement with the words of the Apostle, Rom. ix. 25, that He is God over all, which He can be without being the Father); again, that Hippolytus cannot have said that Christ commanded men to wash away sins, for Christ Himself, according to God's command, has washed away the sins of men. But Hippolytus meant simply that Christ commanded men to wash away their sins in baptism; and when Herr Bunsen declares the text to be *absurd*, and accordingly makes alterations in it at pleasure, all one has to say is, that the absurdity exists for him alone, and that

---

[1] Μηδὲ παλινδρομεῖν διστάσητε.

[2] Τὰς κακοτεχνίας φεῦγε, μᾶλλον δὲ περὶ τούτων ὁμιλίαν μὴ ποιοῦ.

[3] P. 339: Χριστὸς γάρ ἐστιν ὁ κατὰ πάντων θεός, ὃς τὴν ἁμαρτίαν ἐξ ἀνθρώπων ἀποπλύνειν προσέταξε. Herr Bunsen puts in ᾧ after ἐστι, and cuts out ὅς.

his alterations are as perverse as they are unnecessary.[1]

In other respects the partiality for Hippolytus' theology, which Herr Bunsen exhibits several times and in very strained expressions, extends only to single definitions of his with regard to the Trinity, and indeed precisely to those in which he stands in real or apparent opposition to the doctrine of the Church. The false doctrine, against which Hippolytus contended with special zeal, Herr Bunsen takes under his protection; for (p. 176) he reckons the Noëtians among the sects "who, *with regard to God and Christ*, are orthodox, but in other points have some errors." And in the apology[2] Hippolytus has to allow that "the Noëtians stood with us upon evangelical ground;" and has to lament that he "treated them as heretics, although they differed from him in no essential point."

In this apology, which Herr Bunsen causes Hippolytus to make in London on the 13th of August 1851, the old Presbyter first of all overwhelms the English with praise of their power and glory, which they owe above all to their Protestantism, and then assures them that he really was Bishop of Portus Romanus, and there had an ever beloved wife, Chloe, the sister of a sacristan in the temple of Serapis at Portus, named Heron; but she soon died of fever, and soon after that his beloved son Anteros, who likewise caught a fever in the house of Bishop Callistus, whither he had been sent with a message, was torn from him by death. Next he informs the English, in order to inspire them with confidence, that with regard to the Bible he is a true Protestant; but the Book of Daniel

[1] [Bunsen renders the passage thus: "For Christ is He whom the God of all has ordered to wash away the sins," etc. Macmahon (in Clark's *Ante-Nicene Library*) translates: "For Christ is the God (who is) above all, and He has arranged to wash away sin from human beings," etc.]

[2] *Hippolytus and his Age*, IV. pp. 3–117.

is certainly spurious, and forged not earlier than the time of Antiochus, and the Second Epistle of S. Peter is likewise a forgery. And then he goes on to shock them still more by assuring them that their belief in the inspiration of Holy Scripture is a heretical delusion. He declares to them then further, that the Nicene doctrine about the Son of God is unphilosophical and unscriptural. In the doctrine of the Church respecting the Incarnation, and in the Athanasian Creed, he finds the reason why Muhammad and his followers have rooted out the Christian religion in half the world. In his day the baptism of children was quite unknown, and what now takes place under the name is no baptism at all. And after chastising the English establishment in this way with the staff Woe, at the end he brings forward again the staff Gentle,— that is, he falls upon the Catholic Church, and showers upon this mother of all evil (in phrases which he seems to have borrowed word for word from Messieurs RONGE and DOWIAT) all the vials of his wrath, threatens her with inevitable, utter, and fast approaching destruction, and takes leave of the English with the comforting assurance, that before the great second Reformation, now advancing with great strides, and before its divine blaze of light, the apostles of darkness — Catholic bishops and theologians—will sink into their own nothingness.

The reader will understand that after this there is no need of any further examination of Herr Bunsen and his four volumes.

CHAPTER VI.

EXAMINATION OF CERTAIN POINTS IN HIPPOLYTUS' FORM OF DOCTRINE.

THROUGH the certainty which has been now attained that Hippolytus belonged to the Roman Church in the first part of the third century, and the disappearance of so many doubts and obscurities attached to his personality, the rest of his writings still extant, and the witness to Church doctrine which they contain, acquire a new and increased importance. A short notice and discussion of certain passages may serve as a conclusion to this work.

I. THE MEANING OF "PRESBYTER" IN HIS WORKS.

Hippolytus repeatedly calls his teacher Irenæus, Bishop of Lugdunum, the "blessed PRESBYTEROS;" and in one of the two treatises which Photius would attribute to Caius, but which are by Hippolytus,—the one on the Universe and the other called the *Labyrinth*,— the author was designated, or probably had designated himself, as Presbyteros at Rome and Bishop of the heathen (ἐθνῶν). That at that time there were no Bishops without a fixed See has been already remarked. The author was therefore really Bishop of a definite Church, and the only question is, what is the meaning of the addition ἐθνῶν, and of the title "Presbyteros" united with that of Bishop?

It has long ago been remarked that the name PRES-

BYTEROS was, at the end of the second century, still used of Bishops. Most remarkable is this in Irenæus, who not only frequently uses the word of Bishops, *e.g.* those of Rome, or his own teacher Polycarp, but also speaks of the Presbyters who had the Episcopal Succession from the Apostles, and with it the *charisma* of the truth.[1] He mentions also some who were accounted as Presbyters by many, but, being made arrogant by their position,[2] were treated with less respect by others. Again, in Irenæus, and in a well-known passage of Papias, the first immediate disciples and contemporaries of the Apostles are called *Presbyters.* It has been rightly remarked, that here the notion of what is ancient and honourable is associated with the word,[3] and that the name Presbyteros, even when given to a Bishop, was a title of honour; but unmistakably something further must have been implied in this title, viz. the authority to teach, the *Magisterium.* Bishops or others are called Presbyters primarily as the holders and teachers of ecclesiastical tradition and knowledge. Thus the Presbyteri of Papias, and those Asiastic Presbyteri who had heard S. John still teaching, and to whose authority Irenæus appeals, were, independently of any other position and office in the Church, primarily merely the men who held and bore witness to the Apostolic *depositum,* forming the second link in the chain of tradition. In the passage of Irenæus already quoted, the same persons possess as Bishops the Apostolical Succession, as Presbyteri the " *charisma* of the truth," the gift of teaching, and the office of teacher in the Church. And those arrogant persons whom he mentions with reprobation were Bishops, for it was

---

[1] *Adv. Hær.* III. c. 2. 2; III. c. 3. 1, 2; IV. c. 26. 2.
[2] *Principalis concessionis tumore elati.* The Greek word no doubt was πρωτοκαθεδρίας, IV. c. 26. 3.
[3] ROTHE'S *Aufänge der Christl. Kirche,* p. 418.

their ecclesiastical rank, their πρωτοκαθεδρία, which made them puffed up; but they were merely accounted "Presbyters" by many without really being so, *i.e.* without possessing that *charisma*, the knowledge and gift peculiar to the office of teacher in the Church. Therefore, says Irenæus farther on, those who separated from the doctrine of the Church took advantage of the simplicity of the holy Presbyters, viz. their want of philosophical and rhetorical culture, etc. But when he speaks of the Succession, he uses the name Bishop; the heretics, he says, are all much younger than the Bishops, to whom the Apostles transmitted the Churches.[1] We find a similar use in Clement of Alexandria, in the *Eclogues*;[2] the Presbyteri (the old teachers in the Church) had not meddled with bookwriting, because they perhaps thought that the work of teaching and that of composition are not similar in kind. A later contemporary of Hippolytus, Firmilian, Bishop of Cæsarea, in speaking of the synodal meetings of the Bishops there, still uses the expression, "the Presbyteri and Superiors;"[3] and these titles are not synonymous, as Rothe supposes, but express a distinction,—the first meaning those who, among the Bishops themselves, on account of the school in which they had been educated and the work to which they had specially devoted themselves, possessed a *Magisterium*, and on questions of authority enjoyed a special authority.[4]

The same men who bore the honorary title of Presbyteri are several times called *Doctors* (διδάσκαλοι) by

[1] V. c. 20. 1, 2.   [2] P. 996, ed. Potter.

[3] *Seniores et Præpositi, Epist. ad Cyprian*, in Cyprian's Works, Baluz. p. 143. In the Greek, therefore, it stood πρεσβύτεροι καὶ προεστῶτες. Another expression seems to have been used in the following passage, which in the Latin translation runs thus: *Omnis potestas et gratia in ecclesia constituta est, ubi præsident majores natu, qui et baptizandi, et manum imponendi et ordinandi possident potestatem.* Here, no doubt, all Bishops without distinction are meant.

[4] [See LIGHTFOOT'S *Epistle to the Philippians*, pp. 193, 226 *sq.*]

the Roman Hermas; the white stones shown to him in the vision are "the Apostles, the Bishops, the Doctors, and the Church-servants (Deacons), who have holily performed their office;" and again, "The Apostles and Doctors who made known the Son of God" were shown to him under the image of forty stones, which serve to build the tower (the Church).[1] It is clear, also, that among the Priests of the Church, those who had the gift of science and learning (*doctores gratia scientiæ donati*, as Tertullian[2] calls them) were distinguished from the rest. Thus, in the *Acts of S. Perpetua*, the martyr Saturus mentions a *Presbyter Doctor Aspasius*, who was at variance with his Bishop Optatus; and Cyprian tells us that in company with the Presbyters, who were also Doctors, he used carefully to examine beforehand those who were to be appointed Readers.[3]

When, then, Hippolytus mentions Irenæus as the blessed Presbyteros, that is much the same as if he had called him a teacher of the Church. And when he himself in one of his writings is called Presbyteros and Bishop, that is to indicate his double office, which, at the beginning of the *Philosophumena*, he expresses in the words that he "has a share in the same grace as the Apostles, that of the High-priesthood and of teaching."[4]

But why does he call himself ἐπίσκοπος ἐθνῶν?

Hippolytus distinguishes between congregations or churches which, consisting of converted heathens, had nothing at all to do with the old Law, and those in which (as consisting wholly or by a large majority of

---

[1] *Pastor*, III. vis. ix. 21.   [2] *Præscr. adv. Hær.* 3.
[3] *Acta MM.* p. 93, ed. Ruinart. Cypriani, *Ep.* 29, p. 55, ed. Brem. Dionysius of Alexandria makes a similar distinction; he summoned together, he says, in the Arsenoitis the Presbyters *and* the Doctors (τοὺς διδασκάλους) of the Brethren in the villages. *Ap. Euseb.* vii. 24.
[4] Τῆς τε αὐτῆς χάριτος μετέχοντες, ἀρχιερατείας τε καὶ διδασκαλίας, p. 3.

converted Jews) the ceremonial Law was still partially observed. This is seen specially in a remarkable passage in his explanation of the blessing of Jacob. He makes the passage (Gen. xlix. 11) about the two foals, which are of one mother—the ass,[1] refer to the converted heathen and the converted Jews, who are of one faith; but the Elect (κλῆσις) or the Church of the heathen is bound to the Lord, while that of the circumcision is bound to the old Law.[2] In another passage in the same place, he says that the Flesh of the Lord cleanses the whole Church of the heathen.[3] Hippolytus by no means rejects these judaizing Christians; for further on he says of them that they who keep the commandments (of Christ), without giving up the doctrines and regulations of the Law, support themselves (ἐπαναπαύονται) on these as well as on the doctrine of our Lord; and this he regards as admissible, appealing to S. Matt. v. 17[4] ["Think not that I am come to destroy the law or the prophets; I am not come to destroy, but to fulfil"]. Therefore, in calling himself Bishop of the heathen, he means that the Church over which he presided consisted of heathens converted to Christianity, free from all judaizing elements.

II. HIS WITNESS TO THE PRIESTHOOD AND SACRIFICE OF THE CHURCH.

Respecting the PRIESTHOOD and SACRIFICE IN THE CHURCH, a couple of remarkable statements of Hippolytus have been preserved to us. At the end of a small

---

[1] Following the Septuagint, which runs: Τὸν πῶλον αὐτοῦ, καὶ . . . τὸν πῶλον τῆς ὄνου αὐτοῦ.

[2] Or to the *antiquated* Law: τῇ τοῦ νόμου παλαιότητι. The passage is to be found in the Σειρὰ εἰς τὴν ὀκτατεύχον, edited by Νικηφόρος Ἱερομόνοχος, I. 522.

[3] *L.c.* I. 625: Πᾶσαν τήν ἐξ ἐθνῶν κλῆσιν.   [4] *L.c.* I. 530.

treatise,[1] in which he castigates and exhorts the Jews, he depicts the marvellous spectacle of Israel pressing, humbled and penitent, to receive baptism, and begging for the food of grace—the Blessed Bread, while those who formerly offered sacrifice, as Levites or Priests and High-priests, now attend a sacrifice offered by a slave.[2] Hippolytus could make the contrast all the stronger in this way, because at that time it was by no means of rare occurrence that a slave became Priest and Bishop, e.g. Callistus. But wherein this sacrifice consisted he tells us in an extant fragment,[3] in which he gives an allegorical interpretation of the passage in the Proverbs of Solomon (ix. 1–5) about the house which Wisdom builded, and the sacrificial feast which she prepared. "Daily," he says, "is His precious and stainless Body and Blood consecrated and offered on the mystical and Divine Table, in commemoration of that ever-memorable and first Table of the mystical Divine Supper."[4]

A confirmation of this passage is to be found in his interpretation of Daniel,[5] where he says that at the coming of Antichrist, the Sacrifice, which is now everywhere offered to God by the nations, will be done away. Hippolytus is the first among the Fathers to suppose that the last week in Daniel will find its fulfilment in the time of Antichrist and through him. He thinks

[1] MAGISTRIS has edited it in Latin, *Acta Martyrum ad Ostia Tiberina*, Append. pp. 449–458. A fragment of it in Greek also still exists in a MS. in the Vatican.
[2] *Qui Levitæ offerebant, et Sacerdotes immolantes et summi Antistites libantes adsistunt* puero *offerenti*, p. 458.
[3] It is given in FABRICIUS, *Opp. Hippol.* I. 282.
[4] Τὸ τίμιον καὶ ἄχραντον αὐτοῦ σῶμα καὶ αἷμα, ἅπερ ἐν τῇ μυστικῇ καὶ θείᾳ τραπέζῃ καθ' ἑκάστην ἐπιτελοῦνται θυόμενα εἰς ἀνάμνησιν τῆς ἀειμνήστου καὶ πρώτης ἐκείνης τραπέζης τοῦ μυστικοῦ θείου δείπνου.
[5] In the edition of MAGISTRIS, *Daniel secundum Septuaginta ex tetraplis Origenis nunc primum editus*, Romæ 1772, fol. p. 110. Here also Hippolytus is called Bishop of Rome. It should be mentioned that the *Codex Chigianus*, in which this fragment is found, appears not to be older than the tenth century.

that the Prophet has spoken of a double abomination of desolation, a transient interruption at the time of Antiochus, and an utter desolation at the time of Antichrist.[1] Theodoret and Jerome make the words of the Prophet refer to a general cessation of service in the Church; while Primasius, Ephraem, and the Arian author of the work on S. Matthew,[2] prefer the interpretation of Hippolytus;—all, however, suppose that this desolation of the Church will last only four years and a half.[3]

It has been lately maintained [4] that the Fathers, previous to Cyprian, knew nothing of a Sacrifice in which the Body of Christ is offered; when they spoke of a Sacrifice, they merely meant either the prayers which were offered at Christian services and in connection with the celebration of the Eucharist, or the bread and wine *as such* (not that to be changed, and then really changed into the Body of the Lord) as the material of the Church's sacrifice. Here is a Father who lived before Cyprian, and who declares, with a distinctness that defies misinterpretation, that the Body of the Lord Himself is the object and content of the Church's daily Sacrifice. The fond notion that Cyprian was the first person to imagine the doctrine of the Sacrifice of the Body of Christ in the Church is in other respects all the more strange, because we find the same doctrine shortly after Cyprian in the Greek Fathers (who certainly did not obtain it from the

---

[1] *Scriptor. Vet. Nov. Col.* ed. Mai. I. P. II. p. 56.

[2] In MALVENDA, *De Antichristo*, II. 154.

[3] Hippolytus says: $\dot{\alpha}\rho\theta\dot{\eta}\sigma\varepsilon\tau\alpha\iota$ $\theta\nu\sigma\dot{\iota}\alpha$ $\varkappa\alpha\dot{\iota}$ $\sigma\pi\sigma\nu\delta\dot{\eta}$, the Sacrifice and the Drink-offering, with reference to the Eucharistic wine. We have the same combination in PHILO (*Vit. Mos.* 1): $M\varepsilon\tau\alpha\sigma\chi\varepsilon\tilde{\iota}\nu$ $\tau\tilde{\omega}\nu$ $\alpha\dot{\upsilon}\tau\tilde{\omega}\nu$ $\sigma\pi\sigma\nu\delta\tilde{\omega}\nu$ $\tau\varepsilon$ $\varkappa\alpha\dot{\iota}$ $\theta\nu\sigma\iota\tilde{\omega}\nu$.

[4] J. W. F. HÖFLING, *Die Lehre der ältesten Kirche vom Opfer im Leben und Cultus der Christen*, Erlang. 1851. [See J. H. NEWMAN'S Essay on *The Patristical Idea of Antichrist* in *Discussions and Arguments*, Esp. p. 53 sq.]

Latin writings of the Bishop of Carthage) set forth as something long known; so that, for instance, Eusebius of Cæsarea says, " We offer the Blood of sprinkling, the Blood of the Lamb of God, who taketh away the sins of the world, which purifies our souls."[1] And S. Cyril, about the year 344, declares to the newly baptized at Jerusalem, as the ancient universally acknowledged doctrine of this original Apostolic Church, "We offer the Christ who was slain for our sins."[2]

It may be worth while to subject to a more careful examination the celebrated passage in TERTULLIAN, in which he seems to maintain a Priesthood of the Laity, even to the administration of the sacraments and the offering of the Holy Sacrifice. In the treatise on *Exhortation to Chastity*, he endeavours to show that even laymen are under an obligation to withhold from a second marriage after the death of their wife; and as it was objected that the Apostle required this only of the clergy, he answered this objection with the universal Priesthood of all Christians, and then applies this to the actual performance of proper priestly functions. " Are not also the laymen Priests? . . . The difference between the Priesthood and the people is created by the authority of the Church, and the dignity sanctified by the place in the Presbytery. Where, therefore, a regularly ordained Presbytery does not exist, there thou offerest, and baptizest, and art Priest for thyself alone. Where three are, even if only laymen, there there is a Church, for each one lives in accordance with his faith [see Hab. ii. 4; Rom. i. 17; Gal. iii. 2; Heb. x. 38], and before God is no respect of

[1] Ἀλλὰ καὶ τοὺς ἄρτους τῆς προθέσεως προσφέρομεν, τὴν σωτήριον μνήμην ἀναζωπυροῦντες, τό τε τοῦ ῥαντισμοῦ αἷμα τοῦ ἀμνοῦ τοῦ θεοῦ περιελόντος τὴν ἀμαρτίαν τοῦ κόσμου, καθάρσιον τῶν ἡμετέρων ψυχῶν. In Psalm xci. p. 608, ed. Montfaucon, *Coll. Patr.*

[2] *Catech. Mystag.* V. p. 327, Paris 1720.

persons; for not the hearers of the law are justified before God, but the doers of it (Rom. ii. 11-13). . . . If, then, thou hast the right of a Priest in thee when it is necessary, thou must also have the priestly behaviour. Or willest thou, though twice married, baptize and sacrifice?"[1]

Above all things, we must here notice that Tertullian wrote this treatise as a Montanist, for in it he appeals to an utterance of the "holy prophetess Prisca" or Priscilla.[2] If we now compare the view of the Church, as held by Tertullian since his adoption of Montanism, it will be seen that what he here says about the Priesthood was with him merely a logical conclusion. The true Church, he teaches, is a copy of that spiritual Church which exists in heaven, and to which only the three Divine Persons belong. On earth, the daughter and the facsimile of the heavenly Church is to be found where (S. Matt. xviii. 20) three are gathered together in Christ's name,—three "spiritual" Christians ($\pi\nu\epsilon\nu\mu\alpha\tau\iota\kappa o\iota$), or any number of them, who do not, like the great mass of "natural" ones ($\psi\nu\chi\iota\kappa o\iota$), close their ears to the suggestions of the Paraclete, but open their hearts and senses, and willingly obey this new commandment. A Church composed of these $\pi\nu\epsilon\nu\mu\alpha\tau\iota\kappa o\iota$ (believers enlightened by the Holy Ghost through His prophets), possesses the true spiritual and sacerdotal powers, which that Church in which the great number

---

[1] *Differentiam inter ordinem et plebem constituit ecclesiæ auctoritas, et honor per ordinis consessum sanctificatus;* if *constituit* is translated as the perfect (as by NEANDER, *Antignost.* p. 230: "*Only* the authority of the Church *has* created the difference," etc.), Tertullian is made to speak very perversely, for then this difference would be said to be based on something which was possible only in consequence of this very difference. The *consessus ordinis, i.e.* the Presbytery, already presupposes a difference between *ordo* and *plebs.*

[2] *De Exhort. Cast.* c. 10, p. 752, ed. Œhler. Rigaltius was the first to edit the passage, which is wanting in most MSS. and editions. [It is given in Clark's *Ante-Nicene Library, The Writings of Tertullian,* III. p. 11.]

of Bishops is found does not, or at any rate not in the same degree; just as also Peter received his power from Christ not in his hierarchical character, and therefore not with a view to continuation through the Episcopal Succession, but merely personally as πνευμα-τικός.[1] All "spiritual" Christians or members of the higher Church, therefore, bear the right and powers of the Priesthood within them; they could all of them even forgive mortal sins, although they refrain from doing so unless moved to it by a special inspiration of the Paraclete. They can also perform all other priestly offices, baptize, and offer the Holy Sacrifice; but this also they do not do under ordinary circumstances, because they fully recognise the existing arrangements of the Church necessary for the sake of order, and the difference, not to be capriciously obliterated, between a regularly constituted official power in the Church, and the universal Priesthood which dwells in every "spiritual" layman, and therefore are unwilling to cause disturbance and confusion by interfering in the official sphere in the Church. For due respect to *authority* in the Church, viz. that of the Bishop, and to the dignity or office (*honor*) of the Priests assembled in the Presbytery (*consessus ordinis*), demands that a layman should not without necessity or special cause, and merely of his own judgment, perform a sacerdotal or sacramental act, although as "spiritual," as a member of that spiritual Church which exists wherever there are three illuminated souls, he has the power to do so implanted in him.[2]

---

[1] *De Pudic.* c. 21, pp. 843, 844, ed. Œhler.

[2] Thus Tertullian says (*De Bapt.*) of even Presbyters and Deacons that they had the right to baptize: *non tamen sine episcopi* auctoritate *propter ecclesiæ* honorem, *quo salvo salva pax est*. By *honor*, profane writers understand an office united with some special marks of honour. Tertullian means by it the ecclesiastical rank, the clerical dignity; as also in the passage (*De Monogam.* c. 12): *Ne vel ipse* honor *aliquid sibi ad licentiam, quasi de privi-*

Tertullian does not, therefore, mean to say that the difference between the laity and clergy was of later origin, and first introduced by a special decree of the Church, as he has sometimes been understood; so far from that, he expressly places the institution of the various orders in the Church in Apostolical times.[1] What he means is this, that the separation of the clergy from the laity takes place by the exercise of ecclesiastical authority, *i.e.* the selection and ordination by the Bishop and the assent of the Presbytery, as also by the being received into the bosom of this college; not, however, that the sacerdotal power was then first given to the person ordained, for this he already possessed in substance as a layman, but merely that the regular use of it for the benefit of the congregation, and in due hierarchical subordination, was now made a duty.

I formerly thought, and on one occasion stated the opinion, that by the *offerre*, which Tertullian attributes even to laymen, he alluded to the custom in the ancient Church of taking the Eucharistic bread from the Church to one's house, and there partaking of it in successive acts of communion. A private communion of this kind was, of course, accompanied each time by a renewed act of oblation, in which the believer offered as a sacrifice to God the Body of the Lord, then taken in the hand, together with himself, sanctified as he then must be by this very partaking of His Body, and made one with Him. Tertullian mentions this custom frequently,—*e.g.* in the passage in which he recommends men to receive the Lord's Body at the fasting stations and *reserve* It, and thus take part in the

---

legio loci blandiatur. This clerical dignity, which differentiates the official Priest from the layman, is "sanctified by the *consessus ordinis*," *i.e.* by the Presbytery, the members of which, as is well known, had the privilege of remaining seated in the church with the Bishop, while the rest of the clergy and the laity stood.

[1] In the passage quoted above, *De Monogam.* c. 12.

sacrifice.[1] But in his description of the lay-priesthood he certainly goes farther; he means, that where there is no Presbytery, where (for instance) the clergy have been rooted out or dispersed by persecution,[2] or where a believer in prison is cut off from all intercourse with clergy who otherwise were accustomed to offer the Holy Sacrifice for the confessors in imprisonment, then he is "Priest for himself alone," and can therefore consecrate the Eucharist for himself and give himself the communion. That Tertullian does not here speak of an existing recognised custom in the Church, or of a right that was excercised,—that he does not deduce the right from the fact, but *vice versâ* merely maintains the right to priestly functions by virtue of the theory which he has made up for himself, is quite clear. Accordingly, he produces quite in his way the proof that such a right must be admitted; for he appeals (not to the practice of the Church, as you might expect, but) to certain texts (Rev. i. 6; Rom. ii. 11-13), which he quotes verbatim, to his own idea of the difference between clergy and laity, and to the (for him) specially important saying, that where three are, there there already is a Church.

Two deductions from this theory of Tertullian's lay very close at hand. First, it was possible to make women also, who were accounted organs of the Paraclete, into priestesses, as the Montanists somewhat later actually did. Secondly, the official Priesthood must have become a very uncertain and dubious thing; for if the "spiritual" laymen already bore in themselves the sacerdotal power, it would not be very difficult to deny the existence of this internal Priesthood

---

[1] *Accepto corpore Domini* et reservato, *utrumque salvum est, et participatio sacrificii et executio officii* (*De Orat.* c. 19). [Clark, I. p. 193, note.]

[2] He mentions such cases, *De Fuga*, c. 11: *Quod nunquam magis fit quam cum in persecutione destituitur ecclesia a clero.*

(which was the condition of the external) in Presbyters and Bishops, under the pretext that they were not "spiritual," and thus to declare that all their sacramental administrations were null and void.

III. THE "ALTAR" AND THE "HOLY TABLE" IN PRIMITIVE TIMES.

Hippolytus calls the ALTAR on which the sacrifice of the Church was offered the HOLY TABLE. This expression is specially frequent in the Greek Fathers, and that even at the time when altars were already made of stone. It was considered as synonymous with "Altar," as one sees, among other places, from a passage in S. Gregory of Nyssa,[1] in which it is said that the Holy Altar is a common stone; but when it has been sanctified by the service of God, and has received consecration, it is a Holy Table, a stainless Altar ($\theta\upsilon\sigma\iota\alpha\sigma\tau\acute{\eta}\rho\iota\sigma\nu$), which can no longer be touched by any one, but only by the Priests, and by them only with reverence and awe. The Greek Fathers avoided the expression used to designate heathen altars; and, when they did not speak of the Holy Table, chose the word introduced by Hellenists to designate the Jewish altar, and otherwise unknown to the Greeks.[2] On the other hand, the Latin-

---

[1] *Orat. in Bapt. Christi*, p. 802.

[2] Not βωμός or ἐσχάρα, but θυσιαστήριον. Only in a constitution of the Emperors Theodosius II. and Valentinian, in the fifth century, does βωμός occur of a Christian altar. [SYNESIUS also, in his κατάστασις ῥηθεῖσα ἐπὶ τῇ μεγίστῃ τῶν βαρβάρων ἐφόδῳ (about A.D. 412), speaks of flying for refuge to the unbloody βωμός. Both CLEMENT OF ALEXANDRIA, however, and ORIGEN use βωμός in a figurative sense in speaking of the soul as the true Christian altar. Thus Clement (*Strom.* vii. cap. 6, p. 717) says: "Will they not believe us when we say that the righteous soul is the truly sacred altar, and that the incense arising from it is holy prayer?" And Origen (*c. Celsum*, viii. p. 389) admits the charge of Celsus, that the Christians had no material altars. In *Maccab.* i. 54 and 55, we have the distinction between

speaking Christians from the first had no scruples in designating their altars by the words *ara* and *altare*, which hitherto had had only a heathen meaning. And no doubt the name "Holy Table" would have called up the same idea in the minds of the heathen as the use of the word *ara*.[1] When it was thrown in the teeth of the Christians by the heathen, that they had no temples and no altars, as all other religions and nations had, they admitted this in the sense in which the heathen took these words; for they meant that, as a Christian church is something very different from a heathen temple, so also a Christian church was as far removed as heaven from earth from all heathen altars with their animal sacrifices. Thus ORIGEN, while in answer to Celsus he says that among Christians the place of $βωμοί$ is taken by souls and the prayers which they offer, yet, when he speaks before a Christian assembly, speaks of the altars existing in the Christian churches. In the charge which Cæcilius makes against the Christians in MINUCIUS FELIX, there lies certainly no more than this, that the Christians had no public altars which the heathen could see.[2] CYPRIAN, however, gives the heathen Demetrianus plainly enough to understand that the Christians undoubtedly had altars, but in secret; for he makes it a matter of reproach that the altars of the heathen were everywhere covered with bloody sacrifices, while the altars of the true God

$θυσιαστήριον$ and $βωμός$ strongly marked, the former being used of the altar of Jehovah, the latter of heathen altars. *Ara* is usually avoided by the early apologists; Tertullian qualifies it, *ara Dei*, etc. In the Latin Fathers, and in Liturgical language, *altare* is far the most common word. [Article ALTAR, in Smith's *Dictionary of Christian Antiquities*, which contains much information on the subject generally.]

[1] *Mensæ in ædibus sacris ararum vicem obtinent*, says FESTUS, p. 236, ed. Amst. 1699; and Scaliger remarks on this, that in the *jus Papirianum* it was laid down, *mensas arulasque eodem die, quo ædes dedicari solent, sacras esse.*

[2] *Cum honesto semper publico gaudeant*, he says, . . . *cur nullas aras habent?* (c. 10.) [MINUCIUS FELIX (*Octavius*, c. 32) says: *Delubra et aras non habemus.*]

either did not exist (among the heathen) or only in secret (among the Christians).[1]

IV. ASCETICS ALREADY NUMEROUS IN THE TIME OF HIPPOLYTUS.

Hippolytus mentions it as an interpretation that had already been put forth in his day, that the seven pillars on which the house of the Divine Wisdom rests (Prov. ix. 1) are the seven ranks or classes in the Church,—Prophets, Apostles, Martyrs, Bishops, Ascetics, Saints, and Just. It might surprise us that in so early an age the Ascetics are already mentioned as a special class, which, therefore, must have been numerous enough to be mentioned along with the others in this enumeration. It cannot, however, be doubted that the number of those who gave up the business and distractions of the world, and devoted themselves to a strict religious life, celibacy, with constant meditation or frequent prayer, was already at that time very great. This ascetic mode of life had no definitely established form; there was as yet no school for such, no community of many living together. Perpetual virginity was the point most generally observed; some added to this the abstaining from flesh and wine.[2] Not merely laymen, but Bishops and clergy, belonged frequently to these Ascetics; and it often happened that married people by free consent devoted themselves to the ascetic life, and henceforth lived merely as brothers and sisters, sometimes giving up dwelling together, sometimes continuing to do so. Justin even in his time can boast, that in all classes of society he can point out persons who of their own free-will had lived to old age in unbroken continence. Athenagoras

---

[1] *Dei altaria vel nulla sunt vel occulta*, p. 190, ed. Brem.
[2] TERTULL. *De Cultu Fem.* c. 11.

makes mention of those numerous Christians of both sexes, who in order to attain to more intimate union and closer intercourse with God, grew old in celibacy. There are those "elect among the elect," who (as Clement of Alexandria says) have withdrawn from the storms of life into the safe harbour; those Ascetics, to whom Origen in his controversy with Celsus appeals, whose mode of life (as he says) was in its use of means very like, but in its aim very unlike, that of the Pythagoreans.[1] That some chose in addition to this a voluntary poverty, is shown by the case of the Presbyter Pierius of Alexandria.[2]

V. THE DOCTRINE OF HIPPOLYTUS RESPECTING THE DESCENT OF CHRIST INTO HADES.

In two passages Hippolytus bears witness to the common doctrine of the ancient Fathers, that Christ gave the souls in the under-world or Hades also a share in the fruit of His Redemption; that immediately after His death upon the cross His Soul went to that

---

[1] JUSTIN. *Apol.* p. 62; ATHENAG. *Legat.* c. 28; CLEM. ALEX. II. 955 [ἐκλεκτῶν ἐκλεκτότεροι]; ORIGEN, *Contra Cels.* p. 615.

[2] HIERONYM. *De Scr. Eccl.* c. 76. [*Ibid.* c. 41, the case of Serapion, Bishop of Antioch: *leguntur et sparsim ejus breves epistolæ, auctoris sui ἀσκήσει et vitæ congruentes.* Of Pierius Jerome says: *constat hunc miræ ἀσκήσεως et appetitorem voluntariæ paupertatis fuisse.* According to MOSHEIM (*Eccl. Hist.* I. p. 128, ed. Stubbs), a class of Ascetics arose "on a sudden" in the second century. The truth is much better stated by I. G. SMITH (*Dict. of Christ. Ant.*, article ASCETICISM) and by ROBERTSON (*Hist. of Christ's Church*, I. p. 248, 2d ed.). For 150 years there is no trace of a *class* of ἀσκηταί in the Church. Christianity itself is an ἄσκησις. Between 150 and 250 A.D. Asceticism as a profession assumes a more defined position. Neo-Platonism had begun to exert a strong influence on some centres of Christianity, teaching that an imitation of the Divine repose was to be aimed at by avoiding, as far as possible, the evil influence of the body. This was equally the case in the East, where the climate invites to a contemplative rather than an active life. The love of austerity for its own sake is prominent in many of the sects of the second century,—the Montanists, the Syrian Gnostics, the Encratites, and Marcionites. About 250 A.D. the

place where the souls of the departed since Adam were kept as in a prison-house, waiting and hoping for the coming release, and there preached to them the good tidings of His Incarnation and Redemption. He is the first writer known to us who makes John the Baptist go before to Hades, as the one who was destined to serve as forerunner to the Lord not only on earth, but also in the other world, in order to proclaim there the joyful message, that the Lord would soon come thither also, "to free the souls of the saints out of the hand of death."[1] This idea, which occurs in Origen also, has been transferred even to the prayer-books of the Eastern Church: in an invocation of John in the Troparion we have—"Thou, who didst proclaim beforehand to those in Hades the approach of Life through the Holy Spirit, bring life to my soul that is stricken with death."[2]

In another passage[3] Hippolytus wishes (it appears) to impress upon us that it was the Human Soul of Christ which descended into Hades to the souls confined there, while His Body lay in the grave; while the Godhead at one and the same time in Its Essence was with the Father, but also remained in the Body, and descended with the soul into Hades. An unknown writer in the *Catena* on the Catholic Epistles has made

Decian persecution precipitated the effects of causes already at work, and those who had hitherto lived a strict life in society now fled from society altogether, and took refuge in the desert. The history of Asceticism here merges in that of Monasticism. In considering the extravagances of Asceticism we must never forget the frightful moral corruptions of heathendom from which they were a natural reaction.]

[1] Οὗτος προέφθασε καὶ τοῖς ἐν ᾅδη εὐαγγελίσασθαι, ἀναιρεθεὶς ὑπὸ Ἡρώδου, πρόδρομος γενόμενος ἐκεῖ· σημαίνειν μέλλων κἀκεῖσε κατελεύσεσθαι τὸν σωτῆρα λυτρούμενον τὰς ἁγίων ψυχὰς ἐκ χειρὸς θανάτου (*De Antichristo*, c. 45, *Opp.* I. 22).

[2] See this and other similar passages in ALLATIUS, *De Lib. Eccl. Græc.* p. 303.

[3] MAIO has cited it from a *catena* on S. Luke's Gospel, *Scriptor. Nova Coll.* ix. 712.

use of this passage of Hippolytus; both apply the words of Psalm cvii. 16, that the Lord "hath broken the gates of brass and smitten the bars of iron in sunder," to this subject; and later Fathers also, as Athanasius, understood them of the descent of the Redeemer into Hades.[1] By his expression, "the souls of the Lord," Hippolytus shows that he, like his teacher Irenæus,[2] supposed that the benefit of Christ's appearance in Hades was shared only by the believers there.[3]

VI. THE CHILIASM OF HIPPOLYTUS.

From the circumstance that Hippolytus, in his work on heresies, nowhere mentions CHILIASM, it has already been conjectured that he himself may have been inclined to this idea. His relationship to S. Irenæus increases the probability of this, which is raised to certainty by a passage in his interpretation of Daniel.[4] For, proceeding on the assumption that Christ appeared upon earth in the year of the world 5500, he goes on to conclude that a sixth thousand must yet be completed, and then the Sabbath (on the analogy of the Creation) must come. The first Sabbath, the day of divine rest after the Creation, is "the type and image of the coming *kingdom of the saints, when Christ shall come down from heaven, and they shall reign with Him.*"[5]

As a Chiliast, therefore, Hippolytus ranks himself with that section of the ancient Fathers who would

[1] *Catena in Epp. Cath.* Oxonii 1840, p. 66; *Corderii Expos. PP. Græc. in Psalmos*, iii. 185.

[2] *Adv. Hær.* IV. c. 39, 45; V. c. 31.

[3] In his interpretation of Daniel, also, Hippolytus says of Christ: Εὐαγγελιζόμενος ταῖς τῶν ἁγίων ψυχαῖς, διὰ θανάτου θάνατον νικῶν.

[4] *Daniel secundum Septuaginta*, Romæ 1772, pp. 99, 100.

[5] Τὸ σάββατον τύπος ἐστὶ καὶ εἰκὼν τῆς μελλούσης βασιλείας τῶν ἁγίων, ἡνίκα συμβασιλεύσουσι τῷ Χριστῷ, παραγινομένου αὐτοῦ ἀπ' οὐρανῶν, ὡς Ἰωάννης ἐν τῇ ἀποκαλύψει διηγεῖται.

not, and according to their theory *could* not, admit that the souls of the righteous even before the resurrection attained to the Kingdom of Heaven and the Beatific Vision; and who therefore taught that all souls in definite places enter upon a middle state still undecided, and are kept until the end of the present world. Thus JUSTINUS and IRENÆUS, the latter of whom can scarcely tolerate the very different opinion of other Catholics, that the souls of the righteous attain immediately to everlasting life; perceiving in it an heretical turn of thought, because it recalled to his mind the wild fancies of the Valentinians, who confidently expected immediately after death to ascend into the *Pleroma* to the Father, leaving all the heavens and the *Demiurgos* himself far below them.[1] So again TERTULLIAN, who even perceives a kind of arrogance in the fact that Catholic Christians would not tolerate the notion of souls going to Hades; as if, he says, the servants were better than their Master, who Himself went thither. Whereas the Catholics said, "It was for the very purpose of abolishing the necessity for our going down any more to Hades that Christ went thither; and what difference would there be between heathens and Christians, if all after death were kept in the same prison-house?"[2] Yet Tertullian makes an exception in favour of the martyrs, who are to go to Paradise and enjoy the Divine Glory immediately.[3] Accordingly, HIPPOLYTUS also maintains that the great receptacle of souls, created at the beginning of the world, consists of various divisions or dwellings; and that one of these is Abraham's Bosom, the dwelling of the just,—a bright place, in which the pious, in the enjoyment of perfect rest and in the hope of the future joys of Heaven, occupy themselves meanwhile with

---

[1] *Adv. Hær.* V. c. 31. [2] *De Anima*, c. 55.
[3] *Apolog.* c. 47; *De Resurr.* c. 43.

contemplating the things of the visible and living world.[1]

In opposition to these theories, which have their root in Chiliastic views, stand already at that time HERMAS, CLEMENT OF ALEXANDRIA (who assigns to the pious dead, after they have been subjected to the still necessary purification, immediate companionship with the Angels in Heaven),[2] CYPRIAN (who commends himself to the intercession of virgins when they find themselves in the enjoyment of the heavenly reward),[3] and METHODIUS, Bishop of Tyre, who, in spite of his leaning towards Chiliasm, declares that the souls of the departed will have their abode with God before the resurrection.[4] Then follow the anti-chiliastically inclined Eusebius of Cæsarea, Athanasius, Epiphanius, and Jerome; until at last only isolated voices, and these ever more and more rarely, make themselves heard in favour of a general Hades.[5]

---

[1] *Opp.* ed. Fabricius, I. 220. [2] *Stromata*, VII. p. 732, ed. Colon.
[3] *De Habitu Virg.* [4] *De Resurr.* in Photius, cod. 234.

[5] [MOSHEIM (*Eccles. Hist.* I. p. 90, ed. Stubbs) traces Chiliasm to Cerinthus. The only authority for this (none are cited by him) appears to be Caius, the obscure Presbyter noticed at the beginning of this volume (pp. 2–4) as a possible (though not probable) author of the *Philosophumena*. It was perhaps only for the sake of bringing Chiliasm into disrepute that Caius traced it to the arch-heretic. Papias, unless Eusebius misunderstood him, appears to have held Chiliastic views. But the fact of their being ardently maintained by Montanists and other sects brought such tenets into disfavour in the Church. Chiliasm seems never to have been dealt with by Synods; it is in the gradual consensus of the Fathers against it that we find its condemnation. See ROBERTSON, *Hist. of Christ. Church*, I. pp. 63, 160 *sq.* 2d ed.]

APPENDIX A.

DR. SALMON ON THE CHRONOLOGY OF HIPPOLYTUS.

SINCE Dr. Döllinger published his *Hippolytus und Kallistus*, few more important contributions to the subject have been made than the article on *The Chronology of Hippolytus* by Dr. Salmon, Regius Professor of Divinity in the University of Dublin, in the first number of *Hermathena* (1873). The title of his essay shows that he deals rather with the science than the theology of Hippolytus; but as he here and there traverses the same ground as Dr. Döllinger, and in one important instance arrives at a different conclusion, it will be worth while to state some of the main results arrived at in this most valuable dissertation.

Dr. Salmon considers that the reasons stated by Dr. Döllinger[1] for believing that the famous statue dug up in Rome in 1551 represents Hippolytus, that it must have been erected soon after his death or banishment, *i.e.* not much later than 235, and therefore is one of the earliest works of Christian art still remaining to us, are absolutely conclusive. The calendar for determining the Paschal full moons inscribed on one side of the chair of the statue, although in form a 16-years cycle, is really an 8-years cycle,—*i.e.* it proceeds on the assumption that the full moons return to the same day of the month after eight years, an assumption so erroneous that in considerably less than a century the calendar would give full moon when the moon was

[1] Pp. 24–27.

new. Hippolytus was not the inventor of this system; he found it in existence, and added to it an attempt to show the day of the week of the full moon as well as the day of the month. The cycle proves that the author was no mathematician, still less an astronomer, but merely an almanac maker. His cycle is a mere guess; had he tried, he would have found that in eight years the full moons do *not* return to the same day, but a day and a half later. He was content with making eight years contain an exact number of months without any days over, quite overlooking the fact that his months were not all of the same length. To ask how Hippolytus made a name by so blundering a performance is like asking how Wyatt made a name as a first-rate architect at the end of the last century. "A charlatan in an age of ignorance" always finds admirers. Before Hippolytus' day, Christians had been in a great measure dependent on the Jews for determining the time of Easter, obliged *tanquam ignorantes quæ sit dies Paschæ post Judæos cæcos et hebetes ambulare.*[1] They were, of course, grateful to a man who seemed to be able to settle the time of Easter for them for many years to come.

An insight into the chronology of Hippolytus, such as Dr. Salmon gives us with great clearness, enables us to decide with perfect certainty that the chronicle, first published by Canisius in 1602 (*Antiq. Lect.* II. 580), and included among the documents appended to Du Cange's edition of the *Paschal Chronicle*, is the work of Hippolytus. It is written in Latin, but was evidently first written in Greek; for two versions are still extant agreeing exactly in sense, but differing in words. The author was, apparently, but an indifferent arithmetician; his totals do not always agree with the

---

[1] *De Pascha Computus*, in the Appendix to Fell's *Cyprian*, written in Africa about 243.

items given, a fact which affects the present question. Four Passover intervals, as given by him, are—from Joshua to Hezekiah, 864; from Hezekiah to Josiah, 114; from thence to Esdras, 108; thence to the γένεσις (conception) of Christ, 563. The same intervals, as deduced from the table on the statue, are 864, 113, 107, 563. In the production of so inaccurate a worker, the difference of a single unit in two of the numbers need not weigh with us. Such close coincidence between the dates in the chronicle and those deduced from the table of Hippolytus argues identity of authorship. This argument amounts to proof, when we consider that the Cyprianic computist quoted above makes these same intervals 826, 103, 144, 465; Eusebius, 730, 114, 111, 514; Syncellus, 909, 105, 128, 502; modern chronologers also widely differ. Du Cange had already conjectured that Hippolytus was the author of the chronicle on other grounds, and the conjecture may now be considered as an established truth.

The last section of the chronicle originally contained a list of the Bishops of Rome. In the extant table of contents, the title of the last section is *Nomina Episcoporum Romœ, et quis quot annis præfuit*. This section has disappeared; but it is contended by Mommsen[1] and others, that the earlier part of the list of Roman Bishops (ending with Urban, A.D 230), given by the chronographer of the year 354, is from a different source from the remainder, and is based upon the list now missing from the chronicle of Hippolytus. The chronographer's list ends with Liberius, and is commonly called the Liberian catalogue. The earlier part gives the names of the Bishops, time of their government, contemporaneous Emperors, and the Consuls of

[1] *Ueber den Chronographen vom Jahre* 354, "Abhandl. der philolog.-histor. Classe der Konigl. Sachs. Gesellschaft der Wissenschaften," I. 585.

the first and last years of each Bishop; but in such a way that the Consuls of the first year of a Bishop are never the same as those of the last year of the preceding Bishop, but are those of the year following. With one remarkable exception, there are no historical notices. In the part of the catalogue subsequent to Urban, a different method prevails. The days of Bishops' ordination and death are often noted; the death of one Bishop and the accession of his successor usually come under the same Consuls; historical notices, apparently contemporaneous, make the catalogue into a chronicle. Mommsen's theory is, that the chronographer of 354 took the catalogue from the chronicle of Hippolytus, and added to it other lists which he had compiled; that as these contained the names of Consuls, whereas the list of Hippolytus did not, he put in the names of Consuls into this part also, using a table of Consuls still to be found in another portion of his work, and in so doing made several mistakes.

Dr. Salmon confirms Mommsen's argument thus. The opening sentence of the Liberian catalogue is this: *Imperante Tiberio Cæsare, passus est Dominus noster Jesus Christus, duobus Geminis Consulibus* [A.D. 29] *viii. Kal. April., et post ascensum ejus beatissimus Petrus episcopatum suscepit. Ex quo tempore per successionem dispositum, quis episcopus quot annis præfuit vel quo imperante.* Now, whence did the author get the statement that our Lord suffered on March 25th? Not from tradition; for March 25th cannot have been the true day, because the full moon in that year fell on March 18th. And, moreover, there is no trace of any such tradition. Clement[1] of Alexandria, who seems to condemn all attempts at determining the exact day, gives March 21, April 20, and April 14, as the days maintained by various persons in his time. But in

[1] *Strom.* I. 21.

221 the full moon did fall on March 25th, and hence any one living then and believing in an 8-years cycle would conclude that it fell on March 25th in the year 29. And so we find in the cycle on the statue of Hippolytus, opposite March 25th, on the line answering to A.D. 29, πάθος Χριστοῦ. It was Hippolytus, therefore, who made the calculation that the Crucifixion took place on March 25th, A.D. 29, and any one who asserts the same does so on the authority of Hippolytus. And we have thus another independent argument, almost amounting to demonstration, that the earlier part of the Liberian catalogue is derived from the list of Roman Bishops now missing from the end of the chronicle of Hippolytus.

It has been seen that Dr. Döllinger in this work argues against the main part of Mommsen's theory;[1] but on being shown the restatement of it in the *Hermathena*, strengthened by Dr. Salmon's additional argument, he at once admitted its probability.

We may confidently assume that Hippolytus was the first who ever made a chronological list of the Bishops of Rome. The line of succession had been made out more or less correctly, but without any dates attached. The lists of the early Bishops given by later writers, and collected together by Lipsius in his *Chronologie der Römischen Bischöfe*, p. 143, tend to the conclusion that all of them are based on Hippolytus. If this be so, it is all-important to examine his evidence and test its value.

We cannot determine what materials Hippolytus had at his command. No doubt the Roman Church had some records of previous episcopates, and these would be fairly trustworthy, at least as regards the later Bishops. But how did Hippolytus perform the task of working up these materials? Dr. Salmon has

[1] See p. 63.

"no very high opinion of his qualifications for it. It is not merely that he does not seem a computer of much arithmetical accuracy, but that he seems little capable of weighing evidence. Men incapable of asserting anything they do not believe to be true, still differ widely as to the amount of evidence which will induce them to make an assertion. Hippolytus strikes me as one of those arbitrary and self-confident men who have unbounded faith in their own theories, and the confidence of whose assertions is quite disproportionate to the evidence they can produce for them."

The article goes on to show that it is to the chronicle of Hippolytus that we owe the statement, so fraught with consequences to the Church, of the 25 years' episcopate of S. Peter. That chronicle certainly contained the statement of the 25 years' episcopate; there is no evidence that it was contained in any earlier work, and, though it does not actually contradict, it ill agrees with the testimony of Irenæus; but the publication of such an assertion by a man of Hippolytus' reputation accounts for the acceptance of it by the Roman Church, and thus is a full and adequate explanation of the agreement in that statement of a number of writers, the earliest of whom wrote nearly a century later.

Hippolytus himself seems to have arrived at the 25 years' episcopate of S. Peter as a result of some calculations of his own. It can be almost proved, and even without proof the assertion may be allowed as probable enough, that Hippolytus accepted the Pseudo-Clementines as history; in particular, that he accepted the statement that Clement was ordained by S. Peter. It must be remembered that Hippolytus dates the 25 years of S. Peter's episcopate from the Ascension to A.D. 55. Then comes Linus, whom Irenæus places first, from 55 to 67. Next Clement, from 67 to 76;

followed by Cletus, 76 to 83; and Anacletus, 83 to 95. Irenæus places Anencletus next to Linus, and after him Clement. Hippolytus, believing the statement of the Pseudo-Clementines, that Clement was ordained by S. Peter, has transposed Cletus and Clement, in order to bring the accession of Clement within the lifetime of the Apostle; and then, having pushed back Clement's episcopate so far, he found a gap in the chronology after his death, which he filled by making the two forms of the remaining Bishop's name represent two persons, Cletus and Anacletus. After this the lists of Irenæus and Hippolytus unite. We see, then, how the latter arrived at the 25 years of S. Peter. Believing, on the authority of the Pseudo-Clementines, that S. Peter ordained Clement, on the same grounds he would reckon S. Peter as Bishop of Rome. He calculates the interval from the Ascension to S. Peter's death as about 37 years; and the traditional 12 being deducted for Linus, there remain 25 for S. Peter.

The order, Linus, Anencletus, Clement, is therefore the one to be preferred.[1] There was no reason for placing Anencletus before Clement, excepting the fact that he actually preceded him. On the other hand, there were two strong reasons for placing Clement before Anencletus,—(1) that Clement was one of the greatest names in the sub-apostolic age, while Anencletus was an unknown person; (2) that the Pseudo-Clementines bring Clement into contact with S. Peter. The transposition of Anencletus and Clement was not accepted by any Eastern writer, and not even the authority of Hippolytus caused it to be generally accepted in the West. The canon of the Roman mass retains the original order of the Greek diptychs— "Lini, Cleti, Clementis."

[1] See DÖLLINGER's *First Age of the Church*, pp. 298-300, Eng. Trans.

The rest of the essay is mainly taken up with an argument to show that Hippolytus was probably the author of the celebrated Muratorian fragment; and that, at any rate, it was owing to his influence that the *Shepherd of Hermas* ceased to be read publicly in churches in the West.

It will be seen from the above abstract that Dr. Salmon shows Hippolytus to have been as self-opinionated and inaccurate as a chronologer, as Dr. Döllinger shows him to be as a controversialist and theologian. It is one more proof of the obscurity of the early Bishops of Rome, that one of such mediocre abilities should tower above them as a man of immense genius and unrivalled learning.

APPENDIX B.

DR. NEWMAN ON THE AUTHOR OF THE PHILOSOPHUMENA.

In his *Tracts, Theological and Ecclesiastical*,[1] Dr. Newman thus enumerates the theological writers in the West down to the middle of the fourth century:—1. S. Hippolytus of Rome; 2. The Roman author of the lately discovered *Elenchus Hæresium* (the *Philosophumena*); 3. Tertullian of Rome and Carthage; 4. Novatian, also of Rome; 5. S. Zeno of Verona; 6. S. Hilary of France; 7. S. Phœbadius, also of France; 8. Lactantius of Africa; 9. Victorinus of Africa. He thus continues:

"Of the four Roman theologians in this list, three were in direct variance with the Holy See on matters of discipline, which they maintained ought to be stricter

---

[1] P. 219, sec. 14, *The Western Writers* (how far they unconsciously supplied material or support for Arianism before its rise). Pickering 1874.

than the Popes judged to be prudent. The earliest of these three seems to be the author of the *Elenchus Hæresium*, discovered some twenty or thirty years ago, who is so scandalous in his treatment of two contemporary Popes, Zephyrinus and Callistus; a learned and able writer, *but fierce and reckless in his enmities, and incontrollable in his temper.*[1] Another, the African Tertullian, is the most powerful writer of the early centuries. He is said to have lived in Rome, for many years apparently, and was there ordained priest; then, when at length driven to his own country by the hostility of the Roman clergy, he set himself to inveigh against the laxity of morals which he considered to be tolerated by the Popes, and died in the profession of Montanism. The third is Novatian, a Roman Priest, so highly placed and so specially respected, that during the vacancy of the Holy See he was chosen by the Roman clergy to be their spokesman in their correspondence with S. Cyprian of Carthage; a man of unblemished, or rather austere character, and dying for the Christian faith in the Valerian persecution. He, too, scandalized by the relaxation of discipline in his day, became the author of the unhappy schism which goes by his name. His sectaries stood by the Catholics, and suffered with them for the cause of orthodoxy during the Arian tyranny. He is said to be the first Anti-Pope, and to have contrived his own consecration by means quite unworthy of his high character; but, *bearing in mind how Pope Callistus suffers from his unscrupulous adversary, I am slow to admit what may really be a party representation of him. He, as Callistus, has no opportunity of speaking for himself.*

"Greater still in representation, without any slur

[1] The italics are not Dr. Newman's, either here or elsewhere in this quotation.

upon his character or conduct (though some have attributed to him a temporary Novatianism some twenty or thirty years before Novatian), is Hippolytus. He stands, or rather stood while his writings were extant, in point of authority, range of subject, and ability, in the very first rank of theologians in the ante-Nicene times; and perhaps has no rival at all, as a theologian, during that period, except his master, S. Irenæus. At present we have little more than fragments of his writings; and it is a mystery how Origen's works have come down to us, who has been ever in the shade, and not Hippolytus', who has ever been in the brightest light of ecclesiastical approbation. A senator of Rome, as some consider, before he became a servant of the Church, he is said to have become a disciple of the holy Bishop of Lyons, and he followed him in being in succession Bishop, Doctor, and Martyr. Within a century of his death, a church had been erected near the Basilica of S. Lawrence in honour of a martyr of his name, and it became a popular shrine and resort of pilgrims; and there is reason for concluding that he was the Hippolytus to whom it was dedicated. I say so because there it was that, in the 16th century, a marble statue of him was found, which is still to be seen in the Vatican, an historical portrait, as some consider, with a list of his works engraven upon the episcopal chair on which he is seated. He is the first commentator *in extenso* upon Scripture among Christian writers, and his annotations are said to have been used by S. Ambrose in his own *Hexameron*. He is on the catalogue of theologians given us by Eusebius, S. Jerome, Theodoret, and Leontius; and, together with S. Irenæus, is quoted largely by Theodoret in his controversies with the heretics of his day. Moreover, Pope Gelasius, A.D. 500, uses him as one of his authorities in his work against the Eutychians; and Pope Martin, in the Lateran Council of A.D. 649, appeals to him in his own condemnation of the Monothelites.

"That a name so singularly honoured—a name which a breath of ecclesiastical censure has never even dimmed—should belong, as so many men think just now, to *the author of that malignant libel on his contemporary* Popes which is appended to the lately discovered *Elenchus*, is to my mind *simply incredible*,— incredible not simply considering the gravity of tone in what remains to us of his writings, and mainly, indeed, in the *Elenchus* itself; but especially because his name and his person were, as I have been pointing out, so warmly cherished at Rome by Popes of the fourth, fifth, and seventh centuries. Rome has a long memory of injuries offered to her majesty; and that special honours should have been paid there to a pamphleteer, as we now speak, who did not scruple in set words to call Pope Zephyrinus a weak and venal dunce, and Pope Callistus a sacrilegious swindler, an infamous convict, and an heresiarch *ex cathedra*, is an hypothesis which requires more direct evidence in its behalf than has hitherto been produced. I grant that that portion of the work which relates to the Holy Trinity as closely resembles the works of Hippolytus in style and in teaching as the libellous matter which has got a place in it is incompatible with his reputation; in the present discussion, however, it matters not what becomes of a difficulty which is mainly historical or biographical. Here I shall place him first among the Western writers, on account of the weight of his authority in early times, the clearness and terseness of his style, and the completeness of his doctrinal view."

This kind of reasoning certainly appears to be not a little precarious. Substitute the name of Jerome for that of Hippolytus, and the controversial writings which bear Jerome's name for the *Elenchus*, and where would a parallel line of argument land us? Might it not seem "simply incredible" that "a name so singularly honoured," "so warmly cherished at Rome" by the clergy in after ages, should belong to the author of such virulent abuse of the Roman clergy? Granted that portions even of the controversial writings closely resemble the undoubted works of Jerome both in style and teaching, yet the scurrilous "matter which has got a place" in them is wholly "incompatible with his reputation" as a grave theologian and revered saint.

To what extent arguments of this kind are pushed by a certain school of critics against various books of Scripture is well known to every theological student. In the present case, of course, everything depends on the correctness of the statement that the hypothesis of Hippolytus being the author of the *Elenchus* "requires more direct evidence in its behalf than has hitherto been produced."[1] Lastly, did Romans of the third century feel that unbounded reverence for the Popes which is preached and practised in the nineteenth? Would Hippolytus' lips be sealed by the considerations which would silence a modern Cardinal?

APPENDIX C.

THE POEM OF PRUDENTIUS ON THE MARTYRDOM OF HIPPOLYTUS.

FREQUENT allusion has been made in the course of this work to PRUDENTIUS' account of Hippolytus (see esp. p. 51 *sq.*). The works of Prudentius, as the translator knows from experience, are not in every one's hands, and therefore it will be convenient to most

---

[1] It is said that Dr. Barrow, late Principal of S. Edmund Hall, Oxford, was one of the first, if not quite the first, to put forth this hypothesis.

readers to have the whole poem ready at hand for reference. It is No. XI. in the *Peristephanon Liber*, a series of fourteen poems in honour of various martyrs, many of them Spanish. The text here followed is that of Dressel (Leipsic 1860) :—

PASSIO HIPPOLYTI BEATISSIMI MARTYRIS.

Innumeros cineres sanctorum Romula in urbe
    vidimus, O Christi Valeriane sacer.
Incisos tumulis titulos et singula quæris
    nomina ? difficile est, ut replicare queam.
Tantos justorum populos furor impius hausit,   5
    cum coleret patrios Troia Roma deos.
Plurima litterulis signata sepulcra loquuntur
    martyris aut nomen aut epigramma aliquod.
Sunt et muta tamen tacitas claudentia tumbas
    marmora, quæ solum significant numerum.   10
Quanta virum jaceant congestis corpora acervis,
    nosse licet, quorum nomina multa legas.
Sexaginta illic defossas mole sub una
    relliquias memini me didicisse hominum,
quorum solus habet conperta vocabula Christus,   15
    utpote quos propriæ junxit amicitiæ.
Hæc dum lustro oculis et sicubi forte latentes
    rerum apices veterum per monumenta sequor,
invenio Hippolytum, qui quondam schisma Novati
    presbyter attigerat nostra sequenda negans,   20
usque ad martyrii provectum insigne tulisse
    lucide sanguinei præmia supplicii.
Nec mirere, senem perversi dogmatis olim
    munere ditatum Catholicæ fidei,
cum jam vesano victor raperetur ab hoste   25
    exultante anima carnis ad exitium ;
plebis amore suæ multis comitantibus ibat,
    consultus, quænam secta foret melior ;
respondit : " Fugite, O miseri, execranda Novati
    schismata, Catholicis reddite vos populis.   30
Una fides vigeat, prisco quæ condita templo est
    quam Paulus retinet quamque cathedra Petri.

Quæ docui, docuisse piget : venerabile martyr
   cerno, quod a cultu rebar abesse Dei."
His ubi detorsit lævo de tramite plebem   35
   monstravitque sequi, qua via dextra vocat,
seque ducem recti spretis anfractibus idem
   præbuit, erroris qui prius auctor erat;
sistitur insano rectori Christicolas tunc
   ostia vexanti per Tiberina viros.   40
Illo namque die Roma secesserat, ipsos
   peste suburbanos ut quateret populos,
Non contentus humum celsa intra mœnia Romæ
   tingere justorum cædibus adsiduis,
Janiculum cum jam madidum, fora, Rostra, Suburram 45
   cerneret eluvie sanguinis adfluere.
Protulerat rabiem Tyrrheni ad littoris oram,
   quæque loca æquoreus proxima portus habet.
Inter carnifices et constipata sedebat
   officia extructo celsior in solio,   50
discipulos fidei detestandique rebelles
   idolii ardebat dedere perfidiæ.
Carcereo crinita situ stare agmina contra
   jusserat horrendis excrucianda modis.
Inde catenarum tractus, hinc lorea fragra   55
   stridere, virgarum concrepitare fragor :
ungula fixa cavis costarum cratibus altos
   pandere secessus et lacerare jecur.
Ac jam lassatis judex tortoribus ibat
   in furias cassa cognitione fremens :   60
nullus enim Christi ex famulis per tanta repertus
   supplicia, auderet qui vitiare animam.
Inde furens quæsitor ait : " Jam tortor ab unco
   desine ; si vana est quæstio, morte agito.
Huic abscide caput, crux istum tollat in auras   65
   viventesque oculos offerat alitibus.
Hos rape præcipites et vinctos conice in ignem,
   sit pyra, quæ multos devoret una reos.
En tibi quos properes rimosæ imponere cumbæ
   pellere et in medii stagna profunda freti.   70
Quos ubi susceptos rabidum male suta per æquor
   vexerit et tumidis cæsa labarit aquis :

dissociata putrem laxent tabulata carinam
    conceptumque bibant undique naufragium.
Squamea cænoso præstabit ventre sepulcrum   75
    bellua consumptis cruda cadaveribus.
Hæc persultanti celsum subito ante tribunal
    offertur senior nexibus implicitus.
Stipati circum juvenes clamore ferebant,
    ipsum Christicolis esse caput populis :   80
si foret extinctum propere caput, omnia vulgi
    pectora Romanis sponte sacranda deis.
Insolitum leti poscunt genus et nova pænæ
    inventa, exemplo quo trepident alii.
Ille supinata residens cervice : " Quis," inquit, 85
    " dicitur ? " affirmant dicier Hippolytum.
" Ergo sit Hippolytus, quatiat turbetque jugales
    intereatque feris dilaceratus equis."
Vix hæc ille : duo cogunt animalia freni
    ignara insueto subdere colla jugo,   90
non stabulis blandive manu palpata magistri
    inperiumque equitis ante subacta pati,
sed campestre vago nuper pecus e grege captum,
    quod pavor indomito corde ferinus agit.
Jamque reluctantes sociarant vincula bigas   95
    oraque discordi fœdere nexuerant.
Temonis vice funis inest, qui terga duorum
    dividit et medius tangit utrumque latus :
deque jugo in longum se post vestigia retro
    protendens trahitur transit et ima pedum.   100
Hujus ad extremum, sequitur qua pulvere summo
    cornipedum refugas orbita trita vias,
crura viri innectit laqueus nodoque tenaci
    adstringit plantas cumque rudente ligat.
Postquam conposito satis instruxere paratu   105
    martyris ad pænam verbera, vincla, feros :
instigant subitis clamoribus atque flagellis
    iliaque infestis perfodiunt stimulis.
Ultima vox audita senis venerabilis hæc est :
    " Hi rapiant artus, tu rape, Christe, animam."[1] 110

---

[1] There is a reading *rapiunt*, which Dr. Döllinger appears to have had (see p. 54).

Prorumpunt alacres cæco et terrore feruntur,
   qua sonus atque tremor, qua furor exagitant:
incendit feritas, rapit inpetus et fragor urget,
   nec cursus volucer mobile sentit onus.
Per silvas, per saxa ruunt, non ripa retardat   115
   fluminis aut torrens oppositus cohibet.
Prosternunt sepes et cuncta obstacula rumpunt,
   prona, fragosa petunt, ardua transiliunt.
Scissa minutatim labefacto corpore frusta
   carpit spinigeris stirpibus hirtus ager.   120
Pars summis pendet scopulis, pars sentibus hæret,
   parte rubent frondes, parte madescit humus.
Exemplar sceleris paries habet inlitus, in quo
   multicolor fucus digerit omne nefas.
Picta super tumulum species liquidis viget umbris   125
   effigians tracti membra cruenta viri.
Rorantes saxorum apices vidi, optime papa,
   purpureasque notas vepribus inpositas.
Docta manus virides imitando effingere dumos
   luserat et minio russeolam saniem.   130
Cernere erat ruptis conpagibus ordine nullo
   membra per incertos sparsa jacere situs.
Addiderat caros gressu lacrimisque sequentes,
   devia quo fractum semita monstrat iter.
Mærore attoniti atque oculis rimantibus ibant   135
   implebantque sinus visceribus laceris.
Ille caput niveum conplectitur ac reverendam
   canitiem molli confovet in gremio;
hic humeros truncasque manus et brachia et ulnas
   et genua et crurum fragmina nuda legit.   140
Palliolis etiam bibulæ siccantur arenæ,
   ne quis in infecto pulvere ros maneat.
Si quis et in sudibus recalenti adspergine sanguis
   insidet, hunc omnem spongia pressa rapit.
Nec jam densa sacro quidquam de corpore silva   145
   obtinet aut plenis fraudat ab exquiliis.
Cumque recensetis constaret partibus ille
   corporis integri, qui fuerat, numerus;
nec purgata aliquid deberent avia toto
   ex homine, extersis frondibus et scopulis: 150

metando eligitur tumulo locus, ostia linquunt :
   Roma placet, sanctos quæ teneat cineres.
Haud procul extremo culta ad pomeria vallo
   mersa latebrosis crypta patet foveis.
Hujus in occultum gradibus via prona reflexis   155
   ire per anfractus luce latente docet.
Primas namque fores summo tenus intrat hiatu
   inlustratque dies lumina vestibuli :
inde, ubi progressu facili nigrescere visa est
   nox obscura loci per specus ambiguum,   160
occurrunt cæsis inmissa foramina tectis,
   quæ jaciunt claros antra super radios.
Quamlibet ancipites texant hinc inde recessus
   arta sub umbrosis atria porticibus,
attamen excisi subter cava viscera montis   165
   crebra terebrato fornice lux penetrat.
Sic datur absentis per subterranea solis
   cernere fulgorem luminibusque frui.
Talibus Hippolyti corpus mandatur opertis,
   propter ubi adposita est ara dicata Deo.   170
Illa sacramenti donatrix mensa eademque
   custos fida sui martyris adposita
servat ad æterni spem vindicis ossa sepulcro,
   pascit item sanctis Tibricolas dapibus.
Mira loci pietas et prompta precantibus ara   175
   spes hominum placida prosperitate juvat.
Hic conruptelis animique et corporis æger
   oravi quotiens stratus, opem merui.
Quod lætor reditu, quod te venerande sacerdos
   conplecti licitum est, scribo quod hæc eadem,   180
Hippolyto scio me debere, deus cui Christus
   posse dedit, quod quis postulet, adnuere.
Ipsa, illas animæ exuvias quæ continet intus,
   ædicula argento fulgurat ex solido.
Præfixit tabulas dives manus æquore levi   185
   candentes, recavum quale nitet speculum :
nec Pariis contenta aditus obducere saxis
   addidit ornando clara talenta operi.
Mane salutatum concurritur : omnis adorat
   pubis, eunt, redeunt solis adusque obitum.   190

Conglobat in cuneum Latios simul ac peregrinos
  permixtim populos relligionis amor :
oscula perspicuo figunt impressa metallo,
  balsama defundunt, fletibus ora rigant.
Jam cum se renovat decursis mensibus annus 195
  natalemque diem passio festa refert :
quanta putas studiis certantibus agmina cogi,
  quæve celebrando vota coire Deo ?
Urbs augusta suos vomit effunditque Quirites
  una et patricios ambitione pari 200
confundit plebeia phalanx umbonibus æquis
  discrimen procerum præcipitante fide,
nec minus Albanis acies se candida portis
  explicat et longis ducitur ordinibus :
exultant fremitus variarum hinc inde viarum, 205
  indigena et Picens plebs et Etrusca venit.
Concurrit Samnitis atrox, habitator et altæ
  Campanus Capuæ, jamque Nolanus adest.
. Quisque sua lætus cum conjuge dulcibus et cum
  pigneribus rapidum carpere gestit iter. 210
Vix capiunt patuli populorum gaudia campi,
  hæret et in magnis densa cohors spatiis.
Augustum tantis illud specus esse catervis,
  haud dubium est, ampla fauce licet pateat.
Stat sed juxta aliud, quod tanta frequentia templum 215
  tunc adeat cultu nobile regifico,
parietibus celsum sublimibus atque superba
  majestate potens muneribusque opulens.
Ordo columpnarum geminus laquearia tecti
  sustinet auratis suppositus trabibus. 220
Adduntur graciles tecto breviore recessus,
  qui laterum seriem jugiter exsinuent.
At medios aperit tractus via latior alti
  culminis exurgens editiore apice.
Fronte sub adversa gradibus sublime tribunal 225
  tollitur, antistes prædicat unde Deum.
Plena laborantes ægre domus accipit undas
  artaque confertis æstuat in foribus,
Maternum pandens gremium, quo condat alumpnos
  ac foveat fetos accumulata sinus. 230

THE "PASSIO HIPPOLYTI" OF PRUDENTIUS. 351

Si bene conmemini, colit hunc pulcerrima Roma
   idibus Augusti mensis, ut ipsa vocat
prisco more diem, quem te quoque, sancte magister,
   annua festa inter dinumerare velim.
Crede, salutigeros feret hic venerantibus ortus   235
   lucis honoratæ præmia restituens.
Inter sollempnes Cypriani vel Chelidoni
   eulaliæque dies currat et iste tibi.
Sic te pro populo, cujus tibi credita vita est,
   orantem Christus audiat omnipotens: 240
Sic tibi de pleno lupus excludatur ovili,
   agna nec ulla tuum capta gregem minuat.
Sic me gramineo remanentem denique campo
   sedulus ægrotam pastor ovem referas.
Sic, cum lacteolis caulas compleveris agnis,   245
   raptus et ipse sacro sis comes Hippolyto.

Dressel is disposed to accept the whole of this as historical. *Quando id evenerit, parum constat; omnibus autem quæ Prudentius rettulet accuratius perpensis, martyrium ex Decii vel Valeriani temporibus nos ante oculos habere probabile fit . . . Ea igitur Prudentii auctoritatem haudquaquam debilitare poterunt, quamvis plures Hippolytos martyres exstitisse adseverent* (p. 441). Even CASPARI (*Quellen zur Geschichte des Taufsymbols und der Glaubensregel*, III. p. 406) does not think the narrative of Prudentius wholly apocryphal. He does not say, however, very distinctly *how much* of Prudentius' account may be considered historical; perhaps no more than that he survived the exile to Sardinia, and lived two or three years after 235. He refers his readers to Friedr. Nitzsch, *Grundriss der Christlichen Dogmengeschichte*, I. p. 162; and Harnack, *Zur Quellenkritik der Geschichte des Gnosticismus*, "Zeitschrift für Hist. Theol. Jahrg." 1874, p. 194, n. 154.

C. BROCKHAUS (*Aurelius Prudentius Clemens in seiner Bedeutung für die Kirche seiner Zeit*, Leipzig 1872) maintains that the honour paid to the relics of Hippolytus at Rome, and the famous statue found near the site indicated by Prudentius, show that the Hippolytus intended by the poet is the Roman Bishop. He thinks it doubtful whether Prudentius considered him a follower of the African Novatus, or of the Roman Novatian (who, setting out from different points, agreed in resisting episcopal authority); or whether, like Eusebius (*E. H.* vi. 43, and vii. 8), he confounds the two schismatics. Brockhaus regards the description of the catacombs (153–175) to be the most valuable part of the poem to the historian and antiquarian. On the historical value of the account of the martyrdom, he does not seem to think it necessary to express an opinion (p. 142, etc.).

APPENDIX D.

ONE MORE THEORY ABOUT THE BISHOPRIC OF HIPPOLYTUS.

Some notice ought to be taken of the theory first started apparently by Le Moyne, a French writer residing in Leyden in the seventeenth century. He combines the theories that Hippolytus was Bishop of Portus and that he held a See in Arabia,—thus, that he was Bishop of *Portus Romanorum*, the modern Aden. I know not in what author the name *Portus Romanorum* occurs. Aden is commonly believed to be the same as Arabia Felix ('Αραβία εὐδαίμων), or Arabiæ Emporium ('Αραβίας ἐμπόριον), or Attanæ ('Αδάνη), as it is variously called by ancient writers; the third variation, which occurs in Pliny and Philostorgius, being the native name of this flourishing seaport. Le Moyne was supported by some writers of eminence, as Spanheim, also of Leyden, the Port Royalist Tillemont, and others.

But his theory does not now need serious refutation; no one is likely to think it a tenable hypothesis at the present day. The *Philosophumena*, unknown of course to Le Moyne and those who have followed him in this, has placed it beyond a doubt that the scene of Hippolytus' labours was Rome, or its immediate neighbourhood. (See the Introductory Notice to the translation of *The Writings of Hippolytus*, I. 20, in Clark's *Ante-Nicene Library*.)

One more item of evidence may be added to that already given in abundance that Hippolytus was Bishop of Rome. In the *Theologische Quartalschrift*, Tübingen 1862, p. 467, there is an article by Dr. NOLTE of Paris on *Ein Excerpt aus dem zum grössten Theil noch ungedruckten Chronicon des Georgius Hamartolus*. In it occur these words: ὁ θεῖος Ἱππόλυτος Ῥώμης. GEORGIUS HAMARTOLUS to a great extent copied Eusebius; but, as Eusebius did not know of what place Hippolytus was Bishop, Georgius Hamartolus must have had some other authority for calling him "of Rome."

In the same volume of the *Quartalschrift* (p. 624) there is a rather damaging critique by the same Dr. Nolte on Cruice's edition of the *Philosophumena* (Parisiis 1860). He thinks that a few very good emendations and ingenious conjectures are perhaps the most valuable portion of Cruice's work, but that these scarcely warranted the production of a new edition. In the introductory matter Cruice is thought by some to have availed himself largely of the work of Dr. Döllinger, to whom I am indebted for the knowledge of these articles in the *Theologische Quartalschrift*.

APPENDIX E.

ONE MORE THEORY ABOUT THE AUTHORSHIP OF THE PHILOSOPHUMENA.

It was to be expected that the Jesuits would put forth a dissertation on a work which so nearly touches Papal claims; it was also to be expected that they would put forth something more able than the only work on the subject by a member of their Society with which I am acquainted: *De prisca refutatione hæreseon Originis nomine ac philosophumenon titulo recens vulgata commentarius* Torquati ARMELLINI, e societate Jesu. Romæ 1862.

The drift of it is simply this:—

1. The *Philosophumena* cannot have been written by Origen, who was not a Bishop, as the author evidently was.

2. It cannot well have been written by Caius, with whose known doctrine and acts its contents are not consistent.

3. It cannot have been written by Hippolytus; for Hippolytus was always held in the highest honour by the ancient Church, and no mention is made by ancient writers of his having headed a schism. (Compare Dr. Newman's argument in the same direction in Appendix B.)

4. A great deal may be said for Jallabert's conjecture that Tertullian was the author; but the style is that of an imitator of Tertullian rather than of Tertullian himself. Moreover, the abrupt attack on the Montanists is unlike Tertullian, even before he became a Montanist. (The discussion of Tertullian's claims, which might have been dismissed in half a dozen lines, occupies about a quarter of the treatise. The author of the *Philosophumena* lived in or near Rome during

the pontificates of Zephyrinus and Callistus; Tertullian was almost certainly in Africa at that time, and we may take for granted that he would have written such a treatise in Latin; to say nothing of the author of the *Philosophumena* having been a Bishop.)

5. The real author was Novatian. All the arguments which point to Tertullian point equally to Novatian, who is not excluded by the objections which seem to exclude Tertullian. (There is no doubt a certain amount of resemblance between the Trinitarian doctrine of Hippolytus and that of Novatian; but beyond this there does not seem to be much in favour of the Novatian hypothesis, which, so far as I am aware, has been adopted by no one else.)

APPENDIX F.

PROFESSOR CASPARI'S CONTRIBUTIONS TO THE SUBJECT.

These are very considerable indeed; but, unfortunately, they are by no means so accessible as one could wish. They are to be gathered mainly from long and somewhat closely printed and uninviting notes to the third volume of the author's great work on the text of the earliest creeds.[1] This third volume only appeared last year, and has already been for some months out of print; so that, as the present writer knows from experience, to obtain the work at all is a matter of some difficulty: his first acquaintance with

---

[1] *Ungedruckte, unbeachtete und wenig beachtete Quellen zur Geschichte des Taufsymbols und der Glaubensregel*, herausgegeben und in Abhandlungen erläutert von Dr. C. P. CASPARI, Professor der Theologie an der Norwegischen Universität. Christiania 1866, 1869, 1875.

it was made in a borrowed copy. This rapid disappearance of the first edition will perhaps encourage Professor Caspari to issue a second as soon as possible, and thus supply a real want.

The material bearing on the present subject is to be found chiefly at pp. 374–422. In extracting some portions of the substance, it will be convenient to follow the order in which the points occur in the present volume rather than that in which they are found in a series of more or less unconnected notes. It will thus be easy to see, by a glance at the table of contents, how far Dr. Döllinger's conclusions are confirmed by the latest writer on these much-vexed questions.

After a general classification of the works of Hippolytus into exegetical, apologetical, chronological, polemical, etc., Dr. Caspari (p. 377) divides the polemical works into two classes,—those against non-Christians, *i.e.* Jews and heathen, and those against heretics (p. 394). This second class may be subdivided into those directed against all heretics, and those directed against a single heresy or individual heretic (p. 397). To the former of these subdivisions the *Philosophumena* belongs.

1. *He considers it indubitable that Hippolytus is the author of it* (p. 403). The proper title of it is κατὰ πασῶν αἱρέσεων ἔλεγχος. This is shown by the opening words prefixed to each book (evidently by Hippolytus himself) as a table of contents; *e.g.* τάδε ἔνεστι ἐν τῇ πρώτῃ, τῇ πέμπτῃ, κ.τ.λ., τοῦ κατὰ πασῶν αἱρέσεων ἐλέγχου. The title *Philosophumena*, strictly speaking, applies only to the first book, which contains a sketch of various philosophies.

2. That Hippolytus is the author of the Σπούδασμα κατὰ τῆς Ἀρτέμωνος αἱρέσεως (Eus. *H. E.* v. 28), or σμικρὸς Λαβύρινθος (Theodoret, *Hæret. fab. comp.* II. 5), he thinks probable, but not certain (p. 404). If Photius

(*Bibl. Cod.* 48) by the Λαβύρινθος means the σμικρὸς Λαβύρινθος, then it must be by Hippolytus; for Photius says the Λαβύρινθος was by the author of the Περὶ τῆς τοῦ πάντος οὐσίας. If by the Λαβύρινθος Photius means the *Philosophumena* (or the tenth book), then some one else than Hippolytus *may* be the author of the σμικρὸς Λαβύρινθος. This latter hypothesis, though not baseless, has very serious difficulties. Even if it is true, however, there is still much to be said in favour of Hippolytus being the author of the σμικρὸς Λαβύρινθος, which was written against Roman Monarchians by some one living in Rome, and not before the fourth decade of the third century. All this points to Hippolytus, who at that time was the great anti-Monarchian theologian in Rome.

3. The *Syntagma* mentioned by Photius is not the same as the *Philosophumena*, but a shorter work, containing a summary of the lectures of Irenæus, and probably written very early in the third century.

4. Into the difficult question of the relation between the *Libellus* appended to Tertullian's *De præscr. hæret.* and the Σύνταγμα πρὸς ἁπάσας τὰς αἱρέσεις, Dr. Caspari declines to enter. He contents himself with deciding that the *Appendix* is certainly taken from a Greek original, directed against all heresies, and was written in Rome,—most probably soon after the pontificate of Zephyrinus; because the heretics added by the author to those in the original treatise are confined to those who made their appearance in Rome in the latter part of the second century and first decade of the third. Harnack thinks it may have been written considerably later. Döllinger (p. 20) thinks it may have been written after the *Philosophumena*, *i.e.* later than A.D. 230 (p. 116). Dr. Caspari does not think much of Œhler's arguments to show that Victorinus of Petavium (martyred 303) is the author of the *Appendix*, which is really

a long foot-note on the *title* of Tertullian's treatise (pp. 417–422).

5. It has already been mentioned that Dr. Caspari thinks there are some elements of historical truth in Prudentius' account of the martyrdom of Hippolytus, but he does not say what these are (p. 406).

6. He concurs in the view that the dispute between Hippolytus and Callistus ended in Hippolytus being set up as a rival Bishop by his party, and the two leaders excommunicating one another; and that this formal schism lasted during the pontificates of Urbanus and Pontianus (p. 330).

7. All, or nearly all, the works of Hippolytus were written in Rome; and we find him in literary activity there from the last days of Commodus to 235, or even 238, excepting the time spent by him under Irenæus at Lyons. This time probably falls between 195 and 200, shortly before the death of S. Irenæus. It was very possibly during the absence of Hippolytus from Rome on this occasion that Epigonus, the disciple of Noëtus, arrived there and won followers. This would explain the indefinite way in which Hippolytus speaks of him in the *Philosophumena*, as if he did not know much about him. He twice calls him Ἐπίγονός τις (ix. 7, x. 27). That Lipsius (*Zur Quellenkritic des Gnosticismus*, p. 40) is wrong in supposing that Hippolytus originally lived in Asia Minor, and in that country was a disciple of S. Irenæus about the year 170, composed the Σύνταγμα πρὸς ἁπάσας τὰς αἱρέσεις about 190–195, and did not come to Rome until after that, has been convincingly proved by Harnack (*Zeitschrift für Hist. Theol.* Jahrg. 1874, p. 195). The accurate knowledge which Hippolytus has of events which took place at the close of the reign of Commodus (*Philosoph.* ix. 12), shows that he was old enough at that time to notice and appreciate what was going on; and it is quite manifest

that he was active in Rome under Zephyrinus and Callistus, and after the latter's death (pp. 408, 409).

8. The influence of Origen over Hippolytus was the natural one of a stronger though younger mind over a less powerful one. This influence was the result not merely of their intercourse in Rome, but much more of the writings of Origen (p. 353).

9. The *Philosophumena* was written some time after the death of Callistus, *i.e.* 230–235. This is in substantial agreement with Dr. Döllinger, who says about 230, and Jacobi in Herzog, who says about 234. Harnack would place it considerably after the death of Callistus. Anyhow, Lipsius (*Chron. der röm. Bischöfe*, p. 176) is not to be followed in placing it just before or just after the death of Callistus, *i.e.* about 222 (p. 403).

10. The treatise κατὰ Βήρωνος καὶ "Ηλικος (or Ἡλικίωνος, or ἡλικιώτων) αἱρετικῶν is most certainly spurious. For proof of this he refers to Dr. Döllinger's arguments, p. 295 (p. 407).

11. It is worth while adding, that Dr. Caspari does not at all agree with Dr. Salmon's conjecture (which is not noticed by him) that the celebrated Muratorian fragment may be the work of Hippolytus, to which conjecture the much discussed words, "*nuperrime temporibus nostris*," are not the only bar. Dr. Caspari argues strongly in favour of a Latin original. The few Græcisms which occur, occur in Latin authors also; whereas the use of "*Catholica*" for "*Ecclesia Catholica*" is strongly against the fragment being a translation. Καθολική for Ἐκκλησία καθολική occurs (Dr. Caspari believes) in *no* Greek author; but in Latin the adjective used as a substantive is very frequent in *African* writers, elsewhere rather rare. A large number of instances are quoted. The most probable hypothesis is, that the Muratorian Canon is a Latin original by an

African writer living in Rome, and that its date is about A.D. 170, if not somewhat earlier. Among ecclesiastical documents it may be regarded as the most ancient Latin original which we possess. It is, however, possible that the Muratorian fragment, like the *Appendix* to Tertullian's *De præscr. hæret.*, may be a Latin reproduction of a Greek original written in Rome (pp. 151, 410).

These are but a few gleanings from the storehouse of information supplied by Dr. Caspari; but perhaps they are sufficient to induce those interested in the subject to go to the storehouse itself.

There is a complete edition of the extant works of Hippolytus in one volume by Lagarde: *Hippolyti Romani quæ feruntur omnia Græce*, e recognitione Pauli Antonii de Lagarde. 1858, Lipsiæ et Londinii.

www.ingramcontent.com/pod-product-compliance
Lightning Source LLC
Chambersburg PA
CBHW050329230426
43663CB00010B/1797